GHOSTS OF EMPIRE

GHOSTS OF EMPIRE

BRITAIN'S LEGACIES IN THE MODERN WORLD

KWASI KWARTENG

BLOOMSBURY

LONDON · BERLIN · NEW YORK · SYDNEY

First published in Great Britain 2011

Copyright © Kwasi Kwarteng 2011

Map by ML Design

Kwasi Kwarteng has asserted his right to be identified as the author of this Work

Bloomsbury Publishing Plc
36 Soho Square
London W1D 3QY

www.bloomsbury.com

Bloomsbury Publishing, London, Berlin, New York and Sydney
A CIP catalogue record for this book is available from the British Library

ISBN 978 0 7475 9941 8

10 9 8 7 6 5 4 3 2 1

Typeset by Hewer Text UK Ltd, Edinburgh
Printed in Great Britain by Clays Ltd, St Ives plc, Bungay, Suffolk

Liber dicatur hic parentibus meis
amore grati filii piissimo

CONTENTS

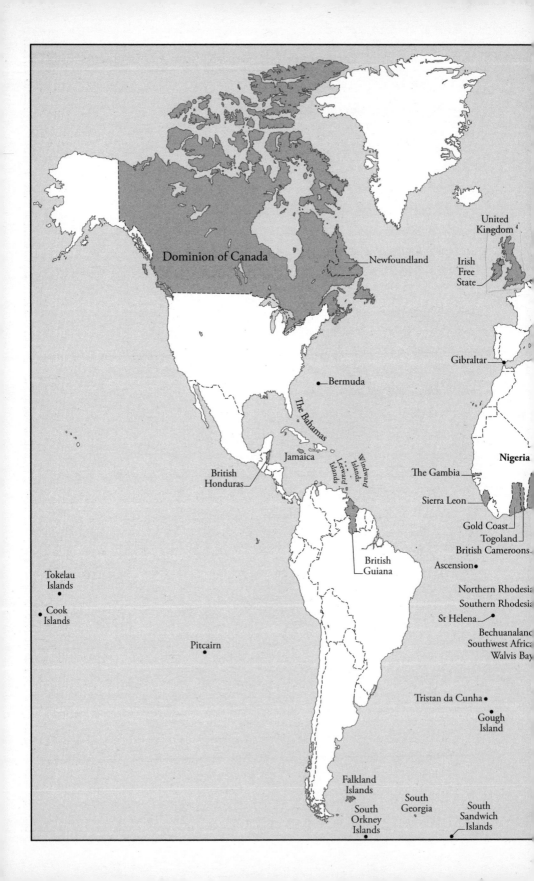

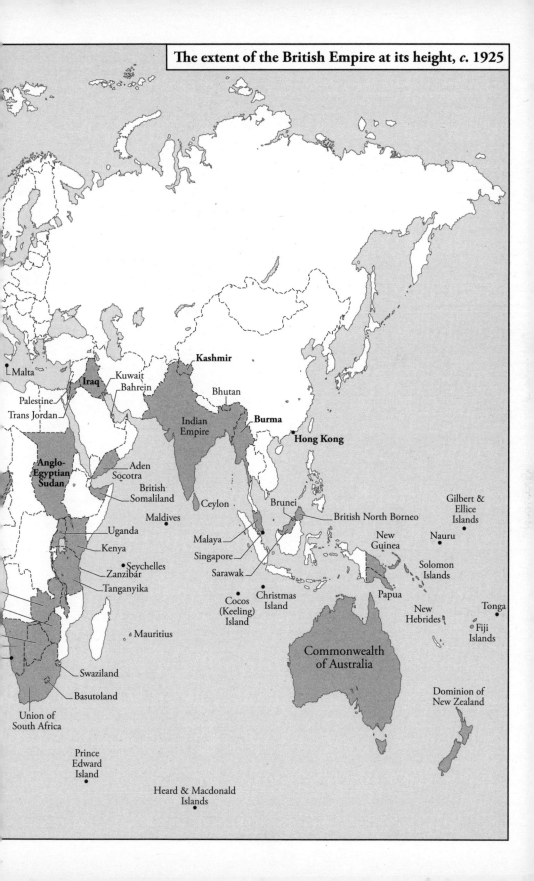

The extent of the British Empire at its height, *c.* 1925

Malta

Kashmir

Iraq
Kuwait
Bahrein

Palestine
Trans Jordan

Bhutan

Indian
Empire

Burma

Hong Kong

Anglo-
Egyptian
Sudan

Aden
Socotra

British
Somaliland

Ceylon

Brunei

British North Borneo

Gilbert &
Ellice
Islands

Maldives

New
Guinea

Nauru

Uganda

Kenya

Malaya

Singapore

Seychelles
Zanzibar

Sarawak

Solomon
Islands

Tanganyika

Papua

Tonga

Cocos
(Keeling)
Island

Christmas
Island

New
Hebrides

Fiji
Islands

Mauritius

Commonwealth
of Australia

Swaziland

Basutoland

Dominion of
New Zealand

Union of
South Africa

Prince
Edward
Island

Heard & Macdonald
Islands

Introduction

The British Empire remains one of the most popular themes in history. We all know, or think we know, about its character. We have a hazy image of officers in pith helmets, pukka sahibs and turbaned and bejewelled maharajas; we have a sense of the grandeur and splendour of the empire, but it remains, at the beginning of the twenty-first century, very remote. The workings of the empire itself are even more obscure, as is the long roll of colonial governors and officials who administered it.

In this book, I have tried to show what the British Empire was really like, from the point of view of the rulers, the administrators who made it possible. As one historian has said, the task is to recover the 'world-view and social presuppositions of those who dominated and ruled the empire'.[1] This does not mean that the 'victims and critics' were unimportant, but it does mean that any understanding of the empire should start with trying to capture the mentality of those who bore responsibility for an imperium which was the largest the world has seen.

Ghosts of Empire takes an unusual approach, in the way it examines aspects of Britain's legacy in parts of the world which are diverse in terms of geography and culture. The countries or territories which form the subjects of this book are, in many ways, still influenced by their connection with Britain. Many of them, like Iraq and Kashmir, have been prominent in the international press for some years; others, like Nigeria and Sudan, have been less widely written about, but all of them, in my view, reveal certain similar characteristics of British rule.

The choice of Hong Kong was the easiest, since the departure of the British from the territory in 1997, watched by millions of people on television, has been understood to symbolize the formal end of the British

Empire. More relevantly, to readers in the twenty-first century, Hong Kong's destiny is now bound up with that of China, the most rapidly emerging superpower of the new century. Iraq's history as a dependent territory of empire was strictly a twentieth-century affair. Handed over to Britain in 1920, after the First World War, Iraq remained under formal British rule for only twelve years. Yet, for the next twenty-five years, it was ruled by a monarchy which affected British manners and style.

In Kashmir, a Hindu family were established as rulers over an overwhelmingly Muslim kingdom. The Dogras ruled Kashmir for a hundred years, and the effects of their rule are still felt today. Monarchy was a particularly British instrument of policy, and the experiences of both Iraq and Kashmir illustrate its limitations. Burma, which, like Kashmir, formed part of the jurisdiction of the Secretary of State for India, was treated in a completely different way. In Burma, an ancient monarchy was toppled and replaced by direct British rule. The contrasting treatment of Kashmir and Burma reveals the many inconsistencies of imperial policy. On the continent of Africa, within the boundaries of both Nigeria and Sudan, there existed ethnic and racial animosities which were only exacerbated by imperial rule. These animosities have haunted the post-imperial destinies of both countries.

The British Empire has always been with me. My parents were born in what was then called the Gold Coast in the 1940s and had experienced the empire at first hand. My father entered secondary school in January 1956, less than fifteen months before the Gold Coast became independent as Ghana in March 1957. This school was designed on traditional Anglican lines, and, although it had been founded only in 1910, it imitated older English establishments. The headmaster was an Englishman, of a type familiar in the colonies, a product of Winchester, England's oldest boarding, or public, school, and Cambridge University.

I visited the school, Adisadel College, in 2001 for the first time. I was struck by the grace and tranquillity of its environment, as the school stands high on a hill in Cape Coast, Ghana's oldest town, which had been colonized by the Dutch in the seventeenth century. I realized that very few schools in Britain enjoyed such a pleasant setting. And yet the story of the school since independence in 1956 reflected the turbulent, unsettled history of the country since that time. In 1960 there had been 600 boys at the school; there were now over 2,000 and yet the facilities and infrastructure had remained the same. The shortage of money had not really changed the ethos of the place. Even though the school tried to shake off its imperial past, and had done this successfully by abolishing, for example, the teaching of Ancient Greek in 1963, there were still many traces of the old order. The school had been transformed, but vestiges of the empire could still be seen, not least in the house system, favoured in British boarding schools, and the honours boards in the dining room. The empire in a certain sense still existed, although it now clung on only in a twilit afterlife that carried an eerie echo of its original character.

This book attempts to describe some of that afterlife, by giving an account of a country's experience before independence and afterwards. The character of the empire is portrayed through the forgotten officials and governors, without whom it would not have survived more than a few weeks. I have not written one of those books that purport to show that the empire was a good thing or a bad thing. I have tried to transcend what I believe to be a rather sterile debate on its merits and demerits. I have simply sought to enter, as best as I could, into the mentality of the empire's rulers, to describe their thoughts and their ideals and values. I argue that individual officials wielded immense power, and it was this that ultimately led to disorder and even chaos.

Officials, as I hope to show, often developed one line of policy, only for their successors to overturn it and pursue a completely different approach. This was a source of chronic instability in many parts of the empire. In many ways, the British were too individualistic, and the vagaries of democratic politics meant that a consistent line was seldom adopted. I have called this 'anarchic individualism', in that there was often nothing to stop the 'man on the spot', as he was called by the Colonial Office officials, from pursuing the course of action he thought best. From Nigeria, where Lord Lugard dominated the scene, to Hong Kong, where Sir Alexander Grantham successfully ended any move towards more democratic institutions in the 1950s, powerful individuals directed imperial policy with little supervision from Whitehall. Such a system was ultimately anarchic and self-defeating, as policies developed over years in Nigeria, Sudan, Hong

Kong and elsewhere were simply put aside when a new governor took his place.

These reversals of policy show that the empire was an intensely pragmatic affair. Apart from a common educational background and a sense of shared style, individual governors and officials had a wide range of interests and beliefs. Some were motivated by a strong evangelical Christianity, others were outright atheists; some governors were highly conservative, while others were more liberal, even radical. What bound these people together was a very similar educational background, which leads inevitably to the notion of class.

Class was central to the British Empire. As one historian has argued, Britons in the imperial age saw themselves as 'belonging to an unequal society characterized by a seamless web of layered gradations . . . hallowed by time and precedent'.[2] The empire was extremely hierarchical. In each colony, there were highly detailed tables of precedent, which showed exactly where everyone stood in the pecking order. These tables sometimes revealed whether the Superintendent of the Botanical and Forestry Department came before the Director of the Royal Observatory, but this hierarchy was not really the kind we associate with feudal society. What tends to be overlooked in discussions about class in Britain is the extent to which it was often merely a synonym for money and education. In a feudal society, class is associated with the idea of family and breeding, yet as early as 1775 Topham Beauclerk could tell James Boswell, Dr Johnson's biographer, that 'now in England being of an old family was of no consequence. People did not inquire far back. If a man was rich and well educated, he was equally well received as the most ancient gentleman, though if inquiry were made, his extraction might be found to be very mean.'[3]

This is an important point which explains the prestige of the public schools. What your grandfather did for a living was, by the early nineteenth century, largely irrelevant. What really mattered was whether you had gone to the right schools and universities. In this respect, there was a clearly defined scale, with Eton and, to a lesser degree, Harrow at the top and perhaps about fifteen other schools which were regarded as acceptable. Education at this sort of school would very often be followed by a stint at Oxford or Cambridge, where, towards the end of the nineteenth century, the class of degree awarded became important, with a first of course being more prized than a second or third. The subject studied was also significant, with Classics, the study of the languages and cultures of ancient Greece and Rome, being the most popular as well as the most prestigious discipline. History was probably the next most sought after, but didn't have quite the same status. Technical subjects were rarely studied by those who aspired to a career in the administration of colonies; the late nineteenth century was, after all, a time when the Professor of Engineering at Oxford was frequently dismissed by his colleagues as the 'Professor of Jam-Making'.[4]

Once admitted to a 'decent' public school, and after obtaining a good degree at either Oxford or Cambridge, or perhaps after a stint in the army, the young man who wanted to make a career in the colonies could really go as far as luck and talent would take him. The system, once the right educational background had been established, was fairly meritocratic. The ultimate imperial civil servant was Alfred Milner, born in Germany in 1854, the son of a medical student who had married a widow twenty years his senior. Milner's background was obscure, but by dint of talent and industry he ended up as a viscount and was elected chancellor of Oxford University, though he died before he could be officially installed. He owed his success initially to his prowess in the examination halls of Oxford University. He had won the top Classical scholarship to Balliol College in 1872 and had steadily picked up awards and prizes during his career there. Armed with his double first, he dedicated himself to a 'life of public usefulness'. His one brush with democratic politics failed, when he was unsuccessful as the Liberal candidate in Harrow, a suburb of London, in 1885. Thereafter he pursued power as an administrator.

Milner's career touches on another important point. It is a mistake to think that administrators were motivated by liberal ideas of democracy. In many cases they chose careers in the empire precisely because they were not democrats. They were elitists, men who could write Latin and Greek epigrams and had sought to wield power without having to go through the inconvenience of being elected. Milner himself remained 'profoundly distrustful of the enfranchised'.[5] To argue that he and his colleagues were promoting democracy stretches the truth. The empire stood for order and the rule of law, but we must not pretend that its character was something other than what it was. The imperial administration was highly stratified and snobbish. It was the very opposite of the egalitarian, plural and liberal institution that some historians have portrayed. As George Orwell remembered of his own education, 'it was universally taken for granted . . . that unless you went to a "good" public school (and only about fifteen schools came under this heading) you were ruined for life'.[6] The people who ran the empire would tacitly have agreed with this statement. Yet the narrow educational field did not preclude men of modest means, brought up in obscure families, from climbing the ladder. Among the administrators there were the sons of parsons, of university lecturers and of civil servants. In fact the majority were from middling, anonymous families, without the pride of lineage associated with true aristocracies. It was at the public schools and, to a lesser degree, at the universities that the elite swagger and famously lofty sense of superiority were cultivated.

This was a manifestation as much of cultural superiority as of purely social snobbery. A first in Greats, the Oxford Classics course, and an education at Winchester ensured that a man would be held in the highest esteem. An interesting feature of this snobbery and sense of superiority was the extent to which native princes and rulers were made to fit the pattern. In the native societies the British administrator encountered, it was often class, money and education that counted more than race. This explains why Colonial Office officials in the 1930s would spend time arranging for a Nigerian chief's stay in Claridge's, one of the most exclusive hotels in London. The hierarchical view of the world was exported to the colonies and, in many ways, the empire was a 'vehicle for the extension of British social structures'.[7] There were certainly notions of racial superiority, but these were mingled with often contradictory ideas about education and wealth. It was a confusing picture.

The empire was not simply a forerunner of the modern pluralist democracy, so valued in the West. It was something entirely different. It is simply misleading to describe the British Empire, as one historian has done, as the champion of 'free-market liberalism' and democracy.[8] Such a judgement pays too little attention to what the empire was really like, or to the ideas that motivated the people who actually administered it. Notions of

FERGUSON

democracy could not have been further from the minds of the imperial administrators themselves. Their heads were filled with ideas of class, loosely defined, of intellectual superiority and of paternalism. 'Benign authoritarianism' would be a better description of the political philosophy that sustained the empire.

The focus of this book is on the colonial empire, not on the white dominions. This recognizes that much of the debate about the British Empire in the early years of the twenty-first century has really been about the role of the United States of America. Some historians and political scientists have suggested that the United States should follow Britain and try to impose its own 'Pax Americana' on the more anarchic parts of the world. The model the United States is being asked to follow is one of administration and military occupation. Even the most strident neo-conservatives, the historians who say that 'empire is more necessary in the twenty-first century than ever before', have never suggested that millions of Americans should emigrate to places like Iraq on a permanent basis and establish their families there.[9] Aggressive modern imperialists do believe that an empire can keep the world safe and better administered. I contend that the example of the British Empire shows the opposite; empires, through their lack of foresight and the wide discretion they give administrators, lead to instability and the development of chronic problems. In any case, the idea of creating an avowedly interventionist American empire now seems, especially after the defeat of the Republican candidate in the 2008 presidential election, as absurd as the notion of absolute monarchy seemed to Britons of the nineteenth century. It also misunderstands the nature of empire. Britain's empire was not liberal in the sense of being a plural, democratic society. It openly repudiated ideas of human equality and put power and responsibility into the hands of a chosen elite, drawn from a tiny proportion of the population in Britain. The British Empire was not merely undemocratic; it was anti-democratic. The United States, on the other hand, despite its difficult history, proclaims itself to be democratic, plural and liberal. Its avowed values could not be further removed from those of the British Empire.

As I hope to show in many of the examples of imperial history I outline in the following chapters, the anarchic individualism and paternalism which underpinned the British Empire led to messy outcomes. Transitions from British rule to independence were difficult, because the Pax Britannica was itself transient and without any firm foundation. The British Empire was nothing more than a series of improvisations conducted by men who shared a common culture, but who often had very different ideas about government and administration. There is very little unifying ideology in this imperial story. It was grand and colourful but it was highly opportunistic, dominated by individualism and pragmatism. The British Empire is a bizarre model to follow for fostering stability in today's world. Indeed, much of the instability in the world is a product of its legacy of individualism and haphazard policy-making.

PART I

Iraq: Oil and Power

I

The Spoils of War

The speaker was self-assured and confident. With a lifetime of public service behind him, Lord Curzon was fully in command of his audience. The Inter-Allied Petroleum dinner, given on 21 November 1918 at Lancaster House in St James's, was a festive occasion. The Great War, which had cost over 900,000 British lives, had been over for ten days. It had been a close-run thing. For a considerable period during the war itself, Germany had looked invincible, with its great coal deposits and manpower. But oil had saved the day for the Allies. One of the most 'astonishing things' Curzon had seen during the war in France and Flanders was the 'tremendous army of motor lorries', all powered by oil. 'Even before the War', he boomed, 'oil was regarded as one of the most important national industries and assets.' It was clear that the 'Allied cause had floated to victory upon a wave of oil'.[1]

Curzon was by now a seasoned imperial statesman. His career achievements had been celebrated, even from his Eton days, where he had been a competitive and successful student; he had finished his time there by becoming the captain of the Oppidans, the senior boy in the school who was not one of the seventy King's Scholars (King's Scholars were from less distinguished social backgrounds but were generally academically more able); as captain of the Oppidans, Curzon was the most academically distinguished of the affluent, fee-paying boys who formed the large majority of the school. At Oxford, Curzon's contemporaries had composed a famous ditty about him which referred to his 'sleek' hair and the fact that he dined at the country seat of the Duke of Marlborough, Blenheim Palace, 'once a week'. In many ways Curzon was an archetypal imperialist of his generation. Unlike many of his fellow aristocrats, he was well travelled and curious about the world. In 1882, immediately after leaving Oxford, he had visited Constantinople, Palestine and Egypt. In 1885, still only twenty-six, he was in Tunis, and in 1887–8 he explored America, China and India. His energy, his curiosity and his ambition were boundless. More significantly, he was wholly committed to the imperial cause. In 1898, he became viceroy of India (that is, the British monarch's representative) at the age of thirty-nine. When Curzon was appointed foreign secretary in October 1919, he was regarded by Harold Nicolson, a Foreign Office official, as 'the last of that unbroken line of Foreign Secretaries who had been born with the privileges of a territorial aristocracy and nurtured on the traditions of a governing class'. An important characteristic of this 'unbroken line' was the narrowness of their education and the certainty with which they held their values. 'Eton and Winchester, Christ Church and Balliol [elite colleges at Oxford University], Trinity and King's [equivalent colleges at Cambridge] had moulded these calm, confident and unassuming men.' They thought the same thing. 'Upon the main principles of Imperial and Foreign Affairs they felt alike; they thought alike; they acted alike.'[2] Not that anyone would accuse Lord Curzon of being 'unassuming'. His manner, according to Nicolson who worked under him at the Foreign Office, 'created the legend of a man, conceited, reactionary, unbending and aloof'. His imperialism 'above everything' was based upon the doctrine of 'responsibility', upon the conviction 'that Great Britain had been entrusted with certain moral and practical obligations towards her subject races'.

Despite this high-mindedness, however, Iraq was different. The Allies' success in obtaining oil during the war had been a result of the participation of the United States of America in the conflict. America had supplied them with 80 per cent of the oil used in the war effort and, as a consequence, the British did not want to be dependent on American oil in the future. Sir Edmund Slade, a retired admiral, who had been born in the same year as Lord Curzon, in 1859, had written a paper for the Cabinet on this very subject that summer. The paper was entitled 'On the Petroleum Situation in the British Empire', and it was dated 29 July 1918, three months before the war's end. Oil was needed – there was no doubt about that. It was 'twice as economical as coal'. The problem was that there was very little to be found in the British Empire. Even before the war, Slade argued, Britain got 62 per cent of its oil from the United States. Romania and Russia were responsible for nearly 20 per cent, while the rest was obtained from far-flung, unreliable places like Mexico and the Dutch colonies in the Far East.

The only way to secure the strategic position, or, in Sir Edmund's stately phrase, to keep 'our hold over the sea communications of the world in the event of another war', was to find oil within the British Empire. If such a source could be found, then 'the predominance now enjoyed by foreign oil corporations will be a thing of the past'. The British would then be 'masters in our own house'. Slade had a pretty shrewd idea where this oil would be found. The oil of Persia (modern Iran) and Mesopotamia (modern Iraq) would in the future, he believed, 'provide a supply equal to that now given by the United States'. The conclusion was obvious enough. Whoever controlled the 'oil lands of Persia and Mesopotamia' would control 'the source of supply of the majority of the liquid fuel of the future'. This memorandum made an immediate impression. The next day, on 30 July, the Cabinet Secretary, Sir Maurice Hankey, wrote to Sir Eric Geddes, who had been a general manager of the North Eastern Railway before being brought into Parliament and the Cabinet in 1917, stating that the 'retention of the oil-bearing regions in Mesopotamia and Persia . . . [was] a first-class British War aim'.[3]

This was all very straightforward. Oil was vitally important to the navy and to the new air force. F. H. Sykes, a major general, and also Chief of the Air Staff, agreed with Slade and told the Cabinet on 9 August, only ten days after the admiral's initial report, that the whole 'future of air power is dependent upon adequate supplies of liquid fuel'. There were a few dissenting voices. Edwin Montagu, a Liberal member of the Cabinet, wrote in December 1918, after the war was over, that the Iraqi state should at least 'participate' in any new company which might be created to get the precious oil out of the ground. In his view, Britain was concerned merely with 'safeguarding' the interests of the new state.[4] Yet Montagu was suspected of being a bit soft on 'natives'; he was Jewish, people muttered, and not all that 'sound' on imperial questions.

It was very clear that oil was essential to Britain. The war offered a great opportunity, because the Middle East had been dominated by the Ottoman Empire; and the Ottomans, to their detriment, had sided with Germany during the conflict. The defeat of Germany and its allies had, therefore, also meant the end of the Ottoman Empire. Britain and France could divide the spoils. The 'most alluring of the Ottoman spoils' happened to be the oil of Iraq.[5]

There were a few problems. There were British officials on the ground who had not been made fully aware of the importance of Iraq in the new world after the Great War. There was also the fact that the Iraqis themselves had been led to believe that, after the defeat of the Ottomans, they would enjoy independence. As T. E. Lawrence, 'Lawrence of Arabia' himself, observed in a letter to *The Times* in July 1920, the Arabs 'rebelled against the Turks [the Ottoman Empire] during the war not because the Turk government was notably bad, but because they wanted independence'. They had not risked their lives 'in battle to change masters, to become British subjects or French citizens, but to win a show of their own'.[6]

There was also the problem that Sir Mark Sykes had created in 1916. He established, in negotiations with his counterpart François Picot, the Sykes–Picot line which had divided up the Middle East between Britain and France even before the war had ended. Sykes had been careless enough to give the French control of Mosul, the northern province of Iraq, where most of the oil was suspected to be. The French hadn't actually taken possession of the province: while the war raged, this allocation was a theoretical consideration. Sykes was not really trusted by the British government, as he was considered to be too imaginative and dreamy, too exotic even. The only son of an eccentric Yorkshire baronet, he had been influenced greatly by his mother, a Roman Catholic, who had a consuming passion for French culture and literature. It was said that she 'could have passed an examination in Balzac' and that she knew French literature as well as a Frenchman. A consequence of this passion was that her son would often spend months on the continent of Europe, being educated unsystematically at various schools there, and consequently avoided the traditional British educational establishments favoured by families of his class and background. She had been estranged from her husband, partly as a result of the wide discrepancy between their ages; they had married in 1874 when he was forty-eight and she only eighteen. They had one child, Mark, in 1879, after which they led separate lives. Mark attended the school of the Italian Jesuits for a few months in Monaco, where perhaps he acquired, in the words of one friend, 'his considerable knowledge of sexual matters combined with innocence'. He had plenty of talent, but no mental discipline. 'The usual monotonous drill in the Classics or Mathematics', his biographer argued, 'creates a certain capacity and aptitude for detail which Mark ever lacked.'[7] He had after all escaped the systematic, rigorous, often pedantic training favoured by the High Victorian education system. He succeeded to his father's baronetcy in 1913.

Sykes had travelled widely in the area which was known at the time as the Near East. He knew only a hundred words of Arabic and he simply 'acted his way through the East'. He had been to Mosul, the northern province of Iraq, as early as 1899, where he found Arabs with the 'minds of mudlarks and the appearance of philosophers'.[8] All this travelling hadn't really tempered some of his more extreme views. He was mildly anti-Semitic and violently anti-Armenian. 'Even Jews had their good points,' he remarked in his book *Through Five Turkish Provinces*, 'but Armenians have none.'[9] At Sledmere, his impressive country seat in Yorkshire, he insisted on attending daily Mass. He was eccentric, unworldly, aristocratic and literary. In the Boer War, he had irritated his soldier comrades by reading Shakespeare aloud while they were digging trenches. While still in South Africa, he wrote to his fiancée, encouraging her to 'read eighteenth century literature a good deal', on the ground that this period was the 'climax of the Christian Era. Now you will find that the French Revolutionary year was the commencement of the present era of progress, grab, commercialism . . . blood, villainy, ignorance, disbelief, and science.'[10] It is difficult to recognize the 'Christian Era' to which he referred, given that Voltaire, Montesquieu, Gibbon and Fielding had all been published many years before the French Revolution.

Sykes was not a materialist. He despised 'grab' and 'commercialism', yet his masters in Whitehall were all too motivated by these considerations.

He had been Conservative MP for Hull since 1911, and was an acknowledged expert, by House of Commons standards, on Eastern and particularly
Islamic questions. His parliamentary career was cut short by the war and
by February 1919 he was dead, killed by the influenza epidemic which
gripped most of Western Europe at that time. He was only thirty-nine.
The Sykes–Picot line didn't last much longer. On 1 December 1918, barely
three weeks after the end of the war, Georges Clemenceau, the French
Prime Minister, had met David Lloyd George, his British opposite number,
at 10 Downing Street. There they both agreed that Mosul should form
part of British-controlled Iraq. By way of compensation, France was to get
25 per cent of the oil produced in the province.[11]

On the ground in Iraq itself, Arnold Wilson, the man on the spot who
'slept and ate in his office', recognized the need for oil but believed that it
should remain the property of the Mesopotamian administration, in
other words of the British government, and not be put in the hands of
any existing commercial company.[12] Wilson, though not an intellectual
man, was typical of the imperial cast of mind. He was practical, not
without idealism, but generally unhampered by reflection or any real
intellectual influences. Born in 1884, he had been educated at Clifton
College, one of the newer so-called public schools which had been established in the Victorian era. He joined the Indian army in 1902, after
winning the Sword of Honour at Sandhurst, an award given to the top
cadet (both academic and practical) in a graduating class. Unusually, he
had also won the King's Medal which is given exclusively for the top
academic performance in the class. He had enjoyed a meteoric career as
an imperial soldier in the East, and would receive a knighthood in 1920,
when still only thirty-six. He was well described, on a brief return to
England in 1907, as 'a self-confident, egotistical, clean-living, intensely
ambitious, rather philistine young man', while his Christianity was
'centred on Clifton chapel'.[13]

As a military man, Wilson recognized the commercial and strategic
interests of the British Empire. Iraq was important primarily because of its
potential oil reserves, but very little oil had actually been produced.
Everyone knew it was there. As a Cabinet memorandum of 2 August 1918
had pointed out, the Germans themselves, in a paper on Mesopotamia

written in 1916, had observed that 'the greatest importance after that of the Suez Canal, attaches to the possession of Mesopotamia', where 'petroleum wells' had been known for 'thousands of years'.[14] More generally, there were wider, strategic considerations too. Britain had an interest in protecting the route to India and the Indian trade. The possession of Iraq made sense for Britain.

It therefore came as no surprise that the San Remo conference of the main Allied powers, which took place at the end of April 1920, should grant Iraq as a mandate to Britain. The term 'mandate' was unusual and, even today, people still think it had less than imperial status, yet it served to disguise the reality of power. Curzon himself admitted this when, in a Cabinet memorandum written as early as September 1917, he had suggested that 'some form of civilised tutelage is required to lead up to the goal of national autonomy'. Clearly, the mandate was precisely this 'form of civilised tutelage'. Curzon expressly declared that the surrender of the Iraqi port of Basra 'would be fatal to the British position in the Persian Gulf which is the maritime frontier of the Indian Empire'.[15] An early political analyst observed as early as 1937 that the British government was 'unwilling to give up its favoured position in Iraq' until it had achieved three aims: 'control of the land route to India', the 'extension and protection of British commerce' and 'control of the existing and potential oil-producing districts of Iraq'.[16] Curzon himself, with characteristic realism, had said that the term 'mandate' could have a 'terminological variant such as perpetual lease', so long as the 'reality which we must not abandon' was safeguarded.[17] Even more explicitly, Curzon had argued, in a memorandum of December 1917, that there 'should be no actual incorporation of conquered territory' but the absorption should be 'veiled' by 'constitutional fictions', as a 'protectorate, a sphere of influence, a buffer state, and so on'.[18]

Behind these fictions, there existed much idealism about the British civilizing mission in the East. There was a genuine belief that British rule was better for Iraq than subjection to the rule of the Ottoman Turks. Curzon, while remaining a clear-eyed champion of imperial interests, could speak as eloquently as anyone about the British achievement in Iraq. In the House of Lords in February 1919, when he had been foreign secretary for little more than a month, he boasted about the 'advance that has been made in the last two years in the development of Mesopotamia'. It had been simply 'amazing', and Britain had done more 'for those places' in two years than the Turks had done 'in the five preceding centuries'. There was no 'more proud experience for any Englishman than if he were now to go to Mesopotamia and see what is being accomplished there'.[19]

Many of the British officials themselves would have agreed enthusiastically with Lord Curzon's high-flown rhetoric. Perhaps none would have been more elated than Gertrude Bell. Much has been written about Bell. Her achievements, which had been overshadowed in the Middle East by those of T. E. Lawrence, are now being celebrated. Women historians feel that Lawrence's fame had eclipsed hers merely because he was a man. Her story was extraordinary. She had been born in 1868, the granddaughter of Sir Lowthian Bell, a self-made Victorian industrialist with brains, titanic energy and drive. The family fortune was impressive, but Gertrude had combined material wealth with learning and physical grace. She was the first woman to gain a first in Modern History at Oxford University in 1888. More remarkably, she was only nineteen years old when she sat the examination, at least two or three years younger than her classmates. She could swim, fence, row, play tennis and hockey. Fluent in Persian and Arabic, she was a passionate archaeologist and explorer, and by the end of the First World War she had spent nearly twenty years in the Middle East. She never married. An early love-match had been thwarted by her father Sir Hugh, who believed that Gertrude's young suitor was too poor to support her in the appropriate style. This doomed relationship had blossomed in 1893, when she was twenty-five, and since then, despite a number of love affairs, she had remained single. Her deepest and most enduring relationship was that with her father. Indeed, the closeness of the relationship might well have been the cause, rather than an effect, of her never getting married.

Sir Hugh Bell outlived his daughter. She died in 1926, aged only fifty-seven, while her father died in 1931 at the age of eighty-two. Gertrude reported to her father on nearly everything she did in Iraq, writing not only about politics and military affairs, but also about cultural issues. She told him, in a letter on 18 December 1920, that 'Mesopotamia is not a civilized state . . . it needs force for the maintenance of internal order.' She was very clear about the nature of the British involvement in Iraq, and the obligations Britain had towards the new state. 'Whatever our future policy is to be we cannot now leave the country in the state of chaos which we have created,' she wrote to her father on 2 August 1920.[20] As a woman, Gertrude Bell was not permitted to exercise ultimate authority in Iraq. That was very much the preserve of the military men like Arnold Wilson and her principal chief, Percy Cox, a tall wiry man of nearly sixty who could keep silence, it was said, in a dozen languages. Cox was the British High Commissioner in Iraq, and Bell was his oriental secretary.

There was no doubting Gertrude Bell's idealism, which meant that she had little interest in the commercial, petroleum side of things. Having made enough money in the steel business, the Bells could devote their lives to liberal imperialism, while others did the dirty work of actually making money. The empire was full of civil servants, polished officials of sophisticated literary education, who turned a blind eye to the more sordid, commercial aspects of the imperial mission. This is perhaps what Harry St John Philby, father of the Soviet spy Kim Philby, meant when he suggested that Gertrude Bell, for all her ability, 'had no half-tones in her repertoire'.[21] Idealism was not far from Humphrey Bowman's repertoire, either. A forty-year-old Eton and Oxford old boy, he was appointed director of education in Iraq from 1918 to 1920. He had fond memories of his first sight of the country in August 1918: 'As the ship steamed slowly up the Shatt al Arab on that hot summer day, the waving palm trees on either bank seemed to give me welcome.' He remembered the happy, jostling crowds in Arab dress as he stepped ashore at Basra. A committed student of Arabic who had spent some of his earlier career in Cairo, Bowman was delighted to hear 'again the Arab tongue' which made him feel that he was coming to a land 'not altogether strange'. All this he recounted in a broadcast on the BBC entitled 'Memories of Iraq', which was transmitted in 1942. His diaries of his time in Iraq paint a vivid picture of the reasonably civilized, enlightened time he spent there. He managed to celebrate 4 June 1919, a date which was remembered as King George III's birthday at Eton, with some fellow Old Etonians in Baghdad. Five old boys of that school attended a dinner at the officers' club, where they dined on 'fish mayonnaise, iced soup, chicken, roast lamb', followed by 'trifle pudding', rounded off with a savoury dish of 'sardines on toast'.[22]

Bowman was fortunate. He missed much of the action which quickly threatened to overturn Britain's position in Iraq. The strange thing about the old boys' dinners and the letters home is the insular world they evoke. The Iraqis themselves seemed to be a sideshow in their own country. Even a relatively genial man like Cox, whose good looks were 'rather marred' by a hooked nose, according to Bowman, was generally quite aloof. Sir Ronald Storrs, the great oriental civil administrator, described the attitude well, in a lecture delivered to the University of Leicester in 1932, when he accused the British of not being 'good mixers'. He went on to say that 'some of our officials, and I regret to say their ladies also, are apt to stand on their dignity in dealing with the men and women with whom they are thrown in contact'.[23]

Humphrey Bowman did not have this problem. Gertrude Bell, in a letter to Lord Allenby, who had led the campaign in Palestine during the war, acknowledged that his departure from Iraq was a cause of 'regret' because he had the 'invaluable gift, which is now more necessary than any other, of making friends with Arabs'.[24] Not being very good mixers naturally meant that British officials were often insensitive to local concerns and states of mind. This frequently led to confusion and sometimes worse.

The Arabs' frustration over the post-war settlement can be easily described. They wanted, in the words Lawrence used in 1920, a 'show of their own'. By now, there were tensions among the British themselves. Some favoured a more liberal approach, in which the aspirations of Arab nationalism would be accommodated; others supported a tougher line. In Wilson's view the people of Mesopotamia 'were obviously incapable of governing themselves'. He proposed only to educate them in 'that art on the municipal level'. It was fine for them to operate independently on the parish-council level. Philby, in a characteristically pompous remark, was not filled with a 'desire to serve in Iraq under his proconsulship'.[25] For her part, Gertrude Bell saw herself as being more liberal, despite believing that force was the best means of 'internal order'. At a dinner in October 1920 she explained to Jafar Pasha al-Askari, a local Baghdad politician, in her excellent Arabic that 'complete independence' was what Britain 'ultimately wished to give'. He replied, 'My Lady, "complete independence" is never given; it is always taken.' A 'profound saying', she remarked in the letter to her father.[26]

The scene of a polite dinner party in Baghdad at the end of 1920, at which British and Iraqi guests exchanged pleasantries in Arabic, belied the turmoil of the preceding months. Cox had departed from Iraq and Wilson had been left in charge. The political discontent and rumblings which Bowman had detected towards the end of 1919 were spilling over into open dissent by the beginning of 1920. Iraq was a country of only 3 million people, split on tribal, ethnic and religious lines. Bowman had observed the relative openness of Basra, where 'Arabs, Indians, Egyptians, Kurds, Armenians, Syrians, Jews' mixed freely, with 'a large sprinkling of the ubiquitous British soldier'.[27] The rest of the country was very different, as it was more sectarian and far less tranquil. Of the 3 million inhabitants, roughly 1.6 million, or 55 per cent, were Arab Shi'ites; 600,000, or 20 per cent, were Arab Sunnis. There were about 600,000 Kurds, while the remnants were Jews, Yazidis and Christians, among other faiths.[28]

Then, as now, the Sunni–Shia divide was the main sectarian split in the country. The background to this political division in Iraq was, of course, the Ottoman Empire. Iraq had been an Ottoman province since 1638 and had marked the eastern frontier of that empire, beyond which lay the Safavid kingdom of Persia, the country we know today as Iran. The Safavids had adopted the Shia Islamic faith, while the Ottomans were proudly Sunni. Iraq had never been under Shia dominion, even though the majority of its people professed that branch of the Islamic faith.

To Gertrude Bell, the Shias were fanatical and irrational, while Sunni Muslims were generally regarded by her and by many of her compatriots as being more compliant. In a letter to her stepmother Florence in March 1920, she had remarked that it was 'a problem to get into touch with the Shiahs [sic]'. Their leaders of religious opinion carried enormous authority and, basing themselves on the Koran, could 'loose and bind with a word'

– though Bell herself dismissed the Koran as 'entirely irrelevant to human affairs and worthless in any branch of human activity'. The Muslims' religious customs had made things particularly difficult for her, a Western woman. She had been 'until quite recently' completely 'cut off from them because their tenets forbid them to look upon an unveiled woman and my tenets don't permit me to veil'.[29]

The potential religious conflicts within Iraq had not, of course, been considered in the negotiations surrounding the San Remo Agreement, which had been signed in the picturesque Italian town just east of Monte Carlo at the end of April 1920. Britain had been granted control over Iraq in the form of a mandate. No one, however, had bothered to ask any of the Iraqis what they thought of the Agreement. The reaction was perhaps predictable, in so far as it stirred religious passions within Iraq, as well as a yearning for independence. More than a year before the Agreement had been signed, Sheikh Muhammad Shirazi, a Shia cleric, had issued a fatwa, in January 1919, proclaiming that 'a non-Muslim could not be allowed by Muslims to rule over the followers of the Prophet'. In March 1920 he was even more explicit, promulgating another fatwa forbidding Muslims to accept any office in the heart of the British administration.[30] Later that month, Ayatollah Shirazi took the decision to launch a general uprising against the British.

The revolt of 1920 has taken on a mythic status among Iraqis. Even foreigners, who have tried to compare the events of that long hot summer with subsequent occupations, have misunderstood it. To the British, it was often depicted as a case of ungrateful, ill-disciplined natives exploiting imperial weakness. To Wilson, the revolt was a typical example of the Arab 'kicking a man when he is down', which he believed was the 'most popular pastime in the East'.[31] Too often British and American historians, often Middle East specialists, have focused exclusively on the Iraqi angle of the revolt. It was, however, part of a general spasm of protest against British imperial rule in the aftermath of the First World War. Revolts, or incipient uprisings, had occurred in Egypt in March 1919, and the following month in India, where at Amritsar soldiers commanded by General Reginald Dyer officially killed 379 unarmed citizens, though Indian estimates put the figure at over 1,000.

The extent to which the Iraqi revolt can be viewed as nationalistic has also been questioned. The one thing that British rule did manage to achieve was the union, if only briefly, of the adherents of both the Sunni and Shia branches of the Islamic faith. General Sir Aylmer Haldane, in his gruff memoirs of the insurrection, published only two years later in 1922, remembered that it 'threw for a time the Sunni townsmen and the Shia country-folk' together, an alliance which he regarded as 'miraculous'. More generally, the insurrection aroused a sense of bewilderment among the British. General Haldane could only speculate on the 'strangely subtle mind' of the Arab, 'a being so vain, so given to exaggerate, and so suscep-tible to propaganda' that it was 'extremely difficult for a European to understand' him.[32] To others, the answer was simple – perhaps the Iraqi Arabs just wanted to be free.

The initial cause of the revolt is now fairly obscure, and many reasons have been given for its occurrence. Some say it was sparked by the arrest of a Shia cleric, others by the arrest of a clerk who recited a 'fiery anti-British poem' in Baghdad. What is certain is that the fury of the Baghdad mob, which has been a frequent participant in Iraqi affairs, was intense. The resistance movement itself was based around Najaf, one of the holiest Shia cities owing to its status as the final resting place of Ali, cousin and son-in-law of the Prophet Mohammed, and Baghdad, a town with a large Sunni population. Bowman noted in his diary, while complaining of the heat and damp, that the month of Ramadan saw the 'first sign of restlessness'. He described how mosques in Baghdad were becoming, for the first time in a long while, hives of political agitation. Meetings which were nomi-nally religious were now, he observed, becoming 'centres of political activity'.

In Iraq in 1920, Ramadan began on 17 May. As head of the education service, Bowman was particularly concerned about the looting of schools in Karbala, another Shia holy place. He also expressed concern that his staff, Iraqi primary school teachers, had fled to Baghdad for safety.[33] There can be no doubt that a nationalist movement existed. The fact that both Sunni and Shia had combined during the revolt surprised British officials like General Haldane and Arnold Wilson, who had clearly underestimated 'the strength of the nationalist movement'.[34] Wilson himself, in his memoirs, readily admitted that the 'deep prejudices which separate the Sunni and Shi'ah sects' had been 'temporarily overcome' during the revolt.[35] Despite the overt nationalism, which we, influenced by President Nasser and the Ba'athists of the 1950s, anachronistically regard as a largely secular movement, there was a strong religious element to the uprising. The Ayatollah Shirazi, the Shia cleric whose fatwa had started the trouble, 'enjoyed unprecedented prestige' among the Shia community, while his fellow Shia clerics clearly saw their struggle as a holy war.[36] Gertrude Bell agreed. Writing to her stepmother in September 1920, she remarked that the British were 'now in the middle of a full-blown Jihad', a term we translate as 'holy war'. She added that this meant that 'we have against us the fiercest prejudices of a people in a primeval state of civilisation'.[37] Of course, the revolt was both religious and nationalistic. St John Philby, in his mischievous way, was convinced of the overtly nationalist impulse behind it. 'What they [the Iraqis] want, like the people of Arabia and Syria . . . is complete independence, nothing more and nothing less,' he asserted in an address he gave in June that year to the Central Asian Society.[38]

The cost of suppressing the revolt was very high. Two divisions of troops had to be sent from India. From October 1920 onwards, British soldiers systematically began to reconquer lost ground; Karbala was occupied by British troops on 13 October, Najaf the next day.[39] The insurgency had lasted three months and affected about one-third of the country. The movement was disorganized, diverse and highly local.[40] The British had lost 426 lives, with 1,228 wounded. Among the insurgents, over 8,000 were killed in those scorching months. In financial terms, the revolt had been disastrous: the cost has been put at £40 million.[41] As control of Iraq was re-established, this made the British highly conscious of any future expenditure they would have to incur in Iraq.

Although a committed imperialist, Winston Churchill, as secretary of state for air and war, argued for more economy in spending in the Middle East. In the summer of 1920, the large number of casualties and the high cost of the military campaign had provoked a political reaction against the mandate and Britain's imperial mission in the Arab world. In August, a *Times* editorial asked, 'what is the total number of casualties we have suffered in Mesopotamia during the single month of July, in our efforts to emancipate the Arabs, to fulfil our mandate, and to smooth the way for the seekers after oil?' In Parliament, the Labour Party were lobbying for a complete withdrawal from Iraq. Churchill, as a senior member of the Lloyd George coalition, was pragmatic enough to suggest that the 'cost of garrisoning Iraq' was 'prohibitive' and 'out of all proportion to its value'.

Combined with high costs, there was also administrative confusion. Britain's empire in the Middle East had come into being only as a result of the defeat and collapse of the Ottoman Empire. There was little infrastructure in Whitehall, the centre of the imperial government in London, from which to administer the new empire in the Middle East. Nominally, the Foreign Office was responsible for Palestine, Egypt and the Sudan, while the India Office was responsible for the Gulf and Iraq. The War Office also had considerable authority in the region. Middle East policy was a battleground, in which each of the three departments sought to gain advantage over the other two.[42] By February 1921, Iraq had returned to a peaceful state. Churchill, who had now been moved to become secretary of state for the colonies, was anxious to create a more stable Iraq, at a much cheaper price. He had also staked a claim for the Middle East for his new department, the Colonial Office. Curzon, still foreign secretary, was anxious to maintain the prestige of his department, and in reality the Foreign Office still retained responsibility for Egypt, Persia and Central Asia. Churchill, with characteristic energy, convened a conference in Cairo in March 1921, after just a few weeks in the job. In the pleasant warmth of the Cairo sun, at favoured colonial-era haunts like the Shepheard Hotel, the Middle East experts of the British Empire gathered and, for three weeks, discussed the various problems which faced Britain in this turbulent part of the world. From Cairo, on 23 March, Gertrude Bell wrote to Humphrey Bowman, the Old Etonian Arabist, that the 'stream of nationalist sentiment' was often 'the only visible movement' in Arab politics.[43]

The most famous man at the conference of the 'forty thieves', as Churchill called it, was undoubtedly T. E. Lawrence, an 'object at once of awe and pity'.[44] Lawrence continues to fascinate Western minds, influenced perhaps unduly by what is perceived to be the romance of the East. His participation in Iraqi affairs was peripheral, despite the fact that regarded himself as a 'foundation-member' of the new kingdom of Iraq.[45] Lawrence famously was convinced of the need for the Arabs to be independent. He boasted as much to Charlotte Shaw, the wife of the playwright George Bernard Shaw, declaring that he had been 'right to work for Arab self-government through 1919 and 1920'. The self-government he had in mind was a figment of his own romantic imagination. Despite his vaunted support for the cause of Arab self-determination, Lawrence told Mrs Shaw in the same letter that the Arabs were not yet ready for the self-government he had so generously conceived for them. 'As for Irak [sic] . . . some day they will be fit for self-government and then they will not want a king: but whether 7 or 70 or 700 years hence, God knows.'[46] He was clear that until the Iraqis proved 'fit' for self-government they would have to make do with a king, provided by Britain.

The monarchy that the British so obligingly gave to the Iraqi people would, in the long run, produce as many problems as it supplied solutions. Faisal, the new king, was a thirty-eight-year-old Sunni from the Hejaz, on the Red Sea, to the west of the modern kingdom of Saudi Arabia, and he had spent his earliest years among the Bedouin tribesmen. As a member of the Hashemite family, he was descended from the Prophet Mohammed in the thirty-eighth generation, and his father, Hussein bin Ali, was the Sharif of Mecca, the keeper of the holy city. The Hashemites had been subordinate in status to the Ottoman Sultan, who presided over the extensive Ottoman Empire from the Topkapı Palace in Constantinople. Faisal, as was the custom for the sons of important dignitaries in the Ottoman Empire, had spent time in Constantinople. He had been educated to play his part as a high official in the empire, not to become a leader of an Arab nation. He had been befriended during the First World War by T. E. Lawrence, to whom he seemed an obvious candidate to be king of Iraq. The British felt that a king would be a convenient stabilizing figure in the country's unsettled political situation. The precise ethnic origins of the monarch were regarded as a minor consideration. Gertrude Bell, in a letter to her father at the end of January 1921, had wondered whether a Turk might not be a better bulwark against the Shias than a 'son of the Sharif'; the Sunnis of Baghdad were worried that they would be swamped by the Shias, and the Ottoman Turks had shown themselves historically to be fierce antagonists of the Shias.[47]

The Cairo conference had set Faisal on the way to becoming king of Iraq. A plebiscite was arranged in which he got 96 per cent of the vote, enough to give a veneer of popular legitimacy to the new dynasty. T. E. Lawrence and Gertrude Bell were proud of their handiwork. Bell wrote to her father on 28 August 1921, in a gushing manner, telling him about the 'terrific week' she had just enjoyed. 'We've got our King crowned.' Faisal's coronation had taken place the week before; at six in the morning of the 21st he had stood in a military uniform and been formally crowned and proclaimed king.[48]

A political solution of a kind had been found, in which Iraq would be a constitutional monarchy, with a constituent assembly, under the aegis of the British Empire. It was a Sunni monarchy in a country most of whose people were Shia. In October 1922, a treaty between Britain and Iraq was signed which proved to be the 'backbone of Britain's indirect rule'. Mindful of the costs of imperial rule, the British government insisted that the Iraqis paid for the costs of the British Residency, where the High Commissioner would live, and other general costs of administration. Over all these arrangements hung the 'smell of oil'.[49] If the political problem of control had now been partially solved, how would the oil itself be obtained? What structure would now be required to serve the British Empire's interest in this important matter?

Gertrude Bell had never bothered about oil. By 1926, she was tired and on Sunday 11 July, after the usual afternoon swimming party, she returned home, worn out by the dust and heat. She went to bed, asking to be woken at 6 a.m. During the night, she took an overdose of pills, from which she died. The circumstances of her death remain obscure. What is known is that she had sent a note to Ken Cornwallis, a British adviser to the King of Iraq, the day before, asking him to look after her dog Tundra, 'if anything happened to her'. Her death certificate, signed off by Dr Dunlop of the Royal Hospital in Baghdad, stated that she had died from an overdose.[50] Her death was widely mourned, as she had been a celebrated figure within the British establishment. She had believed in her personal mission. 'Seven years I've been at this job of setting up an Arab state. If we fail, it's little consolation to me personally that other generations may succeed,' she told her father in January 1923.[51] More than a year after her death, T. E. Lawrence expressed his sense of loss to Gertrude's father. He had never, he wrote, met 'anyone more entirely civilized, in the sense of her width of intellectual sympathy . . . her loss must be nearly unbearable'.[52] Others, less sentimentally, began to wonder about the oil.

2

Rivals

Even before the First World War, many politicians and administrators had realized how important oil would be to the maintenance of the British Empire. At the same time, Arab nationalism was acknowledged to be a potent factor in Iraqi affairs. Trying to create a regime that would allow relatively unhindered access to the oil of Iraq was a delicate operation. By early 1922, a political settlement had been reached, in which a broadly pro-British ruler, foreign to Iraq, had been installed. It was now time to reach a commercial settlement in which Iraq's oil wealth could be efficiently exploited.

Conveniently enough, there already existed a company, the Turkish Petroleum Company, or TPC, which had been formed in 1912 precisely to exploit the oil found in the old Ottoman Empire. The company had been interested in Iraq more as an investment, a medium-term bet rather than a 'get rich quick' scheme. The TPC's initial capital had been £80,000, which made it a relatively small concern even in those days. In the eighteen years from 1910 to 1928 Iraq could 'scarcely be called an oil producer'. In 1929 the annual production figure was still only 800,000 barrels. Iran, Iraq's Shia neighbour, produced 42.1 million barrels of oil in the same year, more than fifty times as much.[1] It was, in fact, only in 1927 that oil was struck. This did not deter the great powers, least of all Britain. A note prepared by the Middle East Department of the Colonial Office on 11 December 1922 was quite clear about the importance of Iraq's oil. The oilfields of Iraq were rich with potential and they had not 'even been properly prospected'. The report confidently stated that there was 'no doubt that there are considerable deposits of oil', particularly in Mosul, in the north of the country.[2]

The successful conclusion of the war had strengthened British political interests in the Middle East and, by diminishing the power of the Turks and the Germans, it had also provided a powerful boost to British enterprise. 'Furthermore, the treaty of October 10, 1922 between Great Britain and the Kingdom of Irak' had conferred 'sufficiently wide "advisory" powers upon the British High Commissioner at Baghdad' to protect the 'economic rights' of British nationals in the country. More particularly, in relation to the Turkish Petroleum Company, the German defeat had strengthened Britain's hand. Deutsche Bank, Germany's greatest financial enterprise, had been an initial investor in the TPC when it was formed back in 1912. Because Germany had lost the war, however, the Deutsche Bank shares in the TPC – amounting to 25 per cent of the company – were simply expropriated in December 1918. The British were already well represented in the company: Anglo-Persian, which would many years later be called Anglo-Iranian and then British Petroleum, or BP, owned 50 per cent. Consequently, when combined with the Deutsche Bank shares, the British stake in the company was three-quarters of the shares. The Anglo-Persian Company itself was majority-owned (51 per cent) by the British government, thanks to a deal brokered in 1914. This deal had been considered 'radical' for the times, since no British government had ever acquired shares in any private enterprise in this way.[3]

This shareholding was not only useful in itself. It provided a bargaining chip with which Britain could keep its wartime allies, who were now potential commercial rivals, happy – the prospect of acquiring shares in the much prized company was an alluring prospect during any diplomatic negotiations. In the aftermath of the war the Sykes–Picot Agreement had been buried and Mosul reverted to British control. In compensation, the San Remo Agreement of April 1920 granted the former German stake of 25 per cent to the French, and the British share was reduced to around a half.[4]

Eliminating the Germans, who had been the principal capitalists and investors in the country before the First World War, from the scramble for Iraqi oil wealth was fortunate for the British. The famous Berlin–Baghdad railway had been a German enterprise, financed by German capital and built largely by German engineers. The Baghdad Railway Company had begun, even before 1914, using local crude oil to fuel its locomotives.[5] As early as 1904 the Germans had prevailed on the Ottoman Sultan in Constantinople, Abdul Hamid, to grant them a railway concession, which gave them the right to survey for oil in Mosul and Baghdad.[6] The Turks had been less obliging on the issue of oil rights. Although they had allowed the German railway company to prospect for oil, they refused to recognize the claim of the actual oil company, the TPC. After intensive lobbying, the oil concession in the provinces of Mosul and Baghdad was finally granted on 27 June 1914, the day before Archduke Ferdinand was assassinated in Sarajevo.[7]

By the end of the war in 1918, the position had become confused. Britain had strengthened its position immeasurably. It now controlled most of the oil in the Middle East. Anglo-Persian was dominant in Iran, the TPC controlled Iraqi oil, while oil in the Gulf had not yet been discovered. Britain's enemies, the German Empire and the Ottoman Empire, had collapsed, allowing Churchill to remark that the end of the war had witnessed a 'drizzle of empires' falling through the rain. There were some annoyances. King Fuad of Egypt claimed that he was now de facto heir of the sultans and therefore the rightful owner of any oil found in the old Ottoman Empire. The exiled Turkish royal family also claimed the oil rights. While their claims could be ignored, a more formidable business negotiator emerged in the shape of Calouste Gulbenkian, an Armenian merchant, as he called himself, who had brokered the initial deal in 1912. His tenacity in holding on to his small shareholding in the company would provoke the ire of the colonial powers and make him tremendously rich. Though his initial stake in the Turkish Petroleum Company had been 15 per cent, he managed to keep hold of 5 per cent during the negotiations of the 1920s and hence earned the sobriquet 'Mr Five Per Cent'.[8]

Gulbenkian was one of those supernaturally wily businessmen who seem to emerge perhaps only once or twice in a generation. He had been born in Constantinople in 1869, the son of an Armenian merchant. Even in the 1880s, Gulbenkian's father had been operating in the oil business and was sufficiently fascinated by it to send his son to King's College London to study engineering. Calouste graduated with a first-class degree in 1888. In 1952 he even received an honorary fellowship from King's College, and he was by then the oldest surviving graduate of the Civil Engineering school, as well as being one of the richest men in the world. This was the only honour he ever accepted.

Gulbenkian was not only wary of honours; he didn't like people much either. His biographer recounts how, because he hated social gatherings, he avoided 'big dinners and receptions unless he thought he might be able to buttonhole somebody useful or pick up an interesting acquaintance'. The time came when he felt he had the best people in the world working for him and did not need to go in search of fresh contacts. He then simply stopped going to parties. Like many interesting characters, Gulbenkian was a mass of contradictions. He insisted on the finest French cooking and wines at home and in restaurants and yet he ate and drank only sparingly. Though he loathed people in general, he was an inveterate womanizer. He was devoted to the Armenian Orthodox Church, but didn't like his own family. A lover of the sea, he never owned a yacht, even when a multi-millionaire. His one guiding principle was his love of work. From the comfort of his armchair, he constantly read reports from associates and subordinates stationed all around the world. His wife, Nevarte, was a socialite and, from 1900 to 1925, her mansion at 38 Hyde Park Gardens became a centre of London social life. Mr Five Per Cent was more interested in pursuing young women. His own son, Nubar, a polished product of Harrow School and Trinity College, Cambridge, recalled that 'on medical advice' his father would keep 'one mistress, of no more than seventeen or eighteen, whom he changed every year until he was eighty'.[9] Calouste was, unsurprisingly, a 'control freak'. Even the sex lives of his children were under his direction. Nubar described how 'father . . . decided it was time my sexual life should start. He arranged for me to call one afternoon on our family doctor.' The doctor introduced Nubar to a 'very respectable-looking young woman of about twenty or so'. They were then taken by taxi to a hotel which Nubar described coyly as a 'maison de rendezvous'.[10]

Gulbenkian's role in the development of oil in Iraq was decisive. He managed to act as a broker who could conciliate the various national interests – British, French and later American – that were represented in the

Turkish Petroleum Company. In his canny way, he was also deeply aware of the position of the Iraqi government and people. The Gulbenkians kept their stake right to the end, even when, as Nubar remarked in 1965, 'the governments and people of the Middle East must eventually have an increasingly larger share of their own wealth' and when the days of the capitalist entrepreneurs were coming, 'no less inevitably, to their end'.[11]

This later view that the governments of the Middle East should be allowed to enjoy some of the wealth in their own countries was not widespread in the early 1920s. The British had secured Iraqi oil, or the rights to it, because they did not want to be dependent on the United States of America. The San Remo Agreement, as we have seen, gave Anglo-Persian roughly a half-share in the TPC (the actual size was 47.5 per cent); France had 25 per cent, an Anglo-Dutch company, Royal Dutch Shell, had 22.5 per cent, and Calouste Gulbenkian had his 5 per cent, which had been assembled out of the holdings of Anglo-Persian and Royal Dutch Shell. This looked like a reasonable settlement to all concerned.

Unfortunately, the initial San Remo Agreement was met with a howl of protest from the Americans. The Italians were also indignant, as they were anxious to turn the Anglo-French oil accord into a tripartite agreement, giving them a fair share.[12] Though the Italians were less successful, the Americans were able to force their way into the deal. A contemporary oil analyst put the matter very bluntly by saying that the only question about Iraqi and Iranian oil that remained to be resolved was 'whether America will be excluded from the division of the spoils'. From the point of view of the Americans, discoveries of large quantities of oil in the Middle East threatened their dominance in the industry, which for 'more than half a century had been pre-eminently an American industry'. France, Britain and Germany had produced nothing, but had consumed a great deal. They were merely 'passive spectators'.[13] San Remo had come as a 'bombshell' to the Americans because they had been effectively barred from participating in Iraq.[14]

The difficulty for the Americans was that, in the immediate aftermath of the war, they had posed as the champions of colonial peoples against imperial aggression. Woodrow Wilson, the US President, had, immediately after the end of the war, been seen as a saviour in Baghdad. In

February 1919, more than a year before the San Remo Agreement was signed, a memorandum from the US Consulate in Baghdad boasted that 'the name of President Wilson is upon the lips of the people of Bagdad a great deal these days. By Moslems, Christians and Jews it is invariably the President who is mentioned as the representative of a disinterested nation which is seeking to secure the liberties and happiness of the oppressed people of the world.' The memorandum continued, without any apparent irony, to suggest that the President would secure 'a reign of justice and righteousness for all'.[15]

But the attitude of the Americans rapidly shifted from idealism to hard-nosed pragmatism. Immediately after the war ended in November 1918, the President had denounced 'the whole disgusting scramble' for the Middle East.[16] After the San Remo Agreement in April 1920, however, President Wilson's Secretary of State, a Missouri lawyer called Bainbridge Colby, was denouncing the British and French, not because of their imperialist greed, but because they had shut out American interests. Colby, who in an earlier life had been Mark Twain's attorney, complained bitterly that the Agreement was 'a monopolistic combination designed to ignore American interests'. He made no mention of the Iraqis. It was simply a case of 'me too'. Starry-eyed Princeton idealism, as represented by the President, had given way to the powerfully commercial instincts of the American Mid-West, as expressed by the Secretary of State.[17]

Other members of Wilson's dying administration joined in the outcry against France and Britain, the old colonial powers. Frank Polk, who would give his name to the Wall Street law firm Davis, Polk and Wardwell, was an under-secretary of state. He wrote a report which reached the Senate on 17 May 1920, only three weeks after the hated San Remo Agreement had been signed. In this document, Polk savaged Britain, observing that the 'policy of the British Empire is reported to be to bring about the exclusion of aliens from the control of the petroleum supplies of the Empire'. The British were grasping and greedy in their 'endeavor to secure some measure of control over oil properties in foreign countries'. The next month, on 29 June, speaking at a dinner given by the International Chamber of Commerce (a group founded in 1919, whose members called themselves 'merchants of peace'), the President of the American Petroleum

Institute, Thomas O'Donnell, was firm but condescending: 'Nobody has a higher appreciation than I of the Englishman abroad or at home. He is a good sportsman, always willing to take a chance in exploring for the world's treasure . . . I am rather surprised that some of my good English friends do not agree with me in advocating that a free opportunity should be given to all people to explore this useful product.'[18]

Other Americans were not so jovial. For the President, despite all the idealism he had shown at the Palace of Versailles during the Paris peace conference in 1919, the world had become a bitter place. He was gloomy. He foretold more conflict, but this time in the field of business. 'It is evident to me', he wrote at the beginning of 1920, 'that we are on the eve of a commercial war of the severest sort, and I am afraid that Great Britain will prove capable of as great commercial savagery as Germany has displayed for so many years in her competitive methods.'[19]

The mood between the former allies, the United States and Great Britain, soured during 1920, as angry memoranda flew across the Atlantic Ocean, between 10 Downing Street and the State Department. What the Americans called the 'open door' policy really meant allowing US interests to exploit the resources of other countries on the same basis as the British and French were already permitted. No one really cared very much about the Italians, as their oil industry was negligible. The Germans and Turks, defeated powers, could be safely ignored, but the Americans grew louder and more aggrieved. In November 1920, Walter Teagle himself, the president of the Standard Oil Company of New Jersey, later known as Esso, addressed the American Petroleum Institute. In his speech he gave an admirable defence of the American position. The Americans were, at that time, already responsible for 70 per cent of the world's oil production, so their attitude could be interpreted by the oil-industry professionals of other countries as one of sheer greed. This was not the case, maintained Teagle. 'Our British friends . . . have argued that if the United States is now supplying 70 per cent of the world's [oil] production, we should be content with things as they are. This is an entirely fallacious view.' Was it reasonable, Teagle asked, 'to ask that Americans go heedlessly on to the quick exhaustion of their own supply and then retire from the oil business'? The American petroleum industry could not 'accept such a conclusion'. American oil interests now would be compelled to look to the 'development of petroleum outside the United States'.[20]

By early January 1921, Congress was beginning to agitate on this issue. A Democratic senator from Tennessee, Kenneth McKellar, was now arguing for an oil embargo on Great Britain in retaliation for the exclusion of US interests from Iraq. McKellar pointed out that the British navy was still heavily dependent on US oil, and that this fact had provided the initial stimulus for Britain to exploit Iraqi oil; but it would take a long time for oil to be produced in Iraq, despite the rich deposits which might be found. In the meantime, McKellar argued, Britain still needed US oil. He went on to explain to the Senate that 'if Great Britain is not permitted to get oil from this country her navy will be severely handicapped'. This was true. Britain would 'be obliged to come to terms' with the US.[21] On the Republican side, Frank Kellogg, a senator from Minnesota who would later serve as secretary of state himself, was equally belligerent. Speaking in the same debate, Kellogg argued that the US government should 'by treaty provide for the protection of American interests in the development of oil lands in foreign countries'. He spoke darkly of 'retaliatory legislation if Great Britain refuses the square deal to Americans'. Serious journals even discussed the possibility of an Anglo-American war.[22]

Against such a storm of protest from the Americans, the British government found itself increasingly impotent. Lord Curzon alluded to the fact that Britain controlled only 4.5 per cent of the world's petroleum supply, while 82 per cent was controlled by the US, because in addition to the 70 per cent that the Americans produced themselves, American companies operating in Mexico supplied a further 12 per cent.[23] As far as the Americans were concerned, however, these facts were irrelevant. The new Republican Secretary of State, Charles Evans Hughes, who took Bainbridge Colby's place in March 1921, even argued that the US enjoyed the same rights as Britain by right of conquest, since America had also been victorious in the First World War. The rights of Iraqis and other oppressed peoples which Woodrow Wilson had been widely expected to champion in 1918 were again completely overlooked. For Hughes, 'in view of American contributions to the common victory over the Central Powers, no discrimination can rightfully be made against us in a territory won by that victory'. Might may well have been right, but it was rare even for an American secretary of state to put the case so bluntly.[24]

In the face of pressure from the American Congress and American business, the British government simply gave up. Winston Churchill, the Colonial Secretary, could not see how he could justify keeping the Americans out.[25] In January 1922, the Colonial Office, still under Churchill's control, decided to admit American oil interests into Iraq, and negotiations between the British champion, the Anglo-Persian Oil Company, and the Standard Oil Company were initiated. Two months later, Churchill persuaded Anglo-Persian to accept a memorandum calling for a minority US shareholding in the Turkish Petroleum Company.[26] The shareholding was agreed in 1923 and implemented fully in the Red Line Agreement in 1928. Under the new dispensation, Calouste Gulbenkian would still retain his 5 per cent. The Anglo-Persian Oil Company, Royal Dutch Shell, the Compagnie Française des Pétroles and an American consortium, led by Standard Oil of New Jersey, would each own 23.75 per cent of the company's shares. The odd number was merely the result of each company giving Gulbenkian 1.25 per cent of the shares from its holding. In 1955, the year Gulbenkian died, his share in the oil company, by then renamed the Iraqi Petroleum Company, or IPC, brought him an income of £5,000,000 a year, a vast sum comparable in £100 million in 2011 prices.

Coupled with the British desire to satisfy American and French interests was the need to keep the Iraqis and Turks out of the company. One Colonial Office memorandum stated that the 'admission of Turkish interests in our oil projects would be extremely inconvenient'.[27] Immediately after the war, liberals like Edwin Montagu, the Liberal Secretary of State for India, had suggested that the Iraqis should participate in the Turkish Petroleum Company, and that the British should control Iraq 'primarily in the interests of its inhabitants'.[28] By the mid-1920s, however, Iraq was already seen as the 'weakest party'. The San Remo Agreement had promised the Iraqis a 20 per cent share of the oil in their own country, but this was difficult to realize since the Americans, the French and, of course, Gulbenkian needed to be satisfied with an adequate stake. There were now too many interests for the Iraqis to be given a share in the company which had been formed specifically to extract their oil.

In the meantime, relations between the various shareholders became fractured and difficult. The Americans, it is true, were not that interested in Iraqi politics, because as long as their dividends kept pouring in, they remained unconcerned about the internal situation of the country. Provided a measure of political stability was maintained, all would be well. Britain, however, was overextended. The British Empire by the 1920s needed helpers or assistants in the enterprise of governing other countries. Sir Robert Borden, the Prime Minister of Canada, had said in 1918 that 'the more we can induce the United States to undertake its just responsibilities in world affairs the better it will be for the world'. And also, he added, 'for the British Empire'. But the Americans were more interested in money-making than in imperial administration. Much of the agitation to secure their oil interests came, as we have seen, from private enterprise. As early as 1910 the head geologist of Standard Oil of New Jersey had visited Iraq and returned convinced that the Euphrates valley contained a large quantity of oil.[29]

The US government of the time merely acted as a cheerleader of American private enterprise. The British had strategic interests in Iraqi oil. They needed oil for their navy which they could control. The Americans had enough oil of their own. Private US companies wanted to make more money and, once those private interests were secured, the State Department simply had no interest in dealing separately with the Iraqi leaders. On at least four separate occasions, Iraqi ministers approached the US Consul in Baghdad, because they wanted to encourage American bids for oil-exploration rights in Iraq. On each occasion, these efforts were disregarded in Washington. The State Department did not wish to disturb the general political situation. The US could be a free rider, while Britain did the dirty work of running the politics. The British knew how to deal with Iraqis, so the Americans believed. The British had people who could speak the languages; they had a historic engagement with Islam and the Middle East.

Yet, despite American disengagement from politics, there were tensions. Individuals who worked for American interests could often be sceptical, and even rude, about British policy. By 1928, a year after the first oil had been struck, Sir Henry Dobbs, the British High Commissioner in Baghdad, was complaining about a 'Mr F. P. Stuart Morgan', a British subject who had once been employed in Teheran by the Anglo-Persian Company and was now working for 'American interests in the Turkish Petroleum Company'. The High Commissioner believed that Stuart Morgan was making a nuisance of himself. He had spoken badly of King Faisal and the British and was generally undesirable. He favoured the Hashemite family's enemies, the Ibn Sauds, who had consolidated their power in the Gulf and would, in the 1930s, found the Kingdom of Saudi Arabia. Stuart Morgan had claimed that the King 'was screwing as much money for himself out of the country as the Turks in their worst days'. He also suggested that this was the general opinion that Americans had of Faisal, and that in the US it was believed that the King was 'intent on making money for himself . . . and did not care for the interests of the people of Iraq'. This was not the case, as far as Dobbs was concerned. Besides, even if it were true, the King was no worse than the Americans themselves.

British officials found it difficult to tolerate men like Stuart Morgan, whom they regarded as 'bounders' and 'cads'. In a letter to Sir John Shuckburgh, Assistant Under-Secretary at the Colonial Office, in December 1928, Dobbs had insinuated that the Anglo-Persian Company had sacked Stuart Morgan because he had 'got too much under the influence of Russian *Wein und Weib*'. The lapse into German is characteristic of the cultured British civil servants of the period; Sir John would know that *Wein und Weib* literally meant 'wine and woman'. Stuart Morgan's predilection for Russian women had not been appreciated in Teheran, and the Anglo-Persian Company conveniently arranged for the Americans to take him on in Iraq 'as a favour'. The man had an 'indifferent moral reputation when out here before, and was unpopular owing to his conceit'. Stuart Morgan was 'now throwing his weight about a great deal and talking as if he had the American group in his pockets'. He had also been 'talking against Faisal in private houses'.

Dobbs identified Harry St John Philby as the chief architect of the anti-British line adopted by Stuart Morgan. Dobbs spoke of Philby's 'mischievous anti-His Britannic Majesty's Government and anti-Faisal ideas'.[30] He openly speculated that Stuart Morgan was 'under the influence of Philby'. In the same letter Dobbs referred again to 'Philby's intrigues'. But who was Philby? What did he want? What did he represent?

Although his fame has been rather overshadowed by that of his son, Kim, who would be revealed as a Soviet spy, Harry St John Philby was a man of distinction. He had been born in Ceylon in 1885. His family were part of the professional, imperial-service middle class, and he was educated at Westminster and Trinity College, Cambridge, where, bored with the Classics, he switched to Modern Languages and graduated with first-class honours in 1907. He joined the Indian Civil Service in 1907 – the 'first socialist' to do so, he said – and was posted to Lahore in 1908. There he added to his impressive command of Latin, Greek, French and German by becoming fluent in Urdu, Punjabi and Baluchi. By the end of the First World War, he had established himself as a noted Arabist, being able to speak two or three Arabic dialects fluently. A distinguished career beckoned. He was made minister of internal security in Iraq after the great revolt in 1920, but he soon became disillusioned. He was transferred to Transjordan, part of the Palestine mandate, and finally left British government service in 1924.

Philby was committed to supporting the family of the Ibn Sauds and that year began acting as an adviser to Ibn Saud himself. The Sauds were the great enemies of the Hashemite dynasty, which the British had installed in Iraq and Jordan. They eventually manage to oust the Hashemites from their traditional role as sharifs of Mecca, guardians of the holy city, in 1924. Their success in regaining Mecca increased Philby's prestige and confidence. His anti-Hashemite stance defined his politics. In the 1930s, his career involved negotiating oil deals with the Americans, and with Germany and Spain, powers hostile to British interests. Those oil deals became the basis of American dominance of the Middle Eastern oil industry, as well as the basis of the vast wealth of the Saudi royal family. Philby is the archetype of the 'Brit who went native'. He converted to Islam and took, as his second wife, a sixteen-year-old girl he had purchased from a slave market. This was in 1945, the year of his sixtieth birthday.[31]

In the 1920s, while intriguing with the Al-Saud family, Philby constantly criticized and mocked British policy, with the Hashemites the principal object of his withering contempt. His career is important because it represented an important strand of British imperial life. Consistently, throughout the empire, there were people who refused to play by the rules. These mavericks were indistinguishable by class and education from their more conventional colleagues; they had been forged by the same elite schools, by Oxford and Cambridge universities; they had been educated in Classics or in the army, but they were often subversives opposed to British policy. In the long run, Philby's support of the Ibn Saud family has proved the more successful: the House of Saud still rules in Riyadh, while the Hashemite Kingdom of Iraq is now hardly even a memory. The story of the insider who, opposed to official policy, gets the right answer occurs frequently in British imperial history.

The various rivalries among the colonial powers, in Middle Eastern politics and the world in general, strained international relations to an extent that is now forgotten. If the United States and Great Britain had been rivals in the decade or so after Versailles, it was the French who continued to annoy the British in their Iraq policy, well into the 1930s. In fact, despite the recent alliance against Germany, France had never vanished from the British imagination as the eternal foe. Curzon, speaking generally about French influence, claimed that 'a good deal of my public life has been spent in connection with the political ambitions of France'. What he had learned over his years of experience was that 'the great Power from whom we may have most to fear in the future is France'.[32]

In regard to the politics of the oil industry, the French had started the 1920s in a compliant, subordinate position. We have seen how the Americans loudly forced their way in to participate in the Iraqi oil concessions. The diplomacy of the French was more subtle. They were allowed a seat at the table. They sat quietly and got used to the game. Then they pursued their interests with tenacity and skill. The problems arose over the pipeline.

The oil in Iraq had to be removed from that country and then taken to be refined elsewhere. That was where the real money could be made. During the whole period of its operations in Iraq, the Turkish Petroleum Company, and the Iraqi Petroleum Company in its post-1929 incarnation, never built a refinery there. Iraq was simply the source of the oil. The oil would be extracted and then carried to refineries outside Iraq. The original San Remo Agreement had anticipated this arrangement: though it allowed the French a seat at the oil table with a 25 per cent stake in the company, the accord also determined that they would agree not to 'put any legal or fiscal obstacles' in the way of the construction of a pipeline. It was clear that the pipeline would transport oil from Iraq and Iran through French spheres of influence to 'a port or ports on the Eastern Mediterranean'.[33] Where that port might be situated was not specified. The French had assented to the treaty. They had not objected to the clause about the pipeline and had agreed not to introduce any obstacles in its way. Once the Agreement had been signed, it was inevitable that the pipeline would have to be built. It was, however, at this moment that a row erupted which would, in many ways, define the French relationship with the British in Iraq.

At least both the British and French were clear about what they wanted. The British wanted the port 'on the Eastern Mediterranean' to be located at Haifa, now in northern Israel, but then a city of only about 22,000 in the British mandate territory of Palestine. The French wanted a port in Tripoli, in northern Lebanon, but then more commonly referred to as Syria, about 122 miles to the north of Haifa. (Lebanon had been carved out of Greater Syria only in 1920 and contemporaries, as is often the case, were slow to adopt this term.) This second location was within their sphere of influence. The debate over which of these two harbours should be the port at which the pipeline terminated continued for years.

In the letter complaining about the 'mischievous' Stuart Morgan, written in December 1928, Sir Henry Dobbs, the High Commissioner in Baghdad, referred to the 'railway and pipe-line question'. He pointed out that he thought the 'port of Tripoli is less suited to the loading of oil tanks than Haifa owing to the winds which prevail in Tripoli'. He was worried that the Americans would agree with the French on this issue. Needless to say Philby was 'pushing the Tripoli line'. The question involved the Foreign Secretary, Sir Austen Chamberlain, and the Colonial Secretary, Leopold Amery, who both took different approaches. Each approach was entirely in character. Sir Austen, a milder politician than his father, 'Radical Joe'

Chamberlain, took a more conciliatory line. Leo Amery, of whom it was said he would have been prime minister if he had been six inches taller and his speeches thirty minutes shorter, displayed the pugnacity for which he was well known.

By 1929, Sir Austen Chamberlain was a very experienced politician. He had been foreign secretary since 1924, in which office he had won the Nobel Prize for Peace in 1925. Educated at Rugby and Cambridge, he was faultlessly polite, charming and elegant. After he had left Cambridge in 1885, his father had arranged for him to spend nine months studying in Paris, followed by twelve months in Berlin, thus equipping him with the linguistic skills which were thought necessary for high diplomatic and political office. He was elected to the House of Commons in 1892 when he was only twenty-nine. In 1903 he started a three-year stint as chancellor of the exchequer at the age of forty. Now, at the beginning of 1929, Sir Austen was enjoying his final months at the Foreign Office. The Conservative government would lose the general election, held on 31 May that year, and in those last months was grappling with Iraqi questions. Chamberlain was a conciliator. At the beginning of February he declared himself 'strongly of the opinion' that an attempt should be made to find 'some solution of the differences which had arisen with the French Government'. He wrote the letter to the Under-Secretary of State at the Colonial Office, William Ormsby-Gore, but the message was clearly meant for the Secretary of State himself, the aggressive Amery. This letter provoked a robust response. Less than two weeks later, Amery complained that 'a definite surrender to the French Government's views' was being contemplated. The views of the two governments, he argued, were 'diametrically opposed'. He thought the difference was 'fundamental'. He also pointed to the fact that, even though the Foreign Secretary might have been gentlemanly about the matter, the French were behaving deviously and were 'directing their energies to detaching the American Group from the British and Anglo-Dutch bloc' in the Turkish Petroleum Company.[34]

Amery, no doubt reflecting the distaste felt by the British in Baghdad for Stuart Morgan, stated that the French government had now 'definitely won' him to 'their side'. The French were equally suspicious of the British. Their representative on the board of directors of the Turkish Petroleum

Company believed that the Iraqi government backed Haifa owing to the influence of the British. For their part, the British were sure that the Iraqis backed Haifa because they had no confidence in the French. Writing from the comfort of the East India Club in St James's Square in February 1929, Dobbs told Shuckburgh, the Colonial Office official, that the Iraqis 'who knew anything about it are rabidly in favour of Haifa'. This was 'partly because they dislike the French and the prospect of French control of the terminus', but also because they thought that the pipeline and railway 'if brought south' would prevent Ibn Saud in the Gulf from expanding northwards.

Meanwhile, from the Foreign Office, Chamberlain rebuked Amery gently, saying that he preferred 'methods of conciliation' as opposed to 'rigid insistence on a line of action which has no guarantee of success'. Chamberlain did not share Amery's view 'that a serious dispute with the French Government over this question is sooner or later inevitable'.[35] Gulbenkian, sitting in Cannes, eagerly followed the dispute and felt that he had to become involved in order to safeguard his interests. It was assumed that, if a pipeline was constructed, a railway would also be built along the same route. The Iraqis believed that the oil company would pay for this development. Gulbenkian was furious. He now fired off a letter, dated 12 February, to Sir Adam Ritchie, the general manager of the company in London. It would be wrong, Gulbenkian argued, for the Iraqis to be under the impression that 'they can later on impose upon us the building of the railway'. He was all for capitalism and a narrow focus on business. He despised what a modern commentator might call development projects. Gulbenkian believed that 'we should make a success of oil exploration'; it was no concern of the company 'to be mixed up in politics'. But the one thing the 1920s should have taught him was that oil was inextricably 'mixed up' with politics. As one contemporary analyst put it, 'cherchez le pétrole [look for the oil] has become as universal an explanation of the tragedies and comedies of international relations as cherchez la femme [look for the woman] is of human relations'.[36]

The Admiralty also contributed its opinions about the preferred port for the pipeline. Its officials felt that the Foreign Office showed a 'strange lack of vision'. The railway and pipeline at Haifa would realize 'advantages of every kind'. What these advantages were they were less specific about. On the other hand, the Admiralty argued, there would be a 'corresponding loss' if the railway and pipeline reached 'a Syrian port'. This would be a 'weak surrender to French interests'. There was only one problem with all this bombast. It was a problem which the Admiralty itself acknowledged. 'The weak spot is that, on purely economic grounds, there is nothing to be said for the Haifa project'; the company 'if left to itself, must opt for Syria'.[37] The French were only too aware of this. Marcellin Berthelot, the French Foreign Minister, was in communication with the Foreign Office right up to the 1929 general election. On the very day of the election, he wrote to the British government that the French wanted to see a pipeline in Tripoli and that it would be 'unjustifiable' for its route to be determined by 'political reasons' ('des raisons politiques').[38]

The dispute over the route of the pipeline rumbled on through 1929 and 1930; it was now being handled by the new Labour administration, which showed itself just as wary of French claims as the Conservatives had been. The company's chairman, Sir John Cadman, a technocrat who, perhaps unusually for the time, had an engineering degree, was worried about the effect the dispute would have on his own position. In a meeting of the Cabinet Oil Committee on 27 May 1930, chaired by Arthur Henderson, the Labour Party's new Foreign Secretary, Cadman told of his nervousness that 'the documents and minutes' on the subject were being 'broadcast round the departments'. The fact that he was 'having consultations with His Majesty's Government' about the pipeline would make his position 'very difficult' with the American and French directors of the company.[39] By February 1931, the dispute still remained unresolved. J. H. Thomas, the Labour Secretary of State for the Dominions, complained about the general direction of British policy since the end of the war. He said Britain had 'been giving in all along the line. We allowed the French to take over the German share in the I.P.C. and then let the Americans in.' Thomas's summation of what had happened was largely accurate.[40] The Cabinet Committee was candid enough to admit that the southern route was 'uneconomical'. The Kirkuk-to-Haifa route was, at 640 miles, 111 miles longer than the route to Tripoli; besides, the countryside in Palestine was 'difficult', in terms of terrain and of its political circumstances.

The Iraqis were adamant that the route had to go to Haifa, and some kind of route remained absolutely necessary. An 'Economic Report' from the Colonial Office, dated July 1929, had noticed that 'leading oil groups' now realized that it was simply not 'a commercial proposition to carry American oil to India and Burma' or to take 'Persian or Burman oil to France and Northern European Ports'. Each market had to be supplied 'with oil from the nearest or most convenient or cheapest source of supply'.[41] But King Faisal was still unprepared to compromise with the French. He was furious with them and, in an interview with Sir Francis Humphrys, the new High Commissioner in Baghdad, in October 1930, he had to be 'calmed down'. The King screamed that the 'Government of Iraq would prefer that the oil should remain permanently under ground [sic] rather than it should be carried to the Mediterranean via Syria'.[42] In the background, Gulbenkian was still stirring. Always the shrewd businessman, he just wanted the cheapest alternative. The French view, in his opinion, was the more practical option. Gulbenkian was clever enough not to identify himself unequivocally with one view or the other. He simply spread the rumour that the French had completely 'won over the Americans and the Dutch to the "Tripoli Alignment" and that Sir John Cadman and the Anglo-Persian Oil Company were therefore isolated'.

The pipeline dispute involved the King of Iraq, the British and the French in a battle of wills. The Americans were spectators and were, by now, more concerned with developing the riches of their new field of oil interest, the Ibn Saud kingdom of Saudi Arabia. Britain and France continued to play a role in Iraqi affairs. In 1935 the pipeline was built and, as a concession to both those imperial powers, the pipeline bifurcated at Haditha, on the Euphrates, in Iraq, with one branch going to Haifa and the other to Tripoli.

Despite nominal Iraqi independence in 1932, the year the mandate expired, the British continued to be a dominant presence. The British had set up King Faisal, and they continued to support his family. Faisal sent his son, Ghazi, to Harrow, the school that had educated Stanley Baldwin, Winston Churchill and Jawaharlal Nehru, among other prominent figures in the 1920s and 1930s. John Galsworthy, author of *The Forsyte Saga*, winner of the Nobel Prize for Literature in 1932, the year the British mandate over Iraq expired, had even been a classmate there in the 1880s of Stanley Baldwin, the ex-British Prime Minister. In the 1920s and 1930s, Harrow was probably at the height of its reputation and prestige. The fact that this was the school patronized by the Iraqi royal family clearly demonstrated the closeness of their relationship with the British establishment. It was this relationship that would eventually doom them and lead to prolonged instability in Iraq.

3

Monarchy and Revolution

The crowd was on the 'point of hysteria'. Hundreds of British and foreign mourners joined in the solemn march through the streets of Baghdad. King Faisal was dead. At the end of the march there was the 'booming of 99 guns'. The crowd, although almost hysterical, behaved 'very well indeed'.[1] The procession took place in November 1933, a delay of two months, because the King's body had to be brought back from Switzerland. Earlier that summer, Faisal, along with three of his ministers, had come to London in order to speak directly with government officials at the heart of the British Empire. The British monarch, King George V, had personally greeted him on his arrival at Victoria Station. As the two kings were driven in their cars the short distance from the railway station to Buckingham Palace, they were cheered by crowds thronging the streets.

During King Faisal's stay, all points of diplomatic etiquette and formality had been observed. Soon after his arrival, Faisal laid a wreath of poppies on the tomb of the Unknown Soldier at Westminster Abbey. He and his ministers were then entertained at a dinner at the Guildhall on 21 June, the day after they had landed in Britain. King George V himself gave the address. He extolled the 'brilliant advance made by Iraq under Your Majesty's enlightened rule'. Iraq was now nominally independent. The mandate had ended in 1932, so King George only gently alluded to the 'progress' which had been 'sustained and assisted during the last twelve years by the friendly co-operation of our respective Governments'. The British monarch expressed his 'earnest hope' that these 'close and fruitful relations' would be 'sustained' in the future. After these polite words, the official part of Faisal's visit soon ended, but the King lingered, enjoying the luxuries of London for a few more weeks, and returned to Baghdad only on 2 August. He left Iraq on Saturday 2 September to go to Switzerland. He was feeling unwell. He died in Berne, the Swiss capital, in the early hours of Friday morning, 8 September. He was barely fifty years old.[2]

King Faisal had been a romantic, even dashing figure. At the peace conference in Paris in 1919, he had charmed the British and Americans alike. To them he exuded all the exoticism and mystery of the East. Robert Lansing, the US Secretary of State, had said of him that he 'suggested the calmness and peace of the desert'. During the First World War, T. E. Lawrence had identified him as the leader and figurehead of the Arab revolt and later recounted their first meeting in a famous passage in his account of the revolt, *The Seven Pillars of Wisdom*: 'I felt at first glance that this was the man I had come to Arabia to seek.'[3] Later he would describe Faisal as his 'very great pride', in a letter to Charlotte Shaw. Lawrence even viewed it as a 'privilege to have helped him [Faisal] to his supremacy, out there'. Even better, in his view, was the fact that Faisal was now a 'person for the English-speaking races'.[4] Whatever else Faisal was, he was staunchly pro-British, 'one of us'. He had been rejected by the French as king of Syria and spent the intervening time polishing his gold daggers and draping himself in silks in a villa on the shores of Lake Maggiore in Italy.[5]

The influence of his friends, such as T. E. Lawrence and Gertrude Bell, enabled Faisal to find another kingdom, Iraq. He had involved himself in the politics of oil, opposing the French insistence on Tripoli as the port for the Iraqi oil pipeline. With Bell and his other English friends about him, he had indulged in the finer things in life. In March 1923, Bell was asking her father to send 'a selection of catalogues or drawings from some of the best London shops by next airmail' because the King was 'in perplexity as to how to furnish a big room in the little palace that has just been built'. Bell, that fearless explorer of the desert, had now, it seemed, become an expert interior designer. She hoped 'we could get chairs and tables' out of the catalogues too. Her father dutifully sent the requisite catalogues. On 10 April, Bell was thanking her father 'a thousand times for all the trouble you took about the King's furniture'.[6]

The taste and style of the Hashemites were distinctly British. This was partly determined by the company they kept. In December 1924, Gertrude Bell described how she had entertained 'little Amir Ghazi', Faisal's son, who was then thirteen years old, at tea with his tutor and governess. 'The train soldiers I had ordered for him from Harrods had arrived last mail and were presented with great success.'[7] More formal relations with the British had been established in treaties signed in 1922 and 1930. These treaties had provided Britain with necessary safeguards, ensuring that it remained the dominant external power in Iraqi affairs. The 1930 treaty had left Britain with 'considerable latitude in matters of defence and administration'. Two airbases were allowed the RAF on Iraqi soil. The end of the mandate, in October 1932, had left a tight clique of Sunni officials and soldiers gathered around King Faisal, but the 'British authorities still retained supreme power, and the vast majority of the population had no power at all'.[8]

Still less did the 'vast majority' have any power over their oil. The Iraqi state under Faisal was chronically short of money and, as a consequence, the country remained underdeveloped in both economic and social terms. In 1920 there had been just three secondary schools in the whole of Iraq, while the population stood at 3 million. By 1930, this figure had gone up to nineteen secondary schools, attended by only 2,100 students. It is not surprising, therefore, that the illiteracy rate before 1950 reached more than 90 per cent.[9] The oil revenues only really started to affect the country's income in the 1930s and, even then, a fixed sum of just £400,000 in gold would be granted to the government by the newly named Iraq Petroleum Company. This sum was fixed in 1931 and remained the same until 1952, when a more favourable profit-sharing scheme was negotiated by the Iraqis. The Iraqi state effectively supported itself by receiving small sums of money from the mainly foreign-owned oil company and, to an even greater degree, by borrowing directly from the British government. Money would be loaned, using Iraq's oil reserves as security, for building railways and equipping the army. In 1939 nearly £4 million was made available at moderate interest rates and repayment was spread over seventeen years.[10] This figure was ten times the amount Iraq received for its oil in a year.

The country itself was largely feudal. It was a place where the scriptural injunction 'an eye for an eye' was still the rule; murder had to be the price of murder. It would be committed by a near relative of the first victim on some member of the aggressor tribe. All that was required of women was to 'produce sons ... to milk, bake, make butter and cheese and weave mats and clothing'.[11] It would be a mistake to describe the landscape as rural, as this conjures up images of rolling fields. The heat in Iraq was its most conspicuous feature. A writer in the 1930s described dust storms as 'frequent'. The 'least breath of wind sets the desert sand in motion', people commonly said. The extreme heat, where temperatures of 120 degrees Fahrenheit (45 degrees Centigrade) were common in summer, meant that it was a harsh environment for people who had just arrived from Europe. Under those sort of climatic conditions, 'a man will leave his bath, dry himself' and find himself, the next moment, 'as wet with perspiration as when in the bath'.[12]

The country was poor. What wealth existed was concentrated in very few hands. During the time of the Hashemite monarchy, only twenty-three banking and manufacturing families possessed between 50 and 65 per cent of the entire private capital of the country.[13] In economic terms, Iraqi society was a narrow oligarchy. In politics, the country was more or less an absolute monarchy. As we have seen, Faisal came from the Hashemite family, whose main distinction was its descent from the Prophet Mohammed's daughter, Fatima. This connection made them 'lord of lords' and the 'grandest family of Islam', although they had been compelled to yield to the caliphs in Constantinople before the caliphate itself was abolished in 1924. Despite the undoubted prestige the Hashemite family enjoyed within the Islamic world, their interests and manners were more Western than Muslim.

Faisal's son Ghazi, who succeeded to the Iraqi throne aged twenty-one in 1933, was hardly a paragon of Islamic virtue. Obsessed with speed and glamour, he was a rather raffish Harrovian with an air of 'reckless and unconventional independence'. As a child, he rode Arab racing stallions. At Harrow, he learned how to dismantle a high-compression engine, even before he learned to speak good English. The *Iraq Times* would comment on his new polo ponies, as he was an excellent horseman who played polo three times a week. New things fascinated him. In Iraq, after his expensive education in England, he bought one 'flashy car after another', a Mercedes in phosphorescent paint being especially noteworthy. His craving for speed took him to the air, and in March 1939 he accepted delivery of a

British plane which could fly at 200 miles an hour. The Prince enjoyed cars, planes, motorcycles, girls and well-cut clothes, in no particular order.

On 4 April 1939, the twenty-seven-year-old King, after having a few drinks, got into his car to drive to the Harthiya Palace, a few miles from Baghdad. He was driving an open-top sports car with two companions in the back. As he sped past a crossing, he lost control of the car, shot off the road and crashed into a lamp-post. His two companions were killed instantly. His own skull was crushed and he died within an hour.[14] The King's sudden death made the political situation difficult for the British. Despite his education at Harrow and his taste for Savile Row suits, Ghazi was the most anti-British of his family. His independent spirit railed against the control that London had imposed on his country. It was widely believed by Iraqi nationalists that his death was not accidental but had been orchestrated by the wicked British colonial power. The King had flirted with European fascism, but his anti-British actions amounted to nothing more than an openly expressed desire to annex Kuwait, which remained a British protectorate under the ruling Al-Sabah family, and to assert Iraqi military independence. Kuwait's sovereignty had been guaranteed in 1899 by Britain in an agreement with Sheikh Mubarak bin Sabah al-Sabah which also bound the Sheikh, his heirs and successors not to 'cede, sell, lease, mortgage or give for occupation or any other purpose any portion of his territory to the Government or subjects of any other power' without the previous consent of the British government.[15]

Those who believed that the young King had been killed by the British suspected the connivance of high-placed Iraqi officials, such as Nuri As-Said, who had been bribed for their support. Crowds began to gather in a number of cities. In Mosul, the oil centre in the north, 260 miles up the Tigris from Baghdad, anti-British feeling was strong. Early on the morning of 5 April, the day after Ghazi's fatal accident, a large crowd gathered at the gates of the British Consulate, where the Consul, George Monck-Mason, and his wife lived. Monck-Mason, 'a trim, clipped civil servant' according to *Time* magazine, appeared on the balcony to placate the crowd. He spoke good Arabic and proceeded to explain what had happened. He said that Ghazi's death had been an accident, which the crowd refused to believe. A group of men broke into the Consulate, wielding pickaxes. In scenes reminiscent of General Gordon's death in Khartoum, more than fifty years previously, Monck-Mason was struck from behind as he stood on the balcony. It was an unfortunate end to a good, if unspectacular, career. Monck-Mason was described in the *Iraq Times* as a 'man of quiet and studious type'. He was, his obituarist noted, 'one of the finest linguists in the Levant consular service'. This was a period when Britons were good at languages, but, even by pre-war imperial service standards, Monck-Mason was exceptional. He was reputed to 'speak no fewer than nine languages', having spent 'nearly all his life in the Near and Middle East'.[16]

Monck-Mason's linguistic skills, and his career in general, point to an interesting feature of the British imperial service. The people dispatched to administer imperial justice in the far reaches of the empire were highly motivated by a desire to be there. They invariably learned the languages and immersed themselves in the cultures of the places they lived in. This meant that, for many administrators, an entire lifetime was spent, far from home, in a strange environment. It was unsurprising that many went native.

Throughout Iraq, the unpopularity of the British had not yet, in the late 1930s, reached the heights it would in the 1950s. Yet many Iraqis detected in British rule an arrogance and aloofness which meant that the reaction, when it came, was likely to be violent. Nubar Gulbenkian, the son of Mr Five Per Cent, had detected the 'first rumblings of change' in 1931 when he was in Baghdad. One small instance of the 'covert resentment' of the British occurred when the British Ambassador had ordered a small Arab hamlet to be removed so that he could 'extend the gardens of the British Embassy' in the city. Nubar remarked, with some understatement, that the 'Ambassador had undoubtedly improved what was already a beautiful residence but he made himself less than universally popular with the Iraqis'.[17]

On the whole, British civil servants and company workers were not adaptable. The businessmen kept themselves apart and socialized with each other, avoiding locals. British habits – clubs, horse racing, boar hunts – were maintained to a remarkable extent. The papers of Sir Harry Sinderson, an Edinburgh-trained doctor who was employed as physician to the Iraqi King and royal family in Baghdad between 1921 and 1946, paint a vivid picture of British life in the heart of Iraq before the Second World War. In Baghdad, Sinderson took a keen interest in the Casuals, a cricket club based in the city, which held its dinners in the Alwiyah Club; it would also play the RAF team at the Alwiyah ground. The Casuals kept up their dinners even after the outbreak of the Second World War, with its toast to the club in verse:

> Our cricket was terrific and we seldom lost a game
> And when we did we always had some unkind fate to blame.

The Alwiyah Club was a large complex. It provided a cinema, a venue for dances, sport, swimming pools and good old-fashioned British gossip. It was proudly referred to as the 'hub of Anglo-Saxon' life in Iraq.[18] There was also the Royal Society of St George which celebrated St George's Day, the national day of England, every year on 23 April. The 1938 dinner was a memorable occasion. The event was diligently written up in the *Iraq Times*, an English-language publication, which referred obsequiously to 'Dr H. C. Sinderson Pasha, this year's President', and declared proudly that the main course had been the 'Roast Beef of Old England', which had been specially imported. For dessert, the 128 guests enjoyed blackberry and apple pie with Devonshire cream. After reading a message from King George VI and Queen Elizabeth, Sinderson went on to give a speech. It was entitled, inevitably enough, 'England'.

Sir Harry, who had represented Edinburgh University at both cricket and soccer, was a fanatical sportsman and enjoyed playing cricket in Iraq well into his fifties. The newspaper cuttings he kept refer to such events as puppy shows or the 'first meet of the Baghdad Boar Hunt' in the 1936 season, of which Mr D. R. de C. Macpherson was the Master. There was the Bromilow Cup for pigsticking, in which people hunted boar with spears on horseback. Pigsticking was a typical imperial sport, popular with maharajas in India and with British officers. Military authorities encouraged it, because it provided good training for cavalry officers. Against a startled or angry wild boar, the pigsticker had to 'possess a good eye, a steady hand, a firm seat, a cool head and a courageous heart'.[19]

To the extent that Ghazi had been regarded as unsympathetic to Britain's interests, his death was convenient for British officials, despite the civil unrest which ensued.[20] His successor, Faisal II, was only three years old when he came to the throne. Strict primogeniture ensured the young Faisal's accession to the throne, but it was customary in Arab countries for respect to be shown to the eldest man of the family, so it was perfectly understandable that King Ghazi's cousin, Abd al-Ilah, a young man of twenty-six, would be chosen as regent. In Abd al-Ilah, the British now had a safe man, a man who was viewed as being 'one of us'. His story, perhaps, more than that of any single individual, may stand as a metaphor for the British connection with Iraq, a connection based on money-making and chronic disengagement from the actual lives led by the ordinary people of Iraq.

Abd al-Ilah had been born in 1913, the son of Faisal I's elder brother, Ali. He had been educated in Egypt at the elite Victoria College in Alexandria, 'a transplanted English public school' which had educated the sons of the Middle Eastern elite since 1902, and whose alumni would later include Edward Said, the Palestinian intellectual, and Omar Sharif, the actor. This educational background had made Abd al-Ilah 'more at home among the English than the Iraqis'. Reticent, suave and 'more English than the English', he became the stereotype of the Anglo-Arab pasha with his well-cut suits and his taste for cricket. He had the 'house party charm and sophistication' which could 'easily be imagined living in well-heeled exile in Sunningdale or Newport, Rhode Island'. He was calculating and smooth, but not as clever as he imagined himself to be. A small, dark, fastidiously tidy moustache testified to his vanity.[21] In the course of the regency, which lasted until 1953, when Faisal II turned eighteen, Abd al-Ilah succeeded in earning a bad reputation with the Iraqis. He was viewed, rightly or wrongly, as a snob, a man who had married three times and indulged in a seedy love life. He flaunted a string of mistresses, though there were rumours of sexual impotence. According to popular legend, he dined every night at the British Embassy, where he and the Ambassador supposedly ate and conversed alone. Abd al-Ilah, remarkably, indulged a passion for fox hunting by importing foxhounds from England. He cruised around Baghdad in a Rolls-Royce. A crowd of social climbers, drawn from the English, American and European community, continually sought his company. Yet much of the excess still lay in the future. In 1939 the full extent of the fragility of the monarchy had not yet been revealed.

Contrary to expectations, the war that broke out in 1939 did not bring forth another figure like Lawrence in the military theatre of the Middle East. Many in the Arab world felt that they had supported Britain against the Ottoman Empire only to be let down at the peace conferences after the First World War, when an independent Arab state failed to emerge from the wreckage of the old Ottoman imperium. In Iraq, even though Abd al-Ilah, the Regent, and his leading minister, Nuri As-Said, backed Britain, a number of army officers were more inclined to support the Nazis, as was a significant portion of the Arab world. The Mufti of Jerusalem, a committed anti-Zionist who would meet Hitler himself in Berlin in 1941, and his pan-Arab circle leaned towards the Axis. On 27 August 1940, Dr Fritz Grobba, the German Minister in Baghdad, submitted a memorandum to an Arab Committee formed under the presidency of the Mufti. This bold memorandum, it was hoped, would form the basis of an Arab–German agreement.

The memorandum directly confronted the central legacy of the post-Versailles settlement in the Middle East. It stated that Germany and Italy would not 'abridge the independence of these Arab countries, e.g. by establishing mandates'; these were described as a 'hypocritical device of the League of Nations and the democracies to disguise their imperialistic greed'. The mandates had indeed been somewhat hypocritical devices. People in political circles in Baghdad decided to act.[22]

The machinations in Iraqi politics in 1940 and 1941 are reminiscent of a storyline from a John Buchan novel. Rashid Ali, a member of a prominent Baghdad family, had been appointed prime minister in March 1940. From the outset, he sought to make life difficult for the British, using the war to further his nationalist ambitions. His faction was opposed by the Regent, Abd al-Ilah, and Nuri As-Said, leaders of the pro-British party. Rashid Ali rejected calls from Britain that Iraq should allow British troops to cross through Iraq to get to Palestine. When Italy declared war on the Allies on 10 June 1940, the British asked Iraq to break off diplomatic relations with Rome, a request that Rashid Ali refused. That November, the British issued a virtual ultimatum to the Iraqi government to drop Rashid Ali, or lose the friendship and support of Britain. British sanctions against Iraq, coupled with military success against the Italians in North Africa, made Rashid Ali's position difficult. He resigned at the end of January 1941, but managed to come back at the beginning of April with the full backing of the Iraqi army, which was largely pro-German. Once their government had been toppled on 10 April, Abd al-Ilah and Nuri fled the country. On this occasion, however, the British responded forcefully. Iraq's oil was now of supreme importance for the Allied war effort, and British forces landed in Basra on 29 April. Rashid Ali sent troops to oppose them. The RAF annihilated the Iraqi air force, destroying twenty-five of its forty planes.[23] The 'Thirty Days' War' started on 2 May and ended with a conclusive British victory on the 31st. Fallujah fell on the 19th, and British forces pressed on to Baghdad, entering the city on the 29th. An armistice was signed two days later, which ensured that the pro-British party was reinstated. Crown Prince Abd al-Ilah and Nuri entered Baghdad in triumph on 1 June.

The short war had cost 1,200 British lives and over 8,000 Iraqi. The attempt to detach Iraq, with its useful oilfields, from the Allied cause had failed. Yet the war had stirred a large section of the Arab world against the British. In a speech broadcast on 9 May 1941, the Mufti declared jihad against Britain and invited every able-bodied Muslim to take part in a war against the 'greatest foe of Islam', the British Empire.[24] Meanwhile the British government had become concerned that the oil of Iraq could fall into the wrong hands. A memorandum on the subject by Major Desmond Morton for the War Cabinet, dated 4 June, argued that even though Abd al-Ilah and Nuri were back in power it might prove safer to destroy the oilfields altogether than to leave things to the hazard of an increasingly volatile political situation in Iraq. Morton found that there 'is no known means of destroying the Iraq oil fields themselves'. Even if the fifty wells were set alight, they would 'burn for about 10 years'. He thought it would be better 'to start work on the destruction of the pipelines'.[25] The British government did not act on this, concluding that the political situation did not warrant such drastic action.

The return of Abd al-Ilah and Nuri As-Said completed the triumph of the British faction in Baghdad. Nuri As-Said, though not as polished an

Anglophile as Abd al-Ilah, was a noted survivor in Iraqi politics and dominated the political scene for much of the thirty-year reign of the Hashemite
monarchs in Iraq. Nuri had been born in 1888 to a middle-class Baghdad
family and was outside the privileged ruling elite. It was his military experience that smoothed his path to power and influence. Trained by a
German colonel in Constantinople, as a young Turkish army officer, in the
years before 1914, he had fought under Faisal in the Arab revolt. He had
got to know T. E. Lawrence at that time, who praised his 'courage,
authority and coolness'. He had first become prime minister in 1930 and
would hold that office a further six times. Nuri's methods were method-
ical, steady and unchanging. He had modest, some might say ascetic,
tastes, rising at six in the morning, consuming grapefruit and coffee, while
listening to the news on Voice of America.[26]

A small man with a chubby face and bushy eyebrows, Nuri was a loyal
friend who delighted in children and always acted as the 'most perfect of
hosts'. To his friends and admirers, he was a statesman in the grand manner.
International strategy 'seems to have been the breath of [his] life in much
the same way as it always absorbed so much of the mind and energy of
Winston Churchill', wrote one British observer in a book published
shortly after Nuri's death.[27] Unlike Churchill, however, Nuri was feared
and hated by his own people.

Nuri's modest tastes contrasted with the extravagance and vulgar
posturing of Abd al-Ilah, the Crown Prince. An incident in America in the
early 1950s captures the difference between them. When out walking in
Washington, the two men looked at men's suits in a shop window, and
Nuri pronounced himself impressed by the seersucker suit; the Crown
Prince merely commented that such suits were appropriate for the 'working
class'. Nuri, nonetheless eager to buy one, was eventually dissuaded, but he
was gratified to see President Truman wearing the same suit the next day.
Despite this apparent modesty, Nuri, the strongman of Iraq, was widely
viewed within Iraq as a British stooge.[28]

He and Abd al-Ilah wanted to keep Britain on their side. They thought
that all would be well as long as the oilwells kept on producing their liquid
gold. The war, in the first instance, had not altered the position in Iraq
significantly. The same people were still in power – the British still had a

strong presence in the country and the Iraq Petroleum Company still presided over the oilfields. Archives relating to Iraq in the period immediately after the end of the Second World War give a striking impression of continuity. In December 1947, Crown Prince Abd al-Ilah could write to Stewart Perowne, the wartime public relations officer in the British Embassy, expressing his pleasure at seeing Perowne while visiting England that summer and stating that hunting had started up again in Baghdad, where the first meeting of the season would take place on 12 December.

After the war was over, it was only to be a matter of time before little King Faisal reached the age of majority and took control of the government. Faisal's education was a very British affair; like any young English boy of the upper-middle classes, he was sent to a British preparatory school, Sandroyd in Wiltshire, which the future Prime Minister Anthony Eden had enjoyed so much in the years before 1914. From Sandroyd, Faisal wrote a letter, in January 1949, thanking Perowne for the parcel of sugar he had sent him, because during the post-war austerity in England 'one has great difficulty in finding such lovely sugar'. Faisal claimed to be enjoying school 'very much', though he missed 'Baghdad and the lovely warm sun'.[29]

The next term, the Lent term of 1949, Faisal entered Harrow, from where he informed Perowne that was he 'getting on much better' as he now had learned his 'way around'. Faisal was a good student at the school, more successful there than his cousin Hussein, later King of Jordan, who was six months his junior. Faisal was attentive, quick and eager. He was, as a consequence of Sandroyd and Harrow, by far the most Anglicized of the three kings of Iraq; his grandfather, Faisal I, had spoken very little English, while his father had been too restless and resentful to pass himself off as a real English gentleman, even if he had wished to do so. Faisal II, by contrast, was a proud specimen of the Anglo-Arab gentleman, and had grown up, after his father's death, in an atmosphere 'unerringly Anglophile'. He had been brought up by a 'proper English nurse maid', as well as by 'a proper English governess'. Young Faisal was popular at Harrow, where he cultivated the 'gentlemanly manner'. He liked sport, art and cheerful living and spoke English 'with an impeccable metropolitan accent. His clothes were Savile Row, and he never looked more attractive or more at his ease than when, in a bowler hat and a duffle coat, he peered at some tweedy open-air function.' His tradition was that of the 'Eton Maharajas', a tradition that had produced urbane sportsmen and gentlemen, rich, smooth, genial young men who were perfectly at ease in the clubs of St James's and Pall Mall, but who couldn't relate, even remotely, to the people they were meant to be ruling. In Faisal II's case, few Iraqis felt close to him. He was born 'cruelly out of his time'.[30]

While Nuri As-Said, the Crown Prince and the young King Faisal II were trying their best to keep internal order, the Iraq Petroleum Company reaped the rewards of the capital investment it had made before the war. Oil production in Iraq had increased substantially from the time of the struggles between the French, the Americans and the British in the immediate aftermath of the First World War. In 1934, Iraq exported only 600,000 tons of oil a year; in 1950 the figure hit 6.5 million tons. Oil production in the Middle East had exploded during that time, with the production figure in 1950 being nine times the total production of oil in 1934. General worldwide production did not experience anything like the same growth, increasing by only 50 per cent between 1934 and 1950.[31] Oil brought riches to the oil-producing states of the Middle East and it altered the relationship between their governments and the West, while also changing the relationship between those governments and the people. Iraq's oil revenues were boosted to a remarkable extent. From £1.5 million in 1941, the figure had reached £5.2 million by 1950, an increase of nearly 250 per cent.

The government of Iraq always had a thorny relationship with the Iraq Petroleum Company. The IPC's annual report of 1936 referred to 'certain difficulties which had arisen between the Government and the Company' in respect of 'lands acquired by the Company'. The same report shows just how wily the company could be in its dealings with the Iraqi government. It entered a deal in 1936 which allowed it to pay rent on government-owned property until 1941 at 'rates in force in 1931'. The years 1931 and 1932 had been the hardest of the global economic slump, as prices and rents reached all-time lows, so fixing rents at 1931 levels was a particularly shrewd move on the part of the company's directors. Towards the end of the war, in the 1943 annual report published in May 1944, the company looked forward to the 'final Victory' which, it believed, was 'somewhere round the corner'. This victory would allow a 'further expansion of the company's activities' and would make the need for plans to 'meet demands for increased production' more urgent.

The 1952 annual report showed that the days when the company could do what it liked were coming to an end, the IPC proudly declaring that a 'number of Iraqi doctors were recruited during the year' while the 'training of Iraqi girls as nurses continued'. This kind of extracurricular pursuit was hardly the sort of thing of which Mr Gulbenkian would have approved. By the early 1950s, Gulbenkian himself was living in the Aviz, a luxury hotel in Lisbon, enjoying his £5,000,000 yearly dividend. Meanwhile, the IPC had to deal with realities on the ground in Iraq. People were on the streets protesting; increased revenues from oil production only accentuated the difference between the middle class, who could enjoy the country's increasing prosperity, and the vast urban poor, who had no share in that wealth. In the meantime, the Iraqi government was successfully lobbying for a greater share in the growing revenues derived from oil production. The 1952 annual report indicated how far things had changed. In February that year a new profit-sharing agreement was ratified by the Iraqi parliament which meant that Iraq now received nearly £29 million from the operations of the company, nearly six times the £5 million earned in 1950, only two years before.[32] The company had to go further in appeasing the Iraqi people.

During the debate on the new profit-sharing agreement in the Iraqi parliament, Nuri is said to have invited any members of parliament who thought they could have negotiated better terms to take his place. There was popular discontent over the arrangement. The IPC still shrouded many of its operations in mystery. Certainly, its accounts from the 1930s through to the 1960s do not accord with more modern ideas of corporate governance. No annual sales figure is provided, and only the amount sold, with the resulting royalty, is revealed. Nothing like an ordinary profit and loss account, or balance sheet, or any of the normal paraphernalia of modern corporate accounting is presented. There were other accusations relating to the company's accounting in these years. Exploration and drilling costs were put under operating costs rather than capital expenditures. This sounds technical, but it had the very practical result that the company's annual profit was shown to be lower than a fair valuation would have ensured.[33] The cost of running the head office in London was also listed under operating costs, further depressing the profits from which the Iraqi government would be paid.

In the 1950s, as oil was beginning to bring tangible wealth to Iraq, large cities were founded, for instance at Kirkuk in the north of the country, while further south Baghdad itself was being filled with grand new buildings; expensive suburbs sprang up; air-conditioned hotels arose, as if by magic, from the desert. Yet the urban masses remained much as they were before, impoverished and illiterate. Even in 1958 only one in seven of the population was literate. By 1950, in a country with a population of nearly 5 million, there were still only 121 secondary schools, with barely 22,000 students enrolled.[34] Iraq remained highly dependent on oil, which provided 65 per cent of the state's total revenue in 1954.[35] The price of Iraqi crude, however, in those pre-OPEC days, was determined by the few firms which dominated the international oil industry, not by market forces.

Meanwhile Nuri was desperately trying to cling on to power. *Time* magazine, in a feature entitled 'The Pasha', described him as looking like a 'grizzled old bear' with his 'big ears and jet-black bushy brows'. He was, in the view of the magazine's correspondent, a 'dictator' who ruled Iraqis with 'an indifference to their opinion that verges on contempt'. He needed to be resourceful and he continued to be what Gertrude Bell had called him all those years before, a 'supple force'. But, for all his suppleness and guile, Nuri had now become cynical and more intolerant. There were new rumours that spoke of his growing partiality to whisky. In 1954, he banned political parties, after elections didn't go as planned; he had become increasingly autocratic.

The decline of British prestige in the Middle East in the course of the 1950s undermined the position of Nuri and his Hashemite masters. The sureness of touch that had characterized British diplomacy in the region had, it seemed to many observers, disappeared. The Hashemites and their Anglo-Arab friends, with their Savile Row suits and Bertie Wooster manners, looked out of date and irrelevant when compared to politicians like Gamal Abdel Nasser, the charismatic Arab nationalist, who had taken power in Egypt in 1952. Under Nuri and Faisal II, Iraq remained isolated from the mainstream of Arab nationalism, although on the streets of Baghdad Arab nationalism was a growing and more conspicuous force.

Nuri had the good sense to create an Iraqi Development Board that would channel 70 per cent of the Iraqi state's oil revenue into infrastructure spending. But this money was directed towards large development projects, dams, bridges and the like, when schools and hospitals were increasingly demanded by the Iraqi people. While the Iraqi Development Board built sixteen dams, the population of Baghdad had doubled to 1 million in the five years from 1952 to 1957. Most of these people lived in shanty towns, while the earth-floored mud hut continued to be a characteristic feature of the Iraqi countryside. The Development Board was a great boon to the economists, planners, architects and engineers who thronged Baghdad from the West. It was said that there were at least a hundred American officials associated with it, whose salaries were paid directly by agencies of the US government. One English economist observed that the Development Board 'in discharging its responsibility has made a skilful use of foreign experience, notably through the employment of consulting firms'. Yet in the 1954 budget the amount of public expenditure committed to the police force was 50 per cent greater than the money spent on education.[36] The consultants and their wives were enjoying themselves. Many thousands of people had come from Britain, Europe and America to gorge themselves, so it appeared to many Iraqis, on funds supplied by the Iraqi taxpayer.

Nuri, despite his political skill, was losing his touch too. He had become even more secretive and suspicious. He was by now nearly seventy years old. He confided in fewer and fewer associates; he never used documents; no records were taken of his meetings. He relied more than ever on his extraordinary memory and kept a revolver close at hand. The conclusion of the Baghdad Pact, or the Pact of Mutual Co-operation between Iraq and Turkey, signed on 24 February 1955, was a watershed. Pakistan, Iran and Great Britain later joined the Pact. Egypt objected, and across the Cairo airwaves radio announcers appealed to the Arab masses 'in the name of millions of Arabs' to save 'Arabs from the menace of military alliances'.[37]

The 1956 Suez debacle, the year after the Baghdad Pact was signed, embarrassed the British and further damaged the reputation of Nuri As-Said.

When Suez broke, the Iraqi ruling order seemed to be decadent and obsolete. There was a general feeling that the Hashemites were passing slowly but decisively from the Iraqi scene. It had been only in 1953 that young Faisal II had taken over his kingdom, and the Iraqi Cabinet, resplendent in evening tails, had greeted the young King at the end of his oath-taking ceremony. That year he had been given a pair of silver candelabra from the Duke of Gloucester on behalf of the young Queen Elizabeth II of Great Britain.[38] By 1957, this all seemed like a distant memory, as restless and volatile crowds gathered menacingly in the streets of Baghdad.

There had been uprisings in the Iraqi capital before. In 1948 and 1952, there had been demonstrations, with protesters complaining about increased living costs and poor wages. These had been quelled, although hundreds had been killed. In 1956, a further uprising had been sparked by the attack on Egypt by Britain, France and Israel in October that year, an external event, which had provoked a large proportion of urban opinion. On 1 November 1956, martial law was declared in Baghdad, and there had been serious riots in Najaf and Mosul, as well as in the capital itself. Nuri now controlled the police, the army and the press. His paranoia was such that he was wary of giving the army the ammunition it needed. He resorted to 'a judicious distribution of ammunition' in order to 'hold the army in check'.[39]

The revolution that eventually broke out in Iraq in July 1958 has been aptly described as a 'landmark in the history of the Middle East'.[40] In May, civil war erupted in Lebanon which Hussein, King of Jordan, Faisal II's cousin and Harrow contemporary, feared would spread to his kingdom. Hussein requested that Iraqi troops be sent to Jordan to protect its borders. Nuri and Faisal II agreed to send two brigades, and these were promptly ordered to begin their march west to that country. Nuri, perhaps reluctantly, agreed to issue the brigades with the ammunition which would be needed to fulfil King Hussein's request. The relevant army units, based in barracks seventy miles to the north of Baghdad, were ordered to march southwards to the trans-desert road. One brigade was under the command of Brigadier Abdul Karim al-Qasim, an austere, non-smoking bachelor.

The other was under Colonel Abdul Salam Arif. The two brigades marched south and converged on Baghdad in the early hours of 14 July.[41]

The night of 13 July was a leisurely affair at the Qasr al-Rihab, the Royal Palace in Baghdad. The King and his court were watching a private performance of the musical *The Pajama Game*, a silly romance, set in a pyjama factory, which enjoyed wide popularity in the 1950s. At about five o'clock in the morning, Colonel Arif's tanks arrived at the palace. Behind them, a crowd of young men started to congregate. The palace was surrounded, but for a while the guards resisted. On hearing gunfire, the King, the Crown Prince and other family members and servants came down into the courtyard to face their enemies. The barber who went daily to the palace to shave the King and the Crown Prince had been admitted at a side door as usual, but escaped as soon as he saw the King and Crown Prince talking in the courtyard to a semicircle of officers on the other side. It was now about 7.45 in the morning. As the royal entourage chattered, a captain of Arif's brigade emerged from the front entrance with a sub-machine gun in his hand and fired a volley of shots. This prompted a 'burst of bullets from every direction'. The King, the Crown Prince and two servants fell, mortally wounded, to the ground. Two of the revolutionary officers also fell.[42]

The events of 14 July stirred the Baghdad crowds to new heights of fury. One witness recalled how the 'mob arrived at the palace in buses, on lorries, on anything they could lay their hands on'; their anti-British sentiments were all too obvious: all that was required to incite them to more acts of violence was a 'few hysterically screamed words about filthy Imperialistic British'.[43] One group of enraged youths seized the Crown Prince's body and dragged it for miles. By the time it reached King Faisal Circle, the body was in shreds. What was left of it was mutilated, cut into pieces and hung from a telephone pole in front of the Ministry of Defence.[44] But where was Nuri As-Said? When news of the revolution first broke, he had immediately gone into hiding. For a day and a night he took refuge with a friend and then, on the morning of the 15th, he left the house in a car, dressed as a woman, in a black chador. The driver was heading for another friendly house but was delayed in congested traffic. At this point, Nuri rashly decided to run for safety. He got out of the car, only to trip in the street, whereupon – as if in grim echo of *The Pajama Game* – a boy of about fifteen glimpsed his pyjamas under the chador. No Iraqi woman would wear pyjamas beneath her chador, and the boy, in amused surprise, half jokingly cried, 'There goes Nuri.' Nuri was immediately shot dead. The mob went wild, and the Prime Minister's body was mutilated and dragged through the streets. Thousands of Iraqis saw the headless, armless, legless trunk of a body being pulled behind a lorry. The body was believed to be Nuri's.[45] The royal palace was pillaged and burned, as was Nuri's home. The British Embassy was attacked by marauding groups of young boys, ranging in age from twelve to twenty. For two days, these gangs, reinforced by older men, roamed wildly through Baghdad, without any restraint from the civil authorities.[46]

Throughout July British families left Iraq, as they no longer felt safe. The British, perhaps dazzled by Lawrence of Arabia and late Victorian romanticism, had been steadfast in their support for the royal family they had established, but Iraq had moved on. The world of the Anglo-Arab Hashemites – their well-cut suits, their Harrow School accents, their easy, urbane charm – had been brutally destroyed by a violent Baghdad mob, who knew nothing of that world. Iraq was now a republic.

4

Saddam Hussein and Beyond

A traditional Anglican service commemorating the life and legacy of the Hashemite rulers of Iraq was held on 30 July 1958 in the Queen's Chapel of the Savoy, just off the Strand. The congregation sang Psalm 23, 'The Lord is my shepherd, therefore can I lack nothing'. The priest quoted Ecclesiasticus: 'Let us now praise famous men, and our fathers that begat us.' The Knights Grand Cross of the Royal Victorian Order gathered to mourn their fallen comrades. King Faisal, Crown Prince Abdullah and General Nuri As-Said had all been honorary Knights of the Order.

In London there was a stunned reaction to the demise of the Hashemites in Iraq. In a letter addressed at the end of August to Stewart Perowne, the friend of the Iraqi royal family, the seventy-five-year-old Sir Kinahan Cornwallis, who had been ambassador to Baghdad in the crucial years 1941–5, spoke of a 'conspiracy of silence as to what [had] happened' in Iraq. London was adapting itself to the new situation. Sir Kinahan, known as Ken, detected 'a strong tendency to decry the old regime and to give them no credit at all in what they did'. He went on to suggest that the 'Royal Family and Nuri and many others [had] served their country devotedly' and added, less controversially, that 'they [had] stuck to us in bad times as well as good'. The old Ambassador recognized that London had 'to get along with the new regime on account of oil and business and politics', but that was no reason for 'showing ingratitude' to the old regime. Such coldness 'disgusted' him.[1]

Other British commentators were less sentimental about the fall of the Hashemite regime. To the writer James Morris, later Jan Morris, who wrote one of his best books on the Hashemite kings, the Iraqi monarchy had been a 'parasitical fake'. Its collapse was just a sign that the empire too was doomed. The Hashemites provoked the young journalist's scorn and inspired some of his most impassioned prose. The Anglo-Arab monarchies, he wrote, 'were born into the swirl of a dying Empire, in the last decades of the Viceroys and the ironclads, and they remained for forty years the friends, allies, wards, clients, pensioners or embarrassments of Great Britain. When she was powerful, they were secure; when she slid into impotence, they crumbled or lost their meaning.'[2] The special connection between Britain and the Iraqi leadership had been broken. The subsequent history of Iraq, with its instability, massacres and wars, shows how completely the attempt to establish a stable regime had failed.[3]

It was only a matter of time before pressure would be applied to the Iraq Petroleum Company, the economic instrument and symbol of Britain's dominance over the country. Although the Iraqi government had, since the 1940s, enjoyed large oil revenues, it had not been allowed to acquire a stake in the IPC. This was a major grievance of the nationalists and the Iraqi people generally. The IPC had been intransigent when the government had asked it to build refineries in Iraq. By 1951, only one small refinery had been built, and that had been completed in 1927. The issue had been important to the Iraqi government. Refineries would increase the country's income, because refined oil could sell for a higher margin than the crude product. All professionals in the oil industry confirmed that it was in the marketing and refining of the product that bigger profits could be realized. Refineries would also provide employment for more workers, and would enable the Iraqis to learn the techniques necessary in the advanced stages of oil production. By the end of 1947, the IPC employed fewer than 15,000 workers, in a population of nearly 5 million. The increase in production of crude oil in Iraq had been impressive, though not as spectacular as in Saudi Arabia or Iran. Events in the Middle East in the early 1950s had altered the climate in which the IPC operated. Early in 1951, the Saudis had reached an agreement with Aramco (the state-owned national oil company of Saudi Arabia) which replaced the existing royalty payment with a 50–50 profit-sharing arrangement. This formed the basis of Iraq's own agreement with the IPC in 1952.[4]

In Iran, the early 1950s had witnessed increasing agitation against the Anglo-Iranian Oil Company (formerly known as the Anglo-Persian Oil

Company, which owned a quarter of the IPC and would later be known as British Petroleum). The nationalist leader, Mohammed Mossadeq, who had tried to nationalize Iranian oil, had been toppled in a plot organized by the CIA in 1953. Any attempt to nationalize the oil in Iraq met with serious difficulties, not least because of the lack of technical expertise among the Iraqis. The IPC had failed to train enough Iraqis to manage the oil industry. There was also a lack of financial resources, as the assumption had always been that only foreign capital could exploit Iraq's rich natural resources.[5]

Yet, by 1960, the oil-producing countries, mainly centred in the Middle East and the developing world, were beginning to flex their muscles. It was in that year that a meeting was held in Baghdad that would change the nature of the oil industry and alter the context of Middle Eastern politics. The meeting itself lasted from 10 to 14 September, only five days, but it gave birth to the Organization of the Petroleum Exporting Countries, more widely known as OPEC. Its founding members were Iraq, Iran, Saudi Arabia, Kuwait and Venezuela. This development weakened the grip of the Western oil companies on the setting of global oil prices.[6]

Iraq's revolutionary regime of 1958 was led eventually by Brigadier Abdul Karim al-Qasim, the forty-four-year-old unmarried army officer who had initially shared power with Colonel Arif. Qasim was noted for his austerity, and the egalitarian character of his regime brought much social reform, especially in the system of landholding, as well as changes in the ownership of Iraq's oil resources.[7] Already in the spring of 1959, the Qasim government had embarked on a series of negotiations with the IPC which lasted two and a half years. They culminated in an ultimatum which Qasim himself delivered on 11 October 1961. The Iraqi government had all along demanded a 20 per cent share in the company, as had been promised in the original San Remo Agreement in 1920. Qasim now undertook that his government would give up the demand for the 20 per cent share if the IPC relinquished 90 per cent of its concession territory and increased the share of the profits given to Iraq. The company, as was by now customary, rejected the proposal.[8] On 11 December 1961, Qasim, the austere brigadier, announced Public Law 80, which dispossessed the IPC of 99.5 per cent of its concession territory.

Iraqi politics became unstable in the years following the revolution of 1958. The Ba'ath Party, which played a significant role in the subsequent history of Iraq, had been introduced from Syria in 1949 by Syrian students studying in Baghdad. By 1951 the party had only about fifty members, but it continued to gain support, particularly among young men whose families had originated in the Shia south of the country. After 1958, military officers began to be drawn to its nationalism and modernizing ideology. The Ba'aths also espoused more radical, socialistic ideas which appealed to a people that had witnessed greater disparities of wealth within society as a consequence of increasing oil money. It was these army officers, predominantly Sunni, who organized the coup that toppled Qasim's government in February 1963. The coup led to the grisly demise of Qasim, shot in front of television cameras 'for the whole world to see'. He asked not to be blindfolded, so that he would be able to 'see the bullet'.[9] It was like a gangland execution.

The people at the top of the government may have changed, but the sense of national grievance against the IPC remained vehement. In early 1965, as the Iraqi government was putting more pressure on the foreign shareholders, the British Prime Minister Harold Wilson was wondering what 'concerted action' could be taken to 'stop the sale in Western countries of Iraqi oil if the Iraqis took violent action' against the IPC. As the control of the Western powers over Iraq's oil diminished, old imperial rivalries were revived. The view in London was that 'French support could not be counted on', because the French were suspected of being more accommodating to the Iraqis than the other IPC shareholders. The British Foreign Office, in February 1965, complained that Paris favoured 'acceptance of the Iraqi terms' while continually urging the British and the Americans to accept the Iraqi government's new demands.[10]

In 1966, the Iraqi Foreign Minister, Adnan al-Pachachi, managed to accost the British Foreign Secretary, George Brown, at the UN building in New York. He wanted the British government to put pressure on the company to come to an agreement. Brown was evasive. He regarded the whole thing as a 'management function', not something with which the British government should interfere. Pachachi, pointing out that oil was inherently political, subtly implied that the absence of a settlement would

be a 'barrier to the development of good relations' between the two countries. By 1968, the dispute between the IPC and the Iraqis, which had
been caused by the draconian Law 80 of 1961, was still unresolved. The
Foreign Office issued a note to 'certain missions' in January 1968 which
described, in diplomatic language, 'oil affairs in Iraq' as being 'confused
and in a state of flux'. The situation was, in fact, much worse than the
memorandum suggested; Iraq's oil had now become a nightmare for the
original colonial powers, whose interests were represented by the IPC.
Dissension between the powers themselves was growing, as each power, in
particular the French, sought to carve its own niche in any arrangement.
The Foreign Office grumbled that the French were 'attempting to exploit'
the political situation, with 'two French Companies negotiating to gain
access' to different parcels of land which had been expropriated from the
IPC in 1961. In the meantime, the Soviet government had been in the
process of reaching its own agreement, promising to provide assistance to
the Iraqis in oil exploration and development. As the old colonial order
tottered, other governments were hovering around Iraq to divide the
spoils. Early in 1967, Eni, the Italian state-owned oil company, approached
the Iraq government with an offer to exploit the most valuable part of the
land that had been confiscated from the IPC. This area was called the
North Rumaila field, where large quantities of oil had been proven to
exist. The British, American and Dutch governments lodged strong
protests with the Italians without any success. Italy was eager to develop
commercial ties to a region from which it had been excluded in the various
treaties and settlements after the end of the First World War.

The Arab–Israeli War in June 1967 made the situation more complicated. The Iraqis passed another measure, Law 97, which gave their newly
founded state oil company, the Iraq National Oil Company (INOC), all
the land which had been confiscated from the IPC by Law 80. The resentment which many in the Arab world felt towards the United States and its
Western allies, as a consequence of perceived Western bias towards Israel,
gave the Soviet Union further opportunity to exploit Middle Eastern oil.
Yet Soviet interest in Iraqi oil was not regarded at all seriously by the British
Foreign Office. The intransigence of the IPC had led to a situation in which
the Iraqis could turn 'to other countries', principally the Soviet Union.[11]

The main source of the dispute remained the North Rumaila fields, which had been on the verge of starting production when the IPC was compelled to relinquish control over them. The Soviet government was eager to take these fields over, with Iraqi consent, having promised to produce 100 million tons a year from them. This would give the Iraqis an added £200 million at a time when Iraq's oil production was only about 60 million tons.

Despite the Soviet threat, a civil servant at the Ministry of Power, Sydney Fremantle, was writing on 19 October 1967 that 'Russia has shown very little desire to invest risk capital overseas.' The Soviets, in the Whitehall view, were not as adventurous and buccaneering as Western capitalists. By the end of 1967, however, it was clear that any Soviet hesitation had given way to greater enthusiasm to exploit Iraq's oil wealth. In November, an Iraqi minister in the oil department announced the arrival of sixteen Soviet oil experts who had been invited by INOC in order to draw up 'an agreement for oil exploration and development' in the northern part of the country.[12]

A deal was reached. *Al-Thawra* ('The Revolution'), a popular Baghdad newspaper, reported on 25 December that letters had been exchanged between INOC and the Soviets. For their part, the Soviets agreed to send 'technicians, equipment and machinery' to transport the exported crude oil to the Soviet Union. The Iraqis and the Soviets enjoyed the first of many warm exchanges of words and vaunted affection; Iraqis, unequivocally decrying the connection between Israel and 'the imperialist' West, spoke of the 'magnanimous political support extended by the Soviet Union to the Arab countries during the imperialist-Zionist aggression last June'. Sayid Adib al-Jadr, the chairman of the INOC Board of Administration, read out a statement to reporters. He enumerated the old accusations made against the IPC and the 'imperialistic-Zionist' powers, emphasizing that 'the oil problem in Iraq began with the imposition of the first oil concession in 1925' and denouncing the 'monopoly of oil exploitation by a single company which resolved to embark on a unilateral limitation of production'. The 1920s settlement had prevented Iraq from benefiting fully from its own natural resources.

In London, *The Times*, in an article entitled 'Russia moves into Middle East oil', asserted that the Russians and the French had deliberately exploited the 'confusion and demoralization among Arab countries that has followed [their defeat by Israel in] the June war'. It was widely known that ERAP (Entreprise de Recherches et d'Activitiés Pétrolières), the French state oil company, had already signed a deal with the Iraqis, earlier in 1967, before that war had even started. Now, the Russians were prepared to finance Iraqi oil expansion, while the French were willing to be its 'contractors'. Encouraged by the support from these two countries, the Iraqi government was now behaving in a more confident and aggressive fashion, *The Times* believed. The Iraqi President seemed determined, according to the report in that newspaper, to provoke a serious quarrel with the IPC. Using the colourful imagery for which the Arabic language is known, he denounced the IPC, with its predominantly British and American directors, as 'bloodsuckers'.[13]

The IPC was being squeezed out, yet the British government was still trying to help the company. By 1968, this attempt was looking increasingly hopeless. The British Embassy in Baghdad was keeping the Foreign Office in London informed of the discussions which were taking place between the IPC and the Iraqi government. It was apparent to British diplomats on the scene that the board of the IPC was sharply divided, as the Americans adopted a tough line, refusing further talks with the Iraqi authorities, while the French were prepared to be more conciliatory.[14] The British Embassy also provided coaching for senior IPC officials in their negotiations with the Iraqis. 'We discussed tactics. Sutcliffe and Macdonald [senior IPC executives] seemed to think that there would be an advantage in their explaining the company's position to top political figures.'[15]

On 17 July 1968 the Ba'ath Party carried out another coup. The party's coup against Brigadier Qasim in February 1963 had brought it to power for only nine months, as Abdul Salam Arif, Qasim's partner in the 1958 revolution, emerged as the dominant figure in Iraqi politics after November 1963 when Arif ousted various Ba'athist members of the Cabinet and was elected president. In April 1966, Arif embarked on a tour of the country in a bid to promote the regime. On the 13th he boarded a helicopter to fly to Basra. Shortly after take-off, the helicopter crashed in a sandstorm, killing all on board, including the President. Four days later, Arif's brother Abdul Rahman Arif was elected president. Abdul Rahman's weak personality and lack of political skill ensured that the regime would be ineffectual.

The coup of July 1968 brought about by the Ba'ath Party inaugurated permanent change in the orientation of government in Iraq. This time the Ba'ath leaders 'instituted the kind of regime they had failed to achieve in 1963', under the presidency of Hassan al-Bakr.[16]

The Ba'athist Revolution openly promoted the policy of 'direct national exploitation of oil'. One manager of CFP (Companie Française des Pétroles), the French oil company which was a partner in the IPC, described Iraq's new rulers as a 'gang of fascist-type thugs' who seemed bent on defending their positions 'with utter ruthlessness'. This, as far as the IPC was concerned, was not necessarily a bad development. It was 'morally distasteful' to deal with these thugs, yet in their ruthlessness they might be just 'the sort of people to show the will and capacity to reach an overall settlement and impose it politically'. The oil company executives had a grudging respect for political leaders as hard-nosed as themselves.[17] This proved to be wishful thinking.

The new Iraqi Minister of Defence, General Hardan al-Takriti, whose cousin Saddam Hussein would soon emerge as the strongman of Iraq, tele-phoned the British Ambassador one morning towards the end of October 1968, asking to see him at six o'clock that evening. As it was a Friday, a holy day in the Islamic world, the call was very unusual. Takriti was obsessed with the idea that the company owed the Iraq government money as a result of the understating of its profits during the 1950s and 1960s. Meanwhile, Sutcliffe and Macdonald, the IPC executives, had a three-hour interview with Dr Rashid al-Rifa'i, the Iraqi Oil Minister, at which the minister harangued the two men, repeatedly raising the question of the 20 per cent Iraqi share in the company which had been promised at San Remo in 1920. When the IPC men protested about Law 80, which had expropriated 99.5 per cent of the IPC's land concession in 1961, the minister played his trump card, complaining of the 'failure of the company to do anything for the people'. If the IPC had managed to build 'only one school a year' their repu-tation in Iraq would have been very different, he argued. Sutcliffe, weakly but truthfully, observed that the company could do nothing right. 'If we built schools, hospitals and so forth, we would have been accused of inter-fering in internal affairs. Now we are being accused of indifference,' to which Rifa'i replied that at least the IPC could have tried.

Three days later, the two oilmen, together with a representative from the American shareholders, went to see General Takriti himself. The General was 'frank and genial' and talked about Iraq's 'current problems'; he told the British businessmen that Iraq needed more money, and that more oil would have to be produced. It was difficult for the Iraqi government to reach a deal with the company, because the company itself, as a symbol of imperialist power, was so widely hated by the Iraqi people. 'The IPC had an appalling image,' Takriti said, but the company needed to produce more oil to boost revenues, since Iraq was a 'developing country and needed help', and, more ominously, the 'armed forces needed equipment'.[18]

Now that Iraq's oil was effectively being underwritten by the Russians and, to a lesser degree, the French, the government could be as rude as it liked to the IPC. By early 1969, the company was clinging on by its fingernails. British civil servants were marvelling that 'in spite of ten years of fairly constant dispute between the two sides, and of much harassment of the IPC by the Iraqis, the IPC still remained in business'. Oil was still the key to the relationship between Britain and Iraq, and the British were fully committed to preserving some kind of role for the company. In a draft of a letter dated January 1969, a British diplomat asserted that 'the position of the IPC is not only of extreme importance in any consideration of Anglo-Iraqi relations', it was 'crucial'.[19]

The Iraqis were by now enjoying their newfound independence. With the Soviets at their side, they continued to treat the IPC with insouciance verging on contempt. In January 1969, Dr Rifa'i spoke to the *Middle East Economic Survey* in language that was partially derived from current Marxist rhetoric about defending the rights of the people against the imperialist powers. He referred proudly to his own government's success in standing up to the Western companies: 'The revolutionary government is forging ahead, and the protection of the people's rights shall not be obstructed by the dreams or wishful thinking of the companies.' Iraq was now 'more powerful than the companies'.[20]

It was into this background of growing Iraqi nationalism, coupled with increased confidence and greater self-assertion, that Saddam Hussein thrust himself in the early 1970s. As vice chairman of the Revolutionary

Command Council and so formally Bakr's second-in-command, Saddam Hussein had been a popular and progressive figure. His career was defined by the steps which he took in finally nationalizing the IPC in 1972. The nationalization was perhaps inevitable. During the 1959–70 period, revenue from the profit-sharing arrangement with the IPC accounted for an average of 80 per cent of the Iraqi government's total revenue each year. The company had a potential noose around the government's neck. Yet it still needed an extra push to bring about nationalization. There were still many associated risks, since the Iraqi government could not be absolutely sure in May 1972 that there would be an international market for nationalized crude oil. A Western boycott of the nationalized oil from Iran in the early 1950s had contributed to the ousting of Mossadeq's government. The possibility of a Western boycott still existed, which meant that the market for Iraqi oil needed a guaranteed outlet, and this the Soviets provided.[21]

Saddam was ruthless. In his role as vice chairman of the Revolutionary Command Council, he assumed direct responsibility from 1971 for dealing with the IPC. To prepare the ground for the nationalization of the oil company he strengthened Iraq's ties with Moscow. Soviet Prime Minister Alexei Kosygin arrived in Baghdad in April 1972. He was given a guided tour of the marble halls of the Presidential Palace, accompanied by a statuesque blonde specially procured by Saddam.[22] While he entertained the Russians, Saddam had shrewdly secured from the French a pledge that they would not join any anti-Iraq boycott so long as French interests were unharmed. On 1 June, two months after Kosygin's visit, the IPC was nationalized. This was arguably the decisive step in the modern history of Iraq. It provided the country with a massive source of revenue at a time when the oil price was about to soar. More broadly it conferred on Saddam Hussein a prestige and authority in the Arab world which only Nasser, in recent times, had managed to enjoy. After all, the nationalization of the IPC echoed Nasser's nationalization of the Suez Canal, sixteen years before. 'Oil for the Arabs' had become the new rallying cry of Arab nationalists since Israel's humiliating victory in the 1967 war. The same cry would become especially resonant in the aftermath of the Yom Kippur War of 1973.[23]

Saddam constantly boasted of his achievement in snatching Iraq's oil wealth from the greedy hands of the imperialists and giving it back to the Iraqi people. In a meeting of oil department bureaucrats on 1 June 1983, the eleventh anniversary of the nationalization of the IPC, he recalled that the real national independence of Iraq had not begun in 1921, nor even with the Ba'athist coup of July 1968; Iraq's real independence, he claimed, dated from 1 June 1972.[24] Always keen to burnish his credentials as an Arab nationalist, he would talk about how his relatives had been killed by the British, how his forefathers had fought bravely against the Turks. He would claim that he had considered himself a nationalist from the time his mother told him of his uncle, Tulfah, who had fought against the British in 1941.[25] Against this background of fierce anti-imperialist struggle, the nationalization of Iraq's oil took on a heroic quality. On the eighth anniversary of the nationalisation, on 1 June 1980, Saddam invited a group of young children to the Presidential Palace. He went on to tell them a sort of bedtime story about the nationalization. He explained to his captive audience that children in the dark days when the colonial powers controlled Iraqi oil could not afford the 'nice clothes you have on now' and could only look at Western children, the children of the British and Dutch oil executives, with envy. Now all the shares were for the Iraqis. There were 'no shares for foreigners'.[26]

At the time of the nationalization itself, Saddam proclaimed that this act had 'crowned a dauntless unremitting struggle that lasted for over half a century against foreign domination and alien exploitation'. These sentiments chimed harmoniously with his much vaunted nationalism, as well as with his socialism. 'The presence of the oil companies did not only arrest the economic progress of the country. It also menaced the country's independence and . . . conflicted with the Revolution's ultimate aim of: unity, freedom and socialism.'[27] The British reaction to Saddam's move was not as robust as might have been expected. Within a year of the nationalization, the Foreign Office was discussing whether to help British companies to get back into Iraq. In August 1973, Tom Boardman, a minister in the Trade Department, was writing to Sir Alec Douglas-Home, the Foreign Secretary, about a move that Shell and CFP, the French oil company, were making in Iraq. These companies had proposed a 'European Consortium involving themselves, Italian, German and possibly other oil companies' to go to Iraq and 'undertake large-scale oil exploration and development'. Shell, it seemed, was convinced of the richness of Iraq's oilfields. It believed, according to the British minister, that there was 'no virgin territory in the Middle East or outside it of equal promise'.

Boardman urged the Foreign Secretary to become more actively involved in this potential development. British involvement would 'improve our economic and political relations with Iraq'. Against the background of the Cold War, it was also important to provide 'an extra link with the West' in Iraq which since 1972 had been in 'alliance with the Soviet Union'. Boardman felt that Shell's proposal needed a 'good deal more study'. He would later tell Shell that the British government 'saw no objection to the group making initial soundings in Iraq, provided no mention is made of possible government involvement'.[28]

Edward Heath, the Prime Minister, cautiously expressed the view that it was a 'very dubious proposition'.[29] The scheme involved the Western governments giving aid to the Iraqis in exchange for access to their oil. Anthony Parsons, a senior Foreign Office official, and an expert on Iranian affairs, felt the scheme was 'imaginative' but would make things difficult for the Saudis and the Shah of Iran. How 'could we begin to explain to the Shah, the Saudis and the Kuwaitis that we were prepared to be far more generous to Iraq (of all countries) than toward any of our friends in the region?' he asked.[30] The potential of Iraq as a rich source of oil was a factor which loomed large in the minds of British civil servants. One Foreign Office memorandum from July 1973 referred to Iraq as perhaps 'the only Middle East country with real hope of discovering very substantial new oil reserves'. The reserves there would be 'maybe greater than those of Iran and perhaps remotely approaching Saudi Arabia'.[31]

The British government and Foreign Office were involved in these discussions about Iraqi oil through the whole of the second half of 1973, while Heath remained guarded. In August, he was wary of being 'bounced', as he put it, into the project by Shell. Displaying the same reticence as the Prime Minister, the Treasury was worried that the Iraqi government would just expropriate the assets when a suitable occasion arose.[32] The Iraqis, for their part, conscious that their oilfields were highly desirable, began to drive a hard bargain. By the end of September 1973, they wanted a 'major agricultural development programme' in exchange for an agreement between Shell, CFP, VEBA of Germany and Eni of Italy, together with the Iraq National Oil Company (INOC), which would provide Europe with a 'new major, stable supply of crude oil'.[33]

The British government continued to worry about the reaction of the US and indeed of the Japanese governments when they found that their own companies had been excluded from the proposed deal. Britain was also concerned about the reaction of its allies in the region, particularly Kuwait, Iran and Saudi Arabia. It was clear that a deal with Iraq would be beneficial for the European Economic Community (forerunner of the European Union), and that it would help stabilize relations between Britain and Iraq. During October, it also became evident that the French government was interested in the project, although it would prefer 'direct involvement'. Co-operation between a 'major British oil company . . . and European companies' would benefit Britain, as it was in Britain's interests 'to help to secure the EEC's long term oil supplies'. The Iraqis, it was recognized by British diplomats, wanted to develop their oil reserves to promote their general economic development.

Unfortunately, the outbreak of the Yom Kippur War in October 1973 delayed Shell's plans. At the end of that month, Patrick Wright, the head of the Middle East Department at the Foreign Office, had the 'impression that Shell were not proceeding actively with this scheme'.[34] But it was simply political circumstance, not any qualms about the nature of the Iraqi regime, which put the brakes on an oil deal with Iraq. Even after the Yom Kippur War, the Foreign Office official Stephen Egerton, an Old Etonian and Cambridge-educated Classics scholar in his late thirties, frankly admitted in December of that year that the 'Iraqi regime is repressive and on occasion hostile; but it is apparently well in control'. Besides, Egerton argued, the Iraqis were 'more anti-Soviet' than they used to be.[35] In the matter of oil politics, and in the context of the Cold War, the nature of the regime was secondary to stability. On 21 November, Wright, in full agreement with Egerton, summed up the situation with startling realism. Yes, there had been a 'history of political unrest in Iraq since 1958', but the present regime had 'remained in power for five years' and had used that power to 'eliminate most potential sources of opposition'. According to Wright, there was 'no strong evidence that the power of the regime [had] declined appreciably'. The Iraqi government was strong and stable. On that basis, Britain could do deals with it. 'Although repressive and singularly unattractive, the present Government seems to be well in control,' Wright contended in language which exactly echoed Egerton's earlier assertions on this issue. Wright was also clear that Western capital and expertise would be needed to achieve Iraq's goals. Even the Shah of Iran, it seemed, would welcome this. The Shah's attitude was that the 'need to counter Russian influence in the area in general and in Iraq in particular' was the most important factor.[36]

The willingness of the British government to deal with Iraq, even after the nationalization, illustrates the highly pragmatic attitude taken by the West towards the Middle East in the days of the Cold War. Money-making and the desire to act against encroaching Soviet influence were primary concerns of foreign policy, long before the days of the neo-conservatives and their more ideologically driven enterprises undertaken in the first decade of the twenty-first century.

The deal with Shell quickly faded into the background. Saddam Hussein, now the dominant personality in Iraq, grew in power and prestige. For those analysts who saw the end of his career in the US-led invasion of Iraq in 2003, it was easy to see him as a villain of the Middle East, a malign dictator who brutally repressed his own people. It is also easy to overlook the extent to which the West had praised and encouraged him. His relations with the French were particularly warm. A French Middle East expert, Charles Saint-Prot, as late as 1987 could describe Saddam as one of the defining figures of the twentieth century. He had undertaken to 'give back life to his country, that is to restart the dialogue with history'. Saddam was a statesman to be compared to 'Charles de Gaulle, Nasser, Nehru, Tito' and even Churchill. The same writer quoted Jacques Chirac, who would later be president of France at the time of the second Gulf War in 2003, speaking in an interview in July 1985: Saddam was a 'sincere and faithful man, animated by a grand ambition for his country . . . He plays an essential role on the Arab scene.'[37]

Increasing oil revenue had raised Iraq's prestige and influence across the Middle East. The country's literacy programme, funded by the oil money, won plaudits across the world. To mark its September 1979 International Literacy Day, UNESCO (the United Nations Educational, Scientific and Cultural Organization) awarded a prize to the Iraqi campaign to eliminate illiteracy. Saddam, having sidelined the hapless Bakr in 1978, was now president and could bask indulgently in the sunlight of international approval. The UNESCO citation claimed that Iraq 'has given the international community an example of determined political will in the field of education'.[38]

With this level of success and adulation, Saddam could pose as the world-historical figure he had always dreamed of becoming. He was avuncular and condescending. Sometimes he engaged in highly personal and charismatic gestures, as in October 1979 when he saw a boy on the street in Baghdad and offered him a lift to school. He then went on an impromptu tour round the school. At other times, he would suddenly appear on the doorsteps of houses, selected at random in Baghdad, accompanied by a camera crew. Saddam was deliberately portraying himself as a modern Haroun al-Rashid, the eighth-century caliph who famously had wandered the streets of Baghdad in disguise in order to learn about his subjects' concerns. Saddam too would go on fact-finding missions and undertake what he called his 'early-morning surprises'. A favourite pastime was to appear at the door of a house and ask any boy who happened to open the door, 'Where is your father?' 'He is asleep.' 'Wake him and tell him that President Saddam would like to share your breakfast.'[39]

Saddam's charismatic style was supported by huge oil revenues. The price of oil quadrupled in the latter half of the 1970s, while Iraq's production of the fuel soared. The Iraqis now owned 100 per cent of the revenues. The Yom Kippur War had induced the Arab oil-producing states to test their economic strength by encouraging them to force up the price of oil, which had been a little over US$3 a barrel on 1 October 1973; oil cost over US$11 a barrel just three months later on New Year's Day, 1974.[40] There now flowed a torrent of wealth into the country: Iraq's oil revenues increased from US$575 million in 1972 to over US$26 billion in 1980, an increase of nearly fifty times, in nominal terms, in just eight years.[41]

These were heady days in Baghdad and in Iraq generally. Oil wealth generated a massive social transformation in the country, where there now existed greater social mobility. The women of Iraq enjoyed a more liberal attitude towards their rights and towards the fashions they were allowed to display in their clothes. The nouveaux riches of Baghdad, the contractors and entrepreneurs, enjoyed all the delights usually found in the more cosmopolitan cities in the West. The 1970s were a period of great expansion and progress. In Baghdad, roads of asphalt replaced dirt tracks; modern hospitals, the envy of the Arab world, and architecturally impressive schools were built.[42] New housing projects and increased social security were also supported by the oil industry. Despite all this investment, nearly 40 per cent of the income derived from oil was being spent on military hardware.[43] Iraq was becoming a significant regional power, envied and feared by its immediate neighbours.

Saddam sat at the top of all this success, hailed by millions of his countrymen as an extraordinary man, a leader of great vision and stature. In his pomp and vanity, Saddam saw himself as a 'new Saladdin', a Nebuchadnezzar or a Sargon the Great.[44] The cult of Saddam began in those years, and he would enter the *Guinness Book of Records* as the world's most frequently painted head of state.[45] The vast increase in oil revenues, the new possibilities which wealth offered the Iraqi people, stirred Saddam's ambition. On 17 September 1980, fully resplendent in the uniform of the commander-in-chief of the armed forces, Saddam stood before the National Assembly of Iraq. He renounced the 6 March 1975 agreement which he had signed with the Shah relating to border and other disputes between the two countries. The Iranian revolution of 1979 had put into power a radical Shi'ite cleric, the Ayatollah Khomeini, a religious figure totally opposed to the secular Arab nationalism that Saddam and, before him, Nasser had espoused. Saddam denounced the Iranians as 'racist' and 'Persian' and launched a war against them.[46] The Iran–Iraq conflict was a new manifestation of the age-old conflict between Ottomans and Safavids, between Arabs and Persians, which had shaped the region for many centuries. But in this act of aggression Saddam badly miscalculated.

The Iran–Iraq War was a disaster for Saddam and marked the beginning of the end of his power. It was a prime example of hubris, of overreaching oneself and bringing about one's ruin. Like Agamemnon, or many other heroes of Greek tragedy, worldly success had pushed Saddam too far. In taking on new projects and fulfilling new ambitions, he would lose everything. The Iran–Iraq War left him crushed by debt. When the ceasefire came into effect on 20 August 1988, he presided over an Iraq that 'had seen most of its major oil exporting capacity destroyed, blocked or closed'. The war left him owing US\$65 billion to Western creditors and to the Soviets. The Arab states, particularly Saudi Arabia and Kuwait, had lent Iraq US\$80 billion.[47] Kuwait was pressing for repayment and, by February 1990, Saddam faced another problem – the collapse of the oil price. In January 1990 the price of oil was US\$21 a barrel. By the summer it was US\$11. At such a low price, Iraq would be bankrupt. Saddam believed that some OPEC producers were flooding the market, not sticking to their assigned quotas, and that Kuwait, in its refusal to keep production down and thus raise the oil price, was the prime culprit. While refusing to decrease production, the Kuwaitis also declined to write off a US\$40 billion loan they had granted Saddam during the Iran–Iraq War.

Saddam needed a dramatic boost to the oil price by which he could obtain more money to pay off his enormous debts, but the Kuwaitis still refused to cut their production. The conquest of Kuwait was the most attractive solution to the Iraqi dictator. Saddam's thinking was brutal but pragmatic: if he annexed Kuwait, he could cut back its production of oil and thereby increase the oil price, enabling him to obtain more revenue.[48] It was the United States' invasion of Iraq, accompanied by its allies, in 1991 that prevented Saddam's dreams from being realized.

In 2002, the year before the second Gulf War, Iraq was exporting nearly 2 million barrels a day under the UN's 'oil for food' programme. This brought in US\$12 billion of revenue, on an annual basis, but was still well short of the 1980 figure. No one knows how much oil there is in Iraq. Since Saddam Hussein's forcible removal from power by the Americans in 2003, the country has not been stable enough for proper geological surveys to be carried out. Under Saddam, Iraq had never been open for such surveys, and no adequate one had been carried out there for more than forty years. Even though the exact amount of oil remains unknown, Iraq still has a huge potential source of wealth. The Iraqi government in 2008 announced that it could be sitting on the largest oil reserves in the world, with 350 billion barrels.[49] This figure is much greater than Saudi Arabia's 264 billion barrels. The official figure of 115 billion barrels still ensures that Iraq is sitting on the third largest oil reserves behind Saudi Arabia and Iran.

The damage done by the second Gulf War has meant that any Iraqi government is desperate to develop its oil reserves. To do this effectively, foreign capital and expertise will be required. The old problems could re-emerge. In June 2008, Iraq threw its doors open to international invest-ment in its oil sector. It announced two bidding rounds for oil- and gasfield development service contracts.[50] Iraq is desperate to boost its production, after the ravages of both Gulf Wars, not to mention the terrible dislocation and suffering caused by the Iran–Iraq War. Interestingly, the Chinese National Petroleum Company has been the first foreign company to begin a project in an Iraqi oilfield.[51] The unsettled state of Iraq, its lack of stability, was deterring foreign investors at the end of the first decade of the twenty-first century. Undoubtedly, the development of Iraq's oil resources remains one of the great questions in the global economy in the coming decades.

But what of the British Empire? To what extent was the settlement in Iraq after the First World War responsible for the wars, the chaos and the confusion that have bedevilled Iraq for many decades? The establishment of the Hashemite kings was a disaster; to set up a monarchy without any antecedent foundation in Iraq was irresponsible, and it may also have been a product of a besetting sin of the British Empire, its snobbery. The IPC, as an institution, was a purely commercial enterprise, and had no political legitimacy or expertise. Its sole aim was to extract crude oil from Iraq, without having any real regard to the welfare of the Iraqi people.

The Hashemites were thrown out in a bloody coup, after which the IPC's days were numbered. The governments that succeeded the monarchy were of an aggressive, nationalist kind which barred foreign companies from Iraq's oil. It was perhaps inevitable that the reaction to the IPC's failure, when it came, would be severe.

Saddam, in his reckless self-regard, used Iraq's newfound oil wealth to build up his army and invade the lands of his neighbours, Iran and Kuwait. In this sense, he was more akin to a conqueror from the ancient or medieval worlds than a sophisticated, modern political operator. The problem can be simply expressed: how can a stable regime be established in Iraq, on the basis of the popular will, while at the same time allowing foreign capital a chance to develop its abundant oil resources? The Hashemite kings did indeed allow foreign capital to exploit Iraq's oil, but they were grotesquely out-of-touch, almost pantomime, figureheads. Saddam and his nationalist predecessors who overthrew the Hashemites were undoubtedly more popular in their appeal; they had come from the people and were more in tune with what the average Iraqi citizen felt and thought. They did not, however, allow foreign expertise to develop Iraq's oil. Saddam abused his abundant oil resources by pursuing a reckless foreign policy that led to war, bankruptcy and the death and ruin of his family. It remains to be seen how the problem of oil and power in Iraq will be resolved. How can Iraq and the international community balance the legitimate aspirations of the Iraqi people with the natural desire of foreign capital to exploit Iraq's native wealth?

PART II

KASHMIR: MAHARAJA'S CHOICE

5

Land for Sale

The battle was over. The Sikhs had been defeated. They would now have to agree terms with the British, in the form of the East India Company. The company, like any modern company, existed to make money. It had only got into politics, making war and signing treaties, to promote its commercial activities. Until 1858, however, it basically governed India. Now, in 1846, it had defeated the Sikh Empire in the Punjab; this meant that the 'English were masters of Cashmere', according to contemporary reports.[1]

Kashmir, or Cashmere as it was spelt until the second half of the nineteenth century, was a beautiful and much prized place. It had been contested by the Afghans and by the Mughal emperors. The physical grandeur of its environment, with its high mountains and stunning valleys, was such that the Afghans, who often invaded, thought of it as a 'mistress'. They enshrined this feeling in a proverb: 'Unto every man his own country is Kashmir.'[2] Kashmir had been conquered in 1819 by Ranjit Singh, the Sikh Raja. He died from a 'stroke brought on by excessive drinking' in 1839, aged about sixty. He had had many wives and concubines, but no strong heir had been found to take over his legacy. With his death the Sikh Empire he had built up over forty years 'began to unravel'.[3] The sons he had were killed and a little boy, aged eight, was now the maharaja. His forces had just been humiliated, so the East India Company, whose job it was to make money, imposed an indemnity of £1 million on the Sikhs for all the trouble they had caused.

They could not afford this sum outright, but a sly cunning man called Gulab Singh, Raja of Jammu and a courtier of Ranjit Singh, came up with a plan. Why didn't the British allow him to rule Kashmir in exchange for a proportion of the money the Sikhs owed? Gulab had served at Lahore, the capital of the Sikh Empire, but he owed little loyalty to the Sikhs. A payment of £500,000 was suggested and then he would be the proud possessor of Kashmir. How he acquired the money for this is still a mystery. At a time, in the 1840s, when the richest men in England, the Duke of Devonshire and the Marquess of Westminster, had an income of £100,000 a year, £500,000 was a huge amount of capital. It would be the equivalent of about £50 million today. Henry Hardinge, the Governor General, was clearly impressed by Gulab's resources and by his cunning. The Raja's income was £600,000 a year[4] – six times, it should be added, the income of the richest peer in England. Like the military men of this period, he was a practical man who once said that he didn't mind enlisting 'native' soldiers since the 'colour of the face cannot be ascertained at 60 yards', the range at which a rifle would be fired.[5]

This was how the Treaty of Amritsar came about. The treaty was signed on 16 March 1846, and is one of the more bizarre documents in the history of the British Empire. It stipulated that Kashmir would be given to Gulab Singh and 'his heirs' in exchange for £500,000 sterling, or 75 lakh rupees, in the Indian currency (a lakh was 100,000), and an annual token tribute of 'one horse, twelve goats (six male and six female) and six pairs of shawls'.[6] The deal was a strange one but it made sense for the East India Company. The company didn't want to have the expense of running Kashmir, so why not get a local feudal lord to govern the province? The local lord could then act as a buffer, a watchdog keeping an eye on the troublesome Sikhs. As a Kashmiri acidly pointed out at the time, 'the grant of Kashmir to Gulab Singh was purposely to create enmity between him and the Sikhs'. Had Gulab refused to take it, the English would have given it to someone else 'to prevent its being in the hands' of the Sikhs.[7] The company needed the money and Hardinge, the Governor General, was 'short of powder'. He didn't have the resources to keep Kashmir.

Sir Charles Napier was in no doubt that selling Kashmir to Gulab was a mistake. 'It is a crime', he thundered, 'to have left the Punjab and Kashmir in the hands of such murdering villains as Gulab Singh and the other ruffians who torment the poor.'[8] Napier was a no-nonsense imperialist of the old school. Now in his sixties, he had been a soldier since the age of twelve. He was now a general, famous for his great hook-nose, his brusque arrogance and his quickness to take offence. He also loathed Gulab Singh and didn't understand why Britain had 'adorned his head with a crown'. His view of the empire was simple and pragmatic. 'It is true we have won that empire most unjustly, but it is now impossible to abandon our position. We may not retreat, and can only hold our ground by skill and courage.'⁹

Everyone, even his best friends, acknowledged that Gulab Singh, the new Maharaja of Kashmir, was a difficult man. He had been born in 1792 and so was in his mid-fifties when he bought his kingdom. He had no formal education, couldn't read and write, but he could shoot and wield a sword. He was savage – he liked, it was said, to flay his enemies alive – but he was also courteous. He knew about power. He recognized that the British were strong and he was perhaps the most obsequious servant the British Empire ever had. The elegant Lord Dalhousie, who took over as governor general after Hardinge in 1848, would laugh at Gulab's cringing sycophancy. In a letter thanking Queen Victoria for his marquessate in July 1849, Dalhousie reported a conversation with Gulab, in which the Maharaja had expressed his delight that 'the British flag has for ever been planted in the sky'. Gulab went on and on, saying that if 'the whole surface of the earth were to become paper, the trees pens, and the rivers ink; they would all be insufficient to express his unbounded pleasure'.¹⁰

By the time Queen Victoria received the letter, two months later, the Sikh kingdom had ceased to exist. After a series of battles which had taken place since the end of the previous year, Sikh ministers gathered at Lahore on the morning of 29 March 1849 and read a proclamation from Dalhousie himself which simply stated: 'The Kingdom of Punjab is at an end. All the territories of Maharaja Dalip Singh are now and henceforth a portion of the British Empire.'¹¹ The last Maharaja, the eleven-year-old Duleep Singh, was taken to England, where he later purchased the 17,000-acre Elveden estate in Norfolk. The initial reason for creating the Kashmir state, as a buffer against the Sikhs, had vanished within three years. After 1849, there was really no reason to keep the maharajas of Kashmir. The kingdom could have been annexed outright. This didn't happen, with consequences which are still felt today.

Dalhousie didn't trust Gulab for one minute: 'I do not, never have trusted, and never will trust him.' He added with the irony for which British imperialists were famous, that 'I am not unskilful enough openly to exhibit distrust.' Dalhousie was a pragmatic Scot, though he had gone through the usual ruling-class treadmill at Harrow and Christ Church, Oxford. He was a short, capable and highly ambitious politician, who had been made governor general at the age of thirty-five. He understood that Gulab Singh's attachment to Britain was one forged purely by self-interest. As he explained in a later letter to Queen Victoria, 'Whatever may have been the character and conduct of this man during his adventurous life, from the time when he ran as an orderly by the side of Ranjeet's horse, till the present day when he reigns over wide dominions, his interests are now too closely and too clearly united with ours.' Britain had cast its lot with Gulab; they sank or swam together. Gulab's sycophancy knew no bounds. Dalhousie relayed to the Queen other obsequious remarks which had poured from Gulab's lips. The British government was 'now seated in the heavens: I have laid hold of its skirts and I will never quit my grasp'. Gulab was wondering if the Queen would accept as a gift the collection of cashmere shawls he had sent for the Great Exhibition in Crystal Palace.[12]

Gulab had been both lucky and shrewd. It was true that he was a clever man, though he almost certainly was not the 'cleverest man ever India produced', which an Indian had told Napier.[13] Hardinge's son, who had visited Kashmir with his father in 1846, remembered Gulab as a 'fine handsome old man with a long beard'.[14] The Maharaja was shrewd in picking his friends. Hardinge, the practical military man, supported him, even though he knew he wasn't an ideal ruler. Gulab was even more friendly with Sir Henry Lawrence, the political officer in the Punjab.

Lawrence was the middle of three brothers who had all gone to serve with the East India Company in the 1820s and 1830s. The Lawrences were a special breed of British hero, Christian warriors who combined deep religious conviction with a tough-minded pragmatism. When Gulab asked Sir Henry how it was that the British always conquered their foes, Lawrence, a little embarrassed, refused to answer. But he then asked for a sheet of paper and wrote 'IHS' on it. He did not explain that these letters stood for the Latin words 'Iesu Hominum Salvator', Jesus Saviour of Men.

The Maharaja thought that the letters were a mystical sign and had them stamped on the silver rupee coins in newly acquired Kashmir. The Lawrences were one of those Anglo-Irish families who were often drawn to service in the empire. Henry, his elder brother George and his younger brother John, who would be viceroy of India in the 1860s, were all educated at Londonderry's Foyle College, which has been described as a 'tough, no-nonsense, God-fearing institution that produced boys ideally matched to the East India Company's needs'.[15]

To the soldier-diplomat Herbert Edwardes, on the other hand, Gulab was the 'worst native' he had 'ever come in contact with'; he was a 'bad king, a miser, and a liar, and the dirtiest fellow in all India'. For the Kashmiris the sale of their homeland to Gulab Singh was a misfortune. The British officials themselves were never entirely comfortable with the decision to support Gulab and his family, a Hindu dynasty, in their rule of a predominantly Muslim state. Napier had written a ditty about Gulab's new kingdom:

> Oh Gulab Sing
> We made you king
> All out of moderation!
> But says Cashmere
> You shan't come here
> And all is botheration![16]

Others were more seriously critical. They knew even in the 1850s that the company had made a big mistake. As early as 1851, Colonel Henry Steinbach, a British officer of German origins, was highly critical of the British policy and even let Lord Dalhousie know what he thought. He had 'a mean opinion' of Gulab's talents. 'In no single thing that he does, can I detect ability.' The whole policy Britain had pursued was wrong. If Dalhousie visited Kashmir, he would find 'the entire population . . . prostrating themselves at your Lordship's feet to beg to be relieved from the Maharajah's rule'. Steinbach's letter was prescient and direct, though he tried to cover himself with an air of tact and diplomacy: 'Far be it from me to animadvert upon the policy of the British Government,' he began. 'I will merely observe, en passant, that the Government made a great mistake in assigning over to the Maharajah so beautiful a country.'

The British had handed over 'a whole people to the Maharajah's oppressive rule'. This had happened even though everyone knew what kind of ruler he would be. Gulab was indeed rich. But there was a catch. He was rich because he was an avaricious, unscrupulous ruler. Steinbach continued, they 'make an outcry in England about the abolition of slavery, whereas the British Government have in reality . . . given over an entire people to a slavery of the most oppressive description'. It was Gulab's greed, more than anything else, which oppressed the people. 'The Maharajah has taken everything into his own hands, and is, with the exception of 5 or 6 shawl merchants, the only trader in Cashmere.' Taxes were exorbitant; from every 100 acres' worth of grain cultivated, Gulab 'takes 90, leaving 10 to the cultivator . . . upon shawls and every other article of manufactured goods he takes exactly half of its sale price'. The result of all this greed was that the people lived in the 'most abject poverty'.[17]

Not that any of this bothered the Lawrence brothers. Sir Henry, who has been described as the 'virtual ruler of the Punjab from 1847', perfected what was known as the Lawrence system.[18] He was a fatherly figure to native rulers. He wanted to keep the region quiet from a strictly external point of view. He was relatively unconcerned about what went on inside the province, as long as it didn't give any trouble to the Raj. Under his younger brother John, this system was dubbed 'masterly inactivity' by its opponents. It entailed a policy, so far as was possible, of non-intervention towards both India's neighbours and the princely states. There was little trust or love involved, but so long as things were quiet that would be sufficient. Along with the inactivity and world-weariness, these imperial bureaucrats sometimes offered penetrating insights into the men and affairs of the region. John Lawrence was bright. In 1829 he had passed out third from the East India College (which later became Haileybury), where he was remembered for having a 'good deal of the Irish element' in his behaviour.[19] He observed of the Afghans that they would 'bear poverty' and 'insecurity of life; but will not tolerate foreign rule'.

In defence of the pragmatists, they were always having to consider the wider picture, the geopolitical situation. Kashmir was an important part of the so-called Great Game – the name, immortalized by Rudyard Kipling in his novel *Kim*, for the battle over Central Asia which was being fought almost continuously, on an informal basis of espionage and posturing, by Russia and Great Britain throughout the nineteenth century. A local ruler was needed to preserve a figleaf of independence. If Britain annexed Kashmir outright, the Russians might be offended. In the 1860s Lord Mayo, who had been appointed viceroy in 1868, was writing to the Duke of Argyll, the Liberal Secretary of State for India under Gladstone, that Russia 'can be truly told that our only object is commerce and peace'. To Mayo, geopolitical manoeuvring in Central Asia was hazardous: 'Russia hardly seems to be aware of the dangerous game she is trying to play in Central Asia.'[20] The term 'the Great Game' describes pithily the strategic dimension of imperial politics in which Kashmir played an important part. It is in the context of this kind of realism in foreign affairs that the granting of Kashmir to Gulab Singh can be more precisely understood.

In this far-sighted letter Mayo pointed out to Argyll something which he felt the Russians did not understand. There were, in India, 'such differences of Religion and Race as enable us to play Mahomedan and Sikh, Hindoo or Buddhist against each other'. In Central Asia, Russia 'is now face to face with millions of poor fanatical and warlike Races inhabiting almost inaccessible mountains or half desert plains – who . . . are to a man almost Sunie [Sunni] Mahometans'. These tribes and warlike people needed only 'some Prophet of influence . . . to lead them against the infidel invader'. This was a shrewd assessment of Central Asian politics, and of the unifying and galvanizing power of Islam. Mayo quoted the *Moscow Gazette* of 5 April 1869, which referred to the Russian plan 'to make Central Asia a strong strategical point against England in the event of an Eastern War'.[21]

What went on inside Kashmir was not nearly as important as its role in the great theatre of Central Asian politics. The Kashmir maharajas were also well aware of their strategic value. Gulab Singh, a diabetic, died in 1857. He was succeeded by his son Ranbir Singh, who irritated the British by trying to curry favour with the Russians, just as his father had been expert at winning the favour of the British. When the Russians occupied the city of Tashkent in today's Uzbekistan in 1865, it was Maharaja Ranbir Singh who was the first Indian prince to send secret emissaries to convey his 'congratulations' to the Russian General responsible for this success. Ranbir was very careful not to enter into any written communications with the Russians. All contact would be oral; he even established a Russian-language school in Kashmir.[22]

Ranbir was every bit as wily as his father. While trying to ingratiate himself with the Russians, he was also keeping the British satisfied. Given his machinations, it is interesting to see that Lord Mayo was not very impressed by his abilities: 'My interview with the Maharaja was satisfactory – he is a very good man but weak.'[23] Ranbir had clearly perfected the art of playing the stupid innocent when dealing with the British, while sending congratulations and marks of affection to the Russians. For the Maharaja, independence was paramount. For the British, a quiet life and the promotion of greater trade were what mattered. Sir Charles Napier had remarked that the British object in 'conquering India, the object of all our cruelties, was money'.[24] This was cynical, but there was a large element of truth in the claim. Lord Mayo was anxious, at the beginning of 1870, to secure a treaty with the 'Rajah of Cashmere which will have the effect of creating a free Road from our frontier to the borders of Eastern Turkestan'. Trade with eastern Turkestan, the area we would call Azerbaijan or Armenia, was of 'daily increasing importance to the subjects of the British Government and those of the Maharaja'. The Maharaja was worried about his independence, whereas Mayo was fantasizing about establishing 'for the *first time* a secure and duty free route from Central Asia to India' within twelve months.[25]

Kashmir was a classic case of extending the empire by franchise, a way of allowing local rulers the freedom to do what they wanted so long as everything was quiet externally and trade routes remained safe and secure. The family of Gulab Singh, in the meantime, were becoming very rich. They had a policy of making 'every product of the Valley a state monopoly'. Even prostitutes were taxed, for which they were divided into three classes, 'according to their gratifications', which were taxed at 40, 20 and 10 rupees a year respectively.[26] According to Walter Lawrence, a British official in the Indian Civil Service (ICS) writing in the 1890s, 'everything except air and water was under taxation'. This policy not only killed initiative and enterprise, it also led to social unrest in Srinagar, the capital of Kashmir.[27]

The hopelessness of the franchise system was exposed during the great famines which crippled India in 1877–9. In Srinagar, a population of 127,000 was reduced to 60,000. 'Oil cake, rice, chaff, the bark of the elm and yew, and even grass and roots were eagerly devoured by the starving people.'[28] The famines ravaged the whole of India, particularly affecting the southern part of the subcontinent. In London the Lord Mayor of London received large donations from businessmen and City financiers anxious to help alleviate the crisis. *The Times* recorded in August that N. M. Rothschild and Barings gave £1,000 each. Truman, Hanbury, Buxton, the brewers, gave £210, while P&O, the shipping company, gave £105. This shows the relative standing of these companies at the time. By October the Lord Mayor's fund stood at £415,000, roughly £41.5 million at today's values.

In Kashmir, however, it was felt that the Maharaja hadn't done enough. Ranbir Singh was under scrutiny, and his death in 1885 gave Britain its opportunity to influence events in Kashmir more directly. The British government immediately told the new Maharaja that the Officer on Special Duty would be replaced by a full-fledged resident.[29] The Resident would be able to keep a watchful eye on the Maharaja, particularly in connection with intrigues with the Russians. It was even suspected that the new Maharaja, Pratap Singh, had been engaged in treasonable correspondence with representatives of the Russian Tsar.[30]

The relationship with the Indian princes is complicated and even now historians are often confused about the degree to which Britain allowed them to be independent. To understand the status of the princes, we can start by looking at certain aspects of British society of the time. British local government had always depended on the resident aristocracy and gentry. In India, the British officials transplanted the status, the petty snobberies and the fine gradations of rank and privilege which prevailed in Britain itself. The class system was replicated in India. The Raj, it seemed, was happiest when dealing with a 'feudal order'. One-third of India was ruled 'indirectly through the princes'.[31] No one has ever been sure of exactly how many princes there were. There were certainly over 500, perhaps nearer 600, and they varied greatly in status and wealth. There were three categories of Indian princely state: at the top there were about

140 large states; then came a little more than 100 or so middling states, followed by about 300 minor states, which were really just landed estates.

The obsession with the princes, their genealogy and the precedence due to each culminated in the publication of a book, entitled *The Golden Book of India*, in 1893. The title was modelled on *The Golden Book of Venice* (the *Libro d'Oro*), which contained the official list of the Venetian nobility, whose members alone could vote and hold office; the *Libro d'Oro* had essentially been closed since 1297. The Indian version, which described itself as a 'Genealogical and Biographical Dictionary', listed in exhaustive detail more than 190 Indian titles of honour, some of which were inherited and others merely honorific. Some of the titles read like something out of *One Thousand and One Nights*: the 'Shams ud-daula' means the 'sun of the state' in Arabic; 'Gambir Rao' means 'sagacious chief'. The standard title was 'raja' for a Hindu prince or 'nawab' for a Muslim. 'Maha' means 'great' in Hindi, so 'maharaja' simply means 'great raja'.[32] There were seven grades of title, like 'the steps of the British Peerage', starting with 'rao' at the bottom, which means 'chief', and ending up with 'maharaja' and 'maharaja bahadur' at the top. This last title was rather formal ('bahadur' means 'brave' in Persian), and distinguished men of this rank were often simply referred to as 'maharaja' for short. The maharajas were at the apex of an elaborate social hierarchy unrelated to democracy or liberalism, but shamelessly aristocratic and deferential. The princes, the top people, seemed to the British to epitomize martial virtues; they were a warrior elite, who rode and hunted. They were Indian society's 'natural leaders'.[33]

In this hierarchy, Kashmir was near the top. Kashmir, or more properly 'Jammu and Kashmir', and Hyderabad were the largest princely states of British India. Kashmir was comparable in size to Great Britain, although it was much more sparsely populated. There was a mystique and a glamour surrounding the princes which greatly added to their mere snob-value. There was also an obsession with protocol, which determined the number of guns they received in salute. At the head of the system was, of course, Queen Victoria, the Queen-Empress herself, who had a salute that rose to 101 guns. Her viceroy would receive a thirty-one-gun salute while the rulers of the five biggest states, Hyderabad, Kashmir, Mysore, Gwalior and

Baroda, each had twenty-one guns; the most minor princes could enjoy only a nine-gun salute.[34] Years later, General Wavell, as viceroy between 1943 and 1947, even invented a mnemonic to remind himself of the order of precedence of the five biggest princely states: 'Hot Kippers Make Good Breakfast.'[35]

The relationship between the 'paramount power', that is Great Britain, and the Indian princes changed over the years. Like many things in the empire, it was essentially a relationship which depended on individuals and circumstances. There were no hard and fast rules. The example of Pratap Singh, who succeeded his father Ranbir in 1885, shows just how flexible the relationship was. On his accession, the man appointed resident in his kingdom was Oliver St John. The installation of a resident where there hadn't been one before was a bad sign if you were an Indian prince, implying a lack of trust between the British and the native ruler. Kashmir had enjoyed a great deal of autonomy. The resident was often a schoolmas-terly figure, a 'paternalistic guide' to an errant ruler.[36]

Pratap Singh was now thirty-five years old. He had never really got on very well with his father, and was suspicious of his younger brother, Amar Singh, who, it was well known, their father would have liked to succeed as maharaja. In March 1888, just two and a half years after Pratap had taken over his kingdom, Oliver St John decided to pay him a visit. The British Resident was not impressed. 'I do not believe he is loyal,' St John observed. Although very polite, the Maharaja, in St John's eyes, was incompetent. The government of India should be 'under no illusion as regards Maharaja Pratap Singh. From first to last I have failed to discover in him any sustained capacity for governing his country, or any genuine desire to ameliorate its condition.' This was a standard complaint that residents made. After all, it was only natural for them to want to increase their power.[37] Yet in this case, the Resident may have had a good case.

Pratap Singh was a strange man. The British might complain of his 'notorious weakness of character and purpose', but his own subjects found his behaviour odd. To modern eyes, he may well have been a 'story-book Indian Prince, vacillating and oppressive, bedecked in silk pyjamas, pearls and a diamond-encrusted turban';[38] to his contemporaries and to the British he was simply a nuisance, an eccentric who was not cut out for the role he sought to play. An opium addict, he was a devoutly orthodox Hindu who in obedience to caste restrictions concerning the crossing of the deep seas would never leave India. He took the Hindu faith so seriously that he kept a dozen cows tethered in the garden outside his bedroom window so he would be sure to see the holy creatures when he woke each morning.[39]

The eccentricity wouldn't have been such a problem if the British had actually trusted him. Throughout his forty-year reign, he was treated in a variety of ways; now threats were made against him, now a more conciliatory approach was tried, but he was always treated as a schoolboy. Lord Curzon, who was viceroy from 1898 to 1905, met Pratap in Peshawar at the end of April 1902. A small dispute had arisen about the coronation of King Edward VII which had been expected to take place that June, but instead was postponed until August. The Maharaja's younger brother Raja Amar had been invited, but the Maharaja had refused permission for his brother to go. The Maharaja had requested the interview because he wished to make his case. He knew that the Viceroy had, in the diplomatic language of the period, expressed 'surprise that he had not allowed Raja Amar Singh to accept the invitation to the Coronation in England'. This was, in Curzon's view, 'almost in the light of a command'.

At this teatime interview (the meeting had started at 4 p.m. sharp), Curzon was curious about the role of the Resident. He wanted to know why a resident had been imposed, and why the Maharaja had lost some of his independence. The Maharaja pleaded that he should be allowed more freedom on the grounds that he was now older and wiser than he had been when the Resident had been appointed in the 1880s. Curzon made no promises about restoring the powers of the Maharaja. In the end, Amar didn't get to visit London. The Maharaja received a sound rebuke from the Viceroy, who would not 'hesitate for a moment to take away any powers conceded' to him if 'anything went wrong'. The Maharaja reacted like a weeping schoolboy. He offered to resign his throne 'in favour of any member of the family whom the Government might select, if he failed to administer to the satisfaction' of the British Raj. Even more humiliatingly, he offered, without being asked, to put his commitment to withdraw 'into writing'.[40]

This little teatime interview demonstrates something of the informal power Britain had over the princely states. There was no real constitution or legal framework. Powers were given and then taken away on a case-by-case basis, as the viceroy or resident saw fit. The residents sometimes liked the princes and got on with them. By the time Francis Younghusband became the Kashmir resident in 1906, Pratap Singh had the measure of his British masters. He would do as his grandfather had done so successfully: he would play the fawning sycophant and would protest everlasting loyalty to the British Crown, while resolutely trying to preserve what little independence he enjoyed.

Younghusband himself has been described as the 'last great imperial adventurer', though many could probably lay claim to that title.[41] He was one of those oddballs who crop up again and again in imperial history. The son of a military family, educated at Clifton College and Sandhurst, he had a passion for travel and adventure. In 1886–7, while still only twenty-four, he had crossed the Gobi Desert and became the first European to go through the Mustagh Pass, where K2, the world's second-highest mountain, is situated. For this achievement, he was elected to the Royal Geographical Society, as its youngest ever member. In his energetic style, Younghusband led the expedition in 1904 to Tibet, which was effectively an invasion of that country. His later career espoused all kinds of causes from 'free love' to a 'religion of atheism', to which he turned after rejecting, in middle age, the muscular Christianity he had so lustily espoused at Clifton College.

Younghusband's time as resident in Kashmir was the most stable period of his adult life. In Kashmir, he did not, as he did in later years, fantasize about his lover giving birth to a 'God-child' who would combine the intense spirituality of its parents and would manifest 'God more completely even than Jesus did'.[42] In Kashmir he lived with his wife and daughter, leading the life of a respectable British civil servant in India, with the endless rounds of garden parties and tea parties. He even espoused liberal views about Britain's imperial mission. In a moment of self-righteousness, he wrote 'Guiding Principles for Conduct as Resident in Kashmir' when he took the job in 1906. It is not clear for whom this little tract was intended; it may have been purely for his own private consumption and it was certainly never published. In this solemn document, he declared his wish 'to allow native talent the means of development'. He 'desired', in his own words, 'to give them [the natives and his own staff] fullest scope for their energies and the gratification of their inclinations'. He wanted to be a paternalistic headmaster; he did not want to 'initiate new measures' or 'assume an autocratic role'. He would be merely a 'guide'; he would 'supervise' the Kashmiris and the young civil servants in his office.

To do all this effectively, Younghusband felt he needed to be 'thoroughly in touch with the Maharaja' as well as being 'very intimately informed of all that goes on'. He wanted debate; he wanted to hear 'matters discussed and thrashed out'. He needed to make himself 'accessible', to get out of the office and 'be out among the people'. That was his choice. Other residents had played things differently; they had been shy or aloof or bookish types who didn't like the endless socializing. The point was that, as in so much to do with the British Empire, there was no right way or wrong way. The empire, as can be seen by the career of the likes of Francis Younghusband, was remarkably tolerant of eccentric characters and misfits who could find no place for themselves in civilian life in Britain. That, in many ways, was the point of the whole thing. Eccentrics were attracted to serve in it, because it allowed great freedom.

Younghusband clearly enjoyed himself in Kashmir. He was a proud imperialist and got on with the ruler. He was briefly made guardian of the Maharaja's nephew, Hari Singh, when the boy's father died in 1909. He gave grand speeches at the state banquets, which he wrote out carefully in his neatest handwriting. At the state banquet given on 26 June 1908, Younghusband issued the imperialist's warning throughout the ages: 'work with us, and all will be well. Oppose us and we will crush you.' The British, in his view, were invincible; sensible native princes and local lords would make peace and work with Britain. He praised Sir Pratap Singh's grandfather, the wily Gulab: 'When others were attacking the British Government and were suffering the consequences which all who beat their heads against stone walls have to expect, Raja Gulab Singh was making terms with them and reaping a reward for his sagacity and foresight.' He contrasted Gulab's wisdom with the folly of others, notably the family of Gulab's erstwhile master, Ranjit Singh, the Maharaja of the Sikh kingdom. 'For crossing the

British the family of the powerful Ranjit Singh . . . disappeared from among the great ruling families of India.'[43]

The Maharaja of Kashmir, according to Younghusband, was the 'possessor of the most beautiful country in the world'. During the Mutiny in 1857, which marked the end of East India Company rule and led to more direct control from Whitehall, with the appointment of a secretary of state for India, the Maharaja had come down 'unhesitatingly . . . on the side of the British'. The British government and people were the best guardians of Kashmir's future. Those Indians and Kashmiris who opposed British rule had 'no practical experience' of governing men 'on the grand scale'; they could not 'be expected to appreciate the exceptional qualities which are essential for men who have to keep three hundred million human beings at peace'. The British had the 'grit and nerve and fibre', 'the resolution, energy and strength' to govern India. He didn't stop there. He praised the British for their mental qualities. They had the 'sagacity, foresight and resource, which are required in those who have to keep India free from internal chaos'.

The confidence which Younghusband displayed was extraordinary. In his mind the empire had absolutely nothing to do with politics. It was really an arena for character, in which the unique qualities of the British could be displayed and brought to bear to the advantage of the subject Indians. Younghusband was a visionary in so many ways. He saw Kashmir's role as being the 'model Native State of India'. As early as 1908, he spotted the potential of Kashmir in developing new forms of energy: the kingdom was a 'great Power reservoir of Northern India', where its 'vast stores of water power' were 'to be converted with electric power' and sold 'all over the Punjab'.[44] At the end of 1909, Younghusband's last year as resident, the Maharaja gave a farewell dinner for Sir Francis and his wife. In response to Younghusband's own farewell speech, he outdid the Resident's fulsome praise of empire of the previous year, describing himself as Edward VII's 'faithful vassal' lifting his hands 'to the Providence that His Majesty's [Edward VII's] paternal protection may continue over us forever'. The dinner had been preceded by an elaborate garden party. To the strains of Wagner and Viennese favourites Schubert and Lehár, played by the Maharaja's orchestra, Younghusband and his wife said their fond farewells.[45]

The goodwill and the entertainment masked the unease that the Maharaja felt. He was always trying to obtain more power and autonomy. Even after the First World War, his status was still under discussion. A secret internal memorandum from 1919 showed that the British still felt that the 'habit of intrigue' was ingrained in 'His Highness' character' and that it would 'be fatal to give him a free hand'.[46] The Germans had even approached him in 1915 inviting him to resist British rule.[47] The Maharaja, despite his protestations of friendship, was not trusted. The Resident had to be in charge, 'particularly in the matter of financial control'. That authority would be exercised in 'a manner least likely to hurt the Maharaja's feelings'. The Resident would be 'in the background as much as possible'. As a sop to the Maharaja, in 1919 his allowance from the British government was increased from £100,000 to £120,000 a year.[48]

The relationship between the British and the Maharaja of Kashmir was therefore defined by trust, and the whole history of Britain's involvement with the kingdom was marked by improvisation and personal interactions. It was a world of splendidly dressed native rulers, of elaborate etiquette, of garden parties and banquets, of makeshift compromises. The Maharaja's character and habits played a considerable role in the Kashmiri political scene for a hundred years after the initial sale of the region in 1846. That land sale itself had profound effects on Kashmir's future. In 1994, nearly 150 years after this event, the President of Srinagar's Bar Association complained that everyone in Kashmir had been 'purchased by the Dogra [the ruling dynasty] ruler for 3 rupees'.[49] The sale was an improvised solution to a particular problem. It was opposed even at the time; it wasn't a plan that was conceived in the corridors of Whitehall or in the Cabinet Room at 10 Downing Street. Kashmir, as a political problem, was the product of short-sighted individuals, often described as 'men on the spot', who were responsible to no one.

6

The World of Sir Hari Singh

Sir Pratap Singh died in 1925 at the age of seventy-five. Hari Singh, his nephew and successor, was the man who would ultimately be responsible for the accession of Kashmir to India in 1947. His career shows the extent to which individuals shaped events in the British Empire. If Sir Hari Singh had decided to join Pakistan, the history of Kashmir might have been just as violent, but it certainly would have been different. Pakistan's main complaint was that a Hindu ruler, without any democratic mandate, decided to attach his kingdom, which was 80 per cent Muslim, to India, a predominantly Hindu state. It was Hari Singh, a bullying, vain and pompous man, who determined Kashmir's future; Whitehall, Lord Mountbatten, the last Viceroy, and the dying apparatus of the Raj ultimately had little say in the matter.

Hari Singh was born in 1895, the son of Amar Singh, Sir Pratap Singh's younger brother. The two brothers did not get on very well. Amar Singh had died in 1909 of what Sir Francis Younghusband described as a 'syphilitic affliction of the brain'. As a boy, Hari Singh played with Eileen Younghusband, Sir Francis's only daughter, who remembered the future Maharaja as a 'most tiresome boy' who persecuted her fox-terrier. As we have seen, Younghusband was initially appointed Hari Singh's guardian, Amar Singh having declared that his wife was an 'illiterate fool' who could not be entrusted with the boy's care.[1] In 1908, Hari Singh entered Mayo College, which had been founded in 1875 in honour of Lord Mayo, the former Viceroy, who had been assassinated on a visit to the Andaman Islands by an insane convict in 1872. Mayo College was a self-consciously elitist institution, conceived from the outset as the 'Eton of India', where maharajas and nawabs would learn the manners of English gentlemen without the expense of travelling thousands of miles to England and spending five years in the Spartan world of the late Victorian public school.

In December 1879, Lord Lytton, the Viceroy, gave the main address at the annual prize-giving day. He invoked the spirit of the English 'system of education' which aimed at 'training, developing and strengthening not only the mind but also the body'. He ended his rousing homage to the 'social and moral ascendancy' of the aristocracy by pointing to a 'very sensible' report which had observed that what was needed for the 'education of India's young rulers and nobles was an Indian Eton'. 'Ajmer [where the school was located] is India's Eton,' he said. 'You', the Viceroy declared, pointing to the rather bewildered boys, are 'India's Eton boys.'[2] Lytton, the son of the writer Edward Bulwer-Lytton, at least practised what he preached. He had been educated at Harrow School, but he sent both his sons to Eton.

The education Hari Singh received at Mayo College would not necessarily have made him more understanding of the needs of his subjects. Snobbish and protocol-obsessed as the late Victorian age was, Hari Singh's own innate pomposity aggravated any such traits he would have acquired at Mayo College. He was status-conscious and proud, but also shy, vindictive and quick to take offence at anything he perceived to insult or belittle him. After leaving Mayo College aged eighteen in 1913, he was bored and quickly fell out with his uncle, who loathed him. Indeed Sir Pratap had been reluctant to accept him as his heir. During the First World War, Hari Singh wanted to travel and see the world, but was nervous that, while he was away, his uncle would disinherit him, so he stayed in Kashmir to protect his position. In 1917, the young Prince nonetheless expressed a desire to travel to 'England via Japan and America', after which he planned to visit the front in France 'if it could be arranged'. British officials realized that the matter needed to be sensitively handled, because if the Prince 'went to the Front on someone's staff it would be all right and not give rise to comment', but if he went on a pleasure trip this would be 'very unpopular with the Kashmir army', who were fighting on the front line in the bloody fields of France and Flanders.[3] Hari Singh's mother and aunts were afraid that 'something might happen to him' on the trip, so in the end he had to stay in Kashmir, which left the British authorities wondering what to do with him. The problem was that Hari Singh was, like many rich young men, idle and pleasure-seeking. One report remarked that 'military work, if he really would go into it thoroughly . . . would give him almost sufficient employment', but 'he does not go into any of the details'. He simply asked a 'few questions' and then affixed his signature to whatever documents needed signing.[4]

Hari Singh, now aged twenty-two, was regarded by British officials – despite his tendencies to idleness – as a 'man of very strong character, considerable ambitions and good intentions'. His uncle, at sixty-seven, was getting more eccentric, and insisted on keeping his nephew in a state of semi-permanent house arrest. A British report of the time described how the Prince had 'neither friends nor assistants of his own standing' but was kept in 'a constant state of repression and aimlessness'. In Srinagar, the state capital, there was a permanent 'atmosphere of intrigue'.[5] The old Maharaja was surrounded by personal favourites and loved plotting and scheming. In a letter to his uncle, at the end of 1921, Hari Singh referred to 'certain persons' who occupied the 'position of Your Highness' confidential and trusted advisors' undermining his own position in the state. That position was becoming 'absolutely impossible and matters were getting from bad to worse'. In a characteristic fit of self-pity, the young man complained of the 'misery' of his predicament which was 'having the most telling effect to the detriment of my health and peace of mind'.[6] His aimlessness induced resentment and, on occasion, clouded Hari Singh's judgement. After the First World War had come to an end, he finally managed to realize his desire of visiting Europe. It was there that his conduct aroused attention in the world's media, when he was involved in one of the most celebrated scandals of the time.

On 4 November 1919 a Victory Ball was held at the Royal Albert Hall in London. This event had been inaugurated the previous November and had started controversially, when Billie Carleton, a twenty-two-year-old dancer and singer, was found dead in her bed of a cocaine overdose, after attending the first Victory Ball. The 1919 event had some startling, though perhaps less fatal, consequences. Hari Singh had taken a box at the Albert Hall. Two attractive women, Mrs Robinson and Mrs Bevan, were in the box next to the Prince. He engaged them in conversation and showed an interest in Mrs Robinson. The next month she followed Hari Singh to Paris, where he was staying at the St James and Albany Hotel, an elegant seventeenth-century building opposite the Tuileries Gardens. One morning Mrs Robinson and the Raja were conversing in his room in the hotel when a man burst in claiming to be Mrs Robinson's husband. The Robinsons appeared to argue, and Mr Robinson suggested that he would divorce his wife, citing the Raja, Hari Singh, as co-respondent in the divorce case. Hari Singh's aide-de-camp, Captain C. W. Arthur, advised his master that the outlook was bleak, because being cited as a co-respondent would bar Hari from succeeding to his uncle's throne. Arthur also suggested that the Prince should buy off the furious husband. Terrified, Hari Singh signed two cheques for £150,000 made out to Robinson and sent Arthur that very day to dissuade Robinson from going to court.

Eventually the truth came out: there was no Mr Robinson, as the episode had been an elaborate blackmail plot conceived by Captain Arthur. In order to spare his embarrassment, Hari Singh had been referred to as 'Mr A' when the blackmail case came to court in 1924, yet this veil of anonymity was ignored by the foreign press, particularly by French and American newspapers, which were not as deferential as British publications. The Raja was humiliated; his own counsel, Sir John Simon, a pompous politician who was a Fellow of All Souls College, a former home secretary and reputedly the highest-paid barrister at the London Bar, described his client as a 'poor, green, shivering, abject wretch'. When he returned home after the case, the Maharaja, Hari's uncle, banished him to a remote jungle estate for six months, where the young man had to perform ritual acts of penance.[7]

The effects of this humiliation on the ebullient Prince were significant, and he became more secretive and suspicious, as well as more self-indulgent and introverted. By the time he finally became maharaja in 1925, he was thirty and had become fat through gluttony, while he pursued his passion for hunting accompanied by a dwindling circle of friends. His treatment of the rajas, who were local dignitaries, and minor officials round his court, was arrogant and often vindictive. He even crossed the British Resident a couple of times at the beginning of his reign.

An example of Hari Singh's insensitivity was his treatment of a Colonel Ward, who had been granted a post as honorary adviser to the old Maharaja in relation to agriculture and industries. Ward had created a retirement career for himself, ostensibly trying to improve Kashmir breeds of cattle and sheep. He enjoyed an estate, Pandrethan, just outside Srinagar, which had been supported by money from Sir Pratap Singh. Hari Singh, wishing to reduce expenditure, summarily evicted Colonel Ward from the estate. The Colonel, however, was eighty-four years old and the Maharaja's hounding of the old man was a public relations disaster. From London, in January 1928, the Earl of Birkenhead, the former F. E. Smith, a swashbuckling lawyer and self-made Conservative grandee, wrote on the matter to the Viceroy, expressing the widely held view that Hari Singh was 'young and bumptious and difficult'. He added that he did 'not like the idea of throwing a British subject to the dogs'.[8] Colonel Ward had been a friend of the Maharaja's uncle and it was this friendship which had incurred Hari Singh's resentment. The British Resident in Kashmir, E. B. Howell, observed that 'His Highness delights in acts of generosity to those whom the late Maharaja depressed and the contrary to those whom he exalted'.[9]

The incident showed the Maharaja's tendency to bully and intimidate. The new Secretary of State at the India Office, Viscount Peel, remarked to the Viceroy, the liberal-minded Conservative Lord Irwin, who in the 1930s became an architect of appeasement as Lord Halifax, that the Maharaja had 'a puzzling blend of good and bad qualities'. There was 'an element of the bully in him', although like all bullies he could be charming among people who were as strong and powerful as he. The Maharaja behaved 'correctly enough when he is under your eye or among his fellow Princes', but when he had only the Resident to deal with 'he tends to assert himself in a domineering way'. The Secretary of State thought the Maharaja suffered from an 'inferiority complex'.[10] In late November 1928, Hari Singh was in London having lunch with Viscount Peel, who was notable as a tall, combative, athletic type with the 'jaw of a fighter'. Now in his early sixties, Peel was 'highminded, well meaning, zealous and able'.[11] He was also tough, arrogant and very wealthy, having married the only daughter and sole heiress of the Ashton linoleum empire. Peel directly confronted Hari Singh about his treatment of Colonel Ward, which he described as 'harsh'. Hari Singh claimed 'he had never heard of the matter'. Peel acidly observed that the Maharaja was either being 'rather disingenuous . . . or else his memory is a pretty short one'. The lunch, in Peel's view, did not 'augur very well for old Colonel Ward'.[12] By April the next year, Hari Singh had sent a letter to Peel in which he backtracked slightly. He claimed that he had been unable to 'acquaint' the Secretary of State with the facts because he had not had his 'papers . . . in England'. Ward had left the house, the Maharaja said, of his 'own accord' when it was decided to abolish the farm. The Maharaja, insensitive to the feelings of others, was very quick to take offence at Ward's campaign against him and his government. The Maharaja even used Ward's advanced age as an argument in favour of his having dismissed him: 'I cannot see on what grounds Colonel Ward deserves any special treatment . . . [he] is about 80 years of age'; this meant that he couldn't have any 'possible grievance against being retired from service'.[13]

The Maharaja was becoming a nuisance, but there was little the British government could do about it. The Resident complained of Hari Singh's delusions of grandeur, his taste for independence, his growing 'tendency towards extravagance', especially the pomp and ceremony he indulged in at court.[14] Hari Singh's pettiness knew no bounds. At a formal dinner held on the night of 15 May 1931 at the Shalimar Bagh in Srinagar in honour of the Maharaja, he was greeted on arrival by a group of notables at the entrance to the garden. The Raja of Poonch, a minor chief in the Maharaja's kingdom, remained in the pavilion and did not form part of the welcoming party. Hari Singh was infuriated by this and ordered that the Raja leave the garden 'at once'; the unfortunate Raja was now to be banned from the Palace and all functions 'until further orders'. The typewritten programme of ceremonials had laid down that, 'on alighting from his motor at the door of the garden, His Highness would be met by the Raja of Poonch'. Technically, Hari Singh was right, but his overreaction was characteristic. The next day the Raja wrote a grovelling letter of apology, but the Maharaja remained implacable. British officials were talking of the possibility of the Raja's 'internment'. On 6 June, nearly four weeks after the dinner, the Maharaja passed an order that the Raja's salute of thirteen guns should be reduced to nine. British officials looked on in bewilderment. Of course they would have 'nothing to do with' the quarrel, which continued throughout 1931. In late November the Raja was complaining to the Resident of the 'consistent series of acts' of 'aggression' on the part of Hari Singh.[15]

The petty feuds and the endless disputes about precedence and protocol reveal the highly fraught, almost surreal conditions in which some of the Indian princes operated. This eccentric, even crazy atmosphere was a feature of the British Empire in India which has often been overlooked. The continual references to precedence and formality would astonish a world that has grown tired of such things. There was a precedent or tradition to regulate absolutely everything. In 1940, an issue at stake was whether 'the Ruling Princes calling on His Excellency the Viceroy should write their names in the Viceroy's Visitor's Book or leave their cards only'. This question was referred to the Committee on Ceremonies, which had reported on just such matters in 1932, when it was decided that 'writing names in the Viceroy's Book is a universally accepted form of courtesy and no exception or modification seems desirable'. This dispute had been stirred by Hari Singh, who had simply left his card while visiting the Viceroy in Bombay and had complained of not having been invited to the garden party which was taking place during the visit.[16]

In 1939 there had been a similar controversy about the issue of gifts being presented to the King and Queen in London by the various Indian princes. Again there was a clear protocol which had been established as early as 1861, but was still being referred to in 1939. Back in early 1860s, Queen Victoria had declared her appreciation of 'every mark of the loyalty and affection of the Princes and Chiefs of India', but it was not her desire 'that they should give expression to these feelings by the presentation of costly gifts'. The Queen would be 'most gratified by the receipt of a simple letter of friendship'. Of course, there had been certain exceptions in the eighty or so years which had intervened. In 1925 and again in 1937, the

Maharaja of Rewa had been allowed to send gifts of albino tiger skins, 'mainly because of their rarity'. Messages from the Indian 'chiefs and princes' to the King Emperor in London were also regulated, according to the status of the prince: 'messages of a purely personal and private nature can be addressed to the Palace direct by Rulers having salutes of 11 guns and over'. Since the lowest-ranked prince was entitled to nine guns and the highest to twenty-one, most of the chiefs and princes could, if they wanted, send Christmas cards, addressed to King George and Queen Elizabeth, directly to Buckingham Palace.[17]

It was inevitable that this kind of formal environment would produce proud and difficult maharajas, who stood on ceremony and were punctilious about their dignity and honours. It was less inevitable that these people ultimately had the power to decide the destiny of millions. It is a tragedy that the fate of Kashmir was in the hands of Hari Singh at such a crucial time as the partition of India and Pakistan. His interests were largely sporting. He was bored by politics and had no desire to engage constructively in affairs of state. Any account of his pursuits is rapidly reduced to never-ending stories from the field of sports and gaming: shooting, fishing, hunting, polo, horse racing and, when he took time off in Cannes or Monte Carlo, a little gambling. His own son, Karan Singh, recalled that his father's shooting parties were 'meticulously planned, each guest provided with cartridges and a packed lunch complete with wine'.

Duck shoots would begin early in the morning, at which time the Maharaja's guests would 'all drive out in a great procession, assemble on the banks of the lake' and then row to the location of the shoot, where the 'whole day would be spent massacring duck of various species'. The Maharaja himself was a superb shot. Black bears, wild boar and even the panthers which roamed the lush jungles of the Maharaja's domain were all shot indiscriminately. His generosity as a host was not matched by even the pretence of sportsmanship. 'Any small setback in shooting or fishing, polo or racing, would throw him into a dark mood which lasted for days,' remembered his son. When this happened, it was best to stay out of the way. His Highness's peevishness would lead inevitably 'to what came to be known as "muquaddama", a long inquiry into the alleged inefficiency or misbehaviour of some young member of the staff'.[18] The Maharaja was known as the 'King of the Indian Turf', an 'uncanny judge of horse flesh' and an 'outstanding horse-breeder'.[19] His scarlet and gold colours were familiar to every 'Bombay race goer', and he was always much happier racing than governing his state.[20] His own riding days were curtailed by his increasing obesity in middle age, but he had excelled at polo, a sport in which he was so anxious for his son to develop equal proficiency that he forced the boy to ride every day from the age of three. This regime didn't work. Today, Karan Singh is a noted writer and academic whose skills at polo are limited.

In the midst of all this outdoor activity, the country over which the Maharaja presided was one of the most economically deprived areas of British India. Levels of literacy, especially among the Muslim population, were very low. Although ancient Kashmir had been renowned as a seat of Sanskrit learning, the capital city, Srinagar, which had more than 60,000 inhabitants, registered only 140 women as literate in the 1901 census. The entire literate population of the city was only 2 per cent. This figure had risen to 25 per cent in 1941.[21] The Maharaja's fabulous lifestyle was funded by heavy taxation of the Kashmiri people, who were described by the Indian civil servant Sir Albion Banerjee as 'dumb, driven cattle'.[22]

Generally, the peasants and lower classes of Kashmir were Muslim and their superiors Hindu. There was a simple reason for this. Under the Mughals of Kashmir who ruled for four centuries till 1752, the vast majority of the population had converted to Islam, and these Muslim converts had been low-caste Hindus who had been consigned to that status by their ancestral religion. Understandably, the Hindus who had refused to convert were, in most cases, the high-class Hindus, the Brahmins, who enjoyed the most prestige in the old religion and would have had nothing to gain from abandoning Hinduism for Islam.

In general, the average British imperial civil servant did have a sense of cultural superiority, but often stopped short of commenting overtly on the racial characteristics of the people over whom he presided. There seems to have been an exception in the case of Kashmir. Memoirs continually refer to the 'excellent physique' of the Kashmiri men and the 'exceptional beauty' of their 'womenfolk'. A Kashmiri would 'handle a load on his back for many hours of the day such as would defeat any of his brothers'.[23] Although the Kashmiris were strong, the British writers were convinced that they lacked physical courage. 'A Kashmiri soldier is almost a contradiction in terms. There is no such thing,' asserted Francis Younghusband, in his otherwise admirable account of Kashmir. Another observer, the missionary Dr Ernest F. Neve, believed that the Kashmiris could 'bear pain much better than Europeans, but owing to want of self-control they make more fuss'. He agreed with Younghusband in praising the physique, while deprecating the courage and temper, of the Kashmiri man: 'in spite of great physical strength and powers of endurance, the Kashmiri is highly strung and neurotic and he will often weep on slight provocation'.[24] Younghusband also commented on two seemingly well-known facts: 'Kashmir is very generally renowned for the beauty of its women and the deftness and taste of its shawl-weavers.'[25]

The charms of Kashmir's women were appreciated not only by British men. Dorothy Hargreaves Burton, the wife of Geoffrey Burton, an ICS man, observed in 1914 that the women in Kashmir were 'decidedly pretty and although Mohammedan do not lead a restricted life'. She was, however, unimpressed by the general character of the Kashmiris and thought that their beauty, both male and female, was merely a veneer: 'Kashmiris are a very good looking race but their beauty . . . is only skin deep.' For her, the Kashmiris always appeared anxious to please the sahib (master), but the majority were 'quite unable to keep promises'. Mrs Burton, in her tour of Kashmir in the summer of 1914, was astute enough to identify the kingdom's fundamental problem: 'It is curious that a Mohammedan people should be ruled over by a Hindu prince.' Yet overall she was deeply moved by the lush vegetation and physical splendour of the Kashmiri landscape; it was 'an emerald set in pearls'.[26]

The anomaly of a Hindu ruler set over a predominantly Muslim population created the inevitable tensions we have come to associate with minority rule. The Hindus dominated the state. The British, who had sold Kashmir to the Dogra dynasty, were mere spectators in the unfolding drama, which cast Hindu against Muslim. Jack Morton, a district policeman who was later stationed in Lahore, recalled that the majority of

Kashmiris were 'lowly Muslim peasants' while the Kashmiri Brahmins 'were the crème de la crème in the Hindu caste system, and ruthlessly maintained their dominance in government and the economy'.[27] The Kashmiri Brahmins, or Pandits as they were known, dominated the administration of the state, and it was only Hindus who were allowed to possess firearms in the Vale of Kashmir itself; Muslims were rigorously excluded from service in the state's armed forces.[28] Visitors acknowledged the refinement and sophistication of the Brahmins and felt that Hindu dominance was part of the natural order. The Christian missionary Dr Neve accepted that the Brahmins' 'intellectual superiority over the rest of the population must be admitted. They are quick of apprehension and have good memories,' though one of their 'besetting faults' was arrogance. By contrast, 'the Mohammedans' were 'grossly illiterate'. The Pandits, as well as being civil servants, could be merchants and shopkeepers but were not allowed to take up handicrafts such as 'carpentry, masonry, shoe-making and pottery', since practising these professions would defile their status.[29]

Kashmir's Muslim population began to organize itself politically, the Hindu Maharaja being increasingly regarded as a tyrant. As early as 1924, there had been labour unrest at the state silk factory in Srinagar, where 5,000 people worked, of whom an overwhelming majority were Muslim. When the Viceroy, Lord Reading, visited Srinagar in October 1924 he was presented with a memorandum signed by many prominent members of the Kashmiri Muslim community calling for an increase in the number of Muslims employed in the state service, for improvements in Muslim education and for land reform.[30] The Hindu basis of the state was reflected in its laws. Gulab Singh, the founder of the Hindu state of Jammu and Kashmir, had been a devout Hindu who, as his biographer observed, reserved 'very brutal punishments' for those accused of 'cow killing', who would have their noses and ears cut off.[31]

Cow killing even in the 1930s and 1940s was illegal in Kashmir. People who committed this act of sacrilege against the Hindu religion could face a seven-year prison sentence. In addition to the prohibition against killing cows, there was a 'special tax on the slaughter of goats and sheep'. Muslims sacrificed these animals once a year as part of a religious ritual.[32] By 1931, the situation was particularly tense. The Maharaja had earlier in the year celebrated the birth of his son Karan, who turned out to be his only child. The succession in Kashmir had been problematic, as the Maharaja had already married three times, without producing an heir. In each case, the wives had died mysteriously, his first wife with her child still in the womb. The Maharaja himself was an only child. The fourth Maharani, the beautiful Tara Devi, a commoner from Kangra, produced a healthy baby boy, the Yuvraj or heir apparent, whose birth triggered a 'delirious wave of enthusiasm' among the Hindu community. The slaughter of animals, including fishing and shooting, was prohibited for three days. There were feasts and free cinema shows; sweets were given to children; there was a procession in Jammu (the predominantly Hindu southern region of the state of Jammu and Kashmir), while Srinagar also witnessed a huge procession.[33] This episode marked the high point of Dogra rule in Kashmir, but it was the events of the summer of that year, 1931, which, in their intensity and suddenness, put the spotlight on the 'communal' issue, the historic divisions between the Hindu and Muslim communities, which would dominate Kashmir for decades.

No one really knows how the disturbance started. It was reported in May that a mosque in Jammu Province had been demolished by Hindus, with the full approval of the Maharaja's government. Rumours swirled of other outrages. At another place in Jammu, it was alleged, Muslims had been prevented from saying their prayers. It was even whispered that pages of the Holy Koran had been found discarded in a public latrine.[34] There was outrage in Srinagar when news of this broke. On 25 June, Abdul Qadeer, a firebrand who had come from the North West Frontier Province, which is now in Pakistan, gave a fiery speech, advocating violence against the Maharaja's rule; he pointed to the Maharaja's palace in Srinagar, which was within view of the crowd, and urged the demonstrators to 'destroy its every brick'. He was arrested, but, as is often the case in such instances, his trial became a showpiece, drawing attention to the defendant's cause. On 6 July, a great assembly of Muslims gathered outside the law court, forcing suspension of the trial. The court proceedings were then moved to the Srinagar Central Jail. The next week, on the 13th, Abdul Qadeer's trial reopened. There was again a huge crowd, and the police were present in strength; stones were thrown and the police responded with gunfire. By the end of the demonstration, twenty-two demonstrators had been killed. This day is known as Martyrs Day and is still celebrated in Pakistan and Kashmir. To the so-called Kashmiri freedom fighters the day marks the beginning of their struggle against Dogra and then Indian rule. In the immediate aftermath of the trial, the Muslim mob regrouped in the Hindu quarter of Srinagar and proceeded to wreak vengeance on the local shopkeepers. Hindus, as could be expected, retaliated and riots between followers of the two faiths broke out. The principal Muslim grievance was well known. In the bureaucracy, Hindus and Sikhs held 78 per cent of appointments, while Muslims held the rest, a proportion that was the exact reverse of the numbers of Muslims and non-Muslims in the state of Jammu and Kashmir, where, according to the census of 1931, Muslims made up nearly 80 per cent of the state's population.

Muslims complained that their share of state scholarships and places in government schools was the lowest of any of the three communities, Hindu, Sikh and Muslim. The cow-killing prohibition was also a source of resentment. The British were shaken by the communal violence which erupted in Kashmir in the 1930s. 'Communalism' is a quaint term that was widely used in the 1930s to describe the sectarian violence that plagued the Indian subcontinent in the years preceding the independence and partition of India and Pakistan in 1947. On 2 November 1931, the British Resident, Sir Courtney Latimer, warned his superiors that communal rioting in Jammu was likely to break out 'at any moment'; he also forecast a 'widespread rebellion in Kashmir' unless the government of India took immediate steps. His attempts to calm the situation didn't work, as the next day, 3 November, the Muslims of Jammu started looting Hindu-owned shops. They attacked the police and set fire to public buildings. Hari Singh responded by telegraphing Simla, the summer residence of the Viceroy, with a request for British troops.

The request was readily granted, but the dispatch of British troops to Kashmir was a significant departure from the traditional policy of the British in India. Since the first decade of the twentieth century, the Raj had followed a consistent policy of non-intervention when it came to the internal affairs of the larger princely states. The policy was prudent, as the British government wanted to rally the princes against the growing forces of Indian nationalism. Giving the princes more power over their states, it was felt, would ensure their loyalty and establish the princely families as a counterpoise to the more radical elements, who wanted the British to leave India for good. The British were caught between two stools. They did not want to alienate the well-to-do Muslim community in the Punjab in general, but neither could they neglect the interests of the princes. Meanwhile, more disturbances took place. A rural revolt spread rapidly throughout southern and western Jammu. There was injury and destruction, shops were looted and dozens of people were killed; over a hundred 'low-caste Hindus' were forcibly converted to Islam.[35]

By January 1932, the Viceroy in Simla had authorized the dispatch of an additional brigade, about 5,000 troops, to Kashmir. In addition, a commission was set up to investigate 'the grievances of Muslim and other subjects of His Highness the Maharaja of Kashmir'. The report of the Glancy Commission was broadly favourable to the Muslim community and it provoked the inevitable backlash, as irate Hindus protested that 'the manner in which the Glancy Commission are injuring the Hindu religion' showed that the British would do anything to 'root out Hinduism from the country'.[36] The Muslim All-India Kashmir Committee nonetheless complained to the Viceroy about the 'harsh and discriminating laws' against Muslims, about the relatively few Muslim lawyers in the state, and about the 'harsh and inhuman' treatment of Muslim political prisoners in Kashmir's jails.[37] The British continued to hide behind the figleaf of 'non-intervention' which was restated in the Viceroy's bland reply. The government of India, the Raj, was 'averse to putting pressure on States to accelerate the process and pace of reforms'.[38]

During this period, Sheikh Abdullah emerged as the voice of Muslim opinion. He was a constant thorn in the Maharaja's side and would be a key figure in Kashmiri politics until his death in 1982. Born in 1905, Abdullah had left Aligarh University with a science degree in 1930 and had settled in Srinagar as a teacher. Once installed in the capital of Kashmir, he threw himself into politics and by the following year was already recognized as a political leader. The events of 1931 defined his career as well as that of the Maharaja. Abdullah, with his scientific, rationalist background, was a committed nationalist even before he was a Muslim. Like many of the leaders of colonial independence struggles, he was attracted by the twin gods of socialism and secularism. In 1931, however, he used the latent power of religious enthusiasm to whip up an agitated crowd.[39] It was then that he realized that 'the Muslim masses appeared to respond to Islamic appeals and Islamic leaders to a far greater degree' than to secular causes.[40] Religion, despite the best attempts of the Indian Congress, under Gandhi and Nehru, was a dominant, and potentially toxic, factor in the affairs of the subcontinent. The harsh fact was that India was in the process of being 'divided on communal grounds'.[41] As early as December 1930, Sir Muhammad Iqbal delivered a speech at the Allahabad Session of the All-India Muslim League, in which he had declared that 'communalism' was 'indispensable to the formation of a harmonious whole in a country like India'. India, he argued, was a 'continent of human groups belonging to different races and speaking different languages and professing different religions'. This diversity meant that each group had to have its own juris-diction; 'European democracy' would not work in India without recognizing the fact of 'communal groups'. The 'Muslim demand for the creation of a Muslim India within India' was, Iqbal believed, 'perfectly justified'.[42]

Religious and ethnic tensions bedevilled British India during the 1930s, and in this febrile atmosphere Kashmir proved to be a focal point for strife. The theme of difference, of Muslim and Hindu incompatibility, was a rallying cry for any Muslims who yearned for their own homeland throughout the 1930s and 1940s. The extreme Muslim view was widely aired in the years immediately preceding the fateful year of independence in 1947. Between Hindu and Muslim, according to extreme Muslim opinion, there was a difference of 'law and of culture', because the two faiths represented 'two distinct and separate civilizations'.[43] Even Sheikh Abdullah, who ended up throwing in his lot with India, mainly because of his secular nationalism and personal friendship with Nehru, had difficulty appreciating the strength of religious feeling among the Muslims of Kashmir. In the midst of these powerful forces, the Maharaja, Hari Singh, was lost, and incapable of providing the leadership that the crisis demanded.

According to his son, the Maharaja 'was not able to grasp the historical dimensions of the changes that were around the corner'.[44] Hari Singh had started his reign attempting to heal the divisions between Hindu and Muslim and, in January 1926, only four months after succeeding his uncle, he had proudly declared that, as a ruler, he had 'no religion; all religions are mine and my religion is Justice'.[45] It was unfortunate that, as his reign unfolded, he came to be more and more identified with the Hindu domination of his state. He was a Hindu monarch, and that was all people could see. The Muslim delegation from Kashmir which had petitioned the Viceroy at the beginning of 1932 had told him that it was 'natural that the rulers of the state should be anxious to maintain its monopoly in the administration'. Those rulers were Hindu. The Maharaja was at the top of that state. Hari Singh, despite his claims to impartiality, when caught between the two extremes of Hindu chauvinism and Islamic fanaticism, sided with the Hindus. In 1931, he had to issue a staunch denial that he intended to revoke the prohibition on the killing of cows. On 9 July that year, shortly before the infamous shootings of the 13th, he declared in a proclamation that the 'malicious rumour now being spread that cow killing is shortly going to be permitted' had 'no foundation whatever'. There was 'no question whatever of making any change in the matter'.[46]

While the Maharaja was being identified purely as a Hindu ruler by his Muslim subjects, the communal forces which eventually created Pakistan were becoming more insistent and powerful. The Muslim League, in its annual session at Lahore in 1940, established the principle that 'geographically contiguous areas' of the subcontinent 'in which the Muslims were numerically in a majority should be grouped to form "independent states"'. Seven years later, this demand was reluctantly conceded by both the British and the Indian Congress Party when the state of Pakistan was born.[47] On this basis, Kashmir should have gone to Pakistan: no one could deny that it was 'geographically contiguous' to other states in Pakistan; no one could claim that it did not have a Muslim majority; and yet none of this made any impression on the somewhat bewildered and frightened Maharaja.

In his mind the ideal situation would have been independence. There is a body of evidence to suggest that the Maharaja had, by the 1940s, become increasingly detached from reality. His uncle, Pratap, had assembled a motley collection of Hindu swamis, gurus, astrologers and assorted holy men round his court whom Hari Singh had for twenty years banished from his presence. Now, in 1944, he summoned back one of the most influential and charismatic of these men, Swami Sant Dev, a mystic who had enjoyed high prestige in the reign of the Maharaja's uncle. Hari Singh restored his allowance and, from May 1946 until October 1947, the Swami was always in residence in various houses within the palace compound in Srinagar. The Maharaja had turned, in the sunset of the Raj, to Hindu mysticism, under whose influence he believed he could build a new kingdom once the British had departed. Some called this fantastical kingdom 'Dogistan', which would, Hari Singh hoped, rekindle the glory of his royal house. This absurd fantasy was nursed by the Swami. The Prime Minister, a Brahmin named Pandit Kak, told the Maharaja frankly that it was a 'futile and impractical' idea, since the nationalism which was pushing out the British would not allow the princes of India to retain their former power. The Maharaja pressed on with his grandiose scheme, though he never forgave or forgot the impertinence of his prime minister. He had already 'at great cost' prepared a new crown of diamonds and emeralds for his coronation as ruler of this new kingdom.[48] He still cut a dashing figure. Though fat, he had a regal style about him. On a visit to Kashmir in 1945, he and his wife dazzled the Viceroy, Lord Wavell, who had been impressed by what he saw as the Maharaja's 'liberal-minded' attitude. Wavell was especially taken with Tara Devi: 'I quite fell for the Maharani who is attractive and has obviously a good deal of character. Her jewels must be seen to be believed; she wore a fresh set every day we were there.'[49] Wavell stayed more than a week.

As independence drew nearer, the fate of Kashmir was still unclear. It had been decided that independence would be granted to India on 15 August 1947. Under the Government of India Act 1935, it was the maharajas and nawabs, the rulers of the princely states, who would decide which country they would accede to. Still the Maharaja of Kashmir had not decided, and it was at this point that Lord Mountbatten, who had replaced Wavell as viceroy in April 1947, made an interesting intervention. In the Pakistani demonology of the tragedy of Partition and the communal violence which followed, Mountbatten plays a special role. Several historians have detected in him a pro-Indian bias, from which the subsequent tragedy of Kashmir is believed to flow. It is true that Mountbatten got on well with Nehru, whom 'he both admired and trusted'.[50] It is also true that Nehru had a very close relationship with Mountbatten's wife, Edwina, to whom Nehru later wrote that 'some uncontrollable force, of which I was only dimly aware, drew us to one another'. A Mountbatten biographer has even opined on the precise nature of the relationship, airily declaring that if 'there was any physical element it can only have been of minor importance to either party'.[51] Whatever the nature of that relationship, the closeness of the Mountbattens to Nehru is well known. Historians have therefore assumed that Mountbatten was on India's side during the Kashmir conflict from the outset. 'The key to understanding Mountbatten's stance over Kashmir . . . was his anti-Pakistan bias,' wrote Andrew Roberts in his acclaimed book, *Eminent Churchillians*.[52] The documentary evidence presents a less clear picture. When Mountbatten visited Kashmir at the end of June 1947, it was to urge the kingdom's accession to Pakistan. He advised Pandit Kak, the Maharaja's beleaguered Prime Minister and, like Nehru, a Kashmiri Brahmin, to 'consider your geographical position, political situation and composition of your population and then decide'. 'That means that you advise us to accede to Pakistan. It is not possible for us to do that,' the Kashmiri replied.[53]

In Srinagar, Mountbatten spent five days from 18 to 23 June with the Maharaja. The Viceroy was a pragmatist and, in keeping with this pragmatism, he frankly told Hari Singh, 'it's up to you, but I think you should consider it very carefully since after all 90 per cent of your people are Muslims'. Even though the true figure was just shy of 80 per cent, the force of the argument remained. 'I don't want to accede to Pakistan on any account,' the Maharaja replied. The problem was that he was unwilling 'to join India either'. Everyone knew that Congress, the dominant party in India, would end the Maharaja's powers, but he could not join Pakistan, because his position as the Hindu ruler of a predominantly Muslim state would surely have been terminated by any Pakistani government. Yet Mountbatten squashed any idea of independence. 'You just can't be independent. You are a land-locked country. You are over-sized and under-populated.'

Mountbatten, to his credit, presented the Maharaja with the facts, however unpleasant they may have been to His Highness's ears. The Viceroy always fancied himself as the imperial statesman and, despite the criticisms of his detractors, in his assessment of the Kashmiri situation he was far-sighted and statesmanlike. He told the Maharaja bluntly: 'What I mind is that your attitude is bound to lead to strife between India and Pakistan. You are going to have two rival countries at daggers drawn for your neighbours. You will be the tug-of-war between them. You will end up being a battlefield. That is what will happen. You will lose your throne, and your life too, if you are not careful.'

Mountbatten spoke truly. Hari Singh spent the next two days fishing, and finally refused to meet Mountbatten formally, as the Viceroy had proposed; the Maharaja was suffering from a 'stomach upset', so he claimed, whereupon Mountbatten left Srinagar without any firm commitment from the Maharaja to join either India or Pakistan.[54] In reality, given Hari Singh's character and the heritage he represented, there was never any question that he would accede to Pakistan. This was the central political fact about Kashmir: it was a state in which a Hindu minority ruled over a Muslim majority and it would have been too much to hope that the ruler of that state would willingly accede to another which had been explicitly founded as a Muslim state. The British, particularly Mountbatten, saw this very clearly. It was obvious to Wavell, Mountbatten's immediate predecessor, that Kashmir should have gone to Pakistan. In a letter written in December 1949, less than six months before his death, Wavell could not have been less equivocal on this question: 'If only this wretched Kashmir business could be settled . . . Of course it ought to have gone to Pakistan from the first, with possibly some adjustments in frontier on the south . . . But I am afraid the prospects of settlement do not look good at present.'[55]

The last two viceroys of India, Lords Wavell and Mountbatten, were at the time convinced that Kashmir's future should lie with Pakistan. That this failed to happen was the result of one man's choice. Under the rules of the game, the Maharaja in effect had the sole authority to decide to which state Kashmir should accede. His possession of Kashmir, his power, was not based on any idea of democracy or of the popular will. It was an accident of birth and, more than that, an accident of history. The Maharaja's power, like that of the other Indian princes, was a product of convenience and snobbery. It was unfortunate that in the case of Kashmir, his decisions mattered. The consequences of his vacillating character and his final decision to accede to India still shape Kashmir and politics in the subcontinent more than sixty years after independence. Yet the Kashmir dispute, in the last months of 1947, would become even more toxic and this was a direct consequence of Pakistan's own folly, not of the Maharaja's stubborn will.

7

Deadlock

India became independent on 15 August 1947, but the position of Kashmir was still unsettled. Despite the persuasive powers of Lord Mountbatten, and the fact that the overwhelming majority of his subjects were Muslim, the Maharaja resolutely refused to accede to Pakistan. Accession to India also posed its own problems. Congress, under the leadership of Nehru and Gandhi, was determined that the power of the Indian princes would not outlive the Raj, which itself had disintegrated more quickly than anyone had expected. As one writer has observed, 'it took the British more than three hundred years to build up their Indian Empire. They dismantled it in just seventy days in 1947.'[1] The parallel to the rapid disintegration of Soviet power in Eastern Europe in 1989 is a striking one.

Hari Singh's dream of creating an independent mountain state in Kashmir was unrealistic and was made more difficult by the significant detail that the Congress leader, Nehru, was a Kashmiri Brahmin. Nehru loved Kashmir like a 'supremely beautiful woman whose beauty is impersonal and above desire'.[2] As he told Edwina Mountbatten, Kashmir affected him in 'a peculiar way; it is a kind of mild intoxication – like music sometimes or the company of a beloved person'.[3] Nehru, as a consequence of his devotion to his native land, desperately wanted India to keep Kashmir, which obviously remained an important object of desire for the new Pakistan government. Through the late summer months of 1947, the Kashmir issue remained in the balance, and the longer it remained undecided, the less likely a peaceful solution would become.

By October 1947, it seemed that some incident or act of spontaneous folly could make the situation worse. Already, at the end of September, Nehru had written to Sardar Patel, a leading figure in the Congress Party, to stress that the situation in Kashmir was 'dangerous and deteriorating'. Nehru was also conscious that some in Pakistan were quite willing to take matters in hand and act swiftly, and by means of violence, to impose their will. 'The Muslim league in the Punjab and the North West Frontier Province are making preparations to enter Kashmir in considerable numbers,' he wrote, adding that the 'approach of winter' would 'cut off Kashmir from the rest of India'. Nehru, at this relatively early date, believed that 'something should be done', before winter conditions set in, by the end of October or, at the latest, early November.[4]

In Pakistan, Sir George Cunningham, who was the Governor of the North West Frontier, expressed similar thoughts in his diary, observing on 6 October that there is 'quite a lot of talk now of the danger of actual war between Pakistan and India'. He noted that the Pakistan government seemed 'to wink at very dangerous activities on the Kashmir border, allowing small parties of Muslims to infiltrate Kashmir from this side'. The religious nature of the dispute was never really in any doubt from the Pakistani point of view, as militants on the Pakistan side were openly courting religious enthusiasm to launch a jihad against the infidel. On 13 October, Cunningham observed that there was 'a real move in Hazara [a district in the west of Pakistan] for *Jehad* against Kashmir'. Two days later, he simply commented that the 'Kashmir affair is boiling up'. That an actual invasion was likely to happen was perhaps the most open secret in international politics at that time. Certainly Nehru, in Delhi, and Cunningham, in Pakistan, knew that an act of aggression was imminent. In India, as early as 7 October, Sardar Patel hoped that 'arrangements are in train to send immediately supplies of arms and ammunition to Kashmir'. He added that there was no time to lose 'if the reports which we hear of similar preparation for intervention on the part of the Pakistan Government are correct'. Patel was confident that such an intervention would be 'true to the Nazi pattern'.[5] How much Cunningham, a British civil servant and therefore supposedly impartial, knew about the Pakistani plans has been a subject of debate. It is clear that he was very well informed of what was happening, although he was powerless to do anything about it. On 18 October he summoned Abdul Qayum, now the Pakistani Prime Minister of the North West Frontier Province, to confront him about the 'Kashmir business'. Cunningham 'told him everything' and 'asked him frankly whether he was in it or not'. A rather cynical and subtle politician, Qayum replied evasively that while it would be a 'very good thing if Kashmir could be filled up with armed Muslims to the greatest possible extent, our line here must be that all officers and our police etc. give no support or sympathy to the movement'.[6]

Everyone, it appeared, knew what was coming, but the news was still shocking when it finally broke. On the evening of Friday 24 October, Lord Mountbatten and the Foreign Minister of Siam were dinner-party guests of Pandit Nehru, the leader of the Congress Party. In the course of the evening Mountbatten was taken to one side by Nehru, who informed him that news had come of 'a large scale invasion of tribesmen from the North-West Frontier into Kashmir'.[7] In Srinagar, at the onset of the invasion, the Maharaja was literally heading for the hills. On the night of the 25th, a Saturday, Hari Singh had been entertaining 200 people in his palace when all the lights suddenly went out. This in itself was quite common, but when the palace was still in darkness after a couple of hours the guests began to feel uneasy. The blackout had been caused by the invading tribesmen burning down the power station at Mohra, only thirty miles down the road.[8] The following night, the Maharaja's servants began to empty his strongboxes of his pearls, emeralds and diamonds. The Maharaja himself frantically searched his palace for the two objects he prized above all others, his two Purdey shotguns. Once these had been found they were packed into his car. Now, accompanied by his friend Victor Rosenthal, a Russian Jewish jeweller and financier, Hari Singh was driven away, never to return to his palace in Srinagar.[9] The palace itself would be sold in 1954 to the Oberoi hotel chain by Hari Singh's son Karan.

The tribal invasion itself has been a subject of intense controversy. What started as an attempt to force the incorporation of Kashmir into Pakistan became, through the intervention of Pashtun (or Pathan) tribesmen, a rallying cry for the new nation of India. The violence of the Pathan invaders is still sometimes referred to by an India seeking to justify its own military intervention in Kashmir. The Pathans, at the outset anyway, carried all before them. In his diary on 25 October, Cunningham remarked that he was 'greatly surprised at the absence of opposition' against people he rather bizarrely called 'our tribesmen'.[10] The remark innocently reveals how closely British officials sometimes identified with the peoples they governed. Many outrages were committed by the Pathan tribesmen, of which the storming of the convent at Baramullah, thirty miles from Srinagar, was the most notorious. On Monday 27 October, as Indian troops who had just flown in were struggling to hold the airport at Srinagar, the tribesmen gave vent to their violent fury. They arrived at the convent of the Franciscan Missionaries of Mary, where an assortment of French, Scottish, Italian and Portuguese nuns resided. In the clinic of the convent, tribesmen found Colonel D. O. T. Dykes, from Somerset in England, and his wife, who had given birth to a daughter only three weeks before. Dykes tried to plead with the invaders. He was shot at point-blank range and died a few hours later. His wife, sitting outside, was also shot and fell dead, crushing the baby she was still feeding. They then stripped her of her clothes and threw her body down a well. Jose Barretto, an Italian whose wife was a doctor at the hospital, was robbed and killed at his wife's feet. Tribesmen raped some of the nuns. The convent's Mother Superior, Sister Mary, died of her wounds, still in her final hours praying for the 'conversion of Kashmir' to Christianity.[11]

The terrible nature of the invasion of Kashmir by the Pashtuns must be placed in the context of the appalling violence which gripped the subcontinent at the end of 1947. At the end of British rule, India was a tumultuous scene of murder and bloodshed. British intelligence reports in October that year may have referred to the 'sufferings of the Muslims in the East Punjab', but the outrages committed by the tribesmen were perpetrated against Muslim and Hindu alike. As one British social worker expressed it, the invading Pathans had sensed an 'opportunity of gaining both religious merit and rich booty'.[12] It was after the excessive violence experienced by Kashmiris at the end of October that the Maharaja acceded to India, though there is a lively debate about when exactly this was done.

The accession of the Maharaja of Kashmir to India is the defining moment in modern Kashmiri history. To the Indians this piece of paper has all the binding legality of a constitutional document, which, strictly speaking, is correct, so far as the letter of the law is concerned. Yet both

India and Pakistan recognized that some kind of popular endorsement of the accession was needed, and both countries, at the time though not subsequently, were committed to a plebiscite on the issue. At the beginning of December 1947, Nehru was writing to the Maharaja about a vote which he clearly thought was likely: 'If there is to going to be a plebiscite, then obviously we have to work in such a way as to gain the goodwill of the majority of the population of the State, which means chiefly Muslims.' At that time, Nehru was enough of a democrat to realize that Indian control of the province could not be maintained 'ultimately except through the goodwill of the mass of the population'.[13] By the end of 1947, both Pakistan and India felt that it made sense for the Kashmiris themselves to decide to which country they should belong. The fact that no plebiscite ever took place to resolve the Kashmir dispute belies some of the wilder claims that democracy was the British Raj's unique legacy to the Indian subcontinent; the Kashmir dispute was a direct consequence of princely rule, and no democratic resolution to the conflict has ever been sought.

The dramatic airlift of Indian troops from Delhi to Srinagar at the end of October 1947 established the deadlock in Kashmir which has persisted to this day. The Pakistanis had been wrongfooted by India's response. Their support, tacit or overt, of the tribal invasion of Kashmir deprived them of any moral authority, while it seemed that they had badly miscalculated by believing that the invasion would put pressure on the Maharaja to accede to Pakistan. On 18 October, before the invasion had even taken place, Abdul Qayum told Cunningham that 'direct action against Kashmir now would tend to make the Maharaja join Pakistan than otherwise'. Yet by the end of the month Cunningham believed that Mohammed Ali Jinnah, Pakistan's first governor general, now saw clearly that the intervention had failed, and had produced exactly the opposite result to its intention. Cunningham, confiding in his diary, believed that 'Jinnah is conscious of having made a blunder (having assumed that tribal intervention would not at once – as seemed obvious to me – throw Kashmir into the arms of India).'[14]

It was perhaps easy for Cunningham to be wise after the event. He had enjoyed a distinguished career in British India. Now nearly sixty, he was a typical member of the public school and Oxbridge elite, upon whom the government of the vast empire largely depended. He had been educated at Fettes College, the so-called Eton of Scotland, which educated a later prime minister, Tony Blair. He had followed this by getting a third-class degree at Magdalen College, Oxford, where he had distinguished himself, not in the stately examination halls, but on the rugby field. He captained the university rugby team in its annual match against Cambridge, and also captained Scotland at rugby before joining the Indian Civil Service in 1911. He retired from the ICS in 1948, only a year after the Raj, to which he had given his working life, had ended. Fittingly, he died on 8 December 1963, on his annual pilgrimage to the Oxford–Cambridge rugby match at Twickenham.[15] He did not manage to get to the game, which Cambridge won.

Now, at the end of 1947, Cunningham, as the governor of the North Western Frontier Province, was in the midst of great events. He had daily contact with all the leading Pakistani politicians as they formulated their response to the Kashmir crisis. His open partisanship of Pakistan is striking, and it is strange that some historians have cited him as proof of Lord Mountbatten's Indian bias, when Cunningham himself was so clearly on the side of Pakistan and 'our tribesmen', as he had called the tribal invaders. At noon on 28 October, only a few days after the invasion, Cunningham went to the house of the Pakistani Prime Minister, Liaquat Ali, where the Pakistani politician was still in bed. Along with Jinnah, he and Francis Mudie, Governor of West Punjab, discussed the Kashmir situation for two and a half hours in Ali's bedroom.[16] The position of British officials in this dispute was unusual; as war loomed between Pakistan and India, a unique situation had arisen 'in which both the opposing armies were led by nationals of a third country' – that is to say, by British generals.[17]

Even in London, there was no clear line or direction on the dispute. The Labour government of Clement Attlee was itself divided into pro-Pakistani and pro-Indian factions. Cunningham himself had been told that the 'Government at Home seemed to be divided', with 'Attlee etc.' favouring Pakistan and a group, led by the Chancellor of the Exchequer, Sir Stafford Cripps, supporting India. Cunningham, in his pro-Pakistan bias, cited his friend General Sir Frank Messervy, a British officer now the commander-in-chief of Pakistan's army, who had visited Delhi at the beginning of

November and had been 'surprised to find Mountbatten directing the military operations in Kashmir'.[18] But this evidence must be set against other sources which show how keen Mountbatten was to get the Maharaja to accede to Pakistan. It was only after the Pakistanis had invaded Kashmir that Mountbatten seems to have been more inclined to take the Indian side. In fact, official papers on the Kashmir conflict, dating from 1948, suggested, as has been confirmed elsewhere, that 'Lord Mountbatten as the Crown Representative pressed the Maharaja very hard to consult the will of his people long ago, in *the practically certain knowledge* that this would result in a vote for accession to Pakistan [italics added].'[19] This official paper, dated 4 November 1947, acknowledged that the Pakistan government had made serious mistakes in its handling of the issue, as it would have been better for it 'to warn the Government of India of the impending invasion'. Mountbatten and the British were powerless, but on the whole, despite internal division, many tended to feel that Kashmir was obviously a state which should have acceded to Pakistan. A note, headed 'Top Secret' and dated 1 December, described the Kashmir situation as 'most dangerous at the moment'. Yet its root cause, according to the memorandum, was simple: 'Whatever errors may have been committed by both sides since trouble started, the basic cause was the action of the Hindu ruler in suppressing popular agitation in favour of Pakistan.'[20]

To other officials, including Lord Mountbatten himself, the logic of the situation was equally straightforward. It was simply 'disingenuous to say, as was said subsequently, that Kashmir had the option to accede to either Dominion. It had that option legally,' but the plain fact was that 'India was divided on communal grounds and the only rational course was for a state if it decided to accede, to assure itself first whether its population would support the accession.' The British police commissioner who wrote these words later observed, in 1955, that 'it need hardly be mentioned that were a plebiscite to be held, it would be nothing short of a miracle, if results went in favour of India'; Hindus would vote for India and Muslims for Pakistan.[21]

Religious enthusiasm, and the strong identification people have with their religion, was a phenomenon which the Congress Party, in its secular liberal way, had never really confronted. As so often, religious feeling had been used as a pretext, an excuse for rape and pillage, but it was still an effective rallying cry. Throughout November, minor Pakistani feudal lords were preaching jihad. The Nawab of Dir, one such petty prince, had persuaded a number of mullahs to issue a fatwa commanding their followers to wage jihad against the Maharaja of Kashmir. A couple of weeks later, the official report referred to the 'mullah element' of a province in Pakistan 'exhorting the general public' to invade Kashmir.[22]

The situation over Kashmir had by the end of 1947 reached deadlock, a position under which it has laboured ever since. It was Lord Mountbatten's idea to refer the dispute to the United Nations, and he urged Nehru to take this step. On 20 December 1947 Nehru succumbed. Given what we know about Mountbatten's views earlier in the year, it seems quite likely that he knew the United Nations would incline towards the Pakistan point of view. He himself had been convinced by the argument that, because the overwhelming majority of the population was Muslim, the people of Kashmir wanted their land to accede to Pakistan. The United Nations, at the beginning of 1948, seem to have taken the same view. On 1 January 1948, India took the issue to the UN Security Council. The received wisdom among Indians is that this was a mistake. They have always felt that they failed to get a fair hearing at the United Nations. It has become part of the Indian mythology that Pakistan, in Sir Zafarullah Khan, had 'a superbly gifted orator', and that Philip Noel-Baker, a member of the British delegation at the United Nations, was a 'vigorous' supporter of Pakistan. One enterprising Indian historian has even stated that British support for Pakistan's position was somehow 'compensation' for the recent creation of the state of Israel, 'after which there was a need to placate Muslims world wide'.[23] The simpler explanation was that, on the face of things, the Pakistanis had a powerful case. As early as the beginning of February 1948, Nehru was complaining that the United Nations was totally dominated by the Americans, whose representative, Senator Warren Austin, in Nehru's opinion had made 'no bones about his sympathy for the Pakistan cause'. For Nehru, Noel-Baker, an athlete who had represented Britain at the 1912 Stockholm Olympics, wasn't that much better, just 'more polite'.[24]

In 1948, Noel-Baker, a Labour MP who would go on to win the Nobel Peace Prize in 1959, was firmly placed in the demonology of India. The

Indians felt isolated and unloved by the international community. Sardar
Patel in a letter of 3 July 1948 to Arthur Henderson, the son of a former
Labour Party leader who was now a Foreign Office minister in Attlee's
government, complained of British bias against India. Patel was wary of
the British, as he believed that 'prejudicial correspondents' from Britain
continued 'deliberately [to] misrepresent our attitude and make it out as if
we are indulging in coercive tactics'. It was his experience 'that the attitude
of an average Englishman in India is instinctively against us'. He believed
that going to the United Nations, where the dispute had been merely
prolonged, had been a mistake. The 'merits' of the Indian case had been
'completely lost in the interaction of power politics'. Mountbatten had
'helped us to his best capacity'. The villain of the piece had been Noel-
Baker, whose 'attitude' had 'tilted the balance against us'. 'But for his lead,'
Patel concluded, 'I doubt if the USA and some other powers would have
gone against us.'[25]

In addition to the argument that the majority of the population of
Kashmir was Muslim, there was the issue of the Maharaja himself. He was
an embarrassment to the Indian case. The Security Council of the United
Nations thought it odd that this one feudal dignitary should have decided
the fate of millions of Kashmiris. Nehru, in his astute way, saw the problem
very clearly. At the beginning of February 1948 he was writing to Sardar
Patel on the subject of Hari Singh. The Maharaja's 'wisest' policy, Nehru
felt, was to 'do nothing at all'. He added that Sardar would surely have
'noticed the repeated references made in the Security Council about the
so-called autocratic rule of the Maharaja' which meant that 'the system of
Indian States finds little favour in foreign countries'. The important role
played by feudal dignitaries like the Maharaja of Kashmir in the period
before independence was exposed and ridiculed by the Pakistani delegation.[26] At the end of January, within a month of the referral to the United
Nations, the Maharaja indulged in feelings of self-doubt and self-pity. In a
long, doleful letter he blamed everyone and everything for the plight in
which he now found himself. He complained that a strong feeling had
grown that 'the UN Security Council will take an adverse decision and
that the state will eventually have to accede to Pakistan'. He threatened to
withdraw the accession that he had made, suggesting darkly that he might

have had 'better terms from Pakistan'. He recognized, of course, that in the long run accession to Pakistan would 'mean an end of the dynasty and an end of the Hindus and Sikhs in the State'. The Maharaja even complained to Sardar Patel, a hero of the Indian Congress Party and an ardent follower of Gandhi's philosophy, that the Indian army had been hopeless in its military engagements in the Kashmir dispute. The Indian army, so he claimed, had done nothing in the three months it had been in Kashmir. He said that the 'name of the Indian Army is getting into the mud' and referred to the Great War when, he argued, the 'name of the Indian Army was at its highest pitch'. It now pained His Highness that the 'name of that Army has become a topic of every tongue during these days and it is daily losing prestige'.

For a man who hoped that India would preserve his authority and the power of his family, the Maharaja was now behaving with a staggering arrogance towards the Indians. His conduct throughout 1948 became increasingly eccentric as he harassed and embarrassed his Indian friends. In the letter he wrote to Patel at the end of January, he candidly said that he had acceded to the 'Indian Union with the idea that the Union' would not 'let us down', in the belief that his 'position and that of [the] dynasty would remain secure'.[27] Years of command and authority had blinded him to where, in post-independence India, real power lay. In April he was ordering Patel, a seventy-three-year-old former president of the Indian National Congress, to charter a 'special plane' to take him from Jammu to Delhi. Urgent decisions needed to be taken, but these had to be delayed, because the Maharaja could not be reached; it appeared that he did not know how to use a telephone 'properly'.[28] Later in the year, in September, the Maharaja was lecturing Sardar on the correct protocol to be observed in celebration of His Highness's birthday. He pointed to the occasions when it was 'usual in the state [of Kashmir] to fire gun salutes', one of which, of course, occurred on the Maharaja's birthday. Naturally, there was 'no difficulty about this when the control of the Army' had been with him, but now the Indian army was in charge. 'My birthday is on the 27th September. Therefore very early instructions may very kindly be issued,' he graciously warned Patel on the 9th of that month.[29]

The sadness was that the Maharaja still believed that his rank and family were important considerations in the political affairs of the new county, even though, as everyone knew, the Raj had ended. He found it difficult to adapt to the new situation, while the United Nations, as would become customary, merely fudged the issue, simply endorsing the current position, which had been achieved initially by military stalemate, without any adjudication of right or wrong. A ceasefire was imposed on 1 January 1949, signed by Messervy's successor General Sir Douglas Gracey on behalf of Pakistan and by General Sir Roy Bucher on behalf of India. The United Nations Commission for India and Pakistan did, however, state that the question whether the State of Jammu and Kashmir would accede to India or Pakistan would be decided through the 'democratic method of a free and impartial plebiscite'.[30]

The position of the Maharaja, at the beginning of 1949, was still not clear. Thanks to his pomposity and tactlessness, he was antagonizing the Indians who were, after all, supporting his throne with their army. By the middle of 1948, Nehru could see that Hari Singh was hopelessly incompetent. 'My study of the Kashmir situation has led me to believe that the Maharaja cannot play,' he wrote to Sardar Patel. The Maharaja was fixated on small things; he didn't get the big picture: 'when there is an obvious possibility of his losing everything he still wants to hold on to relatively simple things'.[31] To secular-minded modern Indian nationalists, the Maharaja had shown absolutely no leadership. He had not led 'his people in the hour of crisis', but had 'left in the night for Jammu', where his winter palace was situated. (His summer palace was in Srinagar.) He had left, moreover, 'in a caravan of cars and trunks carrying his family, his jewels', as well as 'costly furniture and carpets from his palaces'. This had been an 'ignominious betrayal'.[32] The Pakistanis were implacably hostile to the Maharaja, because he had signed his state over to India. The Indians had grown weary of his vanity, his grand airs and his greed, as he kept complaining and asking for money.

In May 1949, Patel proposed to the Maharaja that he should leave the state and appoint his son, the Yuvraj Karan, regent. This suggestion alarmed the Maharaja, who left the audience with Patel in a state of 'shock and bewilderment'. He was, in his own words, 'completely taken aback by this proposal' which he hoped would 'not be a prelude to any idea of abdication', though that is exactly what it turned out to be. In May 1949, Nehru was finalizing the details of a house in Bombay which would be put at the Maharaja's disposal. Throughout the rest of 1949, Hari Singh, Maharaja of Jammu and Kashmir, quibbled about which bits of which properties belonged to him and not to the state of Kashmir. As an Indian politician acidly remarked, 'it would be difficult to find any sane person in India who would agree that fishing rights or fishing lodges . . . were essential to the dignity of a ruler'.[33] Meanwhile, the Maharaja had planned the wedding of his eighteen-year-old son Karan to a Nepalese princess. Tara Devi begged for the Indian state to settle an allowance on the young couple, and to pay for her son's wedding. The letter may have been written by the Maharani, but no one doubted who had inspired the initiative.[34]

The Maharaja stopped being a factor in Kashmir's affairs at the end of 1949, when he departed to live in exile in Bombay. There he sank back into indolent irrelevance, as new political forces emerged to shape the destiny of the land he had once ruled. The Maharaja of Kashmir became a recluse and, in the long days of his exile, loved nothing better than to read 'illustrated books on castles and mansions of England, Europe and America'. He also devoured books on architecture and engineering, on racing and polo. With this sedentary lifestyle, Hari Singh became even more obese, eventually developing diabetes. He died in Bombay on 26 April 1961, aged sixty-five. He had refused to take the insulin injections prescribed for him. A long bout of coughing brought on a heart attack and, when the doctor had arrived, his last words were simply 'Doctor, I am going.'[35]

The death of the former Maharaja moved Kashmir no closer to a solution to its problems. Certainly, as already noted, no popular vote has ever ratified the accession to India, the most important decision the Maharaja ever made. By 1956, Kashmir had been integrated into India, and Nehru had abandoned his earlier commitment to a plebiscite.[36] In addition to the war fought between India and Pakistan in 1948, two further wars, in 1965 and 1971, have been waged between the two countries, in both of which Kashmir was a crucial issue in dispute. Relatively minor incidents have had the potential to aggravate an already volatile situation. In December

1963, the most sacred Muslim relic in Kashmir, a strand of hair from the beard of the Prophet, was stolen from the mosque at Hazratbal. Soon thousands were marching through the streets of Srinagar, demanding that the thieves be caught and punished. Outraged Kashmiris even set up a Sacred Hair Action Committee. Nehru sent the Chief of the Intelligence Bureau to help recover the relic.

The Indian attitude to Kashmir has accorded with the comment of the civil servant V. P. Menon, an ally of Sardar Patel, 'now that we've got it, we'll never let it go'.[37] Pakistani governments have adopted increasingly warlike measures in trying to get back what they feel is rightfully theirs. The current situation has barely changed in more than sixty years. Indian-controlled Kashmir, which includes the stunning Valley of Kashmir itself, has a population of 7.7 million, while Azad Kashmir, the Pakistani-controlled region, has a population of 2.8 million.[38] The boundary between these two regions is a ceasefire line that was determined by the United Nations in 1949.

Today the situation in Kashmir is still tense. In 1989 an insurgency began in Kashmir. On 13 February that year there was a large anti-Indian demonstration, in which the Indian novelist Salman Rushdie was denounced for his book *The Satanic Verses*. Even though the government had banned the book, the whole of Srinagar went on strike.[39] By the following January, the rebellion had grown into a mass resistance to Indian rule. There followed an exodus from the Valley of the Kashmiri Pandits, the people who, under the maharajas, had largely governed the state. According to the 1981 Indian government census, there were only 124,000 Pandits at that time. This represented just 4 per cent of the Valley's popula-tion of a little more than 3 million people. As the uprising broke out in February and March 1990, approximately 100,000 Pandits left the Valley for Jammu and Delhi. Since 1991 bands of Islamic guerrillas, partly funded and encouraged by Pakistan, have fought Indian troops. By the end of 2010, Kashmir was one of the most militarized regions in the world, although Kashmiri aspirations for greater independence remain largely unrealized. The frustration felt by Kashmiris has found expression in violence and in the popularity of the independence movement. The years 1992 and 1993 saw the rise of the pro-Pakistan Islamist guerrilla group

Hizb-ul Mujahideen, which means 'party of the warriors', or 'party of the jihadists' in Arabic. (The words 'jihad' and 'mujahideen' have the same roots.) The continuing war in Kashmir has cost tens of thousands of lives, though Indian and Pakistani figures differ. The circumstances today are very different from those of 1947. The conflict in many ways has, in the words of one commentator, 'taken on a life of its own'.[40] A rampant gun culture pervades what was once a favourite tourist destination, described as a 'heaven on earth', with its 'clear streams, snow-clad mountains and green valleys'.[41]

A story about two friends, both born in Srinagar in 1967, puts the tragedy of Kashmir in human terms. Both members of prosperous, middle-class professional families, Ashfaq Majid Wani and Nadeem Khatib were best friends during the 1970s and early 1980s. Together they attended the best grammar school in the city, where they were both bright students and fine athletes. While Ashfaq's ambition was to be a doctor, his friend Nadeem had ambitions to be an airline pilot. In his late teens, Ashfaq became interested in politics and, fired with this new enthusiasm, he joined the numerous demonstrations that took place in Srinagar at the end of the 1980s. On 23 March 1987, he was one of the hundreds of opposition activists arrested in police crackdowns across Indian-controlled Kashmir. He was released after nine months, but it is now apparent that his period in prison made him bitter. After his release, he was found to have cigarette burns all over his body, and he promptly left home and 'disappeared'. He never came home again, but in 1989 he emerged as a household name in Kashmir. He was now a leading member of the Jammu and Kashmir Liberation Front. By early 1990, when government authority had collapsed in the Kashmir Valley, the insurrection had just started and Ashfaq Wani was one of the most wanted men in India. On 30 March, the Indian security forces tracked him down in the old city of Srinagar. There was a fierce exchange of fire, in which he was killed.[42] He had lost his life at the age of twenty-three.

Meanwhile Nadeem, Ashfaq's childhood friend, was pursuing his dream of becoming a pilot. In March 1992, he left Srinagar to join a flying school near Delhi. From there he went to a flying school in Georgia, in the United States. He returned to Srinagar in 1994, but left again in 1996, telling his

parents that he was going back to the United States, where he would find
a job as a pilot for an American airline. His parents kept in touch. They
received many calls back from their son, who they believed was living a
prosperous and contented life in America. In 1999, there occurred one of
the frequent fierce exchanges of fire between Indian troops and Kashmiri
guerrillas in a remote mountainous area of the region. Nadeem Khatib was
killed at the age of thirty-two. He had left America to go to Pakistan,
where he learned how to be a guerrilla fighter. Ominously, it was his experience in America which had turned him into a radical Islamist. There,
according to his mother, he 'used to brood a lot on America's exploitation
of Muslim countries'.[43]

Beyond the personal tragedies, there lies the dangerous political situation, which continues to have serious implications for international
politics. One curious legacy of the British Empire has been a strong
Kashmiri community in England, which has been described as the 'real
fountainhead of secessionism'.[44] Even more dangerously, the region is one
of the places where the threat of nuclear war is still very real. On 11 and
13 May 1998 India carried out a series of underground nuclear tests at
Pokhran. On 28 and 30 May, Pakistan conducted its own series of nuclear
tests. Some sort of confrontation seemed likely. The Japanese Prime
Minister, Keizo Obuchi, spoke of the urgency of resolving the 'root cause'
of the Indo-Pakistan conflict – Kashmir.[45] More recently, Kashmir has
been host to all types of Islamic terror groups, who find in the state's
lawlessness a convenient cover for their activities. Between 26 and 29
November 2008, Mumbai witnessed more than ten shooting and bombing
attacks, in which 173 people were killed. The group responsible for the
attacks, Lashkar-e-Taiba, had been active in Kashmir for more than a
decade. One of the attackers mentioned Kashmir in a rambling interview
with the India TV news channel during the siege of the Taj Mahal Hotel.
'Are you aware how many people have been killed in Kashmir?' This is an
excuse which in itself proves nothing, except how politically sensitive the
issue of Kashmir still remains.[46]

The Kashmir dispute from the very beginning has been a battle of
different ideas of what constitutes a state. Pakistan was built as an avowedly Muslim state, whose basis is the religion which, it was believed, united

the country. India, under its Congress leaders, has always proudly maintained its secular status. According to one writer, the battle of Kashmir is an 'uncompromising . . . struggle of two ways of life, two concepts of political organization, two scales of values, two spiritual attitudes'.[47] It was exasperating for Indian leaders like Nehru to have to justify India's control of Kashmir, given that the religious argument in favour of Pakistan seemed so obvious. It is ironic that since 1947 religion, in the form of militant Islamism, has, if anything, become a stronger current in international politics. At the end of 1948, Nehru complained that 'people cannot get rid of the idea that Kashmir is predominantly Muslim and therefore likely to side with Muslim Pakistan'.[48] This has always been at the core of the Pakistan case. It was the same argument made by Lord Mountbatten to the Maharaja in the summer of 1947, before Hari Singh's fateful decision to accede to India. It is the same argument that is heard from the mouths of Pakistani politicians today. Secular India, however, sees no reason why a majority Muslim state should not remain as part of India. Recent history has not moved in India's way in this respect. International politics in today's world, especially after 11 September 2001, has been dominated by ethnic and religious conflict, by people identifying with religion to a greater degree than any enlightenment thinker could have imagined. As George Orwell wrote in 1941, the 'energy that actually shapes the world springs from emotions – racial pride, leader-worship, religious belief, love of war – which liberal intellectuals mechanically write off as anachronisms'.[49] The dispute in Kashmir is highly representative of the 'energy that actually shapes the world'.

The role of history, of the British Empire, in all this is clear to see. Accidents and decisions made on a personal, almost whimsical, level have had a massive impact on international politics. The empire in its belief in the individual action of its servants, with very little supervision and without any real central philosophy, created an environment in which a parcel of land was sold to a very rich man, with enormous repercussions. The family of that rich man ruled Kashmir for a hundred years because it was convenient for the British that that family should do so. It is ironic that revisionist historians have pointed to Indian democracy as the British Empire's greatest legacy. Democracy in Kashmir never existed; the system of Indian princes, which is directly responsible for the Kashmir problem, was the absolute opposite of democracy. The personal rule of the Hindu maharajas of Kashmir accorded with the snobbery of Victorian England, the belief in natural aristocrats, the love of pageantry and pride in lineage. These are not modern ideas, but owe their origin more to a feudal, medieval past than to the secular, democratic liberalism of the modern West. In Kashmir, the Maharaja's decision was final. It was that decision which has shaped, and will continue to influence, the fate of this troubled region. As Hari Singh himself wrote, in his clumsy, pompous style, 'to which Dominion the state should accede – strictly speaking – according to the Government of India Act, I alone am the authority to decide'.[50] In many ways, Hari Singh was indeed a modern-day Louis XIV, echoing the famous remark attributed to the French King: 'L'État, c'est moi.'

PART III

Burma: Lost Kingdom

White Elephant

The old King, Mindon, was happy in his palace, from which he had ruled the kingdom of Upper Burma since 1853. Having annexed Lower Burma, the area round Rangoon and the Irrawaddy Delta, in the 1850s, the British were content for Mindon to rule Upper Burma as an independent sovereign. Mindon was clever enough to understand who possessed real power in his part of the world. The old man was a pious Buddhist who had an extensive family; some people claimed that he had a hundred wives, though this is evidently incorrect, because only fifty-three wives have been attested to, thirty-nine of whom bore children. Altogether, Mindon had 110 children, of whom forty-eight were boys and sixty-two were girls.[1]

Mindon, as a local king, had experienced the power of the British at first hand, because his brother, Pagan Min, the previous king, had been an unpredictable and wild ruler who had been defeated by the British in battle. When it took over the southern part of the Burmese kingdom, Britain forced Pagan Min to abdicate. Pagan had been the worst kind of ruler for the British and had begun his reign by massacring a hundred members of his own family to secure his rule. He was devoted to cock-fighting and debauchery of all kinds. According to British observers, the 'acts of cruelty and extortion perpetrated in his reign have never been surpassed'.[2]

The family which now ruled Burma were relative upstarts. In 1752, Alaungpaya, an obscure village chief, launched a successful rebellion against the King of the Mon people, who had deposed Burma's ruling family, the Taungoo dynasty. Alaungpaya then crowned himself king and, in 1755, founded Rangoon. His last campaign was an invasion of Siam (Thailand), during which, in April 1760, he besieged the historic capital,

Ayutthaya. During the siege, a cannon he was watching exploded and wounded him, and he died on the way back to Burma. He was not yet forty-six years old, but his career, though short, had been brilliant. 'In eight years he rose from the position of a petty village headman to that of one of the most powerful monarchs of the East.'[3]

Mindon was a less warlike, more conciliatory ruler than the founding father of his dynasty had been. He was also a pragmatic man who 'knew and feared' Britain's power.[4] Unfortunately, he was deluded in thinking that he could maintain a relationship with the British on equal terms. In his own eyes, and according to the propaganda of the court, he was still 'the lord of all the Great Umbrella-bearing chiefs', the 'King of the Rising Sun', and 'lord of the Celestial Elephant'; most important of all, he was the 'lord of the White Elephant', a phrase which itself has entered the English language to mean something expensive but useless, but which, in Burmese eyes, was the ultimate symbol of royal authority. More widely in Southeast Asia – in Cambodia, Thailand, Laos and Burma itself – the White Elephant was a symbol of royalty. As long as a king possessed a white elephant, he was deemed to be a just ruler. This tradition derived from the time of the Buddha, whose mother was supposed to have dreamed of a white elephant the night before she gave birth. The white elephant gave her a lotus flower, the symbol of wisdom and purity. To be given a real white elephant was a blessing, but it was also a curse. It was a holy animal, a symbol of purity and royal favour, yet, for this very reason, there was no practical use for the animal, which was not allowed to work in the fields or do any other work.

As 'lord of the White Elephant', Mindon felt he had the same status as any monarch in the world. His ambition was to 'establish direct diplomatic relations between himself and the British Government without the interference of the Viceroy', who resided in India.[5] Mindon was very sensitive to breaches of protocol. He demanded respect and anyone entering his presence was required to take off his shoes. Often there were mildly humorous exchanges. General Horace Browne recorded a visit to Mindon's capital, Mandalay, in 1872: 'At the steps of the Audience Hall we had, as usual, to submit to the process of unshoeing, as our Government has not yet seen fit to make a stand against this un-Occidental custom.'[6] Browne was also wearing a hat, and a palace guard kindly asked him to take that off too. He replied, 'No, my friend, give me back my shoes, and I will take my hat off, but I am not going to uncover both ends at once.'

This mildly jocular spirit had hardened by the end of the 1870s, when a greater degree of formality and protocol prevailed in Britain's relations with foreign powers. In Asia, in particular, with its widely differing cultures, diplomats were expected by local rulers to be sensitive to the demands of custom. In 1875, Sir Douglas Forsyth, the head of the mission to Mandalay, had been asked to conform to the Burmese court etiquette and invited to remove his shoes. He complied with this request reluctantly and, afterwards, expressed his indignation. The Viceroy's government in India then gave instructions that, in future, the British Resident in Mandalay should not take off his shoes on entering an audience with the King. This was a humiliation for Mindon.[7] He refused to compromise on the issue. When Robert Shaw, the British Resident (and Francis Younghusband's uncle), was equally intransigent and refused to take off his shoes, he was barred from the palace.

The hardening of British attitudes to Burma in the 1870s formed only part of a progression towards greater imperialism. It was at this time, after all, in 1877, that Queen Victoria was given the title 'Empress of India' by Benjamin Disraeli, the British Prime Minister, whose jingoism was then highly popular. Rivalry between European powers spilled over into contests in Asia and Africa, and Burma was caught up in this competition. Lord Cranborne, who as Lord Salisbury later became prime minister, had declared as early as 1867 that it was 'of primary importance to allow no other European power to insert itself between British Burmah and China', since Britain's 'influence in that country ought to be paramount'.[8] Cranborne's view was that 'an easy communication with the multitudes who inhabit Western China' was 'an object of national importance'.

In the 1860s and 1870s, the prospect of a vast increase in trade with the hundreds of millions who were subjects of the Chinese Emperor was very alluring. Speculators and adventurers dreamed of building railways, which would connect Rangoon to western China. One of these speculators was a crank named Captain Richard Sprye who had badgered the British government with his schemes since the 1850s. British merchants were particularly enthused by the China trade. As Horace Browne wrote in his diary on 31 July 1874, 'the discovery of a north-east passage between Burma and China has long been agitating the minds of the Anglo-Burman and English mercantile world'. Captain Sprye had been the first to draw attention to this possibility. He was dubbed the 'apostle of the overland route to China', an accurate if not very pithy description. His idea was simple. As Browne observed, 'Any schoolboy with atlas in hand can demonstrate that a straight line drawn from Rangoon to the nearest point of the Chinese Empire [in Yunan province] has a length of about 500 miles, half of which lies in British territory.' The line even came to be known as 'Sprye's Route'.

The problem was that Captain Sprye had been in Burma in the 1840s and had never 'explored a single mile of the line himself'. He was the very model of an armchair general. 'From his armchair in London he glorifies himself as the . . . Lesseps of Indo-China.'[9] (Ferdinand, Vicomte de Lesseps was the French engineer who had built the Suez Canal in 1869 and who was very much an international hero of the 1870s.) For his part, Sprye had 'been riding his hobby for fifteen years or more'. He wrote 'interminable letters to every Government office in any way concerned' and was generally viewed as 'an intolerable bore'.[10]

The problem with building a railway which connected Rangoon with the populous El Dorado of western China was the terrain. The route projected may have been only 500 miles, but it would have to cross rugged, mountainous ground. It was extremely difficult territory, as Yunnan itself, the Chinese province closest to Burma, was a land of 'high mountain ridges which were over 8,000 feet even at the lowest points and whose river valleys were sheer crevasses'.[11]

The lure of Chinese riches, then as now, continued to beguile the minds of greedy entrepreneurs. All through the 1870s and early 1880s, self-appointed Burma experts, as well as the British merchant community in Rangoon more generally, were salivating at the prospect of commerce with China. 'Supposing that the entire commerce of south-west China and independent Burma were added to that of British Burma, we may conceive what a vast opening there would be for the merchants of Great Britain.' In Rangoon, merchants had already calculated that 'the Chinese provinces neighbouring Burma contained approximately 103 million inhabitants and that such a vast population was hardly touched by European commerce'. The Chinese trade in tea, silk, tobacco, sugar and oil, everybody felt, would be enormous. Already in the 1870s, the British were clamouring to do business with the 'teeming millions' of China, which was regarded as 'a nation of born traders'.[12]

The logic of trade involved Britain in Burmese affairs to a greater extent, a logic which even King Mindon acknowledged. He was only too aware of the Burmese folk tale of the python and the virgin daughter. This was about an old widow who once found a python asleep under a fig tree. For some reason, she thought it was a bewitched prince, so she brought it home for her daughter. The widow asked her virgin daughter to marry the snake, promising that it would turn into a handsome prince after the marriage. They were put together in the same bed on the wedding night. Soon the young woman cried, 'The snake is swallowing me!' The widow rushed to see her daughter and said, 'Your husband loves you; he is merely teasing you.' The snake swallowed her up to the waist. The young woman again cried, 'The snake is swallowing me!' The widow rushed in and said the same thing: 'Your husband loves you.' After another hour, the young woman had been swallowed up to her neck. She cried out for the last time, but it was too late.[13]

The Burmese King did not represent the only obstacle in Britain's path to riches in South-east Asia. There were obviously colonial rivals whose interests had to be considered. Most notably, the French were eager to be players in that region, where they had traditionally been a check on British schemes to develop relations with the native kingdoms. Colonel Edward Sladen, Commissioner of Arakan in the far west of the country, wrote an assessment of the political situation in Burma in 1885 in which he observed that it was 'somewhat strange that our own first political intercourse with the Burmese Court commenced . . . with an attempt to thwart and anticipate French interests'; in 1795, Captain Michael Symes had been sent by the East India Company to Upper Burma to strengthen 'our commercial relations' and prevent 'the French from gaining a footing in the country'.[14] The French were now consolidating their hold over Vietnam, Cambodia and Laos, causing the British to fear that their rivals would now make their influence felt in Upper Burma.

It was against this background of colonial rivalry and commercial ambition that Mindon, now in his late sixties, entered what would be his final years of illness. In October 1877 his German doctor, Dr Marfels, diagnosed that the old King was suffering from dysentery. His condition was critical, the doctor said, but there was no heir apparent, as Mindon's younger brother, who had been groomed for the succession, had been assassinated in 1866. After this botched palace coup, in which he had been lucky to escape with his life, Mindon was understandably reluctant to identify any one prince as his successor. Of course, he had more than forty sons, of widely different ages, none of whom had been educated in the role of king. The sheer number of sons and wives obviously meant that the situation would become very confused when he died. Various factions, as was often the case in courts with this type of harem structure, would coalesce around different princes and make the court a fraught place, full of intrigue and suspicion. Mindon's favourite queen, the woman he had married earliest, had died in 1872. They had been married for thirty-six years, but she had failed to give him any children. He was grief-stricken by her death, which left Hsinbyumashin, the Middle Palace Queen, as the most senior of all Mindon's wives. She had no sons, but she had daughters, and her plan was to marry one of them to a son of King Mindon by another woman, as it was customary for members of the Burmese royal family to marry their half-siblings, rather like the Ancient Egyptian royal family, or the ruling families of the Incas. The Middle Palace Queen needed to find a suitable prince to succeed Mindon, one who would be pliable and could be easily persuaded to marry her daughter.

The Burmese council of ministers, the Hlutdaw, was also scheming in those months towards the end of 1877 and through 1878. Its members would choose Mindon's successor, and they were resolved not to give the throne to any of his three eldest sons; they too wanted a pliant prince they could control. The Prince whom the Middle Palace Queen wanted also suited the council, and the twenty-year-old Thibaw was chosen by her to be the instrument of their joint ambition. There were rumours about his paternity, but they were widely assumed to be tales told by the supporters of rival princes. Thibaw's mother had been the only one of Mindon's wives who had ever been convicted of infidelity. She had been expelled from the palace thirteen years previously, in 1864, and had scandalously continued her affair with a Buddhist monk.[15] Thibaw himself had been educated in the traditions of the Buddhist priesthood, as well as being introduced to British culture at Dr Marks's Anglican School, where he enjoyed playing cricket. He was remembered for being a terrible loser who used 'unprincely language' when he was bowled out.[16]

Supayalat, the second of the Middle Queen's daughters, was the designated wife of Thibaw. She was a year younger, but, at only nineteen, she was already a forceful personality. She was described only a few years later as being a 'very violent and passionate woman, governed entirely by impulse and caprice'. She was also intensely jealous and ambitious. She duly married Thibaw and took good care of him, but if he 'looked at another woman, woe betide that unfortunate creature'.[17] Dr John Marks, the schoolteacher at whose Anglican establishment Thibaw received part of his education, remembered Supayalat as a wayward girl:

> As a child I had known her to be cruel and vindictive. Her mother knew of her weakness, and instead of correcting it she condoned it. Talking to me one day about her, she said: 'Yes, she is a bad boy. She has always been a bad boy,' using the masculine gender as a term of endearment. As far as I was able to judge, it seemed to me that the mother's idea was that by encouraging her in her badness her daughter would acquire 'authority' (*awza*).

> Supayalat, as a child, used to catch birds and then tear them limb from limb in mere wanton cruelty. It was her way of enjoying herself.[18]

The marriage between Supayalat and Thibaw was potentially disastrous – Supayalat was violent and unstable, while Thibaw was pliable and inexperienced. As 1878 progressed, confusion grew. On 18 September, James Colbeck, an Anglican missionary, was uncertain about what was happening in Mandalay: 'We did not know whether the King was alive or dead, and expected to hear a wild outburst of confusion every moment. I stayed up till the next morning at 3, and then turned in till 6 o'clock – nothing happened.' On the 28th there was yet more uncertainty. 'We are still kept in annoying suspense and do not really know for certain whether the old King is alive or dead; we believe he is dead, but the Burmese Ministers declare he is still alive and improving, and will give a Royal Reception at the end of the Burmese Lent, that is, in about fourteen days.'[19] During this time the plotting and counter-plotting continued.

On 1 October, Mindon finally died. His three eldest sons and their families had been arrested, and then released, on the dying King's orders. The funeral of the old man was stately and elaborate, and was followed by seven days of mourning. The former King Pagan led the funeral procession. He had survived his elder half-brother and was now well into his sixties. Other male members of the extended royal family escorted him, all dressed in brilliant white, the colour of sovereignty in Burma; it was also the colour of death.[20] Foreigners were now allowed to see the King's body, lying in state. They would have been impressed by the splendour of the royal palace at Mandalay. Built only in 1857, Mandalay was a new city, a profoundly Buddhist town where one man in five was a monk.[21] The palace had various 'buildings of wood, completely gilded, and with huge pillars of red lacquered wood, of various sorts, sizes, and shapes'. Visitors would have passed by the throne, in the centre of the palace, under 'a splendid canopy of glittering roofs tapering up like a card house, and having on its top a golden umbrella very elegantly wrought'.[22]

Mindon's death was followed by Thibaw's accession to the Peacock Throne. The Middle Queen had got what she had always wanted, and now her daughter was queen of Burma. Like any new rulers, the royal couple were keen to get a firmer grip on power. They knew that Thibaw, who had not been the first choice as successor of the dying King, was not widely known among the people. On 28 September, James Colbeck reported that 'a very large part of the people are in favour of the Nyaung Yan Prince – and it is also said that many of the officials favour him too'. More ominously, he also reported that 'between 60 and 70 Princes and their relatives are now in chains, badly treated and in terror of their lives'.[23] The Nyoung Yan Prince, who was nineteen years old, had escaped from the palace and was now living in the compound of the British Resident. By November, Thibaw was behaving erratically. He started to throw spears at people who offended him. It was perhaps now that he began the drinking for which he would become famous. In alcoholic matters, it appears, he had refined taste, preferring brands like Hennessy or Exshaw to cruder Burmese spirits.[24] He was, by now, a prisoner in the royal palace, as his ministers, the Hlutdaw, were watching over him, and no one was allowed to see him.[25] It was an eerie atmosphere in Mandalay, as the new year of 1879 arrived. The town itself, abounding with 'pagodas and monasteries', had never looked more impressive. The countryside around the walled city seemed at peace. From one end of the country to the other, 'every hill-top, every plain, every grove of trees, every garden, has its graceful building, in white or gold'.[26]

The calm, of course, was deceptive. The court around the King was isolated and divided. Many of the royal princes and princesses, perhaps a majority of Mindon's 110 children, were still being held captive. No one knew what would happen to them, though some suspected the worst. At the beginning of February, a firm decision was reached. The court acted quickly; between the 14th and 16th of that month, all the imprisoned princes and princesses were executed. It was taboo to spill royal blood, so the method devised was at least scrupulous. The victims were blindfolded and strangled or clubbed to death by criminals who had been released from jail expressly for this purpose. The bodies were then thrown into a ditch and trampled on by elephants to make sure they were really dead. On the night of the 16th, a Sunday, eight carts were seen carrying the bodies of the slain, which were then thrown unceremoniously into the Irrawaddy river. Altogether, thirty-one out of forty-eight of Mindon's sons and nine out of sixty-two of his daughters had been killed.[27] The number of slaughtered among Mindon's grandchildren has never been accurately established.

The people of Mandalay were outraged. The Europeans in the city were worried that they might be the next victims. Thibaw's unpredictable nature was the subject of intense worry and speculation. At first no one knew how many had been killed in the general massacre of the royal princes, with figures ranging from 60 to 250, the 'former being nearer the mark'. Colbeck himself admitted to having had a 'terrible time', but he thanked God that all the Europeans were 'safe and untouched'.[28] The massacres produced a 'wave of revulsion in Rangoon'.[29] People became increasingly resolved to do something about Burma and its mad king. By June, apart from those who lived in the compound of the British Residency, there were only two Englishmen in Mandalay: Colbeck, the chaplain and missionary, and a retired British army officer, Major Halstead, who was described as being 'of weak intellect'.[30]

There have been many theories about the massacre itself, which Thibaw consistently denied having instigated. The council of ministers must have had something to do with the final order, but some of them even denied their part in the crime. One interesting theory, bizarre and rather implausible, was that the massacre had been conceived to cover up another crime. This explanation, coming from a memorandum of the Burmese Minister of the Interior, looks like a false alibi, but it claimed that a minor prince had 'misbehaved' with some of the princesses and had planned the 'death and destruction of the Princes and Princesses' to get rid of 'all proof of his misconduct'. According to this theory, the Prince had influenced Thibaw and urged the execution of potential rivals to Thibaw's throne, as well as the various princesses he had secretly seduced.[31] A more plausible culprit was the King's mother-in-law, who was eager to consolidate the position of her daughter. Queen Supayalat still maintained her hold over Thibaw, a fact illustrated by his reluctance to acquire additional wives. To take wives and beget 'a bewildering number of children' was 'an unwritten task of the Burmese monarch'.[32] It had been customary for the King of Burma to have more wives, at least to make the 'mystic number of four Queens – of the North, South, East, and West', in addition to a number of secondary wives. One of the princes, called the Yanoung Prince, a close friend of Thibaw, encouraged the King to take three additional wives to make up the magic four. Thibaw, it appears, followed his friend's suggestion, but the Prince was promptly arrested and strangled, on the orders of Thibaw's mother-in-law. Thibaw was informed that the Prince had committed suicide with a pair of scissors. The unfortunate wives all died within a year or two. The King was told that 'one of these ladies had died of cholic, another of fever, and that a third had been found dead from violence, but that no one knew who had killed her'.[33] The court at Mandalay increasingly resembled a madhouse.

The received wisdom among historians is that the British Empire in 1879 was engaged in other disputes and crises, allowing Thibaw to pursue his lunatic career for another few years. It is true that Afghanistan and South Africa were areas of great concern during that year. As James Colbeck wrote on 11 May, if 'the Afghan war and Zulu campaign had not tied the hands of Government I suppose we should have had to move before this'.[34] Colbeck was expecting war very soon. Yet it never came. Thibaw was allowed to remain king, and, although the British would later use the massacre of the royal princes and princesses as a pretext for annexing his country, as late as the early 1880s the matter was still undecided.

Charles Bernard was made chief commissioner of British Burma, based in Rangoon, in 1880. Born in Bristol in 1837, he had been educated at Rugby School, from where he had gone into the civil service. He was a moderate, a liberal who 'put great faith in the civilizing nature of British ideals of law and order'.[35] He was in constant correspondence with the Viceroy, Lord Ripon, about the situation in Burma from 1880, but he never felt that a campaign against Thibaw would be appropriate. In July 1880, barely eighteen months after Thibaw had outraged the 'civilized world' with the massacre, Bernard was playing the cool, pragmatic official, so often influential in Her Britannic Majesty's empire. Thibaw was 'indeed a barbarian and a half mad barbarian', but the 'total value of our trade with Upper Burma is now four millions sterling a year'. Bernard quoted the 'decided belief' of his predecessor as chief commissioner in British Burma, Sir Charles Aitchison, that 'the Mandalay Court are extremely desirous to avoid an actual rupture with the British'. This belief was also shared 'by the Rangoon merchants'. Trade and the need to keep the status quo were uppermost in Bernard's mind. The next week he gleefully reported to another official in the Indian government service that 'trade with Upper Burma is going on more briskly almost than ever'. Later in the month, he told the same official that the new Liberal government in London was 'quite disposed to renew friendly relations with the Burmese Government'.[36] Gladstone's new Liberal administration, which had been formed in April 1880, was decidedly non-committal in imperial affairs. The Marquess of Ripon, the Viceroy, a Liberal who was described as being on the left of his party, wrote to Bernard from Simla, the summer capital of India, expressing his pleasure that 'there is little danger of an actual rupture with the Mandalay government at present'.

Ripon, who had been appointed viceroy by Gladstone in 1880, had been a unique child. He was born in 10 Downing Street in October 1827, when his father Viscount Goderich was prime minister. Unlike virtually every other leading politician of the day, Ripon had not been educated at an elite boarding school or at Oxford or Cambridge, so he had the luxury, some said, of being able to think for himself. In his forties, in 1874, he had converted to Roman Catholicism, whereupon he gave up being grand master of the Freemasons. More controversially, as viceroy he introduced the Ilbert Bill in India, which, if it had passed in its original form, would have allowed Indian judges to sit in judgement over Europeans. A storm of protest from the English merchant community in India ensured that it was watered down. Ripon was easy-going and progressive for the times in which he lived. This natural tolerance was expressed in very flexible politics, as Bernard, reflecting his master's tone, wrote in September 1880: 'Whatever may be King Thebaw's bad points, trade with Upper Burma flourishes much under his rule.' Again in December of that year, Bernard could complacently suggest that Thibaw appeared to 'be as peaceably inclined as ever'.[37]

What annoyed the British about Thibaw was not his mad behaviour, nor his propensity to massacre his family members; it was his threat to trade, and, more specifically, his attempt to have dealings with other colonial powers, in particular the French. In 1881, Bernard complained to Lord Ripon that Thibaw's government had established two monopolies, one of sugar and one of salt, which were 'causing disturbances of trade and loss to our merchants'.[38] Colonel Sladen gave an excellent summary of the situation in his report on the state of affairs in Burma in 1885. Thibaw had refused a treaty the British had offered him in 1882. He had then had the temerity to form 'alliances with European States, which have no interests in Burma, and whose presence on the scene, is intended . . . to menace our positions in British Burma'.[39] His attempt to secure monopolies for himself and his parasites outraged the British merchants in Rangoon and its surrounding areas. Yet in 1882 Charles Bernard was still relaxed about the prospect of war with Thibaw, and denied that the British government would 'be justified in making war' in order to 'compel a neighbouring country to reform what we think wrong in their commercial system'. He was very reluctant to fight for trade, though he acknowledged that his pacific views were not shared by the merchants in Rangoon: 'most – but not all – the merchants . . . consider that we might . . . go to war or threaten war in order to enforce observance of the treaty clause regarding trade and monopolies'. He was clear that the 'British Government does not wish to interfere with the internal government of the kingdom of Ava'. What Britain wanted was simply 'freedom of trade between and for the benefit of the two countries'. Trade between Britain and Burma, Bernard kept repeating, was 'about 4 millions sterling a year', and, as a consequence, 'any serious blow or any permanent blow to that trade would be felt in Glasgow, Liverpool and London as well as in Mandalay and Rangoon'. Even if war came, he could say that the British government 'did not intend to annex Upper Burma or to subvert the Native Government there'. That would only infuriate the Indian princes and the King of Nepal, he thought; all Bernard wanted was the 'abolition of the monopolies'.[40]

The 'men on the ground' like Bernard and the Viceroy, Lord Ripon, were measured, cool pragmatists. The real sabre-rattlers were found among the merchant community in Rangoon, where rice-traders, like the Glasgow-born Steel brothers, were already beginning to make large fortunes. Other ardent imperialists were the adventurers and journalists, who often had less actual experience of Asian and Indian affairs. There were men like Archibald Colquhoun, a former ICS engineer and now a *Times* correspondent, who, in books and pamphlets, raised the war-cry in favour of imperial expansion. To men like Colquhoun, war and trade were inevitably linked. In his crude worldview, there were only two languages in the world, war and commerce. The British 'begin with trade and we progress to war'. On the other hand the French 'begin with war, and never get beyond it'. To Colquhoun, Burma was the 'best unopened market in the world'.

Colquhoun, a bachelor in his mid-thirties, enjoyed the swashbuckling side of empire. Fond of champagne, powerfully built and sporting a walrus moustache, he was a copybook imperialist and an 'explorer of the first rank', who in 1881–2 had travelled from Canton to Bhamo in northern

Burma.[41] He also indulged in lofty thinking about strategy and geopolitics. The average civil servant, stationed in Rangoon or Simla, often did not have the time to meditate on such matters. Colquhoun believed that 'the theatre of European jealousies and rivalries has been extended from Turkey and the Levant to the China seas', which meant that the 'eastern problem of the future for England is Russia on the west and France on the east, closing in on her Indian frontiers'.[42] Trying to move public opinion in England in favour of conquering Burma, he now resuscitated the old story about Thibaw and the massacres. 'The present King of Burmah has become infamous through his many massacres,' he wrote, but even Colquhoun understood that the 'monopolies granted by the king' were a 'standing grievance to our merchants in British Burma'. This, Colquhoun saw, was an even 'more formidable indictment' against Thibaw than the 'constantly recurring massacres', which he luridly described. He played on the old themes of the China market and the nightmare of Burma 'still coquetting with France'.[43]

Thibaw thought that he understood European politics. He believed that he could play the British against other European powers. In Mandalay, once the English had departed in 1879, there remained 'a numerous colony of French and Italian' adventurers.[44] An anonymous pamphlet from 1884 expressed alarm that 'France's ambition to become a great colonial power has risen to an amazing height.'[45] The paranoia about the French grew during the early 1880s. One British army major, in a book describing the conquest of Burma, revealed that he had visited Paris in the spring of 1880 and had attended a meeting of what was called 'la société de Cochin-Chine', Cochin-China being a region in the southern part of what is now Vietnam. This meeting was not well attended. The Englishman spoke bad French but he could understand, so he claimed, that the role of the society was to act as a 'sort of private Intelligence Department not ostensibly supported by Government'. Eight years after the meeting, from his desk in London, Major Edmond Browne chronicled the 'feebly supported attempt to establish French influence at Mandalay'. The French, by the time Major Browne was writing, had failed in their attempt to extend their influence in Burma, and their failure induced a feeling of jingoism in Browne, who crowed that the 'French Government, when faced in a frank and conciliatory spirit by John Bull, were obliged to admit that his interests in Burma far exceeded their own'.[46]

In Burma's affairs, the tone in the early 1880s was more combative than it had been a decade before. This change of tone matched a change in personnel and mood. The relatively relaxed, if eccentric, Liberal Lord Ripon had been replaced as viceroy of India in 1884 by Lord Dufferin, an aristocrat of a traditional mould. Dufferin was a dreamer and a romantic. Although he had served in Gladstone's first government in 1868, he had accepted the highly desirable ambassadorship to Russia from Disraeli, the Conservative Prime Minister. As an Irish landowner, who lived well beyond his means, he was very sceptical of tenants' rights and yet, in the 1870s, Gladstone was now championing the tenants in Ireland, as a prelude to Home Rule. Dufferin, in modern terms, was an apolitical career diplomat. He had style and polish. His mother, he often boasted, had been only eighteen when he was born in 1826, and he used to say, as if to explain his eccentricities, 'You see, my mother and I were young together in the reign of George IV. We shared our youth.' This statement involved some poetic licence, as George IV had died only a week after Lord Dufferin's fourth birthday, but it is true he had a close relationship with his mother, though this was strained when she married a man who, fifteen years her junior, was only three years older than Lord Dufferin.

Later in his career, Dufferin served as ambassador in Paris, where Bertrand Russell, the British mathematician and philosopher who had just graduated from Cambridge, stayed with him in 1894. Dufferin, Russell remembered years later, was a 'delicious man – so perfect and well-rounded'. He retired in 1896, aged seventy. His contemporaries never found him so 'delicious'.[47] He was charming, they all agreed, but very spoilt. In contrast to the unusually independent-minded and home-schooled Lord Ripon, Lord Dufferin had gone through the traditional aristocratic treadmill, Eton and Christ Church, Oxford, where he never finished his degree, leaving after only two years, though he served a term as president of the Union. He had spent some years travelling, including a notable trip to Iceland and Norway, when still in his twenties. It was this trip which provided the material for his successful book *Letters from High Altitudes*, a collection of letters ostensibly written to his mother.[48]

A romantic like Dufferin was drawn to the exoticism of empire, and even though he was initially not that enthusiastic about annexing Burma, he had no real ideological opposition to expanding Britain's reach, unlike some Liberals. It was important that, when the final reckoning with Thibaw came, a man who really believed in the imperial mission should hold the reins in India. The individual temper, character and interests of the people in charge determined policy almost entirely throughout the British Empire. There simply was no master plan. There were different moods, different styles of government. Individuals had different interests; centralizing forces were often dissipated by individuals on the ground, even when powerful characters, sitting in Whitehall, were trying to shape events in the empire. More often than not, there was very little central direction from London. The nature of parliamentary government ensured that ministries came and went; policies shifted and changed, often thanks to the verdict of the ballot box, or even because of a minor Cabinet reshuffle.

The circumstances surrounding the final annexation of Burma illustrate the role that chance, the vagaries of the electoral cycle and the idiosyncrasies of personality all played in the extinction of the Burmese monarchy. By 1885, the French were keenly involved in the affairs of Upper Burma. An urgent letter that July from the secretary of the Chief Commissioner of Lower Burma to the Viceroy's government in India gave details of the scale of that French involvement. The French, it seemed, were going to build a railway financed by their government and by a company that would be set up for that purpose. The railway, the British learned, would take seven years to build and would be constructed from Mandalay down to Lower Burma. The concession would be seventy years, so it was hoped that the Burmese would finally own the railway in 1955. The second plan the French had conceived was the establishment of a bank. This bank, it was planned, which was to be called the Royal Bank of Burma, would receive capital from the French government and would be incorporated as a company, which would then raise further capital. Its function would be to lend to the Burmese King and to merchants and it would have offices in Paris, London and Mandalay. It was agreed that this august institution would lend to normal Burmese merchants at 15 per cent, while the King would get a preferential rate of 10 per cent.[49] This was a reasonably high rate even for the time (the British government could borrow at less than 4 per cent from its own lenders), but then again, Thibaw, who everyone believed had massacred more than fifty members of his own family, was not the most reliable credit risk.

The French agents in Mandalay had been busy. The British were afraid that, if both the railway and the bank went ahead, the French would then have firm control over the trade and commerce of Upper Burma and would also control the only railway line in that region. These consequences would be 'disastrous to British interests in lower Burma'. More frustratingly, the French would then be able to open up the Irrawaddy river to all international ships 'on some such footing as the Danube now is'. Something had to be done. Even Charles Bernard, the Chief Commissioner of Lower Burma, cast aside his liberal ideas of non-intervention, stating that if Thibaw's government 'threw themselves into the arms of a foreign power' the British government would be compelled to abandon the policy of non-intervention. He was pragmatic enough to realize that putting another king in Thibaw's place might not work, as the French could always influence Thibaw's successor.

It had not yet been decided to take the drastic step of annexing the country to the British Empire. The French, after subtle British diplomacy, were beginning to relent. As late as October 1885, Bernard's office informed the Viceroy's government that, although annexation had seemed like a good idea in July, the French had now been involved in 'friendly action' towards the British; it was now 'quite possible to stop short of annexation'. E. S. Symes, Bernard's secretary, argued that the 'retention of a feudatory Prince at Mandalay would have advantages over annexation'. It would, Bernard believed, be more popular with the 'Burmese race', in both Lower and Upper Burma. Keeping a feudatory prince would also be cheaper.[50] Dufferin, the Viceroy, was equally unsure about annexation and, in November, he wrote to General Sir Henry Ponsonby, Queen Victoria's private secretary, averring that the 'Empire is certainly large enough, and nothing would have induced me to have extended our territories if it could have been avoided'.[51] On 30 October Bernard's office received a curt and authoritative telegram from the Indian government:

'you will be informed directly it is settled, whether country is to be annexed or not'. Edward Sladen, the Burmese expert, who was fluent in the language, was convinced that annexation was the only answer. In his report on the political situation in Burma, written in September, he suggested that only annexation would provide 'real security against the periodical scares and uncertainties' which were so common a feature of Burmese politics. Even he recognized that this step was a last resort; annexation would not take place without 'exhausting every other course of action'. Sladen was only too conscious that the Burmese people were 'imbued with an almost superstitious veneration for the Royal Family'. He even conceded that a protectorate on the 'Hyderabad system might succeed', if, he added, 'accompanied by a military occupation of the country by British troops'.[52]

Meanwhile a campaign was being prepared. It was now obvious to British officials that the French had to be prevented from spreading their influence and that Thibaw's intention of 'coquetting with the French' had to be thwarted. What remained unclear was the outcome. Thibaw had to be removed, but the fate of the monarchy was still in the balance. It was, as so often happens, a case of 'fight now, think about the future later'. A suitable pretext for the war had arisen in the summer of 1885, when the Burmese council of ministers had imposed a large fine on the Bombay Burma Trading Corporation for illegally exporting timber from Upper Burma without paying the proper royalties to Thibaw. On 22 October an ultimatum was sent to the Burmese government which stated, among other things, that the fine should go to arbitration, and that a British resident should be received at Mandalay with 'a proper guard of honour and a steamer'. Burma in effect would be reduced to a puppet state. The Burmese refused the conditions, giving the British the excuse they wanted to begin the military campaign.[53]

The campaign itself was one of those one-sided colonial wars which have all the air of a tragicomedy. The man in charge of the expedition, Harry Prendergast, was another son of empire, having been born in India. His Burma Field Force, of which Colonel Sladen was appointed chief political officer, consisted of 10,000 troops. On 2 November, as a thunderstorm broke over Madras, a lavish dinner was held to celebrate the arrival of General Prendergast and the coming campaign. Even though it was certain that Thibaw would be crushed by the might of the British forces, the end, when it came, was sudden and unexpected. Thibaw had utterly misjudged the British. On 7 November he issued a proclamation calling for a 'holy war' against 'the English', in which he eloquently denounced 'the English Kala barbarians' who were planning to 'bring about the impairment and destruction of our religion' and the 'violation of our national traditions and customs'.[54] Subsequent history suggests that he may have been justified in his concerns about the future of his country, but the high-flown rhetoric could not save him. In late October, Sladen had been in Rangoon playing the newly invented game of lawn tennis nearly every day and going to dinner parties in the evenings. He confided in his diary on the 29th that he expected 'strenuous opposition and real hard fighting'. Some things in the history of the empire never changed. On 7 November, as Thibaw was breathing fire against the English, Sladen calmly noted in his diary that '33 years ago I was much in the same position with my regiment on board HMS Sphynx prior to the second Burmese War'. He noted hopefully that this would be 'the third and last struggle with Burmese arrogance'.[55]

The kingdom of Upper Burma was taken completely by surprise by the rapidity of the British advance. The Burmese had no time to collect and organize their forces to oppose it. On 16 November the Burmese defensive guns on both banks of the Irrawaddy were taken by a land attack, without any resistance. The next day, however, at Minhla, on the right bank of the river, the Burmese were gathered in considerable force. This position was attacked by a brigade of British Indian infantry on shore, covered by a bombardment from the river. The Burmese were decisively defeated with a loss of 170 killed and 276 taken prisoner, while many others were drowned attempting to escape by river. Harry Prendergast and his flotilla now approached Mandalay, where the General received the unconditional surrender of the Burmese government on 27 November, and the triumphant British forces entered Mandalay at three in the afternoon the following day. Thibaw was shocked by the collapse of his soldiers. Sladen walked into the palace and the council chamber where he sat down for a few minutes, while the King was informed of what had happened, after which Thibaw came to see Sladen in the council chamber. Thibaw's queen and mother-in-law were also present. Thibaw then said, 'I surrender myself and my country to you. All I ask is, don't let me be taken away suddenly. Let me have a day or two to prepare.'[56] Sladen insisted on an 'immediate departure from his capital and country'. Thibaw and his wife were sent into exile in British India, where the ex-King died in 1916, at the age of fifty-nine.

On Tuesday 8 December, less than two weeks after Thibaw had left Burma, his white elephant, the symbol of sovereignty, died. The animal had perished of 'neglect', as Sladen noted in his diary. Some, more romantically, attributed the cause of death to a broken heart. The British had 'great trouble' disposing of its corpse.[57] The animal was dragged pathetically, 'in full view of a shocked public, out of the palace gates'; this was distressing to the Burmese people, who had been brought up to believe in the elephant's near-divine status. Mandalay, a centre of Buddhist culture, had been captured. A system of learning and religious instruction had collapsed overnight. What would the British do now? As Sladen himself observed in his meticulous diary, there had been a massive reversal of fortune. On 16 December, he noted 'what ignorance and want of reason is shown in persons who expect a country just brought under a foreign yoke to settle down in a day!' He observed that a monarchy 'extending over a thousand years has been upset in a day – the whole framework of native government obliterated and brought to a sudden termination'.[58] There was still no final resolution of Burma's future. Thibaw was gone, but who, or what, would replace him remained uncertain.

9

The Road from Mandalay

The fate of Burma was decided, as in so many cases in the empire, by chance and circumstance. It happened that the new Secretary of State for India in the Conservative government was Lord Randolph Churchill, who is better known today as the father of Sir Winston. In the 1880s, however, he was a dynamic political force. Lord Randolph enjoyed one of those careers which shines brightly for an instant and then fizzles into nothingness. Yet, despite the fitful nature of his contribution to domestic British politics and the spasmodic nature of his moods and poses, his impact on the history of Burma was considerable.

After the Indian Mutiny of 1857, it had been an established principle of the British Empire not to annex other countries directly. The favoured way of dealing with native kingdoms was to preserve the façade of native rule, and so maharajas, nawabs and feudal princes were flattered and made to feel important; they were also given appropriate salaries in accordance with their status. Even if Britain exercised the ultimate authority, the sensitivities of local populations were respected. In the case of Burma, Lord Mayo, then Viceroy of India, had effectively ruled annexation out as long ago as 1869. 'The future annexation of Burmah, or any of its adjacent states, is not an event which I either contemplate or desire,' he had declared in a letter written from the summer capital at Simla. Mayo, an orthodox Conservative, who had been appointed by Disraeli, viewed 'with extreme regret any course of action which would impose on the British Government the necessity of occupation'. He did not believe that it would be expedient to incur the added cost of invading the country. Like the good Conservative he was, he simply wished that the 'status quo as regards the relations' between India 'and the kingdom of Burmah should be maintained'.[1]

This was the general attitude until the mid-1880s. It is true that hotheads in British Burma, in Rangoon especially, wanted to get rid of the Burmese monarchy and annex Upper Burma outright. The officials on the ground, however, were more cautious. By coming into the India Office, Churchill changed this situation. In 1885, Lord Randolph Churchill was only thirty-six years old. After a typical, if unspectacular, aristocratic education at Eton and Oxford, where he distinguished himself as a chess player, Lord Randolph's career in Parliament had started in 1874, when he was elected the member for Woodstock in Oxfordshire. The Woodstock seat, being practically in the grounds of Blenheim Palace, the country seat of the Spencer-Churchill family, belonged to him almost by right, but, despite his hereditary advantages, he had spent his first six years in Parliament without achieving much in the way of fame or notoriety.

After 1880, however, Lord Randolph's natural exuberance began to reveal itself. He was a brilliant mimic and satirist, who delighted in poking fun at graver, more seasoned politicians. His energy was as forceful as his mind was scattered and unfocused. In the words of his famous son, Lord Randolph was 'capable upon emergency of prolonged and vehement exertion, of manifold activities and pugnacities, of leaps and heaves beyond the common strength of men', and yet 'he suffered by reaction fits of utter exhaustion and despondency. Most people grow tired before they are over-tired. But Lord Randolph Churchill was of the temper that gallops till it falls.'[2] His attitude to Burma was more in the 'galloping' style. Without Lord Randolph, the annexation of Burma might never have occurred. As Winston Churchill wrote in his hagiography of his father, 'Lord Randolph Churchill was for annexation simple and direct.' The timid bureaucrats of the imperial service might have 'preferred the establishment of a native prince under British advice', the old policy of supporting 'native princes'. Lord Salisbury, the Conservative Prime Minister, fretted about the cost, but, in the end, 'the Secretary of State for India prevailed'.

The annexation itself was announced in a perfunctory way, in a style that was both brutal and clear: 'By command of the Queen-Empress, it is hereby notified that the territories formerly governed by King Theebaw will no longer be under his rule, but have become part of Her Majesty's dominions, and will during Her Majesty's pleasure be administered by such officers as the Viceroy and Governor-General of India may from time to time appoint.' Winston Churchill observed that it 'is one of the shortest documents of the kind on historical record'. The annexation was proclaimed on New Year's Day, 1886, a fitting present for the Queen-Empress. Lord Randolph was good enough to announce this important event at a party, as the clock, ushering in the new year, struck twelve.[3]

The comparative fluidity of British politics in the years 1885 and 1886 meant that there was no firm policy direction coming from Westminster, a political uncertainty that was a key ingredient in the development of imperial policy thousands of miles away in the Irrawaddy delta. The year 1885 witnessed two governments in London. In early June Gladstone's Liberal administration, which had been in office since 1880, was defeated in a vote of the House of Commons on an amendment the Conservatives had moved to the Liberal budget. Seventy-six Liberal MPs were absent from the vote, a sign of lax party discipline, while Charles Stewart Parnell led his cohort of Irish Nationalist MPs into the opposition lobby. An immediate election was not practicable, because the recent parliamentary reforms passed earlier in the year had not been fully implemented. Despite this lack of an election, the Conservatives immediately formed a minority government as a consequence of the Liberal defeat in the Commons. The general election which finally took place in November brought no decisive result, and so the Conservatives continued in office until the end of January 1886, when they, in turn, were defeated in a Commons vote. The ensuing Liberal government proved to be one of the shortest lived in British history, as it fell on the defeat of the Home Rule Bill for Ireland in June that same year.[4]

Against this constantly shifting background of domestic politics, a decisive character prone to bold gestures, like Randolph Churchill, could in the absence of determined opposition affect the direction of the empire. As Gladstone himself remarked, in a speech in the House of Commons at the end of January 1886, 'Parliament usually prorogues at the end of July, and meets again six months after,' which had the result that the whole of the Burma campaign had begun and ended while MPs were in their constituencies or country estates. Churchill had used the Crown's prerogative to annex the kingdom of Burma, bypassing the House of Commons.

As an MP of more than fifty years' standing, Gladstone immediately understood the significance of what had happened. The seventy-five-year-old Liberal leader knew that 'the prerogative of making peace or war is in the hands of Her Majesty', yet he appealed to the common practice and tradition of parliamentary sovereignty on the question of whether to wage war. He argued that, despite the royal prerogative, in practice matters pertaining to peace and war were for the House of Commons to decide. On the whole, 'the wars made by this country are generally, through the privileges and rights of this House, practically under an effective prior control'.[5]

Lord Randolph Churchill, by contrast, had presented the annexation of the kingdom and the prior campaign as a fait accompli. Gladstone protested vehemently against this flouting of parliamentary privilege. 'Under these circumstances, I say that we have no Parliamentary control whatever over these wars.' With regard to the hiatus of six months in the parliamentary year, the 'Indian Forces may be operating to any extent during the whole of that period'. Then there would be 'nothing for the House of Commons to do but say in the subsequent session whether they will or will not pay the bill'. Lord Randolph Churchill, by his impulsive actions, had surprised the Liberals on the opposition benches. Ever the pragmatic politician, Gladstone realized that his party had no 'power remaining, except to condemn the Government'. Other Liberal MPs followed his lead in the last weeks of January and the beginning of February 1886. The brief parliamentary debate over Burma gives an interesting insight into the dynamics of British politics in the last decades of Queen Victoria's reign.

Burma was annexed in a period during which a minority Conservative administration was in power; it is doubtful if such a decisive expansion of the British Empire would have been accomplished under a Liberal government. It is also interesting to note that, during the parliamentary debate on issues arising out of the annexation, it was Liberal MPs from Scotland and Wales who were most vocal in denouncing Randolph Churchill's bold stroke of imperial policy.

William Hunter, the MP for Aberdeen North, was a professor of Roman law at University College London. Born in 1844, he had just been elected to Parliament in 1885, at the age of forty-one. A brilliant Scottish lawyer, he began his parliamentary career by moving an amendment to a bill 'expressing regret that the revenues of India had been applied to defray the expenses of the military operations in Ava without the consent of Parliament'. With his keen lawyer's mind, Hunter spoke very bluntly about the Conservative government's latest imperial adventure. He saw that 'a great territory had been added to this Empire without the consent of the people of Burmah, and without the consent of the people of England'. More particularly, the government had 'met overwhelming defeat in Ireland, Scotland, and Wales' and there had been no parliamentary consent given to use money from the government of India against Thibaw and his cronies in Mandalay. Hunter made an impassioned plea in support of subject colonial peoples everywhere when he said that the 'Burmese people, like all other peoples, would rather bear the vices of their native rulers than the virtues of foreign officials'.[6]

Despite the creation of a new Liberal government in February 1886, the Conservative policy was not overturned. The annexation of Burma had been a major development in imperial policy. In early 1886, having failed to win a clear majority in the general election held the previous November, the Liberals were not strong enough politically to reverse the annexation proclamation. Gladstone appreciated this. His ministers and MPs were not enthusiastic about the situation which Churchill had left them and, in the House of Lords, the new Secretary of State, Lord Kimberley, beat the old Liberal anti-imperialist drum: trade was an 'unjustifiable' reason for war. One senses that Kimberley uttered through gritted teeth his pledge to 'maintain Burmah under the direct administration of the British Crown'. He very correctly observed that recently 'we have wisely made it our policy to avoid as much as possible the annexation of Native States'. The implication was clear: Churchill had not been 'wise'.[7] Yet the Liberal government was in no position to undo what Lord Randolph, in his exuberance, had done.

Some Liberal MPs in the House of Commons were more openly hostile to this latest expression of imperial adventurism than their pragmatic government. Henry Richard, MP for Merthyr Tydfil, is perhaps little remembered today and, although his statue stands proudly in the centre of his former constituency, he remains an obscure figure on the national stage. In the latter part of the nineteenth century, however, he was known not only as the 'Apostle of Peace' but also as the 'Member for Wales', so completely identified was he with the interests of that country. A Nonconformist minister, now well into his seventies, he had represented Merthyr Tydfil since 1868. He has been described as 'not only the consummate Victorian radical, but also the consummate Victorian Welshman'.[8] His intervention in the debate on Burma would provide a fitting conclusion to his legacy of liberal pacifism. He had spent his career denouncing what he called the 'war system'. 'My hope for the abatement of the war system lies in the permanent conviction of the people, rather than the policies of cabinets or the discussions of parliaments,' he once declared.

The debate on Burma was actually about whether the government of India, under the Viceroy, should pay for the campaign. As Gladstone had realized, it was difficult for Parliament to undo what had been executed under the royal prerogative. For Parliament to do this would undermine the Crown. Yet despite this constraint, Richard denounced what had happened in what would in the ensuing decades become a standard liberal critique of imperial wars. He baldly stated that 'the summary annexation' of Burma 'was an act of high-handed violence for which there is no adequate justification'. It was unjust but it was also 'an act of flagrant folly'. 'By suddenly overthrowing the existing government,' he went on, 'it looks as though we had consigned the country to . . . a prolonged anarchy.' The Liberal government, in Richard's opinion, should have 'reversed the policy as they did in Afghanistan and the Transvaal' (a reference to the second Afghan War and the Anglo-Zulu War, fought in the late 1870s). He dismissed the idea that it was Thibaw's misconduct that had caused the war. The truth was simply that 'we coveted his possessions and were determined to have them at any cost'.

Winding up his powerful speech, Henry Richard made the point which anti-imperialists have frequently made – that the costs of invading and occupying a country always exceed, often by a considerable margin, initial expectations. 'We are told it would only be £300,000. But we always begin our wars with very modest demands.' Richard pointed out that when 'we entered upon the Abyssinian War [of 1868] we were assured that the expenditure would not amount to more than £2,000,000 or £3,000,000 whereas it had not been much less than £9,000,000'. When it came to Afghanistan, Richard remembered, the same wildly over-optimistic assessment of the costs of war had been made. 'The Government said the Afghan war would cost £1,250,000 but that had swollen to £18,000,000 or £20,000,000.' What security was there 'that the Burmese War might not lead to such a sum'?[9]

The general principle of annexation worried some Liberal MPs. Although he was Scottish by birth, Lewis McIver was one of the few Liberals representing an English constituency to speak against the annexation of Burma. McIver showed some insight into the relationship the people of Burma had with their king when he observed that in 'the Burmese mind, no social scheme was conceivable without a King'. The King, in McIver's understanding of Burmese culture, was a 'semi-Divine' figure. Britain had respected these sentiments in the past. Upper Burma was, the MP observed, relatively settled. 'Nothing was to be gained by annexation which could not have been equally well secured by a strong Protectorate.' Gladstone felt he had to redirect the debate; the question before the House was about who would pay for the fait accompli, not about policy. Dr G. B. Clark, the Liberal MP for Caithness, another Scottish constituency, agreed with the honourable members 'who felt very strongly at the injustice of the war'.[10] Clark had a 'strong opinion that the war was altogether unjustifiable. It was a kind of freebooting expedition undertaken against Burmah.'[11] Perhaps, in his heart, Gladstone agreed, but he was reluctant to reverse the decisive action Lord Randolph had taken. The Liberals quietly acquiesced in a policy which had not been sanctioned by Parliament and which ran counter to the stated British policy of non-intervention in native states. This had all been due to Churchill's dramatic intervention. Churchill, like modern politicians in the war against Saddam Hussein, assumed that only the best results would ensue. He believed that, once Thibaw was gone, an administration would remain in place that would be stable and that would be amenable to British interests. He thought that it would be a 'cheap war', but the best results did not happen.[12]

Back in Burma, it was the officials on the ground who had to deal with the consequences of Churchill's bold stroke of policy. One of the first problems was what to do with the palace in Mandalay. What would it be used for, once

Thibaw and his wife had been exiled? The palace also contained many valuable objects – gorgeous jewels, finely lacquered furniture and the like. Already in February 1886, only three months after Thibaw's overthrow, tourists were rushing to see it and the various monasteries in Mandalay and the surrounding area. Many of these tourists would have taken trinkets and souvenirs from the precincts of Thibaw's palace, which had already been ransacked by soldiers in the wake of the fall of Mandalay. In 1964, the Victoria and Albert Museum in London returned 154 of these items.[13] Dufferin, as viceroy, gave strict instructions at the end of February 1886 about what should be done with the royal possessions: 'The goods in the palace at Mandalay . . . which it may be desired to dispose of, should be sold to the best advantage either at Mandalay itself, or at Calcutta, or elsewhere.' On the other hand, the high-quality pieces or, in the Viceroy's convoluted words, 'the jewellery that is not manifestly of a comparatively unimportant character' should be 'collected together and sent to England'. The goods dispatched to England also included objects whose value was not yet determined. The British government had been warned by Professor Nevil Maskelyne, the Professor of Mineralogy at Oxford, that there would be 'many priceless articles' found in the palace. The government had made a serious mistake when Ranjit Singh, the Sikh ruler, had been deposed in 1849, as many of Ranjit's treasures had been 'sold through ignorance as to their character much below their value'. This waste should not be allowed to occur again.

Professor Maskelyne believed that the Burmese palace would contain ruby, sapphire and jade specimens of great value, which would be worth retaining. The Viceroy was less sanguine but nevertheless suggested that 'the suggestions of the Professor should be carefully attended to'.[14] Dufferin, as a loyal subject of the Crown, had set aside certain jewels for 'Her Majesty the Queen' and two carved ivory tusks for the 'Prince of Wales'. He was also eager to obtain 'a good bell', if one could be procured 'without in any way offending either the feelings or the religious sentiments of the Natives'. The palace of Mandalay itself 'should be carefully preserved as a Public Building', although it might be 'desirable to transfer to England one or two of the small detached houses which, while they form no essential part of the building, are very fine representations of Burmese wooden architecture'.[15]

Alongside the difficult question of deciding which objets d'art should be sold and which taken back to England was the even more advanced problem of maintaining some semblance of internal order in the country. At the start of the occupation there was the scandal about the abuse of Burmese prisoners. When Parliament opened at the end of January 1886, MPs were already complaining of the actions of Colonel Willoughy Wallace Hooper, the Provost Marshal, a police officer in Burma who was obsessed with photography. The British authorities were then shooting prisoners in order to suppress incipient rebellion in Burma, which had been fomented by bands of young men, dacoits as they were known, still unreconciled to the British annexation of their country. The Provost Marshal wanted to capture the precise moment when the bullet actually entered a prisoner being shot. The story broke in *The Times* on 21 January. The next day, in the House of Lords, Lord Ripon, the former Viceroy and ultra-Liberal, denounced the incident as 'very outrageous'. Lord Randolph Churchill, in the Commons, adopted a pompous tone of outrage. He could not 'bring himself' to believe 'that any officer wearing the Queen's uniform would have allowed himself to perpetrate actions which really would have disgraced the officers of Thibaw'.[16] Dufferin, the current Viceroy, in February could only express his 'deep regret at the unfortunate incident which accompanied certain capital executions which were carried out at Mandalay'. Hooper's behaviour was indeed outrageous. 'The photographing by the Provost Marshal of prisoners in the act of being shot was a most lamentable occurrence.'

Dufferin countered the argument that the act of photographing people who were in the 'act of being shot' didn't actually add to their suffering. As he put it, in the dignified, rather stiff style so often used in these official documents, it is 'no good alleging that the fate of the unfortunate themselves was not aggravated, inasmuch as they were ignorant of what was happening'.[17] The problem, however, was with the policy of executions. After getting rid of Thibaw at the end of 1885, it was clear that the British had immediately adopted a policy of repression. The whole fabric of Burmese administration fell apart; the Burmese army was 'disarmed and disbanded'; the police force was 'dispersed' and there existed 'no centre of administration'.[18] There emerged, as a consequence, a movement against the British which was expressed in general lawlessness and sporadic violence. This was a guerrilla war waged against the British occupation by dacoits. The movement itself became known to the British as dacoity, an Anglicized version of the Hindi word *dakaiti*, meaning roughly 'armed robber'. To the Burmese it was a movement of resistance; to the British it was mere lawlessness. Rudyard Kipling's idealized soldiers in his *Plain Tales from the Hills* were campaigning against dacoits in Burma.

Terence Mulvaney, an Irishman, is the hero of the story 'The Taking of Lungtungpen'. Kipling's tale is interesting in the light it casts on the tough, fighting side of the empire. Mulvaney is an outstanding soldier, whose promotions are denied him because he likes 'one big drink a month'. He and his comrades get hold of a Burmese suspect whom Mulvaney, accompanied by an interpreter, beats with a cleaning rod. By this act of brutality, the soldiers find out that there is a town called Lungtungpen, nine miles away, where the insurgents are based. Mulvaney then persuades his officer not to await reinforcements, but to pay a 'visit' to Lungtungpen that night. Mulvaney and his comrades then cross a wide river ('that stream was miles wide'). When they reach the other side, it is dark. The soldiers find they have landed on the river wall of Lungtungpen. A fierce fight with Burmese insurgents follows, from which the British emerge unscathed. Still naked from swimming the river, Mulvaney and the other British soldiers charge with bayonets and the butts of their rifles and kill seventy-five Burmese men. They hold 'the most indecent parade', with only eight men wearing any clothing. The rest were 'as naked as Venus'.[19]

This may have been a fictional account, but the reality of the violence was scarcely different on the ground in Burma itself where, in the first few weeks after the occupation of Mandalay, the British, according to Grattan Geary, the editor of the *Bombay Gazette*, acted with 'a very high hand indeed, and with complete disregard of Burmese susceptibilities'. So-called dacoits, whom the Burmese would have called patriots, were 'shot out of hand' when captured. This was seen as the best option, as there were few prison places and the 'care of prisoners' was 'irksome to the soldiers'. The guerrilla attacks increased in January 1886, as the 'shootings and floggings' seem to have inflamed the Burmese population. The policy of repression was conspicuously unsuccessful. Grattan Geary, a journalist and traveller, concluded that harsh measures were ineffectual against people who could use the natural landscape in which to hide and regroup. Geary's words have resonance for the course of international history in the twentieth century. 'One grows sceptical about the tranquillizing effect of military executions on the general population. Experience seems to show that where there is a refuge at hand – mountains as in Afghanistan, deserts as in Egypt and the Soudan – an excited population will be exasperated rather than intimidated by such executions.'[20] Repression was not the answer. Geary, misquoting Shakespeare's *Henry V*, observed that 'cruelty and lenity never played for a kingdom but that the gentler gamester proved the winner'.[21] The Burmese were not going to accept the invasion of their country and the deposition of their King.

Burmese institutions were in the process of being dismantled. The issue of what to do with the Hlutdaw, or council, which advised King Thibaw, had been smouldering ever since the palace itself had been captured in November 1885. Edward Sladen, the tennis-playing army officer who was fluent in Burmese, thought that the council should remain to help the British rule Burma. Charles Bernard, the normally liberal Chief Commissioner in Rangoon, disagreed. The important feature of Bernard's liberalism was that he believed in the British mission as a civilizing one. He trusted in British ideas of law and order and sought to impose them on Upper Burma. At the end of 1885, Sladen was writing urgently to Bernard on the issue of allowing the Burmese council to take responsibility for Mandalay and the surrounding country. The council, in Sladen's view, would be part of the provisional government and would help the British in hunting down 'dacoits and dangerous characters'. Sladen and Bernard met to discuss the deteriorating situation on 20 December 1885. Bernard later gave an order which debarred the 'Hlutdaw [from] all control over the City and the suburbs'. This order, in Sladen's opinion, could not 'remain in its present form'.[22] Sladen was now quite firm. He wanted 'respectfully [to] point out that this is not a time for limiting the influence and authority of the council'. His simple argument was that it made no sense to disband the one institution in Upper Burma with any authority when the country was sliding into anarchy. Bernard, in the courteous, formal language of the late Victorian bureaucrat, was equally determined. On the same day he fired back a letter to Sladen in which he said, 'I cannot change my views'; while there were so many British troops employed and 'quartered in the City and while trade and general quiet are still so much disturbed, I must retain the control of the city in the hands of European officers . . . *under your orders* and not under the Hlutdaw [emphasis in original]'.

The next day, Sladen wrote back. He knew how important the council's influence was. 'Knowing as I do, how much this influence depends on the outer formalities of office – on the voice of the people – and on long established custom, I cannot help acknowledging the serious difficulties which must ensue' when the ministers were stripped of power and were 'irresponsible for the criminal state of the capital, in which they reside'.[23] This dispute raged between the two men during January 1886, at the very time when the dacoits were marauding through the countryside. Sladen was now relaying the deliberations of the Burmese council to Bernard, his superior, in Rangoon. The present Hlutdaw desired a 'King and a constitution based on the English monarchical form of Government'. This, the ministers felt, would enable them to restore order and allow 'trade to flourish'. It would also allow the Buddhist religion to thrive. 'Burma has for centuries been under the rule of Burmese sovereigns – it follows therefore that the people can only recognize the existence of a Hlutdaw in connection with Royalty.' The ministers believed that 'if Burma is allowed a Hlutdaw under constitutional restraints, the people will settle down, and the country be easily pacified'. This may have been special pleading, as the Burmese ministers were essentially asking to keep their jobs and status. The British, under Bernard's authority, were unwilling to satisfy the wishes of Thibaw's old ministers. The Chief Commissioner, for all his liberalism, was highly sceptical about the Burmese council's ability to keep order in Burma. In a telegram to the Indian government, he drew a contrast between the districts controlled by English officers and those managed by the Hlutdaw. In the areas controlled by the Burmese, 'the work of pacification has made no progress . . . No police have been organized.'

Bernard's telegram to the government of India on 10 January painted a gloomy picture of the situation in Upper Burma. The Hlutdaw was not to be trusted. To the south-east of Mandalay, in the Shan hills, there was a 'Prince with about 3,000 Shan and Burmese adherents'. To the north-east, there were 'bands of dacoits or rebels'. 'More cavalry' was needed, more mountain guns, more animal transport. English civil officers were needed in every important district, with soldiers, 'to direct, control and support Burman officials'. The Hlutdaw would not 'do the work properly'.[24] Bernard got his way; the Burmese council, the Hlutdaw, was abolished. At the end of February, Lord Dufferin visited Mandalay with his wife, and while he was there he 'took the opportunity of informing the Hlutdaw that the administration of Burma would at once pass under the control of British officers'. The Viceroy loftily thought it 'desirable that the Chief Commissioner should take measures for at once disabusing the whole Burmese population of the idea that there is any chance of the re-establishment of a Native Prince'. In other words, the Burmese were not going to be allowed their own king. 'They should be told that the Queen Empress is now their sovereign.'[25] In his address to the council itself, Dufferin curtly announced, 'Upper Burmah has now been permanently incorporated with the British Empire and you yourselves have definitely become the subjects of the Queen Empress and of the British Crown.'[26]

Sladen had not been successful. In some rather melancholy jottings that February, he drafted a letter in which he declared, 'I have no wish to remain – my position is untenable – my views are so opposed to those of all others.'[27] He was effectively cashiered, although, as he was aged fifty-five, the authorities suggested that he had retired voluntarily. Dufferin dismissed him as a 'foolish, vain man'.[28] The next task was simply to press on and bring the country to order. Throughout the rest of 1886, Upper Burma continued to languish in an unsettled state. Sir Charles Crosthwaite, the man who would succeed Bernard as chief commissioner in 1887, described the situation in this way: in the autumn of 1886 'the country was far from being under our control'. By July it had become obvious that a 'considerable minority of the population, to say the least, did not want us, and that until we proved our strength it was idle to expect active help even from our friends'.[29]

Crosthwaite was chosen as the strongman to replace Bernard, a liberal who had been regarded as rather weak. An arch-Conservative, who would later denounce Liberal governments, Crosthwaite was the type of robust, intellectual reactionary who belied the image of stupid army colonels running the empire. In his seventies, he was to denounce Lloyd George's budget of 1909, which first introduced old-age pensions, as 'rank socialism'. The budget would, in Crosthwaite's apocalyptic imagination, be 'the beginning of a social revolution in this country which will destroy all that is refined and beautiful in the country. The reign of cads it will be and predatory cads' too.[30] Yet for all his Colonel Blimpish bluster, Sir Charles had a keen and efficient mind. Born in 1835, he had gained a first in Classical Moderations at Oxford before entering the Indian Civil Service in 1857. His memoir of the Burma campaign, though grisly and matter of fact, is clearly written. He had literary tastes, formed by his early education in the Classics, and the Roman poet Virgil was a favourite author.

Crosthwaite understood that the invasion and annexation of Burma had been the easy part of the mission to bring Burma under the aegis of the British Empire. As we have noted, there had been only about 10,000 soldiers involved in General Prendergast's initial expedition against Thibaw. 'The work hardly occupied a month,' Crosthwaite observed in his memoir.[31] Yet, in his precise, perfunctory style, he claimed that in 'the following year the subjugation of the people by the destruction of all formidable armed resistance was effected'. This was inaccurate, if the word 'subjugation' implies the termination of all resistance. The year 1886 proved to be a difficult one, during which the need for more troops became more obvious, while it appeared that the capture of Mandalay meant nothing in itself. Burma was 'loosely organized', with the Burmese themselves being 'still free to resist and fight'.[32] The difficulty of the terrain, the wild jungles and swamps round the Irrawaddy river, made Burma an ideal place to wage a guerrilla war. Bands of young, disaffected men, 'egged on by the priests, took advantage of the rainy season, when the jungles were thick and paths impassable', to cause disruption and mischief.[33] There was a feeling that social causes underlay the revolt. In January 1886, some 700 of the dacoits had surrendered to the British on condition of a 'full pardon'. They also demanded work. Dr Marks, Thibaw's old headmaster, even suggested that the government should 'undertake some kind of gigantic measure', like building roads, to suppress the resistance movement by actually giving the young men jobs to do.[34]

Against this background of dissent and resistance, the British did what invading powers often do when faced with such opposition. They carried out a 'surge'; thousands more troops were poured into Burma. In July 1886, *The Times* of London reported that 'we have now some 30,000 troops and military police in Upper Burma', which was twice the 'highest number made before the war'. The *Times* reporter, E. K. Moylan, who generally opposed the government line in Burma, noticed that 'despite the great increase' in the number of troops, British authority did not extend 'beyond rifle-range from our fortified posts'. By the end of the year, there were 40,000 British Empire troops, both from Britain itself and from India, stationed in Burma.[35] The British showed a will and determination in the Burma campaign which would be a source of pride in the veterans, who believed that the rigours they had undergone had shown the soundness of the British soldier, proof of Britian's greatness. In no other campaign was the imperial mission so highly praised as in the Burmese annexation. To some contemporaries, the task of annexing and pacifying was a 'stupendous' one, but it was 'perhaps, the most interesting that can ever fall to a man's lot in life'. The British 'had to make a new country', so they thought, in Burma and, by acquiring this new country, there now arose an opportunity of 'employing large numbers of educated Englishmen – the best men on earth – who would probably be idle'. This, of course, was all for the benefit of the Burmans, and for the 'material good and prosperity of mankind'. 'We must go forward' or else 'we must fall back'. The author of these high imperialistic words, Major Edmond Browne, ended his exhortation to Britain's imperial manhood in fine if overblown rhetoric: 'Let us advance then, with unfaltering steps, facing manfully our mighty responsibilities, and thus fulfill our destiny upon the earth.' Prose being not quite sufficient to capture his sentiments, he then quoted Tennyson's poem, now less well known, 'Hands all round', which had been composed for Queen Victoria's sixty-third birthday in 1882:

> We've sailed wherever ship could sail,
> We've planted many a mighty State;
> Pray God our greatness may not fail
> Through craven fears of being great. [36]

Despite the high confidence and bombast, the reality of the fighting in
Burma was very tough indeed. Contemporary accounts dwell on the difficult terrain, the mosquito-ridden jungles and swamps which covered the
country. Major General Sir George White VC, who replaced Prendergast
as commander of the Upper Burma Field Force, drily remarked that the
'climatic and physical conditions in Burma during the hot weather and
rains are extremely adverse to active operations in the field'. White
complained of the 'extensive swamps, the dense jungle, the heavy rainfall
and the consequent prevalence of malarial fever' which not only hampered
the movement of troops during the campaign but also made them unable
to continue their careers 'if subjected to prolonged exposure'.[37] In their
diaries officials and soldiers described long marches in heavy rain through
paddy fields, where mosquitoes lurked 'of a size and virulence not to be
paralleled'.[38] Through the months of May to October 1886, between 100
and 150 men a month were dying just from disease. In a force of 30,000
in July, not all of whom were out in the field on campaign, this was a high
mortality rate. The soldiers had to contend with the 'ravages of cholera,
malaria, dysentery and heat apoplexy'. The British soldier's life in Burma
was, in the words of one historian, one of 'stifling heat, roads feet deep in
water, flooded rice-fields and swollen rivers'. The soldier's favourite refrain,
during this period, was 'one more river to cross'.[39]

Much has been made of the appalling conditions which soldiers faced
in the First World War, and these horrors have rightly lived on in the
popular mind. This is partly because the Great War affected a great many
people, as almost the whole population, especially after the introduction
of conscription in 1916, was mobilized. The gruelling conditions of many
of the colonial wars in the nineteenth century have been largely forgotten.
Fighting a guerrilla campaign in malarial swamps without any form of
radio or electronic communication is hard to conceive and there is no
doubt that the British professional soldier of those days was exceptionally
tough. This toughness is reflected in some of Kipling's poems, which
evince a brutality and bloody-mindedness in the attitudes of the soldiers
which often surprises modern readers.

The Burmese fought bravely, their leaders rallying the people in the
name of national resistance. Contrary to what British officials believed, the

'armed robbers' felt that they were launching a campaign of national independence. They would have called themselves nationalists if the term had then been current. In October 1887, one of the more notorious dacoit leaders, Bo Swe, was killed in a minor skirmish. His death had a big psychological impact on the resistance movement. Papers were found on his body, some of which outlined various general principles relating to the rebellion. Many of the injunctions were general military-type orders: 'Every man shall obey his superior as a cow obeys a cowherd'; every man shall 'be of one mind with his superior, whether in love or in hate'. Yet in addition to these military orders there were other instructions which unambiguously show the nationalist nature of the insurrection: 'Anyone found to have abandoned his religion, and his national traditions', and to be 'serving the rebel Kalas [the British] by acting as guide, informer, etc., shall be executed or otherwise punished by order of one in authority'.[40] The British were the 'rebels' in a sense, because they had subverted the traditional order in Burma by invading and trying to annex the country.

The natural leaders of the revolt were the princes, of whom there were still many, despite Thibaw's efforts, and the *pongyis* or Buddhist priests. U Oktama, a Buddhist priest, was another leader of the revolt: 'From February 1886 until his capture in July 1889, Oktama continued to be one of the most formidable opponents of the British Government in Upper Burma.' In the eyes of the British, he was a nuisance because of his 'systematic method of pillage'. He and his robbers for long enjoyed 'comparative immunity owing to the impassable nature of the wild forest country and the deadly malaria of the climate'. Oktama ruled a large tract of country 'without check'. In his fiefdom, he assumed the title of *mingyi*, or great minister of state. When he was finally captured, he was hanged.

In Mandalay itself, there were constant rumours of plots to overthrow the British. At the beginning of January 1887, a young prince of the royal family was brought to Mandalay and entrusted to the care of a senior Buddhist priest, the Sadaw (abbot) of the Modi Monastery. On the day the young Prince arrived a fire started in the monastery. The fire consumed about 200 houses in the southern quarter of Mandalay. This fire was interpreted by the monks as a sign of the Prince's supernatural powers. The next week messages were sent out to the Prince's supporters, who were invited to attend a meeting at the monastery, in a building untouched by the fire. The meeting was to take place on 16 January, but was postponed for two days because not everyone could make the earlier appointment. At nine in the morning of the 18th, the meeting started. One monk held a book which contained a list of the conspirators. A charmed image, said to be bullet-proof, and a horoscope were handed round.

At this bizarre gathering, plans for an attack on Mandalay were discussed. The conspirators took an oath of allegiance to the Prince. A wooden image of Buddha was steeped in a jar of water and each of the conspirators, drinking a cupful of the sacred water, took an oath, saying, 'If I fail in my allegiance to the young prince or swerve from it, may I die by the cut of a sword or the thrust of a spear.' About half the conspirators had taken the oath when the monastery was stormed by Burmese police. Twenty-three people, including the Prince and the Sadaw and six of the monks, were arrested; five escaped but one was arrested again almost immediately. Another four people, implicated in the plot, were arrested later. The police found the torn-up list of conspirators, the wooden image, the horoscope and the jar of sacred water, which was still half full. The Sadaw and nineteen of his fellow conspirators were tried and found guilty. They were sentenced to transportation for life.[41]

This failed conspiracy reflects the intense, almost mystical atmosphere that surrounds so much of the 'pacification' of Burma. The country was dominated by religion and folk superstitions. In Mandalay itself there were more than 13,000 monks, which represented nearly 10 per cent of the entire population of the city. It was against this background of rebellion, conspiracies and plots that Charles Crosthwaite became chief commissioner in March 1887. He was systematic and thorough. The measures he used to suppress or, in his own word, 'subjugate' the Burmese were harsh but effective. Looking back at his role from the relative comfort of his Surrey villa in 1912, Crosthwaite could feel satisfied that the subjugation was a job well done. The 'pacification of the country' took four years, from 1886 to 1890, and, in Crosthwaite's memory, it was 'certainly arduous work done under great difficulties of all kinds and, from the nature of the case, with less chance of recognition or distinction than of disease or death'.[42] He imposed a system of fining villages which harboured dacoits. Relatives of suspected bandits were deported. 'I have several times', commented Crosthwaite, 'brought in the wives and families of dacoits with excellent effect. As soon as these relatives were cleared out of a village, that village more or less came over to the British side and, in many cases, as soon as the relatives were sent off, the Bos [Burmese warrior-bandits] related to them surrendered unconditionally with their arms.'[43] The forced removal of relatives of combatants was a technique that would be used in the concentration camps in which Britain housed women and children during the Boer War, twelve years after the Burma campaign. Crosthwaite himself saw the direct connection between the techniques used in Burma and those used later in South Africa. He wrote to Herbert Thirkell White, his younger colleague: 'has it not struck you often how completely this S. African business has followed the different turnings of the conquest of Upper Burma? They have had to follow the methods that circumstances forced on us. Only everything is on so much larger a scale in S. Africa.' More particularly, Crosthwaite commended the use of the 'Blockhouse' system in South Africa which he had used in Burma, by which a series of simple military fortifications were used to divide the open countryside into sectors with fortified lines.[44]

More notoriously, the burning of villages was a technique which ensured that the annexation of Burma was one of the most ruthless episodes in the British imperial story. This drastic measure had been employed in the second Burma campaign of the early 1850s. Thirkell White quoted the government of India's orders, given in the 1850s, on this delicate subject: 'If a band of freebooters . . . have stockaded or fortified in any way a village, the special necessity of preventing it being turned to an evil use again will justify . . . the measure of destroying it.' This was an oblique, rather tortuous, legalistic formula which enjoined British soldiers literally to smoke out the enemy.[45]

The campaign against the Burmese was long drawn out and bitter, and many of the brutalities had absolutely no effect on the Burmese insurgents. Some of the descriptions of incidents in the campaign are striking for their cool, articulate and clear-eyed tone. Geary, the journalist, described how a 'detachment of the Naval Brigade having captured a dozen dacoits, proceeded to execute them one by one, so as to make a deeper impression on the Burmese mind than the shooting of the whole batch at a volley might produce'. Geary continued: 'The first man was placed standing with his back to a wall; a conical ball striking him between the eyes, carried off the whole top of his head, which disappeared in a strange, grotesque, unexpected way.' The reaction of the Burmese to this execution surprised the soldiers of the Naval Brigade. The executed man's comrades, 'standing near, awaiting their turns, screamed with laughter at the sight; they laughed as they went one after the other to be shot in rotation'. They treated 'the whole affair as an extraordinary joke'. The naval men 'returned to their station, much disappointed and not a little indignant'; 'shooting these dacoits, they said, was of no use, for they did not mind it in the least, they thought it great fun'.[46]

Crosthwaite's techniques were more systematic and, ultimately, more effective. The thoroughness of his work was demonstrated in a circular of 4 December 1888 to the effect that no village of fewer than twenty houses would be permitted to exist and that all such villages must be moved into the larger ones. Under this policy, about 6,000 houses were actually dismantled and re-erected; small hamlets merged into larger villages.[47] Yet there was some method in this apparent madness given that, in Crosthwaite's phrase, 'the pacification of Upper Burma was virtually complete by 1890'.[48] Resistance continued in the Chin hills till the late 1890s, but, effectively, Burma was quiet during that decade.[49] Annexation had been hugely expensive. The Liberals were right. The total cost of the annexation was about £5 million, more than twelve times the initial estimate of £300,000.[50] The human cost was also significant. To Kipling, who first saw the Irrawaddy in 1889, it was the 'River of the Lost Footsteps – the road that so many many men of my acquaintance had travelled, never to return, within the past three years'.[51] For the Burmese the annexation was a national tragedy.

As for Lord Randolph Churchill, his brief tenure at the India Office was followed by the chancellorship of the exchequer when the Conservatives returned to power in July 1886. In Burma, British officials could only express relief that he would no longer shape their destinies. 'I see that Lord Randolph Churchill will be Chancellor of the Exchequer,' one official wrote home at the end of July. 'I hope so as it will keep him from the India

Office, where we don't want him, especially we in Burma.'[52] Now chancellor, at the age of only thirty-seven, Churchill seemed an inevitable
Conservative prime minister. He overreached himself, however, by offering
to resign over increases in government expenditure in 1887. Salisbury
accepted his resignation. Churchill never held office again and died of
syphilis eight years later. The annexation of Burma was undoubtedly his
enduring legacy.

Twilight over Burma

The society that the British found in Burma was static. Upper Burma had lived under a monarchy for centuries. The Buddhist priests were numerous and well respected. After subduing the 'natives' in a tough campaign, the British had imposed themselves on Burma and now a Pax Britannica reigned over the country. In the memoirs of retired British civil servants the half-century from 1890 to 1940 was remembered as a period of 'peace and good government'.[1] Burma, in the constellation of British possessions, was no shining star. If India was the jewel in the imperial crown, Burma was nothing more than a bauble, a slight embarrassment, without glamour or pretences. To the English writer George Orwell, who served as a policeman in Burma in the 1920s, the type of British civil servant who ended up in Burma was generally socially inferior. The 'all-important thing', Orwell later wrote, 'in Burma was not whether you had been to one of the right schools but whether your skin was technically white. As a matter of fact most of the white men in Burma were not the type who in England would be called "gentlemen", although they lived like gentlemen' and 'called their evening meal "dinner"'.[2]

For the British, Burma was always a backwater. While the best and brightest Oxbridge graduates competed to get into the Indian Civil Service, Burma had little glamour or even, in Orwell's view, respectability. It was, in the words of a modern Burmese historian, 'never a place where great family fortunes or political careers were made'.[3] The British in Burma were not sentimental about their mission. Herbert Thirkell White had been involved in the pacification of Burma and was a friend of Charles Crosthwaite, the man who had completed that operation. He ended up being the lieutenant governor of Burma between 1905 and 1910, in which role he had been categorical about Britain's mission in Burma. The Burmese, he felt, were a subject people with basic political ideas. 'In Burma there is a comparatively simple social organization,' he noted in his memoirs. It was no use trying 'prematurely to impose representative institutions on people who neither demand nor understand them'. This was the eloquent voice of the imperialist in 1913, when Thirkell White's account, *A Civil Servant in Burma*, was published. 'Above all', Thirkell White warned, 'let us avoid the pernicious cant of thinking that our mission in Burma is the political education of the masses.' Bringing democracy to Burma was not part of the plan for people like Thirkell White. The British mission in Burma was 'to conserve, not to destroy, their social organism, to preserve the best element of their national life; by the maintenance of peace and order to advance the well-being of the Burmese people'.⁴ This point of view would have been shared by many in British India in 1913. In 1912, Lord Hardinge, the Viceroy, had confidently stated that there could be 'no question as to the permanency of British rule in India'.⁵

This attitude was not conducive to the spreading of liberal democracy among the population. Imperialists before 1914 were, to put it mildly, often condescending about the attributes and character of the people they had been called upon to conquer and govern. To Thirkell White, the 'Burman' lacked 'restraint'. He liked to gamble, although the lotteries which were 'exceedingly popular' were promoted for the most part by 'the intelligent Chinaman to the detriment of the guileless Burman'. Despite their guilelessness and lack of self-restraint, the 'Burmans' were 'good swimmers'. In the midst of their 'national character', which was a 'mass of inconsistencies', 'kindness and compassion' were 'noticeable virtues'. No orphan was left destitute in Burma. No stranger asked in vain for food and shelter. There was, however, always the threat of violence. The Burmese were 'quick in quarrel'; the use of the knife in these quarrels was 'lamentably common'. These 'good people' had a 'mixture of original sin', being 'gay, careless, light-hearted, with a strong if uncultured sense of humour', but 'they can be cruel and revengeful'.⁶ This description echoes, perhaps unconsciously, Kipling's famous phrase in the poem 'The White Man's Burden' in which he notoriously described the 'new-caught sullen peoples' as being 'half devil and half child', while urging the 'best' of the imperial race to take up the 'White Man's burden':

> Take up the White Man's burden –
>   Send forth the best ye breed –
> Go, bind your sons to exile
>   To serve your captives' need;
> To wait, in heavy harness,
>   On fluttered folk and wild –
> Your new-caught sullen peoples,
>   Half devil and half child.[7]

The idea that Britain would provide the law and order for Burma was a reason given for the annexation in 1885, fourteen years before Kipling's poem was first published in 1899. The benefits of British rule were obvious: 'If riches and personal comfort, protection of property, just laws, incorruptible judges and rulers, are blessings as a set-off against Utopian dreams of freedom, then Jack Burman has a happy future.' The Burmese citizen, or 'Jack Burman', now a subject of the British Crown, had no need for 'Utopian dreams of freedom'.[8] He needed law and order. The image of the Burmese as helpless children would persist right up to the granting of independence in 1948. Sir Arthur Bruce, the commercial adviser to the Governor of Burma in the 1940s, remembered that everyone thought the 'Burman, on the whole, was a happy-go-lucky sort of chap, the Irishman of the East, free with his smiles . . .'[9] British officials commented favourably on the treatment of women in Burmese society, when compared, so they believed, to other 'Eastern' cultures. To the journalist Grattan Geary, the Burmese were 'free from caste prejudices, tolerant in manners and habits'. More particularly, they allowed 'women their rightful place in social and family life'. Thirkell White observed with approval that 'many girls, especially of the richer classes, learn to read and write', making Burmese women, in his opinion, more literate than women among 'other Eastern people'. He also welcomed the fact that 'no Burmese girl marries except to please herself'.[10]

The relaxed, open nature of Burmese women meant that another danger often presented itself in the eyes of the colonial administrators. As early as 1881, Charles Bernard, the Chief Commissioner in Rangoon, was complaining that 'the habit of keeping Burmese concubines has been rife among civil officers in Burma for many years past'. The ostensible reason for prohibiting this was the smoothness of administration. In 1867, the then Chief Commissioner, Colonel Albert Fytche, had been pressured by the Bishop of Rangoon into circulating a memorandum condemning 'the practice of concubinage among civil officers' on the ground that it was 'baneful to the administration'. This circular, as is often the case, had absolutely no effect. Bernard felt that the practice could not be 'tolerated'. No officer indulging in it would be promoted. Reports were to be made of any officers 'who infringed the rule in this matter'. The problem was that these Burmese women were not hidden away: 'I am afraid that the practice of regular open concubinage still obtains among civil officers in Burma.' So young officers who came 'fresh to the province' saw what their seniors were doing and were 'apt to fall into the same habits'.[11] The threat of no promotion was actually carried out by Charles Bernard, who passed over three senior district superintendents for the job of inspector general of police, one of them – a Major Litchfield – because had 'formed and maintained immoral connections with a native of the country'. The British tended to be pragmatic about such things, however. There is no hint, in the official papers at least, of any of the 'scientific racism' or fears of 'miscegenation' which were common elsewhere in the later part of the nineteenth century. Sir Charles Crosthwaite, the arch-Conservative, who thought that Lloyd George and Churchill were cads and loathed the 1909 'People's Budget', was typically practical on the issue. Writing at the end of 1888 to Herbert Thirkell White, Crosthwaite was frank: 'There is no doubt that many men in Burma keep Burman women.' He then, in his common-sense way, pointed out that 'many men in England keep English women, and many men in India consort with Indian women but as there are more English women and as society is stronger in India than at our small stations, it is not so openly done'. Crosthwaite, perhaps unaware of Fytche's pragmatic argument against concubinage, insisted that it was not 'the duty of Government to enforce morality'. As an officer who was leading the tough campaign to pacify the country, he showed a more tender side in dealing with the issue of sexual relations between British officers and Burmese women. It was, he felt, a 'very difficult question'. The 'real evil of it' was the 'injury done to the children who are deserted in cold blood'. Crosthwaite was certain that the men needed to give 'adequate provision' for the children they sired on Burmese women. Yet it was for the 'women to complain'.[12]

The racial attitudes of the British were not based on any scientific reasoning. British imperialists were not systematic racists like the Nazis. The racism and social ostracism were reflected in crude ways such as by 'colour bars' at clubs, where only Europeans could join or be served. U Tin Tut's experience in one incident showed the petty humiliations sometimes inflicted on the natives. U Tin Tut had been educated in England at Dulwich College and Cambridge before the First World War. In the early 1920s, the Gymkhana Club at Rangoon were playing their only opponents, the garrison, at rugby football. The garrison were unable to find fifteen Europeans to make up their team, so they asked U Tin Tut to play for them. Having been commissioned into the army during the Great War and later being called to the London Bar, he was now a civil servant in Burma. More importantly, from the garrison's point of view, he had played scrum-half for Cambridge and Dulwich. During the game, everyone acknowledged that he was the best player. Afterwards, U Tin Tut was refused the use of the showers on the grounds that only Europeans could use the clubhouse.[13]

The humiliations and resentments were keenly felt by Burmese Buddhist priests, who had never fully reconciled themselves to the foreign rule of the English. Against this background of resentment and an unshakeable belief in supernatural forces, there emerged one of the strangest episodes in the history of the British Empire. At about 11.30 in the morning on 28 October 1930, Saya San, a relatively obscure former Buddhist monk in his early forties, was proclaimed king of Burma. He wore the royal clothes prescribed by ancient usage, and the gem-studded shoes; he carried a gem-encrusted sword; his retinue carried white umbrellas. Two months later, the new self-styled King of Burma entered his palace in Tharrawaddy, a town in Lower Burma, where he had a lavish breakfast with his five queens in the presence of his four ministers. The purpose of the breakfast would become apparent. Saya San was there to declare war on the British. From his ruby-studded banyan-wood lion throne, he exclaimed, 'In the name of Our Lord, and for the Church's greater glory I, Thupannaka Galon Raja, declare war upon the heathen English who have enslaved us.'

Thus began what a contemporary British civil servant observing the events described as 'one of the most extraordinary spectacles of the twentieth century'. In the words of the official British government report, Saya San's rebellion 'was undoubtedly organized to overthrow the existing Government by force of arms'. In the eyes of Maurice Collis, the British official, the scene was medieval. Collis was a brilliant Oxford Modern History graduate from the years just before 1914, which, to many Oxford-educated survivors of the First World War, seemed like a golden age. As an official serving in Burma in his mid-forties, he had perhaps failed to live up to his original promise. 'Was it a pageant . . . an historical play, some reconstruction of the twelfth century?' he asked. The Saya San rebellion would take nearly two years to suppress. The rebels, enthused by the ever-potent mixture of nationalism and religion, were largely peasants who believed in ghosts and spirits, and they killed a Mr V. H. T. Fields-Clarke of the Imperial Forest Service so that his spirit would fight on their side. In subsequent battles, the Burmese peasants fervently believed that his ghost was striding in their ranks against his former employers, the British.

Saya San's rebellion stemmed from many causes, yet at its core was the peasants' 'national dislike of a foreign government'. In Collis's liberal analysis, every 'man and woman in Burma wanted to get rid of the English Government'. They wanted this not because the 'English' were particularly 'oppressive or lacking in good qualities', but because they were 'pro-English instead of being pro-Burman'.[14] Collis's use of the term 'English' is characteristic in that the terms 'English' and 'British' were used interchangeably in the years before the outbreak of the Second World War.

The Burmese peasants, the followers of Saya San, believed in the power of the mind over the body. The mind, according to Buddhist ideas, could make the body invulnerable to violence and pain. Magic, it was widely thought, could be used to great effect in the fight against British imperialism. By the proper use of pills, oils, chants and cabbalistic signs, the

Burmese peasant soldier, so he believed, would have an infallible protection against the weapons of the white man. All over the country, brave Burmese peasant warriors charged against machine guns chanting magical formulas or holding amulets, or in their credulity they would point to aeroplanes in the sky in the vain expectation that these would come crashing down.[15] From the very beginning, Saya San's rebellion was nationalist in inspiration. The symbolism of the coronation, the ritualistic declaration of war and the role of the Buddhist clergy all pointed to this interpretation. One of Saya San's lieutenants, who called himself the 'Holy Lion', put the matter plainly: 'Burma is meant only for Burmans; but the heretics took away King Thibaw by force and robbed him of Burma.' It was interesting that the Holy Lion mentioned King Thibaw, who had been removed forty-six years before and had now been dead for over fifteen. The heretics, the Holy Lion continued, 'have ruined our race and our religion and now have the effrontery to call us rebels. The heathen English are the rebels. We have never robbed another's country.'

The nationalist motive, in the context of the 1930s, was modern, but the means by which the Burmese peasants sought to realize their ambitions was ancient. Shwé Yon, the 'Great Doctor', assured the peasants that the amulets they wore would make them 'sword- and gun-proof'. The Great Doctor also gave them a gong, which he said 'has magic power. Wish for what you want and sound this gong. When you meet Government troops, sound it and they will be stupefied.' All this excitement proved too much for Collis, a liberal intellectual, educated in the best traditions of Rugby and Oxford. The 'East can be too exotic', he wrote. 'There comes a time when one longs for the buttercups and the hedges of May. I sailed for home on 30th April 1931.'[16] The Burmese rebels did not have this option, as they were fighting an uneven contest for their independence. Their motives were patriotic, even if their methods were crude and ineffectual.

The Saya San rebellion spread to about twelve of the forty districts of British Burma. Saya San himself continued to be the charismatic figurehead of this little-known and now almost forgotten uprising. Among his followers, the priest-king was believed to be invulnerable and even invisible. Belief in magic was so strong that, if a tattooed comrade was injured or killed by the white man's bullets, the fault obviously lay with the bad design of the tattoo, and not with the actual bullets. Any failure, as far as the Burmese peasant warriors were aware, was caused by bad magic, not by the uselessness of magic itself. The British, perhaps unsurprisingly, managed to rise above the magic charms of the Burmese priesthood and imposed order on Burma by means of their military forces. In eighteen months, 3,000 rebels were killed or wounded. Perhaps 9,000 more were captured and arrested; 350 were tried and convicted, of whom about 130 were hanged. British troops had to be brought from India.[17] Saya San himself, it is said, went to the scaffold with his head erect. He was, as could only be expected, covered in tattoos from head to foot. He was hanged, along with other rebel leaders, in November 1931.[18]

The Saya San rebellion was driven by a powerful mixture of nationalist fervour and religious enthusiasm. The average Burmese still thought in terms of the revival or restoration of the monarchy. A king was, to many Burmese, the only suitable substitute for British rule. Saya San was a *pongyi*, a Buddhist monk, who had been involved in nationalist plots throughout the 1920s. His rebellion showed considerable skill in organization and propaganda, and his brief success revealed a constant thread in Britain's association with Burma. From the beginning of British rule, there had been a shift away from traditional symbols of authority, but, although the Burmese monarchy had been destroyed, the people of Burma still remained almost mystically attached to the idea of kingship. The nationalist movement, even in the 1930s, harked back to the quasi-mythical and romantic world of Burmese priests and kings. The rebellion of 1930–1 also showed the powerful sway that nationalism held over the peasants who linked their patriotic pride to the 'military and political achievements of Burmese kings and generals'.[19]

While Saya San and his adherents had posed no real threat to the British administration in Burma, the Second World War constituted a far greater threat. The Japanese, by their occupation of large parts of the British Empire in South-east Asia, hastened the end of that empire. The fall of Singapore on 15 February 1942 was a massive blow to British pride and prestige: Churchill famously called it 'the worst disaster and largest capitulation in British history'.[20] Yet the Japanese troops had actually launched bombing raids on Burmese territory on 9 December 1941, only two days after the Pearl Harbor attack, and long before the capture of Singapore. As one member of the Indian Civil Service, himself a veteran of the British army in France in the First World War, remembered, 'Rangoon's Christmas present from Nippon duly arrived in the shape of eighty bombers and twenty fighters.' The year 1941 ended with a massive exodus from Rangoon. The effect of 'the Christmas present from Nippon', the bombing raids, was to terrify the city. There followed the general dispersal of 'half a million people', 'three-fifths of whom were Indians'. One of the consequences of British involvement with Burma had been a large immigration of Indian workers. Without them, activity in the port of Rangoon 'came to a full stop'.

The ordinary course of life in Rangoon had been rudely interrupted. 'Public transport had ceased to function'; shops were shut; trade was at a standstill. The decision to get out of Burma was taken by General Sir Harold Alexander, the General Officer Commanding, who said years later to one of the British civil servants who had escaped from Rangoon, 'Quite simply, as I realized the Japs were in danger of cutting our line of retreat unless we moved fast out of Rangoon, there was the likelihood of another Singapore. Hence the decision to press the button and get out.' The departure from Rangoon was planned and orderly, in so far as these things ever can be. The city was blown up, in line with 'carefully prepared plans'. The power station and telegraph buildings were principal targets of controlled explosions. For those fleeing the city it was 'an eerie drive back through the deserted streets of Rangoon's suburbs'. The Japanese enemy was on the move. 'At any moment turning a corner one expected a burst of Jap machine gun fire from advance parties moving in to the capture of a great city.' To those fleeing Rangoon, the city itself was a sad and unforgettable sight. The power station was now ablaze; the warehouses in the port were charred and blackened shells; the telephone exchange and the telegraph office had collapsed in smoke and ruins.[21]

Most British eyewitness accounts agree that the fall of Rangoon and the Japanese occupation of Burma inflicted an 'acute jolt' on the Burmese way of life, as well as a blow to British prestige.[22] Rangoon itself finally fell into Japanese hands on 7 March 1942. Its fall had been a typical example of British imperial overstretch, as it was 'not possible for the British to be strong in South East Asia while fighting a desperate battle for survival in the West'. The government of Burma was 'deeply humiliated by the way in which the civil authorities had been unceremoniously bundled out'. The fighting, not least in central Burma for control of the oilfields, had left devastation. The 'only safe assumption that could be made', observed Arthur Bruce, was that the scene, if the British returned, would be 'one of nearly total ruin so far as the industrial economy of the country was concerned'.[23]

The speedy collapse of British power in Burma had 'given Burmese officials confidence'. The cause of Burmese nationalism, which had been espoused by Thibaw and Saya San, was inadvertently promoted by the partial collapse of British power in South-east Asia in the face of Japan, which was, in the racial thinking of the time, an Asiatic power. The exit of British officials in 1942 created a space in the administration which the Burmese, under their Japanese overlords, began to fill. To the newly empowered Burmese, 'there was no good reason why, after the war, they should not continue to administer the country', which they were 'confident of their ability to do successfully'.[24] Despite this new confidence, the Burmese suffered many ordeals under the Japanese occupation. It is true that the Japanese granted Burma independence in August 1943, but the new entity was a puppet state of Japan, recognized only by Japan and its Second World War allies, and the Japanese continued to force indigenous Burmese to work on the notorious Burma–Siam railway, where the daily death rate has been estimated to be 'as high as 80,000'.[25]

As the Second World War entered its final stages at the end of 1944, Burma was the scene of a successful British military campaign undertaken by Lieutenant General Sir William Slim's Fourteenth Army, which finally captured Rangoon on 3 May 1945.[26] By the end of the Japanese occupation, Burma had changed to an extent which members of the British expatriate community immediately acknowleged when they returned in 1945. A professor of history at Rangoon University, B. R. Pearn, commented that Burma 'had suffered more from the effects of war than any other part of South-East Asia'. In Rangoon itself, 'economic life was at a standstill; no trams or buses were running; the water and sewage systems were out of action'. Burma had essentially been contended for twice: in 1942 the country had been fought over from south to north; in 1944–5 it had been fought over again, this time from north to south, in a campaign that comprised the 'biggest land operations conducted against the Japanese in any theatre' of the war. The collapse of the rice trade, Burma's most important export crop, had reduced the country to a very straitened condition. Before the war, Burma had been the biggest exporter of rice in the world, sending abroad more than 3 million tons a year, half of which went to India. India was so dependent on rice from Burma that the loss of this source of rice proved to be an aggravating factor in the appalling famine in Bengal in 1943, in which it is estimated that 3 million people died.[27]

In October 1945, at the start of the new academic year, when Pearn found himself the 'solitary non-Burmese member' of the staff at Rangoon University, he found that conditions within the university had completely changed. He complained that 'British standards of work and discipline . . . were no longer respected.' Sir Hubert Rance, who would be the governor of Burma for a short time in 1946–7, noticed that 'a great many changes had taken place in Burma', changes which 'perhaps had not been properly appreciated by the planners in Simla'.[28] Simla, the summer capital of British India, was the location to which the government of Burma under Sir Reginald Dorman-Smith, the Governor, had retreated after the humiliation of the first part of 1942. The altered political climate in Britain, where Labour had won an historic landslide victory in the general election of July 1945, also affected the mood. To traditional Tories like Dorman-Smith, the world had changed immeasurably in a very short time. Dorman-Smith had been born in 1899 in Ireland and, after Harrow and Sandhurst, had distinguished himself by becoming president of the National Farmers' Union at the age of thirty-two, which he used as a springboard to a political career. He had been elected to the House of Commons as a Conservative in 1935, and served briefly as minister for agriculture, before being sent out to Burma as governor, where, it was assumed, his agricultural background would prove useful.[29]

Dorman-Smith was a self-styled Colonel Blimp. In December 1942, Leopold Amery, the Conservative Secretary of State for India, had written a couple of letters to Dorman-Smith expressing their shared attitude to Burma and the fate of the British Empire. In the first letter Amery voiced concern about the ambitions of America and China in Burma: 'Why should these foreigners poke their noses into the British Empire?' In the second he boasted to Dorman-Smith that he was 'at least as Colonel Blimpish as you are'. Amery was a small man, and some said he made up for this by being pugnacious. In the letter he went on to say that he was 'not at all prepared that anyone, Yank or Chink, should poke either projecting or flat noses into the problem of the reconstitution of Burma'.[30] Of course by 1945 the 'Yanks and Chinks' were immeasurably more powerful than they had been in 1886, when Burma had been annexed.

It was not only foreign powers, alien to Burma, that were threatening to 'poke their noses' into Burmese affairs. Significant numbers of Burmese were now beginning to assert themselves in their attempts to win independence from the British. The precipitate collapse of the British position in 1942 was matched by an equally rapid disintegration after the war. Dorman-Smith, although governor, was now subordinate to Lord Mountbatten who had become the supreme Allied commander of the new South-East Asia Command in November 1943. As Mountbatten became a significant player in the region's affairs, it was apparent that the likes of Dorman-Smith and Leo Amery would no longer be dominant figures in determining Burma's future. The Labour victory in 1945 meant that traditional Conservative politicians would, for a period at least, be sidelined. Dorman-Smith himself was summarily dismissed when he went to see Fred Pethick-Lawrence, Labour's secretary of state for India. Dorman-Smith returned to his room at the Burma Office in Whitehall and tersely informed Tom Hughes, an official in the Governor's Office, 'I've been sacked.'[31]

Mountbatten, in contrast to Conservative Party men like Leo Amery and Reginald Dorman-Smith, saw himself as a thrusting, youthful and modern figure who had no bleary-eyed sentimentality about the British Empire. In an interview with the BBC given in early 1969, he portrayed himself as a pro-Burmese figure. He contrasted his liberal attitudes to the views of those 'Civil Affairs officers' who had run Burma before the war. They were keen, Mountbatten claimed, to keep power from the Burmese.

This, of course, was partly true. Churchill himself had declared in 1942 that he had not been appointed the King's first minister 'in order to preside over the liquidation of the British Empire'.[32] Amery and Dorman-Smith agreed with these sentiments, while Mountbatten boasted of his more progressive attitudes. His career was greatly helped by the fact that the Labour government, after the war was over, believed him to be a sympathetic figure, untrammelled by the hidebound Conservatism which they believed would block Britain's path to a new, brighter future. Mountbatten, distantly related to the British royal family and uncle of the man who would marry the future Queen of England in 1947, considered himself grand enough not to be influenced by what he might well have believed to be the cheap, late Victorian music-hall rhetoric of empire. He dealt in power; he had a clear grasp, so he thought, of reality.

In the eyes of those British officials who deplored the end of empire, Mountbatten was the author of many of the subsequent misfortunes inflicted on Burma. He decided to arm and support the AFPFL, the rather long-windedly titled Anti-Fascist People's Freedom League, headed by Aung San, a remarkable young guerrilla leader, only thirty years old. To the hard right, this was the essence of Burma's tragedy after the war. 'In May 1945,' as Sir Arthur Bruce, a director of Wallace Brothers, the well-known finance company which operated in South-east Asia, remembered it, 'the British in Burma were in a position of absolute supremacy – all powerful, all conquering.' How did this change? 'How was it that, within two years, they were forced . . . to hand over effective control to a band of young communists, wholly inexperienced in the arts of government or the ways of commerce and industry?'[33] These 'young communists' were, in Bruce's view, the source of all Burma's subsequent problems.

Whatever the view of the young communists of the AFPFL and Aung San, they had simply stepped into a vacuum which had been created by the circumstances of Burma's history. The monarchy had been abolished. The court and religious authorities had been largely eradicated or marginalized. The British had successfully stamped their authority on Burma, but then this authority had itself been removed by force when the Japanese tanks rolled into Burma at the beginning of 1942. The consequence of these grave upheavals in a period of less than sixty years ensured that there were no leaders of Burmese society. This was noticed by the British officials themselves, such as Bruce, the businessman imperialist, who observed that the circumstances prevailing in Burma were 'unique': Burma had an extraordinary social structure; it had 'no natural leaders, civil or military, no indigenous sources of capital . . . no native experience of the arts of government'. In Burma proper, as distinct from the Shan states on Burma's frontier, there was 'no princely or natural ruling class of any kind'. There was 'no aristocratic or patrician class'.[34] This had been caused by the systematic nature of the pacification sixty years before. Burmese historians would claim that it was the imperialism of both Britain and Japan that had created the power vacuum and the opportunity for the young communists to seize power. Sir Charles Crosthwaite in the late 1880s, together with the Japanese brutalities of the 1940s, had eliminated the 'natural leaders' of Burma.[35]

The young men, often described as the communists of the Anti-Fascist People's Freedom League, did not see themselves as communists. They were more akin to student socialists, young men who had read a smattering of Western political theory and who enjoyed debating at Rangoon University in the 1930s. Aung San emerged as the leader of this group. He had been born in 1915 and had graduated from Rangoon University in 1938. He was a student activist who had only recently gone into politics, and at Rangoon University in the 1930s, as a young nationalist, he was influenced by the usual texts written by revolutionary socialists like Marx, Lenin, Stalin and Trotsky; he also paid attention to the apparently successful movements led by Mussolini and Hitler. After throwing in his lot with the Japanese, Aung San went briefly to Tokyo where he was trained and entertained as a useful ally against British imperialism. At the end of March 1945, in an opportunistic move, Aung San turned on his Japanese friends. Mountbatten's decision to welcome him and his force, the newly christened Burma National Army, or BNA, as an ally against the Japanese infuriated the Supreme Allied Commander's Conservative opponents.

It is difficult to see how Mountbatten could have acted differently. Aung San's movement had the support of the people of Burma, although some perhaps doubted how deep that really was. It was a nationalist movement, but the ideas inspiring it seemed shallow and superficial, and its vaunted socialism was more a rhetorical ideal than a systematic programme. Aung San's speeches of the time were little more than student debating exercises. He delivered one at the meeting of the East and West Association on

29 August 1945 at Rangoon's City Hall. On this occasion he described the 'feudal' system that had existed in Burma before the British came. He acknowledged that British capital had been poured into the country and that railways and roads had been built. He talked in general terms about the 'humanizing influence of Buddhism'. But there was little in the speech that he wouldn't have heard in the debates at Rangoon University.[36] The student warrior-thinker's political philosophy may have been trite and unoriginal, but it is undeniable that Aung San possessed charisma. Small, with high cheekbones and deep-set eyes, he cut a pretty 'insignificant' figure in terms of physical presence. Yet he managed to charm Mountbatten when they met at the latter's headquarters in Kandy, Sri Lanka, at the beginning of September 1945. With his cropped hair and simple Japanese soldier's uniform, he portrayed himself as a man of destiny, the man to bring peace and independence to Burma. A common theme in the memoirs of British officials was a comparison of Aung San with Louis Botha, the South African Boer leader who was reconciled to the British and became the first prime minister of the Union of South Africa, under the flag of the British Empire. Tom Hughes, the British civil servant based in the Governor's Office in Rangoon, remarked that Mountbatten 'continued to placate Aung San by treating him as Botha had been treated in South Africa, i.e. as an ex-rebel who had seen the light'. Sir Arthur Bruce, the Rangoon-based bank director, in his no-nonsense way thought that the analogy was ridiculous. 'Lord Mountbatten, drawing what might be thought a ludicrously false analogy between Boer Leaders [Jan] Smuts and Botha and a small group of communist extremists led by Aung San, disregarded the advice of the men who were competent to know and decided to support Aung San both militarily and by implication politically.'[37]

To Sir Arthur Bruce and other officials who were now 'disturbed that the A.F.P.F.L. was rapidly assuming the mantle of the only political party in Burma', Aung San was no Jan Smuts. He was, in the staunch view of Bruce, 'the leader of a band of Maoist revolutionaries – men who were determined to seize power, and who were well aware that power resides in the barrel of a gun'.[38] John Wise, the counsellor to the Governor of Burma from 1940 to 1946, agreed that Aung San was the wrong man to be entrusted with the future of Burma. He felt that Burma's tragedy was that 'decisions on . . . vital questions came to be dealt with in the end by persons who were unfamiliar with the old political scene'. These new people 'were unduly swayed by the somewhat tarnished glamour of the active resistance fighters'. He held Mountbatten responsible for throwing his 'powerful influence behind the rise to supremacy of a party which was basically undemocratic and traditionally hostile to the British'.[39]

Many British officials such as the Chief Civil Affairs Officer, Major General C. F. B. Pearce, were alarmed by the rise of Aung San, the young man who had enjoyed such a meteoric political ascent. The Burmese politicians whom the thirty-year-old superseded were also incensed. One politician who had dominated Burmese politics in the 1930s was U Saw. He and Aung San were 'uneasy bedfellows'. Aung San had made it known that he would never accept U Saw as leader.[40] U Saw was a lawyer who had defended Saya San, the priest-king, at his trial in 1931, and had been a prominent figure at a time when Aung San was still struggling with Karl Marx's theories at Rangoon University in the 1930s. He had been born into an affluent family in 1900, and in 1945 felt, not unreasonably, that he had a good claim to be leader of an independent Burma. The rivalries between the foremost figures in the Burmese independence movement often spilled over into acts of violence. At about 3.30 on the afternoon of 21 September 1946, U Saw emerged from the Governor's Office and went to the offices of the paper he owned, the *Sun*. At 4.30, he left with a driver, in his own car. Two members of his political party followed in another car. As this small convoy approached a roundabout, U Saw noticed four men, all dressed in uniform, in a jeep which was advancing towards him. He then spotted the muzzle of a gun pointing at his car. There was a shot; a bullet passed through the back of the car. The driver stopped and the jeep sped off. U Saw had not been hit, but the broken glass had cut him very badly about the face and eyes, and he was taken to the General Hospital. U Saw was convinced that his assailants were members of Aung San's AFPFL. Sir Hubert Rance, the governor who had replaced Dorman-Smith, visited the injured man in hospital. The Burmese politician was angry and said that he knew to which party his would-be assassins belonged. He would get even with them one day, even if it meant that 'he had to swing for it'.[41] Aung San, some days later and after being urged by the Governor, visited U Saw in hospital and publicly denounced the attack, but the rift between the two political leaders was there for all to see.[42]

Meanwhile the cause of Burmese independence progressed at a steady pace. In the first week of September 1946, the police in Rangoon and the surrounding districts went on strike. Morale within the force was low, as there had been rampant inflation which destroyed the value of the low wages the policemen earned. The next week other public servants went on strike. It was believed that Aung San and his party were behind these events. The situation in Burma was growing more volatile, and in November 1946 the Governor informed the Secretary of State for India and Burma that 'unless Her Majesty's Government can be brought into direct touch with Burmese politicians, new and novel methods of embarrassing Her Majesty's Government will continue to arise'.[43] It was therefore decided that a Burmese delegation should be sent to London in January 1947 to enter into talks with the British government.

Labour's first secretary of state for India and Burma, after their election victory in 1945 and until April 1947, was Lord Pethick-Lawrence. He had been born plain Fred Lawrence but had added his wife's maiden name to his own, at her insistence. Pethick-Lawrence was now seventy-five and had converted to socialism, again under his wife's influence. Emmeline Pethick had met Fred Lawrence as long ago as 1899, but refused to marry him until he became a socialist. This duly happened in 1901. They had devoted their lives to the usual array of radical causes: women's suffrage, birth control, world peace. When his wife was arrested, Lawrence had caused immense amusement in Edwardian London for pledging the suffragette cause £5 for every day his wife was held in prison. This generous gesture was wilfully misinterpreted as a sign that he was willing to pay to keep his wife behind bars. First elected to the House of Commons in 1923 as a Labour MP, Lawrence himself was a rich man whose 'grandfather and father had made their fortune', remembered one Labour politician, 'in Victorian days by building thousands of those sorts of houses seen from the train on coming into London from Dover or Portsmouth'.[44] Their money had paid for the young Fred Lawrence to attend Eton where, as captain of the Oppidans, the same position at the school which Curzon had held, he had welcomed Gladstone on a visit to the school in 1891; he went on to Trinity College, Cambridge, where he took firsts in both Mathematics and Natural Sciences.[45]

Despite his impressive academic credentials, Pethick-Lawrence showed little curiosity about his political office. The Labour Party, preoccupied with the fate of India, was perhaps not as absorbed in Burma's affairs. Pethick-Lawrence visited India in the spring of 1946, but had been unable to accept the Governor's offer to extend the trip to Burma.[46] The London conference at the beginning of 1947, which set the terms for independence the following year, simply consolidated Aung San's prestige. Ever the ardent intellectual, his first port of call when he arrived in London had been the bookshop, Foyle's, on the Charing Cross Road. U Saw had flown to London on a different flight, such was the bad feeling between him and Aung San's AFPFL. Aung San himself had been in poor health, and there had been doubts that he would be able to stand up to the 'rigours of an English winter'. Yet the visit was a success. Aung San by this time knew English quite well, although he never spoke the language fluently. He held a reception at Lancaster House at which various Labour MPs paid him their respects. He told them, 'Colonies and a Labour government were a contradiction in terms.' At a dinner at the Dorchester Hotel, the Labour Foreign Secretary, Ernest Bevin, regaled his Burmese guests with stories about the Agadir crisis in 1911 provoked by the deployment of a German gunboat to the Moroccan port, when he had been told by Whitehall to 'settle a South Wales Docks strike that night' in view of the 'serious international situation'.[47]

Back in Burma, Aung San's party swept to power in the elections that took place there in April 1947. There were still many unresolved issues. David Rees-Williams, a minister in the Colonial Office, had travelled out to the country in March, where a pressing issue was the question of the frontier areas inhabited by various hill tribes who were not ethnic Burmese. These included the Shan and the Karen peoples (the Karens had remained loyal to the British during the Japanese occupation). These areas, 'lying in a horseshoe to the east, north and west of ministerial Burma, comprised . . . 47% of the total area of Burma'. They included 2.4 million people, or 16

per cent of the population. After 1945, as Burma was edging towards independence, the question of the frontier areas became 'acute', as Rees-Williams
put it.[48] The idea of setting up an independent Karen state was also mooted
at the time, but this was dismissed as a 'beautiful pipe-dream'. In the midst
of these disputes, Aung San, the great national leader, was seen as the man
who could keep the country together. Conditions in Burma and the frontier areas were now chaotic. The war had destroyed the economy and
infrastructure of the country. New political forces had emerged, and the
Karens feared that, with the British gone, and with a resurgent Burmese
nationalism, they would be oppressed by the ethnic Burmese. Rees-Williams
had been sent out to Burma to head a Frontier Areas Committee of Enquiry
to try and settle this latest issue. The secretary of his committee was a
Cambridge Classics graduate named Bernard Ledwidge, a 'clever, tall and
plump young man who spoke with a drawl' and who irritated Rees-Williams
by his insouciant manner. 'His usual daytime wear was a blue shirt, khaki
shorts and a pair of pink ankle socks.'[49] Even at the most tense moments,
English eccentricity and sangfroid seemed to prevail in the far-flung
outposts of empire. Ledwidge's 'style of dress and his languid manner' also
infuriated 'the Governor who thought it an insult to Government House'.
These vexing characteristics did no apparent harm to the young man's career
and, as ambassador to France in the 1960s and to Israel in the 1970s,
Ledwidge enjoyed a successful Foreign Office career.

The Frontier Areas Committee achieved little. The Burmese, above all
Aung San, were not prepared to give the Karens and other tribes the
freedoms they themselves sought from the British. Aung San continued to
be the dominant figure; he was a conciliator but he was also a Burmese
nationalist. His party had won a crushing victory in the April elections,
and, despite the deep divisions within the country, he was the one leader
everybody could rally round. There were signs of danger. On 16 July, the
Governor of Burma, Sir Hubert Rance, spoke to Aung San, telling the
young independence leader about a rumour that U Saw was concealing
arms in the lake close to his house. The Governor even suggested that the
lake should be dredged. Rance himself remembers that Aung San was on
'tremendous form' that day. Three days later, on the morning of 19 July,
the Executive Council (the pre-independence Cabinet) was sitting in its

usual place, in the council chamber on the first floor of the Secretariat in Rangoon. At 10.40 a.m., four armed men dressed in military uniform entered the chamber and sprayed the room with bursts of gunfire. One survivor described how Aung San stood up and received the first burst of fire: he would die like a soldier. The next day U Saw was taken into custody. Seven members of the Executive Council, including Aung San, had been killed. It was Aung San's death, however, which moved the nation and, in the years that followed independence, many Burmese and some British have believed that Burma's subsequent tragedies, the civil war which immediately followed independence and the military dictatorship, stemmed from this tragedy. Sir Hubert Rance remembered Aung San as 'a very young man', still only thirty-two when he died. He was shy and reserved but 'when he laughed his whole face lit up'. Rance asked in his memoirs whether, if Aung San and his associates had lived, 'Burma's troubles in 1949 and succeeding years [would] have arisen'. Rance thought not. Philip Nash, in a BBC Third Programme broadcast in 1952 entitled *U Aung San – A Study in Leadership*, described the young leader as a 'remarkable man'. If he had lived, Nash concluded, 'Burma would not have been engulfed so soon or so deeply in the civil disturbances which followed so quickly after independence.'[50]

U Saw and eight associates were tried and found guilty of murder on 30 December 1947. U Saw and five others were executed the following May. By then, the country was independent. Independence Day had been scheduled for 6 January 1948, the date that Attlee had announced to the House of Commons at the end of October, but 'every astrologer in Burma wrote to the press stressing [that] the 6th was the most inauspicious day'. After a meeting of astrologers, 4 January at 4.20 a.m. was declared to be ideal. Attlee then complied with the astrologers' demands and announced that, for technical reasons, the date had changed. The Governor and his wife inspected the farewell military parade that took place at 6.30 that morning. He and his wife then drove through the crowded streets of Rangoon to the docks, where they prepared to embark on HMS *Birmingham*. The name of the ship was mildly ironic. Birmingham had been the industrial city Randolph Churchill had sought to capture as the candidate in the 1885 election; he failed to win there, but was returned instead for South Paddington.

The day of Burma's independence was for the left-wing *New Statesman* journalist Dorothy Woodman the 'most memorable day' of her life. For Sir Arthur Bruce, that day was only 'the prelude to a desperate Civil War, followed eventually by the suppression of all civil liberties under the military dictatorship of today'.[51] To Bruce, in his retirement, Burma seemed to be 'friendless, creditless, internationally bankrupt, living in a state of sullen isolation, totally withdrawn from what used to be described as the comity of nations'. He wrote those words in 1972.

They are still partially true forty years later, with the only modifying circumstance being the growing prosperity of China, of which modern Burma is little more than a client state. Modern Burma, by any reckoning, has been a disappointment. Civil war between the frontier tribes and the Burmese government raged after independence. In 1965 *Time* magazine could report that 'Burma's countryside has been racked by 17 years of warfare'. In addition to the communists, the Burmese army is battling such dissident tribal groups as the predominantly Protestant Karens and the hill-dwelling opium-smoking Shans.[52] In March 1962 a military leader, Ne Win, who had been Aung San's chief of staff, staged a successful coup. Four years older than Aung San, Ne Win was eccentric, with a firm, traditional Burmese belief in astrology and lucky numbers. Until his death in 2002, he dominated Burmese life. He went to Vienna every summer with an entourage of fifty to see Hans Hoff, one of Austria's most respected psychiatrists, and it was in Vienna in June 1966 that Inge Sargent, née Eberhard, an Austrian woman who had married a Shan prince, confronted Ne Win about the disappearance of her husband four years before.[53] Ne Win did not grant the Shan Princess an interview. He was the archetypal mad dictator: he didn't like interviews; he was 'allergic to visitors'.[54]

Ne Win has also been described as 'xenophobic, capricious, superstitious and fascinated by the occult "science" of numerology'. Important events were staged on dates whose numbers, when added together, made nine. In 1987 he decided that all banknote denominations should be divisible by nine. He then introduced the 45-kyat and 90-kyat notes. Burmese who had hoarded 100-kyat notes lost their savings. While the majority of the people lived in poverty, Ne Win lived like an emperor. He married seven times, twice to the same woman; he loved golf; he was said to bathe in dolphin's blood to regain his youth, but was ruthless or astute enough to amass a fortune estimated at US$4 billion.[55]

Until 2011, Burma was ruled by a long-standing military dictatorship under Ne Win's less flamboyant successor Than Shwe. As well as being more or less a client state of China, the destitute country he ruled over was propped up by a strong narcotics trade and the export of illegal rubies. Rubies had been a motivating factor, if only a minor one, behind the British annexation. The Burma Ruby Mines Company had been floated on the London stock market in March 1889, when it had been the public offering of the year, prompting a scramble for the shares.[56] In 2007, it was estimated that more than 90 per cent of the world's rubies came from Burma. These were cut and polished in other countries to avoid customs duties, but the money derived from their sale supported the military junta.[57] The junta itself had crushed a student-led protest movement in 1988, killing 3,000 students in the process. It had imprisoned, under house arrest, for nearly two decades Aung San's daughter, Aung San Suu Kyi, who won the Nobel Peace Prize in 1991. The army, now 400,000 strong, or four times the size of the British army in 2010, claimed to be the only force that could hold the country together. Burma is composed of more than a hundred ethnicities, some of whom are still waging unofficial war against the central government.[58]

In February 2011 Thein Sein became the country's first civilian president after nearly fifty years of military rule. A career soldier who first joined the military government in 1997, Thein Sein was an ally of the outgoing President Than Shwe and, despite his vaunted status as a civilian, he was merely one of about twenty military chiefs who stepped down from their army posts before the 7 November election in order to run as civilian candidates. This development, critics said, was merely a device to prolong military control of government in Burma.[59]

The army's success and strength has been a function of the power vacuum in Burma. There were no leaders, no real civic society, no institutions after the double shock of annexation and the Japanese invasion. Even in the 1940s, just as in the debates of the 1880s, some British politicians could see that the annexation of Burma had been misguided. As the

Labour politician David Rees-Williams, later Lord Ogmore, observed:

> This annexation . . . I have long felt was a great mistake. It was a mistake
> to snuff out the independence of a proud people, it was a blunder to place
> Burma as a mere Province under India . . . What the British Government
> should have done was to elevate a respectable Burman royalty to the
> Throne and guide him and his officials into the way of sound administra-
> tion and a democratic system . . . declaring the whole of Burma to be an
> independent sovereign state under the protection of the British Crown.[60]

This had actually been the policy in South-east Asia after the Indian
Mutiny of 1857. Ironically, annexation had been avoided in Kashmir,
where it would have made a great deal more sense, as there existed no
traditional indigenous ruling family. In Kashmir, a new, alien dynasty, of a
different faith from the overwhelming majority of the population, was
installed. Precisely the opposite course of action was taken in Burma,
where an old ruling dynasty was deposed, and over which direct control
from India, and ultimately from London, was established. The absence of
any traditional social order made it easier for the British army to impose
its authority on the Burmese people. The consequences of Lord Randolph's
impulsiveness were all too apparent in the second decade of the twenty-
first century.

PART IV

SUDAN: 'BLACKS AND BLUES'

Kitchener: An Imperial Hero

Perhaps no figure represented the British Empire at its late Victorian zenith better than Lord Kitchener. Even today, his image is familiar because of one of the most famous poster campaigns of all time, in which the caption reads, 'Your Country Needs You'. These words, of course, applied to the recruitment of British soldiers at the beginning of the First World War, but the origins of Kitchener's extraordinary fame and success were in mid-Victorian Ireland, where he was born in 1850. Kitchener was not an Irishman and he would have agreed with the Duke of Wellington, who had also been born in Ireland, that 'being born in a stable did not make one a horse'; despite his Irish birth, Kitchener never considered himself anything other than an Englishman. His father had been born on 19 October 1805, two days before Lord Nelson's victory at Trafalgar and, as a tribute to the great admiral, Henry Kitchener had been given the middle name 'Horatio', which he also gave, as a middle name, to his son.[1]

Herbert Horatio Kitchener grew up in Ireland, under the watchful gaze of a doting mother and the stern discipline of a father who was twenty years older than his wife. His subsequent fame was not easily predicted by the rather obscure circumstances of his birth. For a man who 'left an indelible mark on his generation and on British history', Kitchener's beginnings in Gunsborough Villa, a modest Victorian pile near Listowel, County Kerry, were hardly the stuff of imperial legend.[2] His origins were distinctly middle class, perhaps even rather boring. His father had been a middle-ranking army officer who had retired to Ireland, the year before Kitchener's birth, in order to save money. Henry Kitchener's own family was undistinguished, but the young bride whom he married in 1845 was from the Chevallier family, French Huguenots who had settled as minor country squires at Aspall, a charming moated Jacobean manor near Debenham in Suffolk.

The delights of the Suffolk countryside were not found in Ireland, where the damp cold could often prove dangerous to people with weak constitutions. The general severity of the climate was not helped by Colonel Kitchener's eccentricities. He was a martinet, a disciplinarian and general oddball, whose idiosyncratic tastes included an aversion to bed linen, which he avoided by forcing his family to use newspapers instead of blankets. The stories of Henry Kitchener's foibles were often recounted in the countryside around the banks of the Shannon, where he had bought his derelict estate. The domestic staff were terrorized by a ruthless efficiency, and by a pedantic, grinding punctuality. The household was run 'with military order and discipline, backed by forceful language'. A servant who brought breakfast to the dining room one minute after eight, the appointed hour, was scolded pitilessly by the infuriated Colonel. Mrs Sharpe, the young Kitchener's nanny, remembered seeing Sarah, the parlour maid, standing outside Mrs Kitchener's room with the breakfast tray on one hand and a watch in the other, waiting for the precise hour to enter the room. Mrs Sharpe, in the days of the young Kitchener's fame, was not surprised to learn of his reputation as a strict disciplinarian: 'it was bred in him', she sighed.[3]

The picture that emerges of the young Kitchener's upbringing is almost a parody of a Victorian nightmare of a childhood. And yet, through his mother, Kitchener and his elder brother Arthur were taught the gentler virtues. Frances Kitchener, the boys' mother, encouraged them to recount the events of the day and to recite a hymn or read a New Testament passage, which she would explain to them. The Colonel, in his eccentricity, loathed all schools, and it was probably to the boys' benefit that they were not sent to the public schools on the British mainland or their imitators in Ireland. Instead of the usual diet of Classical authors and grammar which was the mainstay of public school education at that time, Herbert Kitchener was taught about estate management and 'rural improvement'. Unusually for their class and for the time, the boys, first under their father and later abroad, had a modern education, learning Mathematics, History, French and German, instead of Latin and Greek.[4]

A defining moment in the life of the young family came in 1863, when Frances Kitchener's tuberculosis worsened and the doctors concluded that the damp conditions of south-west Ireland would never allow her to recover. The Colonel, with characteristic decisiveness, sold the estate and moved the family to Switzerland, which the doctors had recommended for its mountain air. This was a common prescription for tubercular and bronchial diseases in an age before the discovery of penicillin. The Kitchener family soon settled in the little spa town of Bex and the boys started attending a French school near Geneva. The move to Bex failed to improve Frances Kitchener's health, and, in a desperate final attempt to remedy her condition, the family moved once again to Montreux, a town on the north-east shore of Lake Geneva, where a colony of British invalids and retired officers could be found. Unfortunately, this move did not have its intended effect, and Frances Kitchener died in the summer of 1864, at the age of thirty-nine.[5]

The loss of his mother, when he was only fourteen, was undoubtedly the great sorrow of Kitchener's life. Already in Ireland, his mother had been sensitive to the young Herbert Kitchener's shyness and tendency to hide or suppress his feelings. One day he had not told her about an injury he had suffered when a rock fell on his hand, and she remarked to the nanny that 'Herbert is so very reserved about his feelings, I am afraid he will suffer a great deal from repression.'[6] After her death, Kitchener's shyness became even more pronounced. He was teased by pupils at the English boarding school at the Château du Grand Clos, in Switzerland, for his Irish accent and unsophisticated country ways. Yet his unusual education did provide him with a facility for languages, which, in his later career, would give him the opportunities he craved. He spoke fluent French and good German and, by the time he was admitted to the Royal Military Academy in Woolwich in 1868, he was a far more accomplished man of the world, in many ways, than his contemporaries who had emerged from their mid-Victorian English public schools.

Woolwich, or the 'Shop', as it was known, is one of those institutions which defined the British Empire, but which has now been largely forgotten. It had been founded in 1741, more than fifty years before the Royal Military College at Sandhurst, and was closed in 1939, only to be merged with Sandhurst in 1947. Before its closure, the Shop had its own distinct reputation. It was not as socially exclusive as Sandhurst, because it attracted more middle-class cadets, who were often brighter and more motivated than their counterparts at Sandhurst. Woolwich trained engineers and artillerymen, who had to pass exams to gain their commissions, while Sandhurst, before the abolition of the purchase of commissions in 1870, was little more than an upper-class finishing school. The discipline at the Shop was also notorious, provoking a mutiny by the cadets in October 1861, little more than seven years before Kitchener went there in January 1869. The mutiny, it has been noted, was caused by the 'disgusting characteristics of the eggs that were being served'. That day, the cadets wilfully dropped their rifles on the parade ground, for which they were duly arrested. When the call for afternoon study sounded, it was ignored. The so-called mutiny was a series of pranks and minor acts of subordination, but the long term result of these disturbances was an improvement in the conditions of the cadets, particularly with regard to the meals which the Academy served.[7]

The daily timetable Kitchener and his colleagues endured was grinding and monotonous, with a reveille at 6.30 a.m. and lights out at 10.30 p.m. The last meal of the day was served at the absurdly early hour of 3.30 in the afternoon. Kitchener made little impression at the Shop, where he had come twenty-eighth out of fifty-six in the entrance exam. He seemed a mediocrity and there were few signs of future greatness in him. The Duke of Connaught, one of Queen Victoria's younger sons, who had entered the Academy a year earlier, remembered him as 'a tall lanky young man, very quiet and unassuming'.[8] (Kitchener, at this stage, was six foot two.) He had a slight squint, which rendered him useless at games and thereby accentuated his natural tendency to remain aloof from his fellow cadets. It made him a terrible shot at the endless country-house parties to which he would later be invited, and he humorously acknowledged this defect in his shooting abilities by naming three gundogs Bang, Miss and Damn.[9]

Kitchener's early career in the army was steady rather than spectacular and he was not one of those brilliant personalities who shine from earliest youth. In 1870 he was unfortunate enough to be in France, where his father had now moved to Brittany with his second wife on account of the relatively low cost of living there. During the Franco-Prussian War, which broke out that year, the young Kitchener attached himself to a field ambulance unit and saw the battle round Le Mans, where the fighting was fierce. There he witnessed, without 'manifesting any visible sign of emotion', the 'slaughter of large numbers of men and horses'.[10]

Perhaps moved by the destruction he saw in France, Kitchener seems to have become more ambitious in his twenties and more eager to seize opportunities for travel. A decisive turning point occurred when he volunteered to help his friend Claude Conder on the Palestine Exploration Fund in 1874. In a bid for self-improvement, he was spending part of his leave in Hanover polishing his German when he was informed by Conder of the death in Palestine of the young civilian surveyor Charles Tyrwhitt-Drake. Lieutenant Kitchener grabbed his chance to take Tyrwhitt-Drake's place and embarked on what promised to be an adventure, though the surveying work proved to be useful and dull rather than an obvious prelude to exciting military exploits. Palestine gave him the opportunity to learn Arabic, which accomplishment would define his career in Egypt and the Sudan, where he would make his name. Meanwhile, his steady progress brought him back to London in 1876, after eighteen months in Palestine, where he and Conder prepared twenty-six sheets of a great map of Palestine for their topological survey. The following year he went back to Palestine for more fieldwork, and he took to his tasks with an energy and gusto which now began to impress observers. The French archaeologist Charles Clermont-Ganneau noticed the 'tall, slim and vigorous' Lieutenant who had an 'ardour for his work' which 'astonished us'.[11]

The steady ascent in Kitchener's career at this stage may have been a little plodding, but no one could deny the young engineer's ambition. His father, in his idiosyncratic way, had laughed at his son's zeal, saying, 'You're too tall, only little men get to the top.' But this did not discourage the younger Kitchener, and there is a sense by the late 1870s that he was growing into the persona which would later dominate and fascinate contemporaries. He next went to Cyprus in 1878 to conduct a survey similar to the one he had undertaken in Palestine. The outcome of his labours there was a work entitled *A Trigonometrical Survey of the Island of Cyprus*, published in April 1885. This great work is, unfortunately, as dull as its title.[12] Yet it was in Cyprus that Kitchener developed two traits which would distinguish him: his famous moustache and a strange passion for pottery and porcelain, which puzzled his long-lived father, the Colonel – though he recognized, perhaps, in his son's eccentricities the more bizarre traits of his own personality.

Cyprus was an odd outpost of empire, which had only recently been ceded to Britain by the Ottoman Empire at the Congress of Berlin of 1878. Kitchener impressed his commanding officer, Major General Sir Robert Biddulph, with his diligence and attention to detail, but by the middle of 1882 the thirty-two-year-old Kitchener was beginning to feel restless and unfulfilled. He was, he told Biddulph, 'extremely anxious to see service in Egypt' and was concerned that his 'remaining here [in Cyprus] in a civil capacity while military service was offered me might be used against me in my future career'. In a rare burst of emotion, he lamented that his 'greatest contribution up to the present has been to finish the map of Cyprus'.[13] Like the young Julius Caesar, who wept when he saw a statue of Alexander the Great because at an age when Caesar was dallying in Spain Alexander had conquered the world, Kitchener was feeling the frustrations of early middle age. His career, it seemed, was going nowhere.

An opening in Egypt had arisen because Kitchener could speak Arabic. It was his knowledge of this difficult language that distinguished him from his contemporaries in the army and, time and again, gave him opportunities to execute difficult and dangerous tasks. As Winston Churchill, a young officer in the British army of the 1890s, observed, 'in 1874 accident or instinct led him to seek employment in the surveys that were being made of Cyprus and Palestine, and in the latter country he learned Arabic. For six years the advantage of knowing a language with which few British officers were familiar brought him no profit.' Arabic in the 1870s was, in Churchill's judgement, as 'valueless as Patagonian', but the year 1882 brought fresh chances when a British fleet bombarded Alexandria in order to protect British subjects from rioting Egyptians.[14] The British government decided to send an expeditionary force to Egypt, and it was felt that an officer who knew Arabic would be useful. Kitchener was accordingly employed in the Egyptian army and won promotion to the rank of major. His methods, his thoroughness and his general demeanour of measured efficiency began to earn recognition and spread his fame. It was at the beginning of his service in Egypt that an Irish priest heard his name for the first time. The young priest was talking to soldiers in the Royal Irish Regiment in Plymouth, in the mid-1880s, just after their regiment had returned to Britain from Egypt when one man mentioned a remarkable officer: 'Oh, he is not known, sir. But if you wish really to know, he is only a major in a black regiment.' The priest asked the officer's name. 'Kitchener, sir. If you like to follow him, sir, he will run the whole of the British Army.'[15]

By the early 1880s, Egypt and more particularly the Sudan were among the most exciting places in the British Empire. Egypt itself had fallen under British influence in the 1870s, when Disraeli had bought shares in the Suez Canal, and the Egyptian government, under a hereditary ruler known as the Khedive, began to come under the informal influence of the British Consul General, who in 1882 was Evelyn Baring, a scion of the British banking family and another graduate of the Royal Military Academy, Woolwich. Baring was a gruff bear of a man whose nickname, inevitably, became 'Over-Baring' or 'le Grand Ours' (the Big Bear). Egyptian politics were even more complicated by the fact that the Khedive and the ruling classes in Egypt were Turkish and were, nominally at least, vassals of the Ottoman Sultan in Constantinople. The land to the south of Egypt had been known to Arab traders for years as *al bilad as-sudan*, or the 'Land of the Blacks'. In the eyes of the British and the Arabs alike, the history of the Sudan before the Egyptians under Turkish rulers established nominal control over the country was a tale of incoherent blood feuds and chaos. In Kitchener's own words, 'endless wars raged' and the 'blood feud was most bitter'.[16]

The Egyptians' claims on Sudan and their attempt, under British influence, to suppress slave trading had alienated many of the Sudanese tribes, who had thrived on this inhumane, if lucrative, activity. The Sudanese were also beginning to feel the weight of Egyptian rule through the 'self-seeking and unscrupulous tax-gatherers' who were now descending upon them from Cairo.[17] To exacerbate the problem for the Egyptians, there arose, as so often is the case, a national leader of great charisma and force who, through the power of religious enthusiasm, combined the various disaffected elements in the Sudan into one movement.

Mohammed Ahmed had been born in 1844, the son of a boat builder, and his brothers followed their father in that trade. Ahmed, however, found his vocation in religion. His father died on a journey to Khartoum while Ahmed was still a boy and, in a celebrated description by Winston Churchill, which some historians have taken as referring to Churchill himself, the boy 'deprived of a father's care' developed 'an independence and vigour of thought which may restore in after life the heavy loss of early days'. Mohammed Ahmed was certainly an independent thinker. He pursued his religious studies with great diligence and cultivated a personal reputation for austerity, often fasting for days.[18] He started off as a disciple of the renowned holy sheikh Mohammed Sherif, but a dispute with his master made Ahmed strike out on his own, preaching and winning disciples to his austere brand of Islam.

Emboldened by his initial success in attracting followers, Ahmed proclaimed himself the 'Mahdi' in the summer of 1881. 'Al-Mahdi' was an Arabic term, meaning guide or leader; and the expectation that a prophet with special powers would come to earth at the end of the world to purify mankind and bring justice is a belief not exclusive to the Islamic faith. To Victorian generals, the mystical and religious aspect of the Mahdi's mission was especially fascinating. There was a general view that Islam held a particular attraction for the 'native races' of Central Africa, and the natural superstition of the native was often invoked to explain the Mahdi's stunning successes. The Mahdi had to be a 'descendant of the Prophet', the 'Ashraf', and would share the same name as the Prophet, Mohammed ibn Abdullah, Mohammed son of Abdullah, which was the Mahdi's full name if one includes his patronymic. Whatever the general aims of the 'expected Mahdi' might be, Mohammed Ahmed's ambitions in 1881 were more specific. He aspired to 'gain over the whole of the Sudan to his cause, then march on Egypt and overthrow the false-believing Turks'. Only after this had been accomplished would the Mahdi finally establish 'the thousand years' kingdom in Mecca, and convert the whole world', according to a contemporary British account of the Mahdist uprising.[19]

Among the followers the Mahdi managed to gather, there was a man called Abdullah, from the Ta'aisha Beggara tribe of the northern Sudan. Abdullah was a man of determination and force who acted as the Mahdi's practical right-hand man; he was often described as 'the man of the world, the practical politician, the general', and, with the Mahdi providing the religious inspiration, the two men began to rouse the local tribes to rebellion.[20] The Mahdi himself wrote letters to all parts of the Sudan, calling upon everyone to fight for the purity of Islam, for the freedom of the soil and for 'God's holy prophet "the expected Mahdi"'. The Egyptian government, by now increasingly under British influence, sent two companies of infantry – about sixty men – to arrest the religious leader in an attempt to bring the revolt to an end. It was an August evening in 1881 when a steamer with the infantrymen aboard arrived at Abba, near the village where the Mahdi resided. The two companies approached the Mahdi's village by separate routes. It was now dark, and the two units entered the village from opposite directions; in the confusion caused by the uncertainty of where the Mahdi actually was and by the darkness, the soldiers started firing at each other, and the Mahdi, with his small following, seized his opportunity and destroyed both companies of men. Some of the Egyptian soldiers managed to get back to the steamship at anchor in Abba, but its captain quickly left the scene of the debacle, and 'those who could not swim out to the vessel were left to their fate'.[21]

This initial success brought the Mahdi great prestige, and people in Sudan began to wonder if he was indeed the 'expected guide', the genuine Mahdi who would inaugurate a reign of peace and justice. The self-styled Mahdi now began to assume the airs and confidence of a man bent on a divinely inspired mission. He appointed his four successors, or khalifas, in accordance with the precedent set by the Prophet Mohammed himself, and, unsurprisingly, the chief of these khalifas was Abdullah. It was against this backdrop of religious enthusiasm and insurrection that the famous mission of General Gordon was conceived. In November 1883 the Mahdi's troops had achieved a victory even more dramatic than that at Abba, annihilating a force of 10,000 Egyptian soldiers commanded by Major General William Hicks. Hicks's men had been attacked in a savage onslaught, which only 300 of the 10,000 men survived. In keeping with Sudanese custom, the heads of Hicks and his leading officers were presented to the Mahdi and his followers.[22] It was then decided by Gladstone's government in London to evacuate the Egyptian garrison in

Khartoum, an operation that Gordon was dispatched to oversee; he arrived on 18 February 1884.

Charles Gordon is one of those historical figures of whom many people are dimly aware. This is partly because the role of Gordon was successfully played by Charlton Heston in the 1966 film *Khartoum*, in which Gordon meets his end on the steps of the palace at Khartoum, surrounded by spear-wielding dervishes. Despite being the subject of a Hollywood block-buster, Gordon's life was even more spectacular than any work of creative fiction could depict. Born in 1833, he was fifty-one when the final act of his eventful life unfolded. Like Kitchener and many others in the Sudan story, Gordon had been educated at the Royal Military Academy in Woolwich, from which he had been recruited into the Royal Engineers. Requiring a knowledge of mathematics and engineering, this corps compensated for its lack of social prestige by attracting a particularly determined type of officer. Gordon was, however, even more unusual. He was a mystic, a Christian fundamentalist, who became convinced that the Garden of Eden was located in the Seychelles. His religious fervour embraced death as the 'gateway to eternal life'. He despised money, luxury and modern living, and when he left England for the last time in 1884 he sensed that he would never return, exclaiming passionately, 'I dwell on the joy of never seeing Great Britain again, with its horrid, wearisome dinner parties and miseries.'[23]

The circumstances which pitched the Mahdi against General Gordon were out of the ordinary, and both men, as was remarked at the time, were of a remarkably similar type. They were religious fanatics who each believed he was performing God's will, though the sincerity of the Mahdi's protes-tations has been doubted. The Mahdi preached asceticism and worldly renunciation, though the number of wives and concubines he took – some put the figure as high as 110 – undermined his claims to rigorous absti-nence.[24] Gordon, on the other hand, was a genuine ascetic. He was friends with the greatest imperialist capitalist of the age, Cecil Rhodes, and told Rhodes, at a breakfast in South Africa, that in China, where he had served with distinction in the 1860s, he had been offered a 'whole room-full of silver'. He had refused the gift and, in recounting the story to Rhodes, asked, 'What would you have done?' 'Why', said Rhodes incredulously, 'taken it of course! What is the earthly use of having ideas if you haven't got the money to carry them out?'[25]

Gordon immediately tried to rally the garrison in Khartoum, which grew increasingly nervous as the Mahdi's men arrived to besiege the town. Ever rigid in his sense of duty and honour, the General 'considered that he was personally pledged to effect the evacuation of Khartoum by the garrison and civil servants'. Nothing would now induce him to leave until its inhabitants had been rescued.[26] He also formed an 'unshaken determination never to surrender the town to the rebels'. The inhabitants of the city now numbered only about 14,000 out of the original 34,000, since Gordon had immediately on arrival in Khartoum started sending people away.[27] While the siege lasted, the British public, updated by newspaper reports, became increasingly concerned about the impending crisis. As Lord Randolph Churchill told the House of Commons on 16 March 1884, the General was in a dangerous situation, being 'surrounded by hostile tribes and cut off from communications with Cairo and London'.[28] The siege continued, with conditions in Khartoum becoming more and more desperate. The garrison suffered from 'want of food', and by December 'all the donkeys, dogs, cats, rats etc. had been eaten'.[29] The slow response from the Gladstone government to the crisis in which Gordon found himself is well known. The Prime Minister was as stubborn as Gordon and seems to have taken a perverse pride in not heeding the popular demand that he immediately send a force to save Gordon.

Belatedly, a Gordon Relief Expedition was dispatched in August 1884, under Sir Garnet Wolseley, another powerful figure of this militaristic age. In Khartoum, Gordon was having sleepless nights and was only too aware that his ability to withstand the siege was limited. The denouement came in January 1885, when, at about 3.30 a.m. on Monday the 26th, the Mahdi's troops made a 'determined attack' on the south side of the town. Khartoum fell, according to Kitchener's account (though he was not there to witness it), because the garrison were too exhausted by their sufferings to put up a proper resistance. Once the rebels had entered the town, there was a general massacre, and the exact fate of General Gordon remains unclear. He was killed, certainly, but differing accounts of his death have been related to this day. It is likely that he died near the gate of the palace, but the dramatic accounts of his confronting the mob on the steps of the Governor's palace may derive more from the imagination of subsequent storytellers than from what actually happened. After his death, there unfolded a macabre scene. Since none of the tribesmen knew what the General looked like, there was uncertainty about which was 'Gordon's body, and great confusion occurred in the Mahdi's camp at Omdurman' – a town on the western banks of the Nile on the other side from Khartoum. When the heads of various Europeans were presented, some were identified as Gordon's, only for other tribesmen to deny the attribution. The General's body itself was never found.[30]

The massacre, in which 4,000 people were killed, ended at about 10 a.m. when the Mahdi ordered the slaughter to stop. Kitchener's description of the siege is written in a characteristically dry, matter-of-fact style but, at the end of his account, he did allow himself an uncharacteristic rhetorical flourish: 'The memorable siege of Khartoum lasted 317 days and it is not too much to say that such a noble resistance was due to the indomitable resolution and resource of one Englishman.' Kitchener's assessment was that the Mahdi was now in control of the whole of the Sudan, and it would be difficult for the time being to envisage a government without him: 'The Mahdi's personal influence is paramount in the country and unless he leaves it I hardly think the people could free themselves.'[31]

The Mahdi himself, however, was soon stricken with a dangerous disease and, in June 1885, only five months after the fall of Khartoum, he failed to appear at the mosque for prayers for several days. At first, his followers thought nothing of this, for had it not been revealed that the 'Mahdi should conquer Mecca, Medina, and Jerusalem' before his earthly mission was done?[32] The rule of the Mahdi had been strict, but there is no evidence that he was particularly unpopular. He had forbidden 'dancing and playing', which he denounced as 'earthly pleasures', and anyone who was found disobeying his rules was liable to punishment by flogging and confiscation of all his property. The use of bad language was strictly forbidden, with a punishment of eighty lashes prescribed for every insulting word uttered. To the usual Islamic prohibition against alcohol, there was added an equally strong injunction against the smoking of tobacco. Thieves would be deprived of their right hands for a first offence, and of their left foot for a second.[33] The Mahdi was perhaps the first Islamic fundamentalist of the modern era, as earlier fanatics, like Mohammed ibn Abd al-Wahhab in eighteenth-century Saudi Arabia, were unmolested by the modern Western world of machine guns and organized military campaigns. On the seventh day of his illness, the Mahdi, stricken with typhus, knew that his end was near. Summoning his followers by one last effort, he named Khalifa Abdullah his successor, declaring, 'He is of me, and I am of him; as you have obeyed me, so you should deal with him. May God have mercy upon me.'[34]

While the Mahdi was treated by the British as a figure of some importance and dignity, his successor, the Khalifa, has been portrayed in all the most lurid colours of late Victorian sensationalism, as a monster of human wickedness and depravity. In 1890 he was described in an intelligence report as a 'tall, stout man' whose hair was beginning to turn grey. At that date, the Khalifa would have been in his mid-forties, as he was roughly the same age as his former master, the Mahdi. The British depicted him as an ignorant, cunning savage, and tales of his sexual depravity titillated both the official classes and the wider public. It seems strange that a description of the Khalifa's seduction techniques should find itself in a 'General Report on the Sudan', but the intelligence agent could not resist recounting how Abdullah employed an agent, Haj Zubeir, to find out all the 'good looking women', whereupon the 'husband of the woman is strictly advised to divorce his wife who is at once brought to the Khalifa'. Once ensconced in the Khalifa's harem, the women 'are carefully guarded and are not permitted even to see their parents'. In this way, the report claimed, the Khalifa collected a harem of thirty-four wives, one of whom was a daughter of the Mahdi himself. It is difficult to see how these details affected the general security situation. Britain, and its puppet state Egypt, had withdrawn from the Sudan, leaving the country at the mercy of the Khalifa and his marauding army. Abdullah himself was an archetypal despot, which made hating him so much easier for the British officials. People brought into his presence were 'obliged to enter . . . on all fours', as no one was permitted to look at the Khalifa's face; they had to address him as 'Ya Sayeedi' (O my Lord) and they were compelled to retire backwards, with their heads bent and their eyes fixed to the ground, when they left his presence.

The Khalifa's intelligence, in British eyes, was impressive; he was a man of force and power with whom the British of the late Victorian era could identify, but he 'neither reads nor writes and is said to be a man of exceptional ignorance', which was compensated for by his 'great determination' and his being 'well versed in every art of fraud and deception'.[35] The British response to the disaster Gordon had suffered at Khartoum was to sit and wait. Sir Evelyn Baring, later Lord Cromer, who for so many years effectively ran the nominally independent Egyptian government, later remarked that the Sudan had been 'left derelict, not so much because the cargo was altogether valueless, but rather because no hands were available to effect the salvage'. He was convinced that any British attempt to reconquer the Sudan would only take place after about 'twenty-five years', in 1910 or 1911.[36]

Cautious and pragmatic, Baring believed that 'any attempt to negotiate with the Mahdist leaders' would prove 'barren of result'. He took the view that, while the Mahdi could inspire his followers with a genuine religious fervour, the Khalifa was a different case. It was true that the Khalifa had the ability to 'raise large numbers of men by preaching a "jehad"', but the 'fanaticism inspired by Mahdiism will never have the force it possessed during the early days of Mohammed Ahmed'.[37] Baring, in his clear-cut way – he was yet another product of Woolwich, but had left the army in the 1870s – believed that the Sudan 'cannot and should not be permanently separated from Egypt'. There were powerful reasons for the reconquest of Sudan. These included the 'stimulus of commercial interests, a desire to aid in the suppression of the Slave Trade' and humanitarian 'pity and commiseration for the inhabitants of the Soudan, who, without doubt, groan under the Dervish yoke'. The British government would have to pay for this campaign, as the resources of Egypt, financial and military, were 'wholly inadequate for the accomplishment of the task'.[38] It was simply a matter of timing.

Kitchener, meanwhile, who had been an intelligence officer on the Gordon Relief Expedition which arrived in Khartoum two days late, was slowly climbing the ladder of preferment within the Egyptian army, gathering honours and titles. He had time to join the Freemasons in 1883 and kept up a lifelong involvement with the organization. In Cairo, where he was stationed before setting out to relieve Gordon, he is even believed to have fallen in love. Hermione Baker was the elder of the two daughters of Valentine Baker, a senior army officer, who lived with her mother and sister in the city's Shepheard Hotel. Kitchener visited the Bakers often in Cairo in 1883 and 1884 and, it was rumoured, had been engaged to Hermione, a young lady in her late teens. But Hermione died of typhoid fever on 13 January 1885, two weeks before the fall of Khartoum, and at a time when Kitchener himself was deep in the Sudan, trying to save Gordon. Ever since this supposed love affair, there have been rumours about Kitchener's sexuality, with a remark of a contemporary journalist being often cited – that Kitchener had 'the failing acquired by most of the Egyptian officers, a taste for buggery'. Hermione's younger sister, Sybil, was never in any doubt that her sister's death was the great tragedy in Kitchener's life.[39] Kitchener destroyed most of his personal correspondence, so the depth and nature of his feelings for Hermione, as well as his other passions, homosexual or otherwise, are likely never to be known.

Posterity does, however, have a much fuller record of Kitchener's promotions and his achievements as an officer. His success in the field, his knowledge of Arabic, the stories of the disguises he adopted while operating as an intelligence officer, began to build up a picture of a glamorous, even magnificent British officer, made more mysterious by the mask of impenetrability he always wore. Kitchener was also adept at making friends with powerful people. He quickly became a favourite in Lord Salisbury's family circle and was invited to Hatfield House as early as spring 1888. It was at this time that Queen Victoria pleaded for him to be appointed one of her aides de camp. The secret of his networking and ability to win influential friends remains something of a mystery, given his shy, rather gauche personality. While in Britain, Kitchener led the life of a Victorian bachelor, passing time in the grand houses of friends and spending innumerable evenings and nights in the clubs of Pall Mall and Piccadilly. The late nineteenth century was perhaps the heyday of the gentleman's club, an institution which grew out of the coffee houses of nearly 200 years before. Kitchener's favourite haunt was the United Service Club, at 116 Pall Mall, which was founded for the use of army and naval officers above the rank of major or commander. Like many others, the club ran into difficulties in the 1970s and closed its doors for the last time in 1978. Kitchener also frequently stayed with his friend Pandeli Ralli, the wealthy scion of a Greek trading family, whose house in Belgrave Square practically became Kitchener's home when he was on leave.[40]

In September 1888, at the precocious age of thirty-eight, thanks to the influence of his new friend the Prime Minister Lord Salisbury, Kitchener was appointed adjutant general of the Egyptian army, the effective deputy in command of that force. This army was run by the British, even though it was nominally controlled by the Khedive, a descendant of the ethnic Albanian Mohammed Ali Pasha, who had been appointed governor of Egypt, under the aegis of the Ottoman Empire, in 1805. In April 1892, Kitchener was promoted to be head of the Egyptian army, or sirdar, at a time when the situation relating to the Sudan was still relatively undecided. Intelligence reports in the early 1890s referred to the Khalifa's efforts to rebuild the wall of his capital at Omdurman, which now looked like a besieged town. None of the inhabitants was permitted to pass the wall; only Beggara tribesmen and the Khalifa's fighters were allowed in and out of the city.[41]

The shift in policy towards the Sudan, a move from containment to active involvement, occurred during the second half of the 1890s, as a result of a change in attitude in Britain. According to Evelyn Baring, now ennobled as Lord Cromer, there had been a 'rapid growth of Imperialist spirit' in England. More particularly, Italy's failure in its imperial mission finally forced Britain to reveal its hand in the Sudan. In Cromer's acerbic words, the Italians 'had shown but little skill, either political or military, in the management of their newly acquired possession [Abyssinia, modern Ethiopia]', and when they were totally defeated by the Ethiopians at Adowa, the situation in Sudan was brought 'to a crisis'.[42] The Italian Ambassador in London urged that a diversion should be made in Italy's interests and it was at this point, in 1896, Cromer asserted, that Lord Salisbury's Conservative government decided to intervene. The Italian excuse may just have been a pretext for a more aggressive action against the Khalifa, but it was a useful figleaf, and the broader point, that the British, under Salisbury's Conservatives, now supported a more energetic form of imperialism, is uncontroversial.

As head of the Egyptian army, Kitchener was the only candidate for the command of the force which would reconquer Sudan. His hour had come. As Lord Cromer remembered, Kitchener at forty-six was 'young, energetic, ardently and exclusively devoted to his profession'. He also observed, as many others did, that the Sirdar's qualities did not inspire love among his troops. According to Cromer, the 'bonds which united' Kitchener and his subordinates were those of 'stern discipline'. Kitchener had a 'strong and masterful spirit', which he used to dominate his men and bully them into submission to his will, instead of obtaining from them 'the affectionate obedience yielded to the behests of a genial chief'. Kitchener left 'as little as possible to chance' and was, in the language of the period, a 'rigid economist', which meant that he was very careful with money, suppressing with 'a heavy hand any tendency towards waste and extravagance'.[43]

The most famous description of Kitchener from this period comes from the stirring account of the Sudan campaign written by G. W. Steevens, entitled *With Kitchener to Khartoum*, which was a bestseller in 1898. A brilliant Oxford Classics graduate, Steevens was a journalist of genius who worked for the newly founded popular newspaper the *Daily Mail* and wrote with a vividness and fluency which brought him early fame as a war correspondent, before he died in South Africa at the premature age of thirty. His sketch of Kitchener included the line: 'You feel that he ought to be patented and shown with pride at the Paris International Exhibition. British Empire: Exhibit No. 1 . . . the Sudan Machine.'[44] The 'Sudan Machine' was a name that stuck. Steevens referred to the Sirdar's 'unerring precision', and it was clear that his characteristics were beginning to fascinate the wider public, as the final resolution of the Sudan conflict became more widely anticipated. A great popular journalist, Steevens appreciated the Victorian public's appetite for supermen and imperial heroes. For him, Kitchener was quite simply 'the man of destiny'.[45] Against such a man, with the backing of the resources of the imperial government in London, the Khalifa and his followers, it was believed, stood little chance. Lord Cromer had mentioned the inevitability of a British triumph in a letter to

Lord Salisbury written in 1892: 'The very name of England is far more feared by the Khalifa and his Beggara than either Turkey or Egypt, and it is practically admitted that they cannot hope for success in fighting against the British.'[46]

The details of the Sudan campaign, which were recounted in numerous memoirs and descriptions, were once familiar to the British public. The one episode that is still renowned is the Battle of Omdurman, the final stand of the dervishes, made famous by the Charge of the 21st Lancers, the last occasion on which the British army made use of a cavalry charge in battle. Winston Churchill, a young cavalry officer who had cajoled and bullied his way on to Kitchener's campaign, would refer to the charge frequently as one of his repertoire of dinner-table anecdotes. It has become part of British military folklore. The Battle of Omdurman itself, which took place on 2 December 1898, was a heavily lopsided affair: at about six in the morning, the dervishes began their advance on the British position. Their 'array was perfect', and a great number of their flags, which had been covered with texts from the Koran, were visible on the horizon. To the young Churchill, 'their admirable alignment made this division of the Khalifa's army look like the old representations of the Crusaders in the Bayeux tapestry'.[47] The outcome of all this medieval pageantry and theatre was grisly, and, in accounts of the battle, one can almost detect the sense of wonder and shame the British felt in inflicting so much damage on a brave enemy, since the Victorian cult of the hero was more than matched by a passion for 'sportsmanship' and 'good form'. These were, after all, times when the veneration of cricket was perhaps at its height, when the cricket legend W. G. Grace was arguably the most famous man in Britain. The dervishes had been sportsmen: 'our men were perfect, but the Dervishes were superb', recounted Steevens.[48] Churchill admitted that the 'Dervishes fought manfully'.[49] The famous charge, in which 400 cavalrymen of the 21st Lancers attacked a force of what turned out to be 2,500 dervishes, made very little difference to the outcome of the battle, though it led to the award of three Victoria Crosses. In reality the dervishes were 'swept away in thousands by the deadly fire of the rifles and Maxims'. Their losses were 'terrible': out of an army whose strength was estimated at from 40,000 to 50,000 men, some 11,000 were killed, and about 16,000 wounded.[50] The British casualties had been negligible: twenty-two men and NCOs killed, and a hundred wounded, while only two officers lost their lives, one of whom, Lieutenant Robert Grenfell, had been the 'life and soul of the joyous Christmas festivities' at Lord Cromer's house in Cairo the year before. Grenfell had been killed by a 'Dervish broadsword' while taking part in the charge. Colonel Frank Rhodes, a *Times* journalist and Cecil Rhodes's elder brother, was also wounded in the battle. The Khalifa struggled on for another year before being killed in the Battle of Umm Diwaykarat in November 1899.

The Battle of Omdurman marks the end of an era of military adventurism and battlefield heroics. It was a day of frightful carnage for the dervish tribesmen, but it would, perhaps ironically, be dwarfed by the 20,000 dead the British themselves suffered on the first day of the Somme, less than eighteen years after Omdurman. Later observers reflected on this macabre symmetry. The constant theme of the battle is the contrast between what the British called civilization, on the one hand, and barbarism on the other. Churchill summed this up when he described Omdurman as the 'most signal triumph ever gained by the arms of science over barbarians'. Tales of barbarism and savagery sold newspapers. Steevens, the great journalist, with a good eye for sensationalism, threw sex into the mix, and one understands how the Victorian journalist often used exotic barbarians and their customs as a means of titillating the prurient tastes of his reading public. On arriving in the town of Omdurman after the battle, Steevens gave a graphic account of the women of Omdurman:

> Yet more wonderful were the women . . . There were at least three of them to every man. Black women from Equatoria [the southern province of Sudan] and almost white women from Egypt, plum-skinned Arabs and a strange yellow type with square, bony faces and tightly-ringleted black hair . . . the whole city was a huge harem, a museum of African races, a monstrosity of African lust.[51]

Steevens, the sophisticated Classical scholar, would have appreciated the irony of his describing 'African lust' in such vivid colours to bored commuters from Bromley and other London suburbs, the 'office boys', in

Lord Salisbury's sneering phrase, who read the *Daily Mail*. This type of mock indignation, combined with a secret titillation, has informed mass-market newspapers ever since. Kitchener, of course, would have regarded himself as being above such basic impulses. As the victor of the Sudan, he reached his apogee as a national hero. At the end of 1898, following the Battle of Omdurman, he was raised to the peerage as Baron Kitchener of Khartoum, and was known as K of K ever after. He was given £30,000 to support the dignity of his new status, and, because of his frugal bachelor lifestyle, he hoarded considerable wealth. There was the slight scandal of the destruction of the Mahdi's tomb, when it was reported that Kitchener had taken the dead man's skull as a trophy of war, while throwing the rest of his remains into the Nile. Even Queen Victoria expressed concern about these reports, writing to Kitchener to say that the 'destruction of the body of the Mahdi who – whether he was very bad and cruel – was a man of a certain importance ... savours ... too much of the Middle Ages'.[52] Kitchener justified his action in destroying the body and tomb on political grounds, and denied ever taking possession of the Mahdi's skull.

The cult of Kitchener now reached its most vivid expression. The *New Penny Magazine*, a publication which catered for the burgeoning lower-middle-class public, for whom the *Daily Mail* had been launched, included a lengthy profile of the newly ennobled Kitchener of Khartoum in its edition at the end of November 1898, less than three months after the Battle of Omdurman. Kitchener's looks were dilated on at some length; he is 'as dark as an Arab, with a fine figure and commanding presence'. This description was a good excuse to recount tales of his adopting disguises while wandering the Sudan as an intelligence officer. Although Kitchener led a dull private life, the *New Penny Magazine* tried to present a more human side to the great warlord: he collected porcelain and was a devoted numismatist, possessing an 'unrivalled collection' of Eastern coins; 'though a bachelor, he is noted in Cairo as a host', while in London the 'Sirdar spends most of his time at one of the well-known service clubs'; 'his knowledge of foreign languages is exceptional'.[53]

In addition to his status as a cult figure, Kitchener enjoyed warm relations with Queen Victoria. In 1899 the Queen asked him to sit for the Austrian Heinrich von Angeli, whom she described as the 'greatest living portrait painter'. Victoria was gratified when she duly received the portrait in November that year. She also asked for and received a white donkey from Egypt, which delighted the eighty-year-old monarch. Such was her solicitude for Kitchener that Victoria offered him dates on which to stay at her Isle of Wight retreat, Osborne House: 'would it be most convenient for you to come here from the 1st to the 3rd, or from the 7th to the 9th?' – an unprecedented degree of flexibility from a monarch to a subject who, under normal circumstances, would be summoned to the royal residence on a particular date, without having any choice in the matter of timing.[54]

Kitchener was made governor general of the newly conquered Sudan in January 1899 and served for the rest of the year. He was not really a civilian administrator and the task of actually building the Sudan was left to others. His greatest legacy in the Sudan was the establishment of the Gordon Memorial College which later formed the basis for the University of Khartoum. He was adept at raising money for the institution, and was generally concerned about the education of the local inhabitants. His reputation scaled even greater heights after the Boer War, though his actual successes in that conflict were muted. When war broke out in Europe in 1914, it was to Kitchener that the British public turned as a national saviour. He remarked that most of his experience had been in the Near East, and that he knew little about conditions in Europe. But, almost uniquely among high-ranking officials, he realized that the war would last at least three years, at time when many believed that it would come to a victorious conclusion in a matter of months. Kitchener died on 5 June 1916 when the ship on which he was travelling struck a German mine off the Orkney Islands. Like that of General Gordon, his body was never found, which gave birth to strange myths that he was hiding in a cave in the Hebrides, or that he was a prisoner of war in Germany. Such was the fascination of the man that many simply refused to believe he was dead.

His career had been extraordinary. It combined exoticism, glamour and bravery. He enjoyed incredible success, being raised successively to a viscountcy and then to an earldom, being made a Knight of the Garter and a member of the Order of Merit, and being given the grant of an estate, Broome Park, near Canterbury. Unusually, an act of Parliament permitted his elder brother and his heirs to inherit the numerous titles he had acquired, although, at the time of writing, his ninety-two-year-old great-nephew was still unmarried, making the imminent extinction of the title likely. More generally, Kitchener's career reveals certain truths about the nature of the British Empire.

Kitchener was a great individualist, and it was this individualism that captured the imagination of his contemporaries. He enjoyed the vast spaces and solitude of the desert. Steevens, the ever fluent journalist, conveyed this appeal of the desert to a certain type of solitary but tough Englishman, perhaps too reserved for more active social life: 'the very charm of the land lies in its empty barbarism. There is space in the Sudan. There is the fine, purified desert air, and the long stretching gallops over its sand . . . You are a savage again. You are unprejudiced, simple, free. You are a naked man facing naked nature.'[55] Cromer understood, perhaps better than any other contemporary administrator, the importance of individualism to the British Empire at its Victorian zenith:

> It has indeed become a commonplace of English political thought that for centuries past, from the days of Raleigh to those of Rhodes, the position of England in the world has been due more to the exertions, the resources, and occasionally, perhaps, to the absence of scruple found in the individual Anglo-Saxon, than to any encouragement or help derived from British Governments.[56]

In Cromer's view, everything about the British pointed to individualism. 'Our habits of thought, our past history, and our national character all, therefore, point in the direction of allowing individualism as wide a scope as possible in the work of national expansion.'[57] Like so many imperial administrators, he distrusted democracy. 'Parliamentary institutions' were an 'exotic system' which provided no 'real insight into native aspirations and opinions'. Democracy would enable 'a small minority of natives to misgovern their countrymen'. As far as imperialism was concerned, the Frenchman allowed no 'discretionary power whatever to his subordinate', and this meant that the junior administrators in the French colonies relied 'in everything on superior authority'. The British official, however, 'whether in England or abroad, is an Englishman first and an official afterwards. He possesses his full share of national characteristics.' The Englishman was 'by inheritance' an 'individualist'. The British system, according to Cromer, bred 'a race of officials . . . sympathetic to individualism' and gave 'a far wider latitude than those trained in the continental school of bureaucracy would consider safe or desirable'.[58] This may have been an idealized picture, but, if it was a myth, it was something the British imperial classes felt strongly about themselves.

Colonial administrators tended to share Cromer's view. Empire was about individualism; it was about character and personality, about the rule of the strongman, who, through a mixture of personality, intellect and leadership, could dominate his peers and the world around him. Kitchener was the model imperialist in this respect. As one biographer has noted, Kitchener was an 'individualist of great conceptions' who centralized 'every species of authority in himself'. Such a man was 'useless at teamwork'.[59] During the First World War he was frustrated by politicians and could not relate to them, because he was an imperialist, not a democrat; he was an individualist who believed in his own destiny, and in the power of strong-willed individuals to shape the world. This view would become more prevalent, with fateful consequences, in other European countries as the twentieth century unfolded.

'The Finest Body of Men'

If the skill and industry of one man had been largely responsible for the reconquest of the Sudan, it was obvious that the vision of many more people would be needed to rebuild the country. Kitchener left Khartoum in December 1899, and a man of a different stamp, Sir Reginald Wingate, was appointed governor general of the Sudan and sirdar of the Egyptian army; the two posts were thus combined in the same person for the first twenty-seven years of British rule in the Sudan. The arrangement under which the Sudan was administered was unique in international relations. It was called a condominium, or shared ownership, the same word Americans use for a joint ownership of a block of apartments. The British and Egyptian governments were the two partners in this unusual system.

The condominium was known as the 'two flags' policy, and was adopted in July 1898, even though the formal agreement was not signed until the following January.[1] That the Egyptian government, though nominally independent, was in reality under the influence and control of Britain did not seem to concern the British officials who maintained the fiction of a 'shared ownership' of the Sudan. The reason for this was simple. The Egyptian government, or rather taxpayers, could be expected to share the cost of running the Sudan (they had paid £750,000 by 1930). So the condominium arrangement saved the British government money, although people who objected to the unusual arrangement pointed out that the Egyptian share of the cost amounted to no more than an eighth or a seventh of a single battleship in 1930 currency terms.[2] Even though the sovereignty of the Sudan was shared between Egypt and Britain, the supreme civil and military command was vested in the British-nominated governor general; Kitchener was the first man appointed to this eminent position, and Sir Reginald Wingate was the second. Kitchener had begun the rebuilding of Khartoum, which had been razed to the ground by the Khalifa, and for this purpose he adopted the Chicago gridiron system for the street-plan. This system had introduced into urban planning a series of diagonal roads, whose object was to shorten the distance from one part of the town to another. The effect of this was that Khartoum was laid out in a series of Union Jack patterns, which people erroneously believed had been designed by Kitchener for patriotic reasons. Kitchener, of course, although extremely patriotic, was a pragmatist before all else and merely wanted 'quick and easy communications' in the newly built city.[3]

Wingate, physically a small man, was a much less impressive figure than Kitchener, lacking the Sudan Machine's striking looks and mysterious personality. Like Kitchener and so many of the leaders of the late Victorian army, Wingate had been educated at Woolwich and joined the Royal Artillery after graduation. To a much greater degree than Kitchener, his social provenance was poor and obscure. He had been born in 1861, the son of a Glasgow textile merchant who died when Wingate was a one-year-old baby. His family, in straitened circumstances, moved to Jersey, whence the young Wingate was lucky enough to enter Woolwich in 1878, after which his career prospered.[4] He graduated from the military academy a respectable tenth out of thirty-nine, and, with characteristic opportunism, got himself attached to the Egyptian army, where promotions were known to be more rapid, in 1883. Again like Kitchener, Wingate quickly realized that knowledge of Arabic would open doors, and he spent every spare moment he had learning the language.[5] The opportunities for self-improvement for young officers in the late Victorian era were clearly considerable if one had ambition and talent. Wingate and Kitchener spent their leisure hours learning exotic languages, while, in the 1890s, Winston Churchill would use his own ample leisure time as a young officer in India devouring Gibbon and Macaulay in order to sharpen his English prose style.

G. W. Steevens, the tabloid journalist, gave the best description of Wingate in the late 1890s and described him as the 'type of the learned soldier' who, under different circumstances, might have been professor of oriental languages at Oxford because of his ability to 'learn you any language you like in three months'. This ability was particularly useful when dealing with untrustworthy natives. 'As for that mysterious child of lies, the Arab, Colonel Wingate can converse with him for hours, and at the end know not only how much truth he has told, but exactly what truth he has suppressed.' If Kitchener was the practical man, Wingate represented the intellectual side of the team.[6] Intellectualism, in Wingate's case, was combined with assiduous record keeping, meticulous filing and a taste, some said, for the macabre. Wingate's papers, now kept in the University of Durham Library, occupy 190 boxes; he was a prodigious letter-writer and a keeper of a voluminous diary, and he constantly wrote reports, minutes and records of meetings and conversations, which reveal him to have been the consummate Victorian colonial administrator.[7] He conceived a high opinion of his historical importance, which resulted in his keeping all his records with admirable method and exactness. Wingate's sense of the macabre was demonstrated by his rumoured possession of the Khalifa's skull as a personal trophy, from which, it was alleged, he would drink champagne on the anniversary of the Battle of Omdurman until his death, aged ninety-one, in 1953.[8]

Like many other military rulers, Wingate enjoyed his status. As governor general he was said to be an autocrat, while civil government, in the early years of British rule in the Sudan, followed a military pattern.[9] As late as 1919, after Wingate had left the Sudan, the official handbook published by the Foreign Office repeated the old mantra, 'supreme military and civil command is vested in the Governor-General', as concise a description of autocracy as any.[10] Humphrey Bowman, an Old Etonian education officer who had gone to the Sudan as part of the Colonial Education Service in 1910 and would later serve in Iraq, mentioned Sir Reginald Wingate's grand manner in his diary: he 'has got a wonderful "manner": never forgets a face or a name . . . Here he is absolute ruler; he travels in kingly state, and is always accompanied by native orderlies and attendants.'[11] There was never any doubt about Wingate's love for the pomp and majesty of absolute power. Of course, no autocrat can govern a country purely by himself, and so a bureaucracy is needed, and this, in the case of the Sudan, was provided by a group of men described by Lord Vansittart, a Foreign Office veteran, as the 'finest body of men in the world'. In Vansittart's later recollection, these young men were 'best fitted by character to bear early and lonely responsibility for thousands of square miles in a climate which might use them up in twenty years'.[12]

To understand the culture of imperialism from the point of view of the people who actually ran the British Empire, the Sudan Political Service is as good a place as any to start. The SPS was instituted in 1901, and a regular system of recruiting young university graduates was in place by 1905. These recruits, unusually for the time, were chosen on the basis not of examinations but of a series of interviews. It was the duty of the Sudan government agent in London to sift through hundreds of application forms and letters of recommendation, and then invite a short list of candidates to the selection board in London. Wingate, as governor general, took a personal interest in recruitment, and was bombarded with letters from friends asking him to take on this or that particular candidate. In most cases, he politely refused the requests, but he was certain of the qualities needed if one was to be admitted to the SPS. One candidate was accepted after Wingate wrote a glowing endorsement: 'his father is the archdeacon of Exeter and all the boys are athletic, public school boys, and brought up under the best influence with strong religious belief'.[13]

This summed up the ethos of the service. Public schoolboys were strongly favoured, as were athletes, and it was this particular feature which gave rise to the saying that the Sudan was a country of 'Blacks ruled by Blues'. 'Blacks' referred to the original Arabic name for Sudan, *al bilad as-sudan*, the Land of the Blacks, while 'Blues' referred to the distinction of getting a Blue by representing either Oxford or Cambridge in a match against the other university. Athleticism was greatly valued because of the supposedly sapping nature of the climate. The Sudan, in the words of one later governor general, was not a land for 'weaklings to master'.[14] The Sudan Political Service was regarded as the elite of the African Service, and enjoyed a prestige comparable with the Indian Civil Service. It conferred even greater distinction, because it was known that getting in was not simply a matter of passing examinations, as was the case for nearly every other branch of the civil service. Service in Sudan was very much about character and not merely brains; Sudan was where the 'best of the imperial breed' could exercise an unlimited sway over natives. In the layered, hierarchical mindset of the time, 'Imperialist England requires, not the mediocre by-products of the race, but the flower of those who are turned out from our schools and colleges.'[15] The chosen men in Sudan would have satisfied Lord Cromer's stern requirements. They were not the mere 'by-products of the race', but 'excellent specimens of our academic and athletic culture'.[16] Of the fifty-six recruits taken on between 1902 and 1914, twenty-seven had a Blue from Oxford or Cambridge. Because only between seven and ten people were recruited each year, the service quickly gained a reputation for exclusivity and tightly bound camaraderie. There was a need, it was said, for 'sound, competent, steady men', which resulted in a strong esprit de corps, with men of similar intellectual outlook and background almost invariably being chosen.[17]

The interview process in London was not particularly rigorous, but involved a series of questions designed to show mental toughness; cranks and people with foreign accents were firmly rejected. When asked 'What made you want to serve in Sudan?', one candidate replied, 'I always wanted to serve in the Sudan, Sir, ever since seeing *Tarzan of the Apes* [the 1918 film]'; he was not selected. Wingate personally rejected another candidate on the less substantial pretext that there was 'something Levantine about him and as you know that fact alone makes him undesirable'.[18] The public school ethos was overwhelming. Colonel Sir Stewart Symes, Governor General of the Sudan from 1934 to 1941, remembered that there was always 'a strong public-school flavour about the members of the Sudan Political Service'.[19]

In addition to the Blue, preferably in a manly sport like rugby or boxing, as opposed to hockey or soccer, a degree in Classics or History from either Oxford or Cambridge was highly valued. In the early days, before 1914, the average man in the service could be said to have a '2nd in History from Oxford' and a rugby Blue. In an analysis of the 500 or so men who made up the service between 1902 and 1956, it was found that over 70 per cent were from Oxford and Cambridge.[20] Even in 1952, in the final year of recruitment, every successful candidate was a graduate of Cambridge University. One entrant from the 1907 intake remembered his colleagues fondly: 'We were athletes ... [there was] a former Rugby captain of Oxford and Scotland, an ex captain of the Cambridge cricket XI, a member of the Oxford soccer team, a member of the Oxford cricket XI and a Middlesex county rugby player.'[21] Interestingly Winchester College, an English school traditionally known for its intellectual, rather than sporting, prowess, proved to be the school with the most members in the service, a total of thirty, or about 6 per cent of the entire intake. Eton and Rugby were second and third with twenty-one and twenty members of the service respectively.[22] As one former member revealed, 'the really important thing about a public school background was that you virtually couldn't get into the SPS without it. I can't think of any of my SPS colleagues who didn't have one.'[23]

Analysis of the backgrounds of members of the Sudan Political Service modifies and deepens notions of class in imperial Britain. A staggering one-third of all the men who joined the SPS were the sons of clergymen. This shows that the imperial elite was certainly not, as has been true of some other imperial cultures, an elite of money or social status; rather it formed a clerisy, noted for its education and cultural values.[24] The clergyman's son would have been educated at an independent, or public, school, but did not expect to inherit much money or even land. This needs to be remembered as a corrective to the simplistic popular idea that the British Empire was run by the upper classes. Empire was largely a preserve of a tiny elite, but that elite was middle class and professional; it was not particularly aristocratic, in the sense of a landed, hereditary caste who enjoyed wealth and power in Britain.

The recruitment of public school sportsmen left very little room for people who did not at least outwardly conform to the behaviour expected of the ruling class. Once selected, however, recruits were given considerable freedom. Again, it was individualism and character that were prized above all else. The greatest attraction of the service was the reputation it acquired for placing new recruits in positions of responsibility 'with little interference from above'. The job was physically demanding, as the young district commissioner would spend much of his time trekking on foot. Sudan itself covered a vast area, there were poor communications and the young recruit was spared the reams of paperwork with which other civil servants had to grapple.[25] The 'Information for Candidates', reprinted in January 1933, offers a clear indication of the official mentality of the period. It stated that only candidates 'over 21 and under 25 years of age on October 1st of the year in which they stand for selection' would be considered. Voluntary retirement would be allowed at the age of forty-eight, provided the official had completed fifteen years' service. This allowed some to start other careers in teaching or even academia, if they were so inclined. 'General character' would be given a prominent role in assessing the suitability of candidates.[26]

Once chosen, the successful candidate would be on probation for two years, until examinations in Arabic and Law were passed. These exams were not generally very demanding, but they did require some private study. During the probationary period, the government could give the probationer three months' notice before discharging him. In the 'Information for Candidates', it was specifically stated that district commissioners and assistant district commissioners would sit as 'Magistrates to deal with criminal and civil cases'. They would be expected to 'lead an active life' and much of their time would be 'spent in travelling'. Service in the Sudan came with its own perks and privileges; a very generous annual leave of ninety days a year was granted, and because no leave was granted to first-year probationers, recruits could enjoy 122 days' leave in their second year.[27] Distances across the Sudan were notoriously vast, but when, at the beginning of the twentieth century, a young officer on leave in England complained to Lord Kitchener that it had taken him three weeks to get from Cairo to Khartoum, he got little sympathy from the great man. 'I don't think you have much to complain about,' said Kitchener. 'It took me three years!'[28]

The first year's study would have to be paid for by the probationer out of his own salary, and would take place at Oxford or Cambridge. A special course of Anthropology was added in 1908. Later, training would take place in the field. Wilfred Thesiger, an Eton-educated Oxford boxing Blue, joined the service in the summer of 1934 and went almost immediately to the Sudan, and though he passed the initial Arabic exam after two years, he 'always regretted' that he had not become 'proficient in Classical Arabic'.[29] A repressed homosexual, Thesiger spent time in the south of the Sudan, which was distinctly more African and less Arab than the north.

The tribal, and less urbanized, south of Sudan was, in many ways, a more challenging district in which to serve as assistant district commissioner and it tended to attract more eccentric, solitary types. Generally, the quality of the Sudan Political Service was praised even by people who were not naturally well disposed to the British or their empire. One journalist, the Frenchwoman Odette Keun, a former lover of H. G. Wells, remarked on how absurdly foolish the young university-educated Englishman generally was in the 1920s. 'Most of us Continentals, at one time or another, have met the young Englishman abroad – on his holidays in Switzerland or on the Riviera; tramping in Italy and Spain.' The impression she formed of this creature was not exactly favourable. The Englishman on holiday in Europe was 'an exceedingly silly, rowdy and obnoxious young animal. He is carelessly dressed. His manners are loutish or intolerably casual. His recreations are purely sportive or childish . . . He drinks too freely and smokes endless vile pipes . . .'[30]

The sort of Englishman who 'tramped' around Italy and Spain in the 1920s would invariably have been drawn from the class of people who ran the empire, because travel on the continent of Europe before the Second World War was the preserve of a small minority of the population. Odette Keun never hid her contempt for this type of English upper-middle-class young man: 'after you have listened to his conversation, you go about in a state of hyper-amazement, asking yourself what the English Universities imagine they are doing in the manner of educating English youth'. She added, 'Whatever it is they have implanted in his brain, he conceals it with utmost success.' But when it came to the officials in the Sudan, the French journalist had nothing but praise. The same Englishman who drank too much on the Riviera or showed himself grossly ignorant of literature or philosophy to his more sophisticated continental counterparts became transformed in the Sudan. There the British official had 'to be well-groomed and dignified in his person'. He was invariably 'unselfish professionally', a stoical individualist, who could also be a team player. The 'youth we know in Europe as a Nuisance and a Stupid had to become one of an order of Samurai'. One feature of the young 'Samurai' which seems to have impressed Keun was the 'sexual austerity' of the young members of the SPS. She describes how the 'English social code . . . vetoes liaisons with native women pitilessly'.[31] This was not strictly true; like many other foreigners, Keun was fooled by outward show and missed much of the hypocrisy which prevailed in this area. In the more remote districts, British officers were known to take mistresses and wives from among the local women.[32]

Odette Keun's reference to the 'sexual austerity' of British officers reveals the masculine nature of the service. Wives were regarded as an encumbrance at best, or a nuisance at worst. Sir John Maffey remarked on the appointment of a governor of the western province of Darfur in 1927 that he 'was a bit perturbed at the idea of a newly married man going to Darfur', as it was 'a land for energetic bachelors'. The lady concerned, however, was 'of a suitable age and of considerable medical attainments'.[33] She could be useful. The rules were quite simple: 'no member of the Political Service may bring a wife out to the Sudan until he has completed five years' service or reached the age of 28, whichever happens first'. As a consequence of this edict, married men were not selected for the SPS, and 'the Government [would] probably dispense with the services of a probationer who gets married during his period of probation'.[34] The shortage of European women in Khartoum, the capital, which itself was not as inhospitable as some of the more remote areas, was often remarked in the early years of British rule. One early probationer who went to the Sudan in 1907 remembered the dances at the Grand Hotel in Khartoum, to which everyone went in full evening dress, or what would be termed white tie, at which most of the men 'had to dance together as there were few women in Khartoum in 1907'.[35]

For women who did finally accompany their husbands to Sudan, the conditions could be tough. There were the diseases, such as malaria and black-water fever, and their husbands were often not very tolerant of their wives' complaints. One bride, when she remarked on the heat, was told by her husband, 'If you want to enjoy this country, never, ever mention the heat.'[36] Wives commented on the degree of exclusiveness the service fostered, talking about its elitism and its remarkably close-knit structure. Rules seemed absurdly petty and restrictive; the service seemed, to one young woman, to have a 'definite preoccupation with seniority'. Another young wife remembered a journey from Port Sudan to Khartoum by train in 1927, in which she found herself sharing a sleeper with another wife who was unknown to her. The younger woman was told in no uncertain terms, 'My husband is senior to yours, so you will have the top bunk.'

Darfur province was a particularly feudal jurisdiction in the 1920s and 1930s, where the Governor enjoyed almost despotic power. His palace in El Fasher, the provincial capital, was an 'imposing white-washed, castellated building, approached up wide steps, at the foot of which on either side were two small cannons'. There the Governor imposed rigid protocol, and guests were told, on arrival, that no one, however senior, could 'wear a blue shirt until he had been in the Province for two years', as blue shirts were deemed to be more casual than white ones; 'our reaction', said one of the wives, was 'unprintable'. The Governor showed similar arrogance towards the US Army Air Force, during the Second World War, when he wired a message to the effect that the Americans could not land at the time they requested because he would be playing polo on the landing strip that afternoon. Indeed, the ability to play polo became so important in Darfur that it often dictated who was to be transferred there.[37] In Khartoum, there were the balls at the Grand Hotel and the garden parties at the Governor's palace, and there were two clubs, the Sudan Club and the Khartoum Club, membership of which was determined by income and status. Higher earners were invited to join the Sudan Club, while the Khartoum Club was reserved for people of lower rank and income. Needless to say, the most junior Political Service official, 'however poor, always belonged to the top club without question'.[38]

During most of the time this regime continued, British rule was hardly ever disputed. Sir Stewart Symes, the Governor General, in a report on the situation in the Sudan in 1935 could remark with some complacency that no one had 'seriously challenged' British rule since 1898.[39] That is how the scene looked in 1930s, but, behind the façade of tranquil, unquestioned British supremacy, there lurked the menace of religious fanaticism. The British always had the Sudan Defence Force in the background, a highly mobile and well-equipped force for 'frontier protection and military operations'.[40] Through much of its history, the Sudan had been a turbulent place. Arab tribesmen had engaged in the lucrative slave trade, which the British had suppressed in the early twentieth century. There was always the threat that another holy man, like the Mahdi, could inspire the masses to topple the rule of the English infidels and return the Sudan to the path of pure Islam.

This danger of religious fanaticism and insurgency is often faintly alluded to in the memoirs and even in the official documents relating to British rule in the Sudan. To the journalist G. W. Steevens at the end of the nineteenth century, the Sudan was the 'home of fanaticism' and had always been called the 'Land of the Dervishes'.[41] Sudanese religious enthusiasm had been particularly vexing to Wingate at the beginning of the twentieth century, and he had done all he could to assuage the religious sensitivities of the Muslim population. In 1901, in one of his first actions as governor general, he appointed a council of twelve ulema – doctors of Islamic law – to advise him on religious matters. To appease the Muslims of the north, Christian missionaries had been forbidden in that region, while the government had itself undertaken the building of mosques. 'The policy of the Sudan Government', boasted the official Foreign Office handbook of 1919, had always been, 'and remains, that of encouraging Islam in all its legitimate modes of expression'.[42] The British knew, from the experience of confronting the Mahdi, the havoc which could be caused by a charismatic, religiously inspired political leader. The catalogue of Sudanese who tried to imitate the Mahdi's success was long, and many of these aspiring prophets are recorded in the handbook, which told of various abortive insurrections with almost tedious exactitude: 'In February 1901, Ali Abdul Karim claimed to be the Mahdi; he was arrested and imprisoned'; 'In the autumn of 1902 Mohammed el-Amin ... declared himself the Mahdi in Kordofan ... He was captured at Dar Gimma and executed at El Obeid'; 'In 1904 Mohammed Adam declared himself the prophet Isa [that is, Jesus] ... He was killed in a skirmish.'[43]

During the First World War Britain became deeply concerned about the prospects of Muslim nations following the Turkish Sultan – who, as caliph in Constantinople, was the designated head of the Islamic world – in siding with the German Kaiser. This atmosphere of fear at the prospect of a religious war, a jihad, finds its most vivid expression in the John Buchan spy novel *Greenmantle*, published in 1916. Buchan describes Islam as a 'fighting creed', represented by the mullah who 'still stands in the pulpit with the Koran in one hand and a drawn sword in the other'. Sir Walter Bullivant, a Foreign Office grandee, warns Richard Hannay, the hero, that 'there is a jehad preparing. The question is, How . . . ?'[44] Buchan's belief that this jihad would come from Turkey or the Middle East was belied by actual events. In the Middle East, under the influence of General Edmund Allenby and, to a lesser degree, T. E. Lawrence, a large body of Islamic opinion was ranged against the Turks. It was in the Sudan that a local leader heeded the call for jihad and was, for some months in 1916, an irritant to the British cause.

When Ottoman Turkey entered the war against the Allies in November 1914, the British authorities in the Sudan quickly rallied local opinion as well as influential religious leaders to their side. A curious production of the early months of 1915 was the *Sudan Loyalty Book*, a published account of all the professions of friendship and loyalty from the Sudan's Islamic leaders and local chiefs. 'From the depths of our hearts and sentiments . . . we proclaim our loyalty and adhesion to our beloved British Government in all events,' wrote Ahmed El Mirghani, a leading Islamic cleric from Kassala, on 13 November 1914, little more than a week after Britain and France had declared war on the Ottoman Empire. Mirghani extolled the British administration as a 'just Government that has rescued the inhabitants of the Sudan from the trials and misrule of former years'.

The circumstances in which this extraordinary book was written were unusual. On 6 November, the day after the British declaration of war on Turkey, 'His Excellency Reginald Wingate . . . called together a number of leading chiefs in Khartoum and the vicinity and explained to them the state of affairs.' Immediately afterwards, 'these notables met together and drew up and solemnly signed a declaration of their loyalty to Great Britain'. The *Sudan Times* then published these messages of loyalty, and finally collected them all in a book which, in the proud words of the introduction, would 'remain as a memorial both to the wisdom and beneficence of the British administration in Sudan'. The book also bore witness to the 'practical intelligence and the high sense of honour and duty on the part of the people of the Sudan'.[45]

These protestations of loyalty meant nothing, however, to Ali Dinar, the hereditary Sultan of Darfur, who used the opportunity of war to attack

British interests and to denounce those Sudanese who had made common cause with the British infidels. Under the terms of the Condominium Agreement of 1899 Ali Dinar had been allowed to remain independent in return for payment of an annual tribute to the Sudan government. In the middle of 1915, this recalcitrant figure was beginning to become a major irritant. The British authorities kept abreast of his movements and that year issued a damning portrait of the ruler himself. Ali Dinar was, as far as the British were concerned, 'totally illiterate' and had 'imbibed all his knowledge of government and his views and conduct of life from his period of detention' under the barbarous Khalifa at Omdurman in the 1890s. In this state of primitive captivity, he had 'neither opportunity nor desire to learn anything of western civilization'. The memorandum identified three main traits of his character as personal pride, innate suspicion and fanaticism. If all this were true, it raises the question of why the British recognized him as Sultan of Darfur in the first place.[46]

Ali Dinar believed, perhaps correctly, that the British would use the pretext of war to take over his sultanate. He tried to anticipate this by writing an official letter to Wingate in December 1914 which asserted that, as a Muslim sultan, he was quite prepared to 'fight against Christian domination' of Muslim states.[47] An independent ruler whose authority depended on British acquiescence, Ali Dinar had been misbehaving even before the outbreak of the First World War, by refusing to allow any Europeans to enter El Fasher, Darfur's capital, or indeed the sultanate itself; all business between the Sultan and the Governor General's office in Khartoum was conducted by correspondence.[48] As a consequence of Dinar's lack of co-operation, the outbreak of the European war made the government in Khartoum particularly suspicious.

By early 1916, after an exchange of increasingly hostile messages, the Sultan had declared the inevitable jihad against Britain and had announced his intention of invading the Sudan, to the east of Darfur, with a large 'army of believers'. This act of folly sealed his fate; a small field force was prepared finally to end the threat of this troublesome figure from a feudal age. The British were contemptuous of Ali Dinar's ignorance and stupidity and believed that 'enemy intrigue' had been the principal factor in his disobedience. In the Sudan, at any rate, it seemed that Buchan's nightmare

Herbert Horatio Kitchener, 1st Earl Kitchener of Khartoum by Sir Hubert von Herkomer and Frederick Goodall (1890). This highly romanticized portrait of Lord Kitchener (1850–1916) outside the walls of Cairo was painted at the zenith of the British Empire. More than any other individual, Kitchener symbolized the British empire. He would be immortalized in one of the most famous posters in history for the slogan, 'Your country needs you'.

Rajah Gulab Singh by an unidentified Indian artist, *c.* 1840. Gulab Singh (1792–1857) bought Kashmir from the British in 1846 for the enormous sum of £750,000. His descendants would continue to rule as sovereign Maharajas of Kashmir until independence in 1947.

Henry John Temple, 3rd
Viscount Palmerston (1784–
1865) was Foreign Secretary
during the 1840s when the
British Crown acquired
Hong Kong. An advocate of
British expansion, he would
later serve as Prime Minister.

Hercules Robinson, 1st Baron
Rosmead (1824–97). In 1859,
at only thirty-four years of
age, he was appointed the
youngest Governor General in
the colonial history of Hong
Kong. Robinson instituted
the cadetships under which
young men from Britain would
begin their service in the
administration of Hong Kong.

SIR HERCULES ROBINSON.

Frederick Hamilton-Temple-Blackwood, 1st Marquis of Dufferin and Ava (1826–1902). A romantic Irish aristocrat, Dufferin was a diplomat of conservative instincts; he was also Viceroy of India when Upper Burma was finally annexed by the new Conservative government in 1885.

Painting of a scene in Mandalay, the old capital of Upper Burma, from *c.* 1908 by Gerald Kelly. Mandalay's capture in 1885 caught the imagination of the public in Britain, and Rudyard Kipling took the city's name as the title for one of his most famous poems.

he Charge of the 21st Lancers at the Battle of Omdurman by Richard Caton Woodville (1898).
he charge at Omdurman in 1898 is remembered as the last cavalry charge of the British
rmy, in which Winston Churchill, then just twenty-three, took part. It marked the end of
ie revolt, which cost 10,000 Mahdist lives, but fewer than fifty British deaths.

eneral Charles George Gordon (1833–85).
 brave and committed soldier, Gordon was
 nt to Khartoum to quell the Mahdist revolt.

Mohammed Ahmed (*c.* 1844–85), a
religious leader who claimed to be the
'Mahdi', the successor to Mohammed,
was portrayed as a wild fanatic by the
British popular press. The Mahdi's troops
famously killed Gordon on the steps of
the palace in Khartoum.

George Nathaniel Curzon (1859–1925) (*second from left*) was, according to an undergraduate ditty about him, a 'most superior person' who enjoyed a gilded imperial career, appointed Viceroy of India aged just thirty-nine.

Gertrude Bell (1867–1925), the daughter of a family of industrialists based in Tyneside. She was self-willed, highly intelligent and focused – and one of the founders of modern Iraq. She supported the Hashemite monarchy and was a key figure in building such institutions as the National Museum of Iraq in Baghdad.

T. E. Lawrence, or simply Lawrence of Arabia (1888–1935). Lawrence saw himsel[f] as one of the founders of modern Iraq, yet he enjoyed celebrity while avoiding any official positions of responsibility in the Empire.

Flora Shaw (1852–1929) was a well-known journalist who married Lord Lugard in 1902. The pair, who both believed fervently in Britain's imperial mission, became one of the most influential couples in the Empire.

Lord Lugard (1858–1945) (*centre*) benignly extending hospitality to Nigerian chiefs at London's Regent's Park Zoo. Back in Britain, Lugard fraternized with, and entertained, visiting chiefs, while never questioning the basis of British rule.

Rudyard Kipling (1865–1936), the bard of empire, whose poems such as 'If' and 'Recessional' captured the spirit of the British Empire better than those of any other writer. By 1928, when this photo was taken, Kipling was tired and disillusioned. As Orwell remarked, 'somehow history had not gone according to plan'.

Men fishing from their boats on Dal Lake, near Srinagar by R.B. Holmes & Co. (1921). A rural scene in Kashmir of the kind Kipling describes in his work.

Faisal I (1883–1933) alongside T. E. Lawrence (*third from right*) and Nuri al-Said (*second from left*), amongst others, at the Paris Peace Conference in 1919. Faisal was crowned King of Iraq in 1921. Faisal and Lawrence were friends and allies in the Arab Revolt against Ottoman rule during the First World War.

The bustling town of Basra in the 1950s. Basra, in the south of Iraq, was a religious centre, as well as a hub of the oil business and trade. Increased prosperity masked popular unease about the monarchy and the pervasiveness of British influence, which led to the Revolution of 1958 and the collapse of the Hashemite monarchy.

Aung San (1915–47) with his young family at the beginning of 1947. Aung San Suu Kyi, the baby girl in the photograph, would grow up to be a notable figure in Burmese politics in her own right, winner of the Nobel Peace Prize in 1991.

Aung San (*centre*), the young Burmese independence leader, with the Labour Prime Minister, Clement Attlee, and other Burmese politicians in the independence talks held in London in January 1947. Independence came a year later in January 1948, but Aung San did not live to see it.

The close relationship between Lady Mountbatten (1901–60) and Jawaharlal Nehru (1887–1964) has intrigued historians. Whatever the exact nature of the relationship, their affinity was obvious to everyone who met them, not least to Lord Mountbatten.

Hari Singh (1895–1961), the last Maharaja of Kashmir, whose decision determined Kashmir's accession to India in 1947. Difficult and proud, Hari Singh was exiled in Bombay and then formally deposed by Nehru's Congress-led Indian Government.

Sir Abubakar Tafewa Balewa (1912–66), a Muslim from the North, was the first Prime Minister of independent Nigeria between 1960 and 1966. His assassination in January 1966 in a military coup marked the beginning of the crisis which led to the Biafran War of 1967–70.

Chukwuemeka Ojukwu, the son of a wealthy businessman, was educated at Oxford University. He described his years there as the 'happiest in his life'. A career soldier, he would lead the briefly independent state of Biafra during the Biafran War. Here, he is pictured introducing Biafra's new currency in January 1968.

Colonial life in Hong Kong in the 1940s. The British were known for transplanting a 'little corner' of England to every outpost of the Empire. Here, people are playing bowls, a quintessentially English game.

. disciplined former soldier and graduate of Cambridge University, Alexander Grantham (1899–1978) had a less idealistic approach to democracy in Hong Kong than his predecessor, Sir Mark Young. Grantham reversed Young's reforms, postponing the advent of democratic government in Hong Kong by at least a generation.

Sir Robert Hotung (1862–1955), a long-lived businessman of European and Chinese attraction. Hotung chose to live his life as a Chinese gentleman, and was excluded from the British Hong Kong Club on account of his race. Undeterred, he formed clubs for ethnic Chinese, despite craving the honours of Empire.

Ne Win (1911–2002), an eccentric general, who became Prime Minister of Burma in 1962 and President in 1974. He was the leading figure of postwar Burma, but died under house arrest in 2002.

Saddam Hussein (1937–2006), attired in the American business suit which was an international status symbol in the 1970s. Saddam was a charismatic nationalist politician, before he gambled and lost everything by antagonizing the United States of America. He was hanged in 2006.

Gafaar Nimeiri (1930–2009), the army colonel who led the 'May Revolution' in Sudan in 1969. A dynamic figure, Nimeiry was himself toppled in a bloodless coup in 1985. He died in his home in Omdurman, in 2009.

Chris Patten (1944–), the 28th and last Governor-General of Hong Kong, receives the Union flag after it was lowered for the final time on 30 June 1997 marking the end of 156 years of British rule. He was fervently pro-democracy, believing, perhaps mistakenly, that this was what the British Empire had been all about.

After the handover, Hong Kong's skyline remained an impressive monument to the success of its capitalism. An energetic, bustling city, Hong Kong managed to preserve its status as a key financial and commercial hub in Asia.

Kirkuk oil field, one of the largest in Iraq, a country whose modern history has been dominated by oil.

The referendum held in Southern Sudan in January 2011 marked a turning point in the country's history. The establishment of Southern Sudan was a repudiation of the attempt to create a united Sudan from two very different elements, the Muslim North and the Christian South. This development shows how contentious many legacies of the British Empire remain of a 'Turco-German Jehad' had been realized.[49] Turkish encouragement of jihad within the frontiers of the British Empire was no idle illusion. None other than Enver Pasha, Commander in Chief of the Ottoman army, had written to Ali Dinar personally as early as February 1915, claiming that the aim of the British and French was 'to extinguish the light of Islam'. Enver Pasha praised Ali Dinar for being 'renowned for [his] religious zeal', and urged him to join 'the Great Jihad' which the 'Emir of the Faithful and the Khalifa of the Prophet', the Ottoman Sultan in Constantinople, had proclaimed.[50]

Ali Dinar, for his part, played the role of pantomime villain to perfection. His florid style, or rather that of his secretaries, so highly praised in Arabic literature, when translated into English seemed bombastic and almost comical: 'You Christians are infidels and dogs . . . You have accepted death . . . you shall taste at our hands the bitter cup of death . . . Sorrow and annihilation shall befall you, and your souls shall be cast into fire and Hell.'[51] Despite some low-key warnings from the French, who were worried about British involvement in Darfur threatening their position in neighbouring Chad, the military campaign against the Sultan was swift and conclusive. The campaign showed how skilful the British were at playing the propaganda war, as their proclamations incited the people of Darfur against their despotic ruler, whom the British had installed in the first place. The Governor General, in his proclamations, also skilfully adopted the florid rhetoric of classical Arabic prose: 'Verily you know', he declared to the natives of Darfur, 'that Ali Dinar has killed your chiefs, plundered your property and sold your women and children . . . you should therefore forsake him . . . and surrender yourselves to my victorious troops whom I have sent to punish that unjust and tyrannical person . . . When you surrender you will be given the "Amen" of God and his Prophet, and you will be saved . . . from the humiliation of servitude to Ali Dinar.'[52]

The campaign against the Sultan was led by Colonel P. W. Kelly, who commanded a small force recruited from the Egyptian army. This force crossed the Darfur frontier on 20 March 1916 and managed to pin down the Sultan's army in El Fasher by blocking the main road east which led to the Sudan itself. On 23 May, Kelly's force successfully occupied El Fasher, after a small battle on the 21st in which 1,000 soldiers, out of a force of between 2,000 and 3,000, of the Sultan's army were killed or 'incapacitated'. As in other colonial skirmishes and battles, the casualties were utterly one-sided; three British officers were wounded, three men were killed, a further two men died of their wounds, and eighteen were wounded.[53] As late as the middle of May, immediately before the decisive battle, Ali Dinar – now utterly deluded – threatened the Governor General personally with a bitter death: 'it is my earnest hope to kill you in the worst possible manner, to let you taste torture and to hang your head and the heads of your troops in the public market as an example'.[54]

As usual, there was a wide gulf between the Sultan's high-flown rhetoric and his capacity to realize his threats on the ground. His tune changed markedly after the defeat on 21 May; now he was suing for peace and blaming everything and everybody for his own rash actions: 'I beg to submit to Your Excellency that all the disputes and dissensions which took place between you and myself were simply the result of intrigues and of the cunning policy of the . . . notables of Darfur.' It was they who had 'induced me and cheated me, by their advice and talk, not to listen to your wise counsels and admonitions'. Like many unsuccessful generals, before and since, the Sultan blamed the cunning and treachery of his followers who 'promised to fight and die before surrendering', but who 'on the arrival of the Egyptian and British troops' all 'forsook' him. Ali Dinar was now willing to give up his sultanate for 'peace with His Excellency the Governor-General', to 'keep my own family and property'. It was a pathetic attempt to save his own skin after the inflated boasting and pompous, blood-curdling rhetoric of only two weeks before.[55]

Ali Dinar now fled with some of his immediate relatives and about 2,000 of his men. It seems that he still harboured hopes for some kind of guerrilla campaign against the British, despite his earlier protestation that he only wanted peace. As his situation grew more desperate during the summer of 1916, Dinar's men began to surrender and desert their leader. Mass defections had occurred by the beginning of November, as hunger now afflicted the Sultan's isolated followers. As troops commanded by Major Hubert Huddleston encircled the Sultan, men, women and children flocked to the British troops and it was reported that, by 5 November,

200 men and 300 women had surrendered with 6,000 head of cattle, 70 horses and 300 camels. The list of prisoners included two sisters of the Sultan and several of his children. The end for Ali Dinar was bloody: on the 6th he was surprised in an ambush with about fifty of his remaining followers. There was some shooting and the Sultan's body was found about a mile from the camp, where the ambush had taken place, with a bullet through his head.[56] Like the Khalifa, the last Sultan of Darfur had learned a harsh lesson in the folly of opposing British rule.

Darfur was annexed in 1916 and incorporated into the regular government of the Sudan. It was made into a province with its own governor, who was subordinate to the Governor General in Khartoum. The problem of dealing with Islamic fanaticism would remain a difficult one for the British administrators, and it was fear of Islamic subversion which led to the next, fateful step in the Sudan's history. The 1920s saw a resurgence of nationalism in Egypt and the Sudan, which was almost always couched in Islamic religious terms. A letter to Saad Zaghloul, the Prime Minister of Egypt, in July 1924, spoke of the English as the 'rulers', and of the Egyptians and Sudanese as the 'subjects', adding, 'God knows we do not want them for they are not of our religion and are unbelievers and their tyranny in the Sudan is not hidden.'[57] In the Sudan itself, there occurred a mutiny at the Khartoum Military School, where cadets refused to go on parade in August 1924 and took up arms instead. A cordon of British troops confined the armed cadets to the school area before any real harm could be done. In the view of the Sirdar's private secretary, this incident 'must definitely put an end to the present system of providing native officers for Arab and Sudanese units'. British officers were needed to keep the volatile native troops in check. More specifically to the mutiny, the 'arrival of another British Battalion and aeroplanes' would have its 'fullest value in its stabilising effect on the civil opinion'.

The mutiny in Khartoum, small though it was, was yet another symptom of the crisis which gripped the British Empire in the 1920s. After the First World War, nationalist movements had sprung up, or had been strengthened, in Iraq, India, Egypt and Palestine. In the Arab world, it was immediately recognized that militant Islam was the principal threat to British authority. In the Sudan, there had always existed two distinct cultures: the northern part of the country was Islamic and Arab, while the southern was more African. The threat that subversion from the Islamic north would undermine the loyalty of the southern region, coupled with the fact that the 'Southern provinces had never produced anything but a loss', led to the formulation of what later became known as the 'Southern Policy'. The man who was most closely associated with this policy was Harold MacMichael, who had graduated from Cambridge in 1904, with a first in Classics and a Blue in the esoteric sport of fencing.[58] He had entered the Sudan Political Service in 1905 and had spent all his career there. MacMichael, known as 'MacMic' to his friends and 'horrible Harold' to his detractors, was yet another driven servant of the state, a type with which the history of the British Empire seems to abound. 'He never tired of work, and while his colleagues slept in the long siesta of a Sudan afternoon, MacMic worked, read, reread, minuted, and responded to the files of government, mastering their contents, remembering their trivialities.' His personal coldness was legendary and it was, perhaps, compounded by his close connection with the very highest circles in the British Empire. His mother had been the Honourable Sophia Caroline Curzon, the elder sister of George Nathaniel Curzon, who served as viceroy of India and foreign secretary, only narrowly failing in achieving his ambition of becoming prime minister. MacMichael, though then a fairly junior member of the SPS, corresponded regularly with his famous uncle about foreign affairs. Contact with Curzon 'placed him in a unique position among the members of the Sudan Political Service', and no doubt added to his aloofness and his sense of superiority.[59] Like nearly all his peers in the service, MacMichael was no democrat. Far from being harbingers of liberal pluralism, the servants of empire were naturally at home with the idea of human inequality, with notions of hierarchy and status. In the context of Africa, MacMichael, in his 1935 book *The Anglo-Egyptian Sudan*, had written: 'Men are not equal in any practical, obvious sense, and the fact is so patent to the African that to deny it by word or deed is merely proof of wrongheadedness. A sense of homage is natural to him. It is a good and sensible instinct, and it must be given scope.'[60]

The natural corollary of human inequality was the building up of a machinery of government in which the native chiefs 'should play an important part'.[61] This was at the heart of the idea of 'indirect rule', through which local chiefs, the 'natural leaders', were given power over their subjects by British overlords. Harold MacMichael had no real affinity with the pagan south of the country, being, like so many other imperial servants, a keen student of Arabic and Islamic culture. As civil secretary, the effective deputy to the Governor General, he issued a statement on 'Southern Policy' in 1930, in which he declared that the administration of the south was to be developed along 'African' rather than 'Arab' lines, and that the future of the southern Sudan might 'ultimately lie with the countries of British East Africa', like Uganda, Tanganyika and Kenya, rather than with the Middle East.[62] This 'Southern Policy' has been well documented, but what is less understood is the exact background to its adoption in 1930. In a paper entitled 'Spread of the Arabic Language in the Southern Sudan' dating from June 1929, Lord Lloyd, the Resident in Cairo, wrote to the Foreign Secretary, the Labour Party's Arthur Henderson, stating that the 'pagan blacks' in the south of the Sudan were 'in a very early stage of civilisation, differing in every respect from the more sophisticated Arab tribes of the north'. Among the tribes of the south, the Dinka, Lord Lloyd continued, 'show us pre-historic man at home in the twentieth century, as uncontaminated by outside influence as any race that can be found in the world today'. He used the imagery of the noble savage; the Dinka were 'flourishing, virile, pastoral and in the early Iron Age'. A confirmed Conservative imperialist, Lloyd reported that MacMichael had argued 'very forcibly that the encouragement of Arabic in the South would serve to promote the spread of Islam', leading perhaps to Islamic fanaticism. 'Islam, though on a higher plane than their present pagan beliefs', was nevertheless in MacMichael's opinion a 'stationary and therefore retrograde faith'. The general conclusion reached was that Arabic as a general language should disappear from the southern provinces, except in those places where it had become the vernacular. MacMichael was then quoted as referring to the 'wide gulf' between the north, where the slave trade was extremely profitable, and the south, where memories of 'slave raids are vivid'.[63]

Once the 'Southern Policy' had been announced in 1930, officials lost no time in defending it. Sir Stewart Symes, the Governor General, spoke in 1935 of 'the distinction between the peoples of the northern and southern Sudan' as being 'real and fundamental'. The people of the south were 'for the most part primitive and pagan' and needed a 'simple education system', in furtherance of which Christian missions would be encouraged and 'northern subversive influences' excluded.[64] By the early 1930s, governors of southern provinces would now be empowered to eject 'immigrant undesirables from the North' who could be a 'possible source of propaganda' in the 'primitive' south. Under the Passports and Permits Ordinance of 1922, some southern governors were already empowered to expel from their provinces 'individual natives of the Northern Sudan whose continued presence [was considered] undesirable from an administrative point of view'.[65] MacMichael's 'Southern Policy' merely made more explicit the fear of militant Islam corrupting the still largely pagan south and subverting British rule there. The policy was viewed sceptically by northern Sudanese politicians who believed that the 'Southern Policy' was a deliberate attempt to divide the Sudan for the purposes of establishing imperial authority more easily over its peoples.

North and South

The Second World War had very little effect on the Sudan. By the early 1940s the 'Southern Policy' had become so entrenched that it seemed likely that 'in the fullness of time' the country would be divided, with the north becoming an 'independent Arab state' and the south perhaps being joined to the British East African network of states, such as Uganda, Kenya and Tanganyika.[1] Certainly, there was a steady confidence in the British mission in the Sudan, and no one thought that independence would happen so soon. The British Civil Secretary, in effect the Governor General's right-hand man, was now Douglas Newbold, a cerebral man who was a popular workaholic. Newbold was lauded as a man of liberal disposition who once confided to a friend that he did not 'hate or despise Dagoes' and that 'colour' did not 'worry him at all'. He boasted of his advanced views, suggesting that 'as far as general appearance goes the average nonwhite is, I think, better looking than the average white, and usually more friendly'. His professed liberalism did not, however, stretch to matters of the internal government of the Sudan. Comparing Gilbert Murray, a well-known Greek scholar and humanitarian of the day, to Winston Churchill who, in the 1930s, had moved to the right of the Conservative Party, Newbold remarked, 'What would Gilbert Murray do if he were Governor of Kassala [in the northern Sudan]? I'd rather have Winston Churchill – he *would* hang murderers and collect his taxes.'[2]

Newbold's pragmatism, when it came to matters of administration, was matched by the other members of the Political Service who, by the 1940s, were stuck in their ways and seemed to younger men to embody the conservatism and reactionary tendencies associated with retired army officers between the wars. Graham Thomas was a young recruit to the service in the late 1940s and he remembered being distinctly out of step with the majority of his colleagues. He had been educated at a Welsh grammar school and had even been a Labour Party candidate. Sir James Robertson, a bluff Scottish rugby Blue from Oxford, who had succeeded Newbold as chief secretary, befriended the young Welsh firebrand, but was clearly puzzled by him. Thomas remembered Robertson as 'physically a big man, with tremendous energy and a strong personality'. Robertson was surprised when Thomas refused to join the Sudan Club on the grounds that he considered it 'repugnant to have a club based on race'.[3] Sir James replied that the Egyptians, the Lebanese and the Indians all had their own clubs, so why should the British not have one?

His other colleagues, Thomas remembered, were 'almost totally composed of Oxbridge "blues" from upper middle class family backgrounds', quite a few of whom had 'joined the service before the General Strike', which had taken place in 1926. These men had 'no knowledge or understanding of the social changes which had taken place in Britain'.[4] Even the officials back in the Foreign Office in London (Sudan, because of the unusual condominium arrangement, fell under the Foreign Secretary's jurisdiction rather than that of the Colonial Secretary) complained of the 'Sudan Civil Servant, who, with all his admirable qualities, has a rather limited and parochial public-school outlook'.[5] As in other parts of the empire, it seemed that nothing had changed, as officials complacently believed that their lives would simply continue as they had before the war.

Thomas's recollections of the mood and style of Khartoum in those years after the Second World War would have been recognized by Sudan veterans of an earlier vintage. The Grand Hotel in Khartoum still put on lavish entertainment, and there was the usual endless circuit of cocktail, lunch and dinner parties, with the traditional formalities of protocol: Thomas and his wife, Ismay, were informed, when they told a middle-aged woman that they were attached to the education department, that 'you won't be invited to the Palace for years'. This turned out to be false, but the mood of stuffiness still very much prevailed. The Grand Hotel itself was remembered as a 'multi-racial' meeting place and it was there, for the New Year's celebrations in 1951, that Prince Aly Khan and the Hollywood actress Rita Hayworth took the whole first floor to stay with their entourage.[6]

Despite the occasional glamour of Khartoum, there were signs that the imperial system was under strain. The 'Southern Policy' had resulted in neglect of large parts of the south, which were administered by a particular type of British official who enjoyed the relative freedom that the remoteness of their postings had given them. The highly individualistic nature of the administration in the Sudan is revealed by the startling fact that there were only 140 officials in the whole country, at a time when the population was 9 million.[7] The sparseness of the population meant that, in the southern Sudan, immense tracts of land were ruled 'by just a handful of men'. This feeling of openness and independence was compounded by the fact that the man who ruled 'with paternal despotism vast and populous territories in the Southern Sudan' would have been, under normal circumstances, 'just another London commuter swept along with the flow of mankind, emerging from the tube to a job'.[8] The delusion of grandeur entertained by district commissioners in the south of the Sudan was aggravated by their tendency to remain in the same district for years, even decades. These men, often coming from a military background, were a 'tough, motley' crew, and were given the nickname 'Barons of the Bog' by their colleagues in the Muslim northern Sudan. The unorthodox methods of these district commissioners in the south by the end of the 1930s often led to administrative chaos.[9] The Bog Barons supported the 'Southern Policy', because it protected their power and independence from officials in the north, and many of them were believers in the system of 'indirect rule', of building up self-contained ethnic or tribal units in the south of the country, which could then be used as bulwarks against the encroachments of Islam and Arab culture.

Robertson, appointed civil secretary in 1945, did not share these views. He disliked what he felt to be the obscurantism and eccentricity of the southern district commissioners, and believed that the southern Sudan had to be 'opened up and brought into touch with reality'.[10] The nature of this 'reality' was probably as unclear to Sir James as to everyone else. He certainly misjudged, as did so many others, the pace of change in the colonial empire and the speed with which parts of it were hurrying along the path to independence. While Robertson was directing the political affairs of the Sudan, the governor general became a figurehead who, in many cases, had not served much time in the Sudan. The men appointed under this arrangement were very different from the soldier administrators like Kitchener and Wingate who had served in the region for decades and were fluent in Arabic. Yet even the more desk-bound administrators like Robertson were allowed to direct policy themselves, in much the same way that MacMichael had done in the 1930s; as always in the British Empire, it was the individual that mattered. A strong, masterful governor general like Sir Reginald Wingate could direct his own government, but when the governor general was less forceful, or more ignorant of Arabic and the Sudan in general, as Sir John Maffey had been in the 1920s and 1930s, the civil secretary took charge and imposed his vision on the country. Robertson, a powerfully built man with a strong independent will, did not foresee in the 1940s the 'sudden change in the world situation which led to the rapid colonial emancipation of the 1950s and 1960s'.[11] He did, however, succeed in reversing MacMichael's 'Southern Policy', just before independence was granted to the Sudan, which upset the precarious balance that prevailed there.

In the words of a modern expert on the Sudan, Robertson 'rushed in where Mandarins feared to tread'.[12] He announced the effective end of the 'Southern Policy' in 1946. As the Sudan groped its way to self-government, it was decided that the only basis for progress was for the two parts of the country to be welded together to form one country, which might then, over time, move towards full independence. The forum where all this was decided and put in place was a conference held in the capital of the southern Sudan, Juba, in June 1947. The conference lasted only two days, but the fundamental decision to combine the south with the north was taken. There had been an initial difficulty because the southern delegates had stated clearly that they did not feel their region was ready for self-government, while the northern delegates were insistent that they needed self-government immediately. Robertson himself realized the danger in which the southerners were placed, since the south was less well developed and had fewer educational facilities, with little infrastructure of any kind. Without 'safeguards' to their culture, he believed that the south would be 'overwhelmed and swamped' by the north. The ideal safeguard would, of course, be the 'maintenance of a British controlled administration with British governors and District Commissioners'.[13] This judgement was naive given that, in 1947 when the independence of India was imminent, it was becoming clearer that the British might have to leave the Sudan at some time in the not too distant future, and what would become of the south then?

Privately, Robertson was not too optimistic about the ability of the south to compete in the united Sudan, as there were still 'limited facilities for education above the elementary level' in the region. From what he had seen, he had concluded that the educated southern Sudanese made 'good clerks', but that a large proportion failed 'when given positions of financial responsibility'. Many of the educated southerners, in his view, showed an 'instability of character and proneness to alcoholic excess which is a little disturbing'. This, he believed, was due to the fact that education lifted them out of their 'tribal environment' and thus disorientated them. Robertson recognized that very little advance had been made in the 'evolution of social equality' between north and south, and he did not hesitate to blame the south for this disparity and lack of progress. In the same report, dating from 1950, Robertson railed against 'Nilotic Conservatism' which regarded cattle as a 'social institution and a means to the acquisition of wives', instead of as an economic asset. He was quite open about his anti-southern bias. The lack of 'social equality' was partly the fault of the average southern Sudanese man, who was 'not readily responsive or companionable outside his own immediate circle'.[14]

Although the Sudan was still nominally under the dual sovereignty of Britain and Egypt, the British were firmly in the dominant position. It was under British auspices that a Legislative Assembly was convened in December 1948, though this hardly represented the people of Sudan. As one British official remarked in 1950, the Legislative Assembly is 'not a fully representative body' and 'a large and important section of the Muslim population has no share in the government of the country'.[15] The Legislative Assembly appealed to the old official prejudices in favour of 'natural leaders', the sheikhs, chiefs and petty princes. It was this predilection for natural leaders which, perhaps more than any other political impulse, defined the British Empire. The publicity agent for the Sudan government, E. N. Corbyn, based in London, could not conceal his delight at the new Sudanese Legislative Assembly as he observed its first session in the spring of 1949:

> Looking down the list of names anyone who has long known the Sudan will find the sons of the tribal leaders, with whose fathers he used to ride on camel-back over their wide tribal areas years ago. These men who have come to Khartoum to the Legislative Assembly are the natural leaders of the real Sudan . . . Thus the Sudan's first Legislative Assembly is a wholesome one.[16]

Furthermore, these natural leaders were 'men of strong personality and independent minds', exactly the kind of men who, if they had been British, would have been recruited to the Sudan Political Service.

The natural leaders were also generally men of property who wielded influence as tribal leaders. They were decidedly not part of the urban intelligentsia or effendia class, whom most British officials despised. 'Effendi' is a Turkish term, widely heard in Egypt and the Sudan in colonial times, which now, in modern Turkish, is used where an English-speaker might say 'Mr'. In the colonial period, the effendi were the educated classes, the intellectuals, who often adopted a strongly nationalist stance against British colonial rule. Years later, when reflecting on mistakes made by the British in the Sudan, Sir James Robertson accepted that this class of person had been foolishly overlooked. The Sudan government had 'tended to put too much emphasis on the Nazirs and the Sheiks and not enough on the small educated class'. The British 'were much more friendly with the country members than with the "effendia"'. Sir James went on to suggest candidly, 'I suppose we thought that the "effendia" were aiming to take our place.' Other 'grave errors' included the failure to do 'anything until 1944 to create some central body in which the Sudanese could voice their opinions', and, lastly, the failure to 'develop the South' after the 'Southern Policy' of MacMichael had been adopted in 1930.[17]

Meanwhile, the Sudan accelerated towards independence, prompting Robertson, who by 1956 was safely ensconced as Governor General of

Nigeria, to regret 'the haste and untidiness of it all'.[18] The rapidity of the move to full independence, which occurred only eleven years after the end of the Second World War, surprised British officials in the Sudan more than it did the civil servants in Whitehall. The process was certainly 'untidy'. The date for independence had been set for 1 January 1956, but disturbances and serious unrest had taken place even before the British had left. The 'Southern Policy', described as a 'comprehensive plan to build up a series of self-contained racial and tribal units . . . based upon indigenous customs, traditional usage and beliefs', had been hated by the Arabic-speakers of the north, who saw it as a symbol of the British tendency to divide and rule. In the south, the Juba conference was resented, because it sealed the emergence of a single, unitary state. The south, as independence drew near, wanted a federal system, which the northerners rejected, while the British were increasingly anxious to get out of the Sudan, even before the Sudanese had agreed on a permanent constitution.

The situation was heading towards a crisis. The 1950s saw a rising tide of Arab nationalism across the Middle East, as people struggled to free themselves from what they saw as Western imperialism, or from feudal constitutions which, as in the case of Iraq and Egypt, placed countries under monarchical rule. The abolition of the Egyptian monarchy by the Free Officers' coup led by Gamal Abdel Nasser in July 1952 was followed by the new Egyptian government's abandonment of any lingering claims of sovereignty over Sudan.[19] Arab nationalism had its effect in making northern Sudanese politicians more focused on achieving independence and less willing to accommodate the south, which, in terms of population, comprised only a quarter of the country. As the British Foreign Office drily observed, the 'nationalistic self-confidence which is now the mood of all independent Middle Eastern states is not conducive to successful colonial rule'.[20]

The explosive situation reached its climax in August 1955 when troops of the Sudan Defence Force based in the south mutinied. The structure of the Force had made such an event likely, as it was split into battalions which had been selected along ethnic lines. There were 'black battalions' from the south and then there were the Camel Corps and the Eastern Arab Corps, which, as their names implied, were units composed exclusively of

Arabic-speakers.[21] The south protested, in a violent way, against the increasing dominance that northern Arabic-speakers began to wield in their territory. As the British began to leave the Sudan in the early 1950s, the vacuum which had been left in the south of the country was filled by officials from the north. This arrangement led to even more confusion. The Sudanese civil service was now dominated by northerners to such an extent that, in 1954, only six out of 800 senior officials were from the south. The presence of northern administrators, teachers and traders in the south was resented, and rekindled old fears which stemmed from the days when northern raiders would literally hunt down the peoples of the south to take them into slavery.[22]

On 18 August 1955 a company of soldiers from the Equatoria Corps staged a mutiny at Torit. This southern unit had been summoned to Khartoum, where the men believed they would have been rounded up and executed, before being replaced by soldiers from the north. Instead, the soldiers began turning on Arabic-speaking northern officers, administrators and merchants and their families. The situation was aggravated when the majority of the 400 or so police officers in the region joined the mutineers. Ismail al-Azhari, the Sudanese Prime Minister, still under the jurisdiction of the Governor General, ordered northern soldiers to be transported to the south to restore order. The troops were taken in British aircraft, which caused resentment towards the British on the part of the southern Sudanese. The northerners, in turn, were furious that the British authorities in Uganda refused to extradite people whom they believed had instigated the coup. The mutiny itself was viewed in sections of the northern Sudan press as part of an imperialist plot. Omdurman Radio was explicit about this: 'The rash sedition in the South was deep-rooted, as a result of 50 years during which Imperialism filled the hearts of Southerners with spite and hatred against the Northerners.' The radio broadcast even suggested that the 'Southern Army mutinied under a premeditated plan which we believe was perpetrated by a foreign hand'.[23]

The British, according to the broadcast, were duplicitous, offering to help the Sudan on the one hand while shielding the mutineers on the other. The newspaper *Ayam*, a northern Sudanese publication, stated that it was the Governor General's job 'to see to it that the mutineer refugees in

Uganda are brought back to the Sudan at the first opportunity for their trial', and that, if the Ugandan government refused to hand them over, the 'whole affair' would reveal 'Britain's conspiracy against the Sudan'.[24] Those mutineers who had escaped to Uganda were the lucky ones, as many others surrendered believing the Governor General Sir Knox Helm's promises of 'fair trial, clemency and safe conduct'. He left the Sudan for good on 13 December 1955, and the mutineers were simply tried by courts martial; the courts martial handed down about 180 death sentences, most of which were subsequently carried out.[25] Yet for northerners to complain about Britain's actions was unfair. Throughout the crisis, the Foreign Office in London had been determined that the north's desire to keep the country united should be realized. An 'independent, unified and stable administration' was needed in the Sudan as a buffer and a barrier against Egyptian expansion. For this reason, 'Her Majesty's Government must do all that is in its power to retain the confidence of the present Sudan Government and of the Northern Sudanese.' This would entail 'some temporary sacrifice of effective administration in the Southern Sudan and possibly of the interests of the Southerners'. In short, the Foreign Office view was that anarchy in the south was preferable to the disintegration of the new state that the British were leaving behind.[26]

In the last months of 1955, British control of the Sudan had more or less collapsed. The northern Sudanese were moving into positions of power in Khartoum and elsewhere in the northern regions, while in the south the 'two and a half million inhabitants' were, so far as the British authorities in London were concerned, now 'virtually unadministered'.[27] It is clear from the sources that the British themselves felt some responsibility for the events in the Sudan. In a report to the Foreign Secretary, Selwyn Lloyd, written in October 1956, Chapman Andrews observed that the 'policy pursued over a long period by the British Administration and [the] influence of Missionaries were also important causes of the trouble ... For whatever reason, and however justifiable, both combined to separate the South from the North and therefore to make the rule of the Northerners unacceptable.' The problem, in all this confusion, as British officialdom saw it, was the old bugbear of Arab nationalism and the 'unstable emotionalism which affects all Arabs', which 'must certainly have an adverse effect on the Negroid Southerners'. Andrews concluded that 'we are not solely responsible for that past', but it was inescapable that 'for 50 years, or two generations, we were in charge and the policy that inspired our steward-ship during that period cannot be left out of account'.[28]

For the southern Sudanese, the events of 18 August 1955 quickly became a symbol of their struggle for independence. In August 2007, the *Sudan Tribune*, a southern publication, could state proudly that 'what happened in Torit on August 18th, 1955 is a great part of Southern Sudanese history that will live with people of South Sudan for centuries to come'.[29] The mutiny was an important symbol of southern resistance, but more significantly it marked the beginning of a nightmare for the Sudan, during which civil war raged for nearly forty of the country's first fifty years of independence. The various wars which plagued the Sudan during that time assumed different guises, but always, underlying the fighting, was a fundamental conflict between the Arabic-speaking north and the African south – despite the reluctance of northern politicians to see matters in such starkly racial, or ethnic, terms.

It was clear from the outset of the first civil war, which continued sporadically from 1955 until 1972, that the conflict had a racial dimen-sion, and many commentators observed the 'race war' element with fascination. Sudan's first civil war has been characterized as 'secret, silent and hidden', a war that was 'smothered by a grass curtain'. Vague rumours filtered out from the south at times, telling of 'northern atrocities, of harassed refugees . . . even of deliberate genocide', but such reports were vehemently denied by the government in Khartoum.[30] Yet the war was known about in the West. A report in the *Daily Telegraph* in March 1967 spoke of 'Khartoum's Arab Army' which had been 'systematically killing men, women and children of the Southern Sudanese Nilotic tribes and burning their villages and crops for over three years'. The reporter, a 'special correspondent', indignantly observed that it was an extraordinary comment on 'international values that a war of racial extermination (the genocide of Nuremberg) has been going on for years in Central Africa, without anything being done or even very much written about it'. Right-wing apologists for Ian Smith's illegal regime in Rhodesia were quick to point out the double standard in the seemingly complacent attitude of the

West to Sudan and the moral indignation felt by many towards the racist government in Rhodesia. In a letter to *The Times* on 7 April 1967 headed 'Where Racialism is Ignored', Sir David Renton, a Conservative MP, referred to the Sudanese Arab army 'systematically killing the Nilotic people of the Southern Sudan, most of whom are Christian'. He went on to compare the situation in Sudan with that of Rhodesia: 'compared with that [Sudanese] brutality the refusal to allow the principle of one man one vote in Rhodesia would be insignificant'. Renton then drew the conclusion that it 'would be a sad world if coloured people could do what they like to each other while the United Nations declines or is powerless to intervene'.[31] In the same month, the BBC's *24 Hours* painted a grim picture of government 'repression and squalor' in the southern Sudan, a broadcast which brought a complaint from the Sudanese Ambassador in London, Jamal Mohammed Ahmed. A couple of days later, the Ambassador also made a formal complaint to the Minister of State at the Foreign Office.[32]

Some African politicians were quick to exploit the troubles of the Sudan for their own ends. In 1969, Hastings Banda, the leader of Malawi, used the civil war in the Sudan to beat the drum of African nationalism, defining the conflict in purely racial terms: 'if Malawi was to fight anyone, such enemies would be the Arabs of the Sudan, because they oppress Africans'. In Banda's crude view, skin colour should determine where people lived: 'If whites in South Africa, Mozambique or Angola belonged to Europe, then Arabs in Africa should also belong to Asia.' It was an unsophisticated view, but it captured the mood of racial strife across Africa in the late 1960s.[33] The war which was fought in Sudan from 1955 lacked the intensity or ferocity of other orgies of violence which subsequently scarred the continent of Africa, like the Rwanda genocide of 1994, but, by early 1971, the UN estimated that over 500,000 people had been killed in Sudan in the previous sixteen years.[34]

In 1972, a peace agreement between the Sudan's north and south was signed. The Addis Ababa Agreement, which allowed a measure of autonomy to the south, was an initiative promoted by Colonel Gaafar Nimeiri, who had launched a successful coup in Khartoum in May 1969. Nimeiri was aged thirty-nine at the time of the coup and had been born the son of a postman in a district of Omdurman. A football fanatic, he graduated from

Khartoum Military College in 1952 and had travelled widely, taking various military training courses, including a two-year spell in the United States at Fort Leavenworth, Kansas.[35] Like many other leaders in developing countries at the time, Nimeiri came to power on the back of communist support and his military coup was described as a coalition between a military junta, the Sudan Communist Party and Arab nationalists. This led to a period in which the influence of the Soviet Union in the Sudan was significant.[36] The agreement was fragile and, during the 1970s, new tensions arose, while the desire of the southern Sudanese for greater independence was openly acknowledged by foreign diplomats. In his valedictory dispatch, written in September 1977, to David Owen, the new British Foreign Secretary, the British Ambassador to Khartoum observed that a member of his staff had called on a southern politician and found the man studying designs for a new, separate flag for the south.[37]

Tensions were increased by the discovery of oil in the south of the Sudan in 1978. The southern regional government was anxious that an oil refinery be built in the south close to the oilfields. Nimeiri ignored its protestations and ordered that the refinery be built in the north, combined with a pipeline to the Red Sea, from which the crude oil could be directly exported.[38] In the south itself, a demonstration occurred in Juba in September 1978 when 3,000 secondary school pupils protested, demanding that the oil located in the south be used exclusively for that region. Although, during the summer of that year, the topic was 'never mentioned officially', it was clear to Foreign Office officials in London that some of the southern leaders were thinking in 'regional rather than national terms'.[39] The final cause of the outbreak of the second Sudanese civil war in 1983 was the general drift of Nimeiri's government from a secular Arab nationalism, which was strongly influenced by socialism, to a more overtly religious, Islamic ideology.

Already in 1977, Nimeiri had sidelined his erstwhile communist friends and begun to flirt with Islamic ideologues. After an abortive communist coup in July 1971, he purged the communists from his government and banned the Communist Party. In 1977 he expelled the last Soviet military advisers from the country.[40] Needing to broaden the base of his support, he then brought two prominent Islamic politicians into his government:

Sadiq al-Mahdi, the great-grandson of the nineteenth-century Mahdi, and Sadiq's brother-in-law Hassan al-Turabi, leader of the Muslim Brotherhood and founder of the National Islamic Front, a militant Islamic party. Turabi was appointed attorney general and immediately pressed for Islamic reform of the legal system and for greater Islamic influence throughout the country. When the British Ambassador, D. C. Carden, met him in December 1978, he was struck by Turabi's charm, but also by his insistence on the 'Islamisation of the Law', and even more by his stated desire to 'push Islam in the South', a region which had not been penetrated by the Islamic faith.[41]

With his new friends, Nimeiri embarked on a radical programme of Islamization of the Sudan which culminated in 1983, when he declared an Islamic revolution in Sudan, which would now be a country governed by Islamic law. The traditional penalties – amputation for theft, flogging for alcoholic consumption and death for apostasy – would be rigorously applied across the whole country. To show his determination in enforcing this strict regime, Nimeiri made the lavish gesture of pouring $11 million worth of alcohol into the Nile, and 'European-style' dancing was banned.[42] The attempt to impose sharia law in the south proved highly controversial and led to the founding of the Sudan People's Liberation Army (SPLA), whose declared aim was not a separate state of southern Sudan, but rather more democracy in the whole country. The second civil war was an obscure conflict, largely forgotten by a wider world which had tired of concerning itself with wars in Africa. Sudan earned its reputation as 'Africa's most dysfunctional country', a title used as a headline by the left-leaning *Guardian* newspaper in its obituary of Nimeiri in June 2009.[43] Nimeiri himself was deposed in a bloodless coup in 1985, and elections were held the following year which were won by Sadiq al-Mahdi's Umma Party, the heir to the Mahdist tradition. This tradition, perhaps ironically, was dominated by moderate Islamists, compared with other parties in modern Sudan. Graham Thomas has even suggested that the 'Mahdist state of a century ago was comparatively liberal and compassionate compared with the present Islamic Fundamentalist Military Regime'.[44]

The history of the modern Sudan is dominated by Islamic fanaticism. This would hardly be surprising to people like G. W. Steevens, the journalist who described the Sudan as the 'home of fanaticism', more than a hundred years ago.[45] The moderate Mahdi was himself toppled in a bloodless coup in 1989 led by Omar al-Bashir, a colonel in the Sudanese army. This coup proclaimed an even more vehement form of Islamic fundamentalism and sharpened the conflict with the south by emphasizing the hegemony of Islamic culture. The war against the south was 'reaffirmed as jihad'. Breaking with precedent which was almost as old as Islam itself, Christians were denied special status; women's relative freedom in public and the workplace was severely restricted. To some historians, the approach of the new militant Islam in the Sudan was similar to the concept of 'Manifest Destiny', adopted by nineteenth-century Americans who aspired to colonize and subdue the entire continent of North America. In much the same way, Sudanese nationalists embarked on their divine mission to 'spread their civilization to non-Muslims'.[46]

The leading intellectual figure behind this recrudescence of militant Islam was the man whom Nimeiri had appointed attorney general in the 1970s, Hassan al-Turabi. Turabi is a figure who has not only had an effect on Sudanese politics, but, through his brand of militant Islam, has had a wider impact in the field of international relations. It was he who first invited a Saudi Islamic dissident, Osama bin Laden, to Sudan in 1990. Turabi was a small man, with a white wisp of a beard, who, unlike many Islamists, was familiar with Europe and the United States. As a student in 1960, he had wandered across America, even staying 'with Red Indians and farmers' – an experience that had shown him the folly of capitalism and secularism. After this trip, he returned to London, where he obtained a master's degree in Law from the London School of Economics in 1961, followed by a doctorate in Law from the Sorbonne, in Paris, in 1964. Turabi now wanted to create an international community – the ummah – which would be based in the Sudan, and could then transform other countries in the region. The Sudan, in this highly ambitious scheme, would become the intellectual centre of an Islamic reformation. To further this plan, Turabi invited all Muslims, regardless of nationality, to the Sudan. He represented the moderate face of the Islamic revolution, while Prime Minister Bashir was portrayed as the military strongman.[47]

Attracted by Turabi's idea of establishing an 'Islamic international', bin Laden spent many happy years in Sudan, where he indulged his passion for horse-breeding, while his wealth was appreciated as a source of investment, as Sudan's economy gradually crumbled under the pressure of civil war. At a reception given soon after bin Laden's arrival, Turabi even described the Saudi as the 'great Islamic investor'.[48] Sudan's embrace of Islamic fundamentalism led to the country being listed by the United States as a 'state sponsor of terrorism' in 1993. Despite tensions between Bashir and Turabi, the Sudanese government continued to back terror attacks, most notably the 1995 assassination attempt on Egypt's President Hosni Mubarak, as he drove from Addis Ababa's airport into the city for a meeting of the Organization of African Unity. Turabi openly boasted about this attack, proclaiming that 'the sons of the Prophet Moses, the Muslims, rose up against him' and 'sent him back to his country'.

Such overt enthusiasm for acts of terror contributed to the growing sense of isolation which permeated the Sudanese government in the late 1990s. The consequence of this growing isolation was the expulsion of bin Laden from the Sudan in May 1996. The Sudanese, to repair their credit with Washington, even offered to hand bin Laden over to the Americans. The Clinton administration did not see bin Laden as the mortal threat he later became and declined the offer.[49] Bin Laden, after remonstrating with his former friends and arguing that he had commited no crimes against the Sudan, then progressed to Afghanistan to continue his jihad against the United States. In the Sudan, militant Islam had more local battles to fight. The doctrine the Islamists espoused in the Sudan was infused by a racial arrogance, which is foreign to Islamic fundamentalism. In the Islamic faith, adherence to Islam is of paramount importance, whereas issues of race and ethnicity are comparatively unimportant. It was this relative tolerance which led to the rapid spread of the religion in Africa and Asia, from its earliest days in the seventh century to more recent times. In the Sudan, the racial element was often regarded as being a key factor, even though intermarriage had made the distinction between Arab and African blurred to the point of being meaningless.

Yet the 'race war' element of the struggle was what characterized the latest manifestation of the conflict in Darfur, in the west of Sudan, which, as already noted, had been an independent sultanate before 1916. It was incorporated into the government of the Sudan in January 1917, but remained a backward and uncultivated region. In 1935, Darfur had only one primary school, while in 1956 it had the lowest number of hospital beds of any Sudanese province.[50] It emerged as a problem in 2005 just as the second civil war between the north and south was coming to its conclusion. In January that year, a Comprehensive Peace Agreement was signed in Nairobi that finally ended the war between Khartoum and the Sudan People's Liberation Army, which was intended to lead the way to full independence for the south. The cost of the war, in terms of displacement of people and lives lost, has never been accurately measured. International agencies reported a figure of 1 million dead, but the consensus figures have crept towards 2 million in more recent estimates.[51]

The crisis in Darfur began as a sideshow to the seemingly never-ending conflict between north and south. After a severe famine in the province in 1984–5, the mid-1990s saw an increasingly chaotic situation develop, embittered by virulent Arab Islamism. It was this fervour which inspired the activities of the gangs of marauders, known as the *janjawid*, a word whose precise meaning is disputed but has generally been understood to signify 'an armed man on horseback' in Arabic.[52] Tensions and violence had been simmering in Darfur until 2004, when an operation by the African rebels killed seventy-five Sudanese government soldiers. It was at that moment that Omar al-Bashir, who had elevated himself to the presidency in 1993, called on local tribes in Darfur to fight the African insurgents. Despite the general truce, signed in Nairobi in 2005, the Darfur conflict continued to the point where, regardless of ethnic labels, gangs of armed thugs simply used the confusion as an opportunity 'to grab land and livestock', under the banner of a 'state-sanctioned military operation'.[53]

In March 2009 an extraordinary warrant was issued by the International Criminal Court in The Hague. For the first time in history, a serving head of state was indicted for war crimes and crimes against humanity. A panel of three judges accused Omar al-Bashir of personal responsibility for 'murder, extermination, rape and other crimes' in the country's western province, Darfur, 'where an estimated 300,000 people had been killed and millions displaced since 2003'. This indictment was spurned by the Sudanese government, which swiftly responded by revoking licences for Oxfam and other aid agencies to operate in Darfur.[54] Darfur was described by UN officials as early as 2004 as the 'worst humanitarian crisis in the world', but it was only the latest episode of a recurring conflict which had paralysed the Sudan for nearly forty years. For as long as the country remained a united state, seeds of future conflict existed; the conflict between Arab and African, between north and south, seemed never ending.

Between 9 and 15 January 2011 a referendum was held in the southern Sudan in order to determine whether the region should remain part of a unified Sudanese state. The referendum gave a decisive result, as 99 per cent of voters supported the creation of an independent state of southern Sudan. The Sudan, after fifty-five violent years of independence, seemed destined to be formally divided into two independent states. Yet whether this solution would finally end the bloodshed and turmoil experienced in the region over so many decades remains unclear.

It is perhaps unfair to judge Britain's contribution to the Sudan purely in terms of the conflict which has plagued the country almost continuously since 1955. British achievements in Sudan were undeniable. Theodore Roosevelt remarked as long ago as 1910 that he doubted if, in any part of the world, there was 'a more striking instance . . . of genuine progress achieved by the substitution of civilization for savagery'. This was a bold claim, but estimates of the population decline during the time of the Mahdi and his bloodthirsty successor, the Khalifa, from a figure of about 8 million to some 2 million, showed that Sudan had enjoyed some benefits from the stability provided by colonial rule. A note of self-congratulation, combined with an awareness of the ingratitude of the natives, was expressed most eloquently by Rudyard Kipling, the unofficial poet laureate of empire, in 1913: 'In due time the Sudanese will forget how warily their fathers had to walk in the Mahdi's time to secure even a bellyful. Then, as happened else-where, they will honestly believe that they themselves created . . . the easy life which they were bought at so heavy a price.'[55]

Yet, whatever the material benefits of British rule, the most enduring imperial legacy in Sudan was the policy incoherence. The British adopted a 'Southern Policy' only to reverse it after sixteen years. The Sudan is an outstanding example of how the enormous degree of individualism which imperial government fostered often led to policy inconsistency and tragedy. That theme is a central argument of this book: individualism, the reliance on individual administrators to conceive and execute policy, with very little strategic direction from London, often led to contradictory and self-defeating policies, which in turn brought disaster to millions. As one historian observed, 'the British administration had certainly vacillated between uniting the south with the north and making the south a black Christian buffer region against the spread of Islam in the north'.[56] Another observed, at the end of the first Sudanese civil war in 1972, that 'even pro-British historians admit that British policy at the time was not consistent or far-sighted' with regard to the Sudan.[57]

Back in the 1890s, Lord Cromer identified lack of policy coherence as a prominent trait in British administration: 'The absence of consistency which is so frequently noticeable in the aims of British policy is indeed a never-ending source of embarrassment to those on whom devolves the duty of carrying that policy into execution.'[58] Cromer saw democracy as the principal cause of this inconsistency. Like so many of his contemporaries, he believed in personal rule and influence. He was an individualist, who fundamentally distrusted democracy, and yet the subsequent history of the empire he spent his life serving shows that it was the very individualism he praised that created instability, as it provided no over-arching framework under which consistent policies could be conceived and executed. The adoption and rejection of MacMichael's 'Southern Policy' was a tragic example of the shortcomings of individualism, devoid of any strategic aim.

PART V

NIGERIA: 'THE CENTRE CANNOT HOLD'

Indirect Rule

Perhaps no other country in the modern world is more a creature of empire than Nigeria. Even the name 'Nigeria' was a consciously invented one, first appearing in an article of the London *Times* on 8 January 1897, at the beginning of the year in which Queen Victoria celebrated her Diamond Jubilee. Flora Shaw, a journalist and commentator on colonial affairs, suggested the name, which she thought would be a good title for the 'agglomeration of pagan and Mohammedan states which have been brought . . . within the confines of a British protectorate'. For the 'first time in their history', these states needed to 'be described as an entity by some general name'.[1]

Flora Shaw was the very model of Victorian womanhood. Her friend and younger contemporary Mary Kingsley described her as a 'fine, upstanding young woman, as clever as they make them, capable of any immense amount of work'. She was also, according to Kingsley, 'as hard as nails', and she talked 'like a *Times* leader all the time'. She was a committed patriot and was 'imbued with the modern form of public imperialism' which was 'her religion'. Unusually for her time, Flora Shaw was a professional woman. She had been born into a middle-class family in Ireland in 1852 and, in 1897, looked a good deal younger than she actually was. She had written a popular novel based on her Irish childhood, *Castle Blair*, which had been published as long ago as 1877. As yet unmarried, she had turned herself into a crusading journalist, after giving up writing novels in her thirties. Early in 1892 she had gone to South Africa, where she went down both diamond and gold mines. Nothing, it seemed, could stop her; she asked questions, investigated and then wrote hundreds of letters about labour conditions, agriculture and other aspects of colonial development.

Her letters so impressed the management of *The Times* that she was sent to Australia and New Zealand. On her return from the round-the-world trip in 1893, she settled in London to take up a permanent position on the newspaper as colonial editor. She was given an annual salary of £800 a year, much higher than other women journalists of the time.[2] She had become one of the best-travelled women of her day.

By the standards of the time, Flora Shaw was a minor celebrity. Like many writers of the late Victorian era, influenced as they often were by the writings of Thomas Carlyle, she worshipped strong, heroic men. This was the age of popular Darwinism. It was the age in which an obscure German philosopher called Friedrich Nietzsche spoke of the 'superman', a being 'beyond good and evil', whose destiny was to impose his will on weaker specimens of humanity. In the world of the 1890s, the 'superman', at least as far as the British could conceive the idea, was more often than not a colonial administrator, who usually took the form of a soldier versatile enough to turn his hand to administration and give law to the natives, a strongman who could speak native languages and write clear, 'manly' accounts of his achievements for his desk-bound political masters at home.

The other woman strongly associated with the beginning of British colonial rule in Nigeria was Mary Kingsley. She would have recognized and applauded the description of the 'superman'. She was another strong female who had been born into the middle class – into a family of academics and clergymen – in 1862. Her uncle was the famous novelist Charles Kingsley, author of the children's classic *The Water Babies*, who died in his fifties in 1875. Mary's parents had neglected her education, so she had been compelled to absorb scraps of information from her father's library. Both her parents died in 1892, when she was thirty, and, with the small inheritance she had been bequeathed, she reinvented herself by packing her bags and setting off for West Africa. There she considered herself an explorer and anthropologist but paid her way by trading, obtaining food by selling fish-hooks and matches, and even engaging in the rubber trade.[3]

Mary Kingsley was striking, if not conventionally beautiful. Tall, slim and blonde, she had big blue eyes, a large mouth and weak chin. Her smile was described as 'crooked'. It was when she opened her mouth, however, that the full power of her extraordinary personality revealed itself. With her deep voice and cultivated speech, she made a strong first impression. Her interlocutors would then be rather surprised, even charmed, by her dropped aitches and her very individual way of expressing herself, as she frequently used slang and other seemingly uncouth terms she had picked up from sailors and West African traders. As a child she had, like many toddlers before and since, shocked her father by picking up and repeating his large stock of swear-words. Rudyard Kipling met her at a tea party in South Kensington in the 1890s. Afterwards they left the house together and were clearly fascinated with each other, talking for hours. She spoke of witch doctors, of rubber and oil trading, of cannibal preferences in 'joints of human flesh'. Any further association, however, was strictly curtailed by the social constraints of the time. Kipling said to her, 'Come to my rooms and we'll talk it out there.' She agreed, then suddenly said, 'Oh I forgot I was a woman. 'Fraid I mustn't.'[4]

Both Mary Kingsley and Flora Shaw were committed imperialists. Kingsley died tragically young, succumbing to typhoid at the age of thirty-eight, while working as a nurse in a prisoner-of-war camp in South Africa in 1900. Yet in her short life she articulated as well as Kipling himself the unapologetic imperialism of the 1890s, the decade of her brief career and fame. For Kingsley, imperialism was a 'good and honest thing', which sought a world 'wherein just, honourable, respectable men of all races, all colours, all religions, can live, worship, trade, labour, or live quietly, unhampered by a lot of pettifogging arbitrary rules and regulations and persecutions'.

For imperialists like Kingsley, the British Empire was an ideal; it was not primarily about glory or money. England had seen 'Venice rolling in riches' and then 'Spain magnificent', but had also witnessed the decay of both those once mighty empires. The English 'must have the world, a free and open world'. Having welcomed the prospect of a world where all colours and races could live freely, Kingsley acknowledged that only the Northern European could make the world free. 'We know from centuries of experience that the ideal of making freedom for the world is not to be expected from any race save the Teuton.' According to Kingsley, there was nothing wrong with this kind of imperialism, which would free Africans and Asians from their superstitions and despotic rulers. In the same address, Kingsley asserted that this 'Imperialism, our Imperialism, is the thing that is not ashamed of wanting all the world to rule over'.[5]

This aggressive imperialism was what brought Nigeria into the colonial fold in the first place, and it is no surprise that the single individual who did more than anyone else to bring this about was a hero to both Mary Kingsley and Flora Shaw. George Goldie was a volatile, tempestuous man, who had been a soldier before becoming a trader. To Mary Kingsley, Goldie was 'one of that make of men who gave Britain India – namely a soldier-statesman'. It was unfortunate that in Africa those men had not been so attracted to founding empires. Goldie was the exception. In Kingsley's opinion, the empire needed more people like him. 'Had we but had a line of these men in Africa acting in conjunction with our great solid under-staff – the Merchant Adventurers – our African record would be both cleaner and more glorious than it is.'[6] For Flora Shaw, who had hoped to marry Goldie after his first wife had died in 1898, his exertions alone had prevented a territory passing 'into the possession of France and Germany' which was 'no less than half the size of British India'.[7]

George Goldie, or George Taubman-Goldie, had been born on the Isle of Man in 1846 and had been spared the usual treadmill of public school. This contributed perhaps to his eccentric, aloof and highly private manner. He was arrogant, but his arrogance was not of the sort that wanted monuments to be erected in his honour, or long biographies to be written about him. Indeed his 'wish to remain unrecognised amounted almost to a mania'. He had, in addition to this wariness of publicity, no 'literary ambition, no desire for popularity, no desire whatever to make money'.[8] In this he stood in stark contrast to Cecil Rhodes, who desired, and achieved, fame, immortality and a colossal fortune. The suggestion that Nigeria be called 'Goldesia', in recognition of George Goldie's achievements, and along the same lines as Rhodesia's celebration of Cecil Rhodes's achievements, met with a flat refusal from Goldie himself.

Yet, despite his seeming self-denial, Goldie's ambition was as intense as that of Rhodes. Dorothy Wellesley, who later wrote a book about Goldie, remembered her childhood friend fondly, particularly as Goldie himself was well into his seventies when she met him. As a small girl, she had called him 'Rameses' because his old, wizened face reminded her of the mummies in the British Museum. 'Rameses, will you tell me the story of your life?' asked the little girl. Goldie stared into the fire and laughed. After a couple of minutes, he replied, 'All achievement begins with a dream. My dream, as a child, was to colour the map red.'[9] He had taken a rather bizarre route to fulfil his boyhood dream. Starting out in a way typical of the late Victorian empire-builder, he had attended Woolwich, from which in 1865 he passed into the Royal Engineers. He was a wild man, claiming to be blind drunk when he passed his final examination. Two years later, as he himself recounted, a rich relation died, leaving him a fortune. Excited by his new freedom, he left the Engineers and all his belongings, heading straight for Egypt, where he fell in love with an Arab girl who taught him 'fluent colloquial Arabic'.[10]

He lived in the desert for three years, but he ordered books from England, which he picked up in the local town, Suakin. It was while spending time with his Arab girlfriend, in what he termed the 'Garden of Allah', that he obtained and digested Barth's *Travels*, five hefty volumes packed with historical and geographical information on the western Sudan.[11] Still only in his early twenties, Goldie returned to England, after setting up a trust fund based in Cairo to provide for his Arab companion. He was restless and turbulent, and plunged into another passionate affair, this time with his family governess, Mathilda Catherine Elliott. The couple ran away to Paris in 1870, where they were caught up in the Franco-Prussian War and had to live in very straitened circumstances, as the city was besieged for four months. In February 1871, Goldie returned with his new mistress to London, where they were married in July of that year.[12]

From the adventures he had enjoyed when only in his teens and early twenties, it was clear that Goldie was going to lead an eventful life. In the early 1870s, however, it was still uncertain how he would make his mark in the empire. His opportunity came when Holland Jaques, a small trading company that operated around the River Niger, ran into trouble in the 1870s. The company was run by the father-in-law of one of Goldie's brothers, and it was agreed to send George Goldie himself to West Africa, where his formidable energy would be employed. After taking over the company, the then thirty-three-year-old Goldie re-formed it as the United Africa Trading Company on 20 November 1879 and, from the beginning, set his heart on obtaining a Royal Charter for it. This would allow the company a monopoly of trade in the region of the Niger delta and further up-river.[13]

This development was an instance of the British Empire following trade. Even in the high imperialistic days of the late nineteenth century, it was British business and enterprise which so often forged a path that was only later followed by the bureaucrats and pith-helmet-wearing district commissioners. British commentators of the late nineteenth and early twentieth centuries commonly referred with pride to the commercial origins of their empire. The belief in the 'superiority of the Teuton' accompanied an aggressive free-trade ideology. Before Joseph Chamberlain's entry into the Colonial Office in 1895, the 'merchant was expected to create empire'.[14] Far from being something despised in official circles, business and trade were revered by the leaders of the British Empire in London. In the Jubilee year of 1897, the British Prime Minister and Foreign Secretary, the third Marquess of Salisbury, used his speech at the Guildhall to launch a paean of praise for British business, playing down strategic motives or motives of sheer glory-seeking behind the growth of empire. The colonial mission in Africa, according to the Prime Minister, was about money and commerce:

> The objects we have in our view are strictly business objects. We wish to extend the commerce, the trade, the industry and the civilization of mankind. We wish to throw open as many markets as possible, to bring as many consumers and producers into contact as possible; to throw open the great natural highways, the great waterways of this great continent. We wish that trade should pursue its unchecked and unhindered course upon the Niger, the Nile, and the Zambesi.[15]

For Goldie, although money was not a primary motivation, 'the opening up of Tropical Africa' was a significant achievement of the Victorian age. The empire, he noted in 1898, was dependent 'on the condition of the national fibre'. From the library of the Naval and Military Club, in

London's Piccadilly, he wrote that 'although it may be that the British Empire has now reached its zenith, and must gradually decline to the position of a second-rate power, we are not bound to accept such assertions without the production of more valid evidence'.[16]

To men like Goldie, imperialism was a highly businesslike matter. Although he did much to suppress slavery in West Africa, where Arab and Fulani raiders were still trafficking in human slaves at the end of the nineteenth century, Goldie was pragmatic even about this evil trade. As early as 1886, he wrote to the Foreign Secretary, the Conservative Earl of Iddesleigh, formerly Stafford Northcote, arguing that even 'domestic slavery, repugnant as it is to modern European ideas, cannot safely be repressed by force at present . . . intertwined as it is with the whole social system of Central Africa'.[17] Goldie's flexibility was shown by how in the early to mid-1880s he managed to grow the National African Company (which had taken over the assets of the United Africa Trading Company), finally acquiring a Royal Charter for it in July 1886, at which point it became known as the Royal Niger Company. During this period, he persuaded local chiefs to sign away many of their rights over their country in a series of treaties which, it seems, were often imperfectly understood by the chiefs themselves.

Between December 1884 and October 1886, a period just short of two years, the company had signed 237 separate treaties with local chiefs. The treaties followed a typical formula: 'We the undersigned King and Chiefs of Sengana, with a view to the bettering of the condition of our country and people, do this day cede to the National African Company (Limited) for ever the whole of our territory extending from the boundary of Akassa territory to Kolama territory.' Not only would land be signed over in this way, but legal authority was likewise handed over. 'We also give to the said National African Company . . . full power to settle all native disputes arising from any cause whatsoever.'[18] In return for this generous concession, the company would allow the chiefs considerable autonomy. It would be given 'full power to mine, farm, and build in any portion of our territory', while it would promise not 'to interfere with any of the native laws or customs of the country, consistent with the maintenance of order and good government'. The treaties were always signed by interpreters like

James Broom Walker Apre, native of Akassa, who would solemnly declare that they were 'well acquainted with the language of the King and people of the country . . . [and had] truly and faithfully explained the above Agreement, and that they understood its meaning'.[19]

These treaties were resented by the French and the Germans, who were involved in empire-building and trading of their own. The Germans protested to the British Foreign Office about the treaties. The case of the King of Nupé rumbled on for years. In 1888, the Germans wrote to the British Foreign Office, complaining that the 'King of Nupé emphatically denies having sold his kingdom to the company'. The company had imposed duties and taxes on other merchants trading in this area, but it had no right to do this, as far as the Germans were concerned. They argued that the King of Nupé had 'never ceded to the Royal Niger Company nor to anybody else any of his lands or territories'. They added that the King 'alone as Sovereign King of Nupé [had] a right to levy duties'. Goldie fired back to the Foreign Office his riposte that the Germans had long been a nuisance to the company. The dispute had been the outcome of the 'German intrigues which have given the Company so much trouble during the past few years'. The Germans, Goldie believed, had poisoned the 'minds of the native rulers, especially as rumours pass rapidly in Central Africa from district to district and acquire strength by repetition'.

In the wake of the international Conference of Berlin in 1885, which precipitated the controversial 'Scramble for Africa', the Germans, the French and the British were all vying for trade and dominance in West Africa. Goldie complained to his political masters in the Foreign Office in London that the Germans had claimed that 'wherever the English went they subjugated and oppressed the populations, that the native laws and customs would be overthrown, and that the power of the Chiefs would be abolished'.[20] The company, as far as Goldie was concerned, had no 'desire to interfere more than is absolutely necessary with the internal arrangements of the Chiefs of Central Africa'.

Goldie's shrewd dealings with the chiefs secured the Royal Niger Company's position as the dominant force in the commercial affairs of the region round the Niger delta and the banks of the river further inland. He not only blamed foreigners, the French and the Germans for interfering in the company's business. The native chiefs often relapsed into their 'old uncommercial pursuits of slave-hunting and inter-tribal war'. This problem was aggravated by the fact that, in every tribe, there were 'almost invariably to be found the influence of the numerous semi-civilized negroes – subjects of Great Britain or a British Protectorate'. These 'semi-civilized negroes' had been educated by missionaries or had picked up some literacy and knowledge of English by commerce. It was Goldie's view that, despite their 'very limited education', they exercised a 'deplorable influence over the native tribes'. 'These foreign negroes have persistently endeavoured, and will doubtless continue to endeavour, to shake the influence of the company with the natives.'[21]

Goldie's Royal Niger Company was beset by enemies and rivals. The monopoly of trade he was trying to establish not only opposed the interests of natives and Germans, it also aroused the anger of British merchants who had been trading in the Niger delta area for years. As the *North German Gazette* complained in July 1888, 'It is well known . . . here that the merchants who are established in the Niger Territory . . . Germans and English, irrespective of nationality, have for a considerable time made bitter complaints about the conduct of the Royal Niger Company.' The company was 'trying to monopolize trade in those parts'.[22] The merchants of Liverpool, some of whom had been trading in West Africa since the 1850s, objected to the dominance the Royal Niger Company sought to establish over commerce in this part of the world. Like the Germans, the Liverpool traders lobbied the British government, and their local Members of Parliament, to curtail the company's powers. The Liverpool firm Messrs Stuart and Douglas had written to their MP, W. F. Lawrence, at the end of 1886 to complain about the company's monopolistic practices: 'Healthy competition does not suit the policy of the Niger Company, hence the monopoly they have set up.' The Liverpool traders objected to the level of duty the company charged other traders. They also argued that 'The action of the Niger Company is no benefit to the natives, not to the civilization they so much vaunt nor to European merchants, but is intended to crush native traders . . . and English merchants who have hitherto so long dealt with the natives, to the great benefit of this country . . .'[23]

What they wanted was to 'induce the Foreign Secretary to either greatly modify the powers of monopoly conferred upon the Niger Company by the Royal Charter, or to revoke the Charter; the latter course being, according to the general opinion, the most desirable'. Lawrence, a dutiful MP, continued to lobby hard for his constituents. He wrote to the Foreign Office, on behalf of the Liverpool Africa Association, urging the 'revocation of the Charter'. The Foreign Office replied that the company was fulfilling its mission and that the Liverpool merchants had not 'given due consideration to the altered circumstances of the African continent, under which the whole of the West Coast, with a few unimportant exceptions, is now under the Protectorate of European Powers'. This new reality meant that the 'old unchecked licence of trade is a thing of the past'. The company was simply doing the job of the British government at a much less burdensome cost to the British taxpayer: 'the Royal Niger Company in offering to undertake the administration of the vast and hitherto almost inaccessible districts adjoining the Niger . . . has rendered good service by relieving the Imperial revenues of the heavy expense of direct administration'.[24] This was empire on the cheap.

In addition to commercial rivals, both British and foreign, there were the do-gooders, the missionaries and temperance societies, who made life difficult for traders by objecting to such activities as the liquor traffic, which the Royal Niger Company promoted. From a lofty height, the Duke of Westminster, President of the United Committee for the Prevention of the Demoralization of Native Races by the Liquor Traffic, wrote to Lord Salisbury to express 'his gratification at how great a diminution [has] taken place in the amount of intoxicating liquors introduced into the Niger Territories, and of the benefits which have resulted from this diminution'.[25] It was against this earnest background of rather absurdly named committees that imperial adventurers like Goldie had to operate. The activities of these committees and activists are redolent of the world of Gilbert and Sullivan or, in a slightly later form, of P. G. Wodehouse.

Assailed by the strictures of such bodies as the United Committee for the Prevention of the Demoralization of Native Races, and by difficulties put in his way by the Germans, Liverpool merchants and local 'semi-civilized negroes', Goldie required an iron nerve to push through his schemes for the company. Every inch the imperial hero, at five foot nine he was not particularly tall, even by late Victorian standards, but was a 'fair blue-eyed man, with piercing eyes, which seemed to bore holes into one'. The piercing glance was a characteristic which endured 'to the end of his life'. His intellect was of a 'kind born to dominate and impress'. He was a particularly hard taskmaster, never taking no for an answer. As the first office boy of the Royal Niger Company, Joseph Trigge, remembered, those 'who did not carry out his instructions, or showed slackness, were severely dealt with'. 'Don't tell me that anything cannot be done. Go and do it!' Goldie would scream. He had a coterie of devoted followers who helped him, but essentially the Royal Niger Company was a one-man show.[26]

Goldie's single-mindedness was an important characteristic which enabled him to get things done, but it also meant that he was cantankerous and difficult. His biographer, generally biased in his favour, admitted that he 'combined uncontrollable passions, ruthlessness, indifference to individuals, contempt for sentimentality in any form, with the excitability and sensitiveness of a child'. He was 'a violent and uncompromising man', a defiant self-willed atheist who 'represented the intellectual attitude of the Huxley and Darwin period'. Fond of women, he was never a faithful husband, though he had developed a close bond with his wife, the governess with whom he had fled to France in 1870. She died in 1898, by which time his work in West Africa was drawing to its close. The company could not hold its charter indefinitely. As the Conservatives were re-elected in 1895 and Joseph Chamberlain took control of the Colonial Office, a new spirit of imperialism would overturn the world of freebooters like George Goldie. In many ways a modern man, an enthusiastic lover of Ibsen's plays and Wagner's music, Goldie was overtaken by events. Towards the end of the 1890s, as the Charter was not renewed, Lord Salisbury thanked the Royal Niger Company for its work, expressing his high esteem for the 'adventurers and patriots to whose efforts the preparation of this territory' was due. Goldie came back to England, but never held another post linked to the empire. When he died in 1925, aged seventy-nine, he remained unshaken in his belief that there 'was no God and no life to come'.[27]

The country over which Goldie had presided as the unofficial leading statesman was not really a country at all. The mad scramble for Africa had been notoriously careless of ethnic boundaries and tribal distinctions. As Lord Salisbury himself described it, the partition of Africa was haphazard and disorganized. After an agreement with the French in 1892, Salisbury wrote that 'we have been engaged in drawing lines upon maps where no white man's foot has ever trod; we have been giving away mountains and rivers and lakes to each other, only hindered by the small impediment that we never knew exactly where the mountains and rivers and lakes were'.[28] In the eyes of the British the country which we would later know as Nigeria was, like Julius Caesar's Gaul, split into three parts. In simple terms the British understood, there was a northern region, which was predominantly Muslim, a western region, which was dominated by the Yoruba tribe, and an eastern region, where the Igbo were the predominant ethnic group. This was an oversimplified view, but it informed British attitudes about Nigeria.

For the British, the division of Nigeria into three parts was a crucially important fact in its short history. The north was dominated by feudal, Islamic lords known as emirs. In the west, the Yorubas had a society in which chiefs were powerful. In the east, the Igbos were widely known to be less feudal. Perhaps the best description of Igbo culture in the years when the British first arrived as committed imperialists is Chinua Achebe's celebrated novel *Things Fall Apart*, which chronicles the reaction of an Igbo village strongman, Okonkwo, to the arrival of the British. Achebe illustrates the relatively open nature of Igbo culture. In the east, in the Igbo villages, age 'was respected among his people, but achievement was revered. As the elders said, if a child washed his hands he could eat with kings.'[29]

The novel shows a world in which warriors lived in compounds with their wives and children. The wealthy man in Okonkwo's village had 'three barns, nine wives and thirty children'. The men wrestled to establish their prestige. Achebe, in an unsentimental way, reveals how the arrival of British missionaries and officials affected the lives of the Igbo for ever. A white man suddenly arrives in this unnamed Igbo village. 'During the last planting season a white man had appeared in their clan.' 'An albino,' suggested Okonkwo. 'He was not an albino,' replied Obierika, Okonkwo's friend. 'He was quite different . . . The first people who saw him ran away, but he stood beckoning to them. In the end the fearless ones were near and even touched him. The elders consulted their oracle and it told them that the strange man would break their clan and spread destruction among them ... And so they killed the white man ... For a long time nothing happened. The rains had come and yams had been sown ... And then one morning three white men led by a band of ordinary men like us came to the clan.' The men then went away. For many 'weeks nothing else happened'. Then market day came round. 'The three white men and a very large number of other men surrounded the market ... they began to shoot. Everybody was killed, except the old and sick.' The Igbo clan was now 'completely empty'.[30] The violence of this outcome was not typical. The missionaries were more widespread, particularly in the south, that is among the eastern Igbo and the Yoruba in the west. At the end of Achebe's book, the young District Commissioner decides to write a book about his experiences in Niger; 'after much thought' he settles on the title 'The Pacification of the Primitive Tribes of the Lower Niger'.[31]

The role of missionaries was well known in late Victorian Britain. As one contemporary writer remarked, the boys at the St Mary's Redcliffe School in Bristol were asked one day to write an essay on a British colony. One of the boys wrote, 'Africa is a British colony. I will tell you how England makes her colonies. First she gets a missionary; when the missionary has found a specially beautiful and fertile tract of country, he gets all his people round him and says, "Let us pray," and when all the eyes are shut, up goes the British Flag!'[32] The commentator realized that the 'great mass of the people of Nigeria [had] come under the protection of the British flag with their eyes shut'. It was for the servants of empire to see that 'when their eyes are opened to appreciate the significance of the raising of that flag, they may have reason to be grateful for its presence'.[33]

The problem in Nigeria was that the missionaries operated only in the coastal areas, in the south, among the Igbos in particular. In the north, the Muslim emirs were left untouched by the zeal of Christian missionaries. The northern emirs were allowed considerable autonomy, which would soon become enshrined in policy. Once the Charter of the Royal Niger Company had run out at the end of the 1890s, the British government decided to take an active role in colonial affairs. This new approach was adopted against a background of fear and uncertainty. Africa, for the

Victorians, was the great unknown continent, where, it was widely believed, cannibalism and paganism were rampant. The traditional stereotypes of the 'dark continent' were not founded on pure fantasy. West Africa was known as the 'white man's grave', and the mortality rates there were extremely high. More than forty years before Goldie set foot in West Africa, scores of sailors had died of fever and other illnesses. Of forty-eight Europeans who had steamed up the Niger river in three ships in the years 1832–4, thirty-eight had died of fever. Later Nigerians would joke that the mosquito should be recognized as a national hero, as it had prevented the mass arrival of white settlers, which no doubt smoothed Nigeria's political path.[34] As Mary Kingsley observed, 'Britain's greatest enemy in West Africa . . . is death.'[35] Tales of cannibalism were not wholly fanciful either. When the warriors of the Brass area on the Niger delta launched an attack on an outpost of the Royal Niger Company in 1895, they justified eating some of their prisoners on the ground that it was 'their custom under such circumstances to kill and eat those captured', particularly as it was 'thought advisable to have a big human feast in order to get rid of an epidemic of small-pox'.[36] Nigeria could not be colonized in the way that Rhodesia, South Africa or Kenya could – countries which would attract white settlers willing to live there for generations. It needed tough men, who could withstand the climate, to administer the country and keep the natives at bay.

As was so often the case in the story of empire, the right man came at the right time to do the job. The next figure after George Goldie who imposed his personality on Nigeria was the colonial administrator Lord Lugard, one of those imperialists who enjoyed tremendous fame and renown while they were alive, only to be forgotten as memories of the empire faded in the years after the Second World War. The son of a Cambridge-educated clergyman, who had 'rowed in his college boat when it was head of the river', Lugard was tough and, though not academic, highly intelligent. As a priest, Lugard's father had the reputation of always volunteering for postings which had 'the worst reputation for mortality'. The Reverend Lugard spent twenty-seven years in the sweltering heat of Madras, where his son, Frederick, was born in 1858. He attended Rossall School in Lancashire, one of the newer English public schools, which had been founded in the nineteenth century to educate the sons of clergymen. There Lugard did not excel in the narrow Classical curriculum, but ended up, as did so many of the empire-builders of the age, in the army, after only eight months at the Royal Military College at Sandhurst. Lugard and his contemporaries were hastily given their commission and sent out to Afghanistan, where the frontier was especially turbulent in 1878.[37]

Despite service in Uganda, Afghanistan and India, it was in Nigeria that Lugard found his vocation. Joseph Chamberlain, the Colonial Secretary, who had deserted Gladstone's Liberals over his opposition to Irish Home Rule in the 1880s, was, by the 1890s, a particularly bellicose imperialist with a seat in the Conservative Cabinet. He wanted to establish a West African Frontier Force. When it was formed, Lugard was appointed to head it with the temporary rank of colonel commandant. In 1900 he was appointed high commissioner of Northern Nigeria. There he conducted a series of military campaigns which successively reduced the independent emirs to a subordinate status. His staff was small and his finances restricted, but his energy and determination were immense. His biographer, Margery Perham, fell into hero-worship when describing his 'almost incredible feats of endurance'. He was small in stature, and his physique 'allowed him to do two men's work in a climate and in conditions which halved the capacities of most men'.[38] For hour upon hour he would toil away at his desk, writing letters and memoranda to the officials he so despised in Whitehall. It was inevitable that he ended up meeting and falling in love with Flora Shaw, the woman journalist of *The Times* who had first given Nigeria its name in her article of 1897. The only problem was that Shaw, as we have seen, was in love with George Goldie and was upset not to have married him after his wife had died in 1898. Goldie refused her offer of marriage, but four years later, on the island of Madeira, Flora Shaw, in accepting Lugard, finally married an imperial administrator and superman worthy of her hand.

The marriage, which took place in 1902, was in many ways extraordinary. The fact that Shaw was now forty-nine and her husband forty-four was not, in itself, out of the ordinary. The most unusual feature of the marriage was that Miss Shaw was a famous professional in her own right. As Lugard's biographer observed, if 'the Victorian age had been as rigidly conventional as some members of later generations have pictured it, this young woman's career would have been not merely remarkable but impossible'. The union of the imperial soldier and administrator with the brilliant and beautiful *Times* journalist who, though not in the earliest bloom of youth, still captivated men, by always dressing in black and by her cleverness, clearly titillated the imperial classes of Edwardian England. In a written note to Lugard, Lord Curzon could not resist offering his praise and congratulations, expressed in a characteristically well-turned phrase: 'If it be the Miss Flora Shaw I congratulate you. If it be another may she be equally brilliant and not less charming.'

The Lugards would form a powerful couple, equally devoted to one another's interests. Flora's death in 1929, at the age of seventy-seven, was a blow from which Frederick, now Lord, Lugard would never recover. He kept her room in their Surrey house untouched until his own death at the age of eighty-seven, in 1945. Lugard had reached a ripe old age, but his family were unusually long lived. His father had died in 1900, having been born in 1808, while his brother reached his hundredth birthday in 1960.

Both Lugards were official experts of empire and extremely well connected. Flora Lugard was a staunch Conservative who, like many Conservatives of the time, knew a great deal more about, and was actually more liberal about, imperial questions than many Liberals of her time. May 1906 saw her at Blenheim Palace, the home of the Duke of Marlborough, where one morning she was talking to the Duke about railways in Nigeria. In the course of this conversation, the Duke's cousin Winston Churchill walked in and proceeded to give his views. At this point, Churchill was under-secretary of state for the colonies in the Liberal government which had taken office in December 1905. Flora Lugard, with the keen journalist's eye, thought Churchill 'so hopelessly ignorant in regard to colonial affairs and at the same time so full of personal activity that the damage he [might] do appears to be colossal'. She also noticed, like many other contemporaries, that the young Churchill 'spoke all the time as if he and not Lord Elgin [his superior at the Colonial Office] was the Secretary of State'.[39]

Lugard himself had very strong views about Nigeria. He was a believer in deeds and, like so many of the most ardent imperialists, mistrusted cerebral indulgences. He was committed to the British Empire and to

British supremacy, although he happily entertained Nigerian friends at home in Surrey in his retirement in the 1930s. The ambiguity of Lugard's position was common to imperial servants. They were often friendly with 'natives', while maintaining openly the superiority of the British. It is very easy to discover what Lugard thought about the empire because, in his retirement, he was one of the most prolific authors and theorists of imperialism. He coined the phrase the 'dual mandate' in the colonies, which simply recognized that the colonial powers, particularly Britain, had not colonized Africa and Asia merely through philanthropy. One part of the mandate was to make money, the second part was to develop the colonies for the benefit of the indigenous peoples themselves. It was quite a neat formula which suggested that both the subject peoples and the imperial power could benefit from colonialism: 'Let it be admitted at the outset that European brains, capital and energy have not been, and never will be, expended in developing the resources of Africa from motives of pure philanthropy; that Europe is in Africa for the benefit of her own industrial classes, and of the native races in their progress to a higher plane.'[40]

An attractive feature of this notion of dual mandate was that the 'benefit' of colonialism 'could be made reciprocal'. It was the 'aim and desire of civilised administration to fulfil this dual mandate'. Even though his book *Dual Mandate* was published as late as 1922, Lugard showed himself to be an imperialist of the old school. His ideas, though organized and systematic, had shown no development from the 1890s, when it was accepted without question that the British were the best imperialists, blessed by innate talent to excel other nations. In his book Lugard happily quoted Lord Salisbury speaking in the House of Lords in 1895, when Salisbury had shown no reticence in boasting to his fellow peers about British superiority in business and investment: 'Our people, when they go into possession of a new territory, carry with them such a power of initiative, such an extraordinary courage and resource in the solving of new problems . . . that if they are pitted against an equal number – I care not what race it is, or what the part of the world [it] is – and if you keep politics and negotiations off them, it will be our people that will be masters.' No matter what the opposition did, British commerce would prevail: 'it will be our capital that will rule'.[41]

For Lugard, the empire had offered a unique avenue of opportunity. For men of energy and drive, worthy sons of an imperial race, empire offered a vast scene in which they could employ their talents. In many fields of activity, 'openings [were] afforded for every class of youth of England, whether from the universities, the technical schools, or the workshop'. To a man of Lugard's energy it was difficult to 'realise how severe would be the blow to the life of the nation if these thousands of avenues to independent initiative and individual enterprise and ambition were closed'. This is what had happened to Germany 'by her crime against the world' in starting the First World War.[42]

Lugard was a great theorist of imperialism and his greatest legacy to the British Empire and to Nigeria was the doctrine of indirect rule. In many ways, Goldie had anticipated this, in his eagerness, as early as the 1880s, to keep the chiefs and local rulers happy. As long as trade was unimpeded, he was content for local rulers to enjoy their traditional powers. Lugard translated this into a deliberate doctrine, even though, once again, it was the actual circumstances, the prevailing shortage of money with which to govern Nigeria, that drove the policy in the first instance. Indirect rule was a function of necessity more than it was an attempt to allow people to govern themselves. It was a practical, not a theoretical, commitment to self-determination or to any other grandiose idea. Lugard himself saw indirect rule as a better policy than a 'regime laid down by regulations from Whitehall'. The old individualistic spirit, the spirit of 'anarchic individualism', is always present in his life and work. The 'all-pervading love of freedom' which Lugard believed was the 'most notable characteristic' of British colonial policy was derived from the 'individual instincts of each Englishman from the highest to the most junior'. This spirit of individualism meant that each of the fifty dependencies of the Crown, which Lugard distinguished from the 'self-governing Dominions of Canada, Australia, New Zealand and South Africa', had 'its own policy adapted to the character and traditions of its people'.[43]

Indirect rule worked because it meant that the 'fifty or a hundred different Native administrations' in Nigeria were free to develop in their own way, 'subject only to a general scheme of policy'. As far as Lugard was concerned, democracy had taken several centuries to develop in Britain itself, and was not even an 'unqualified success in Europe' in the 1920s; Mussolini's Italy had 'discarded' it. Democracy simply was not 'adapted to the mentality or traditions of Eastern or of African races'.

In a lecture at London's Birkbeck College in 1928, Lugard stated firmly that 'only those institutions will survive which are in harmony with native mentality and tradition'.[44] He praised what he called the 'African system of Indirect Rule', in which rulers would continue to be under the guidance of a 'higher civilization'. He recognized that they would 'not be fitted for independence within any period of time now visible on the horizon'. His attitudes to race shared some of the patronizing assumptions of his time: he urged that native culture should be protected from the 'disintegrating effect of the impact of civilization'. Ever the military man, Lugard loved order and wanted to preserve the 'fabric of native society' by protecting the power of the chiefs. He wanted to prevent the 'chaos which follows on the premature destruction of tribal authority'. Although his lecture was given in 1928, Lugard was still beating the drum of 1890s imperialism. He told the students of Birkbeck College, many of whom would have been too young to have fought in the First World War, that England was 'writing our epic on the world's surface', which he believed would be a mark that would 'endure even if England herself should cease to be'.[45]

By the 1920s Lugard was a noted theorist of empire, but earlier in the century he had been a man of action. As high commissioner of Northern Nigeria, he had conquered the emirs in the field of battle. Kano had been captured in 1903. There, Lugard took pictures of the dungeon where the Emir had kept his enemies. He conjured up the scene where there was no 'standing room' and 'victims were crushed to death every night' and 'their corpses were hauled out each morning'. He remembered the stench from the dungeon as being 'intolerable'.[46] The emirs who ruled the Hausa people of Northern Nigeria were not particularly liberal or enlightened. They were absolute rulers who were nearly always at war with one another. Yet these were the very people whom indirect rule benefited. Once the British had subjugated Northern Nigeria, they gave back to the emirs and chiefs many of the powers which they had taken away. These feudal lords were allowed to remain in office, but were now responsible to the British

High Commissioner. Any emir who refused to obey these rules would be deposed, and another member of his family put in his place.[47]

The results of all this were very clear: the same despotic rulers now had even more prestige and authority, as their power was backed by the official sanction of the British Empire. The 'most significant product of Indirect Rule was the enhancement of the status of the various Emirs', who became more autocratic in their attitude towards the mass of the people.[48] Lugard was quite pragmatic about this. In 1922 he observed that 'we are dealing with the same generation, and in many cases with the identical rulers, who were responsible for the misrule and tyranny which we found in 1902'. Yet he was wary of subverting these indigenous institutions. Like Goldie, he mistrusted Westernized natives, who were trying in India and, to a lesser degree, in Africa to bring democracy to their countries. The aim of education in Africa was to 'enable the African to "find himself" – to emerge from the habit of mind which has through centuries marked him out as the slave of other races, to show him the higher rungs of the ladder which lead from mere obedience to cooperation'. A purely intellectual system of education would be, as it had been in India, a great mistake. In India, 'a purely secular and intellectual training, which rated the ability to pass examinations above integrity and good citizenship', had produced an educated class that had nothing to do with the 'vast illiterate masses'. The Westernized Indian was 'politically minded', and was 'a prey to the agitator and the anarchist', because the 'Western knowledge' which he had acquired 'had no roots or foundations in his own traditions, beliefs or environment'. Education in Africa had continued along these lines, with equally bad results. In Africa too, by the 1920s and 1930s, there had emerged 'an educated class' which was 'out of touch with the people, imbued with theories of self-determination and half understood catch-words of the political hustings'.

What Lugard called a 'purely intellectual type of education' undermined 'respect for authority, whether of the State or of the parent'. What he advocated was the 'training of the character'. This, to Lugard and many other administrators, was 'more important than the training of the intellect'. Only by training character could the native develop the qualities of 'integrity, self-reliance and a sense of responsibility' required of the individual citizen. His ultimate model for such an education was the English public school, which nearly always represented the ideal type of education in the minds of the imperial civil servants, most of whom had been educated in establishments of this kind. The qualities Lugard listed could 'only be created and fostered in the atmosphere of the residential school [boarding school], where the influence of the British staff can be brought to bear continuously'. Rather like the Duke of Wellington, who was reported to have said that 'The battle of Waterloo was won on the playing fields of Eton', Lugard believed that it was in 'recreation hours more especially that the public school spirit can be evolved'.[49] The ideals of this system were best expressed, in his view, in the war memorial at Cheam, a famous preparatory school: 'Trained to play the game, without self-seeking, to face life without fear or boasting . . . they faced Death with courage and simplicity.'

Lugard believed that the Boy Scout and Girl Guide movements could assist in this role. To him the English public schoolboy had 'from infancy been habituated to the standards which 2000 years of Christian ethics have created in the society in which he lives'.[50] Among primitive people, he considered, this ethical code had to be created by force of example, which was why 'a strong British staff of the right type' was needed, who 'in the daily social intercourse and in the play-fields will impress on the boys what the school expects of its members'. He drew up a list of the public-school virtues which the young native children would learn: 'self-respect devoid of vanity, truthfulness, courage, good manners, self-control and honesty – because these qualities are the necessary essentials which make a gentleman'.[51]

The ideal of the gentleman was a cardinal concept of empire. Behind indirect rule was the notion that the natural rulers of society, if they could be educated as gentlemen, formed the best type of ruling class. Westernized natives, the examination passers, didn't have the character to rule. The keynote of reform in education was to 'get away from the examination paper'. Even Muslim emirs, if schooled in character, could rule better than a native who had had the misfortune, like Nehru, of being educated at Cambridge or qualifying as a barrister in London. Lugard disliked the phenomenon, already common in the 1920s, of students from Africa and

Asia coming to Europe to complete their education. He hoped that a 'university college in each group of dependencies [colonies] – east and west – may be inaugurated in the near future, where youths may attain a proficiency which will reduce the period to be spent in Europe to the minimum'.[52]

Lugard's ideas were essentially aristocratic and were shared by many members of the imperial class who were mistrustful of democracy, even in Britain. A later Foreign Office memorandum on Nigeria summed up his ideas well: 'self-government for the African masses' should be achieved 'by the education of their own rulers and the gradual extension of their power' rather than by the 'introduction of an alien rule by British-educated and politically-minded progressives'.[53] Relying on hereditary princes in Northern Nigeria was a regressive policy. It meant that the 'educated native' would be excluded from government. Lugard confessed that the 'educated native very naturally dislikes it [the system of indirect rule] for it places the native chief, who has no schoolroom education, and is probably ignorant even of the English language, in a position of authority over his people'. The system also made the ruler independent of the 'educated native lawyer or adviser'.[54] The chiefs and the emirs of Northern Nigeria enjoyed the system. In the north, the emirs, as feudal lords, commanded absolute authority. Even when conversing with his own son, the Sultan of Sokoto, the most powerful of the Muslim emirs in the north, had the 'advantage of being able to watch his son's reactions as the young man did not once look his father in the face when answering his father's questions'. This was a 'custom among the Sultan and the Emirs when talking to their sons'.[55] Pandering to the emirs in this way retarded the progress of education in Northern Nigeria.

More fatefully, Lugard decided to amalgamate Northern and Southern Nigeria in one administration in 1914. This act defined modern Nigeria. The two distinct regions had totally different traditions and peoples. This fact was admitted by Lugard himself. The north was dominated by Islam; the south, in his words, was 'for the most part held in thrall by Fetish worship and the hideous ordeals of witchcraft, human sacrifice and twin murder'. In his biased view, the 'great Igbo race to the East of the Niger . . . had not developed beyond the stage of primitive savagery'. In this hierarchical vision, the Yorubas to the west had 'evolved a fairly advanced system of Government under recognized rulers'. In Lugard's own account, on '1st January 1914 the former governments of Southern and Northern Nigeria were formally amalgamated with some fitting ceremonial'. A 'durbar was held on the great plain at Kano', in which 'not fewer than 30,000 horsemen took part'. Each horseman marched past, then 'gave the salute of the Desert, charging at full gallop with brandished weapons'.[56] The aristocratic and hierarchical traditions of the north were easy for a military man like Lugard to understand. The amalgamation of Northern and Southern Nigeria was officially sanctioned by Whitehall. Lugard admitted that he was 'intimately acquainted with the method of Administration' in Northern Nigeria, but had no real understanding of the Igbo, Chinua Achebe's people. As he wrote in the report he prepared on the amalgamation of the two parts of Nigeria, the 'Southern provinces were populated by tribes in the lowest stage of primitive savagery, without any central organisation except in the west where the Yorubas . . . had developed a social organisation'. In contrast, the north had 'under the influence of Islam' developed an 'elaborate administrative machinery'.[57]

The Yoruba chiefs in the west quickly accommodated themselves to the empire and enjoyed its trappings; the northern emirs were flattered and fawned upon. In 1934, the Emir of Kano and his son were received by King George V in London, where the Emir seems to have been impressed by the sanitary conditions and by English food.[58] Not to be outdone, in 1935, the Yoruba chief, the Alake of Abeokuta, was anxiously lobbying the Colonial Office to plan a trip to London, where he was anxious to see King George V, as his father had been personally received by Edward VII as long ago as 1904.[59] The beleaguered civil servant at Government House in Lagos had to inform the Colonial Secretary that the Alake would be 'accompanied by his two daughters and by three members of his Council'. The elaborate preparations made for his visit show the pageantry and pomp of empire. The Alake wanted to see Paris during his trip to Europe and was keen to travel there by air. A. E. F. Murray, the Resident of Abeokuta Province, was writing to the Under-Secretary of State at the Colonial Office about the arrangements in early 1935. 'I have approached Imperial Airways,' he wrote, 'and have ascertained that they will be prepared to give every assistance.' Meanwhile Murray was making the requisite arrangements for the Alake's stay at Claridge's, the Mayfair hotel. In March the Alake himself was writing directly, in an informal style, to Sir Philip Cunliffe-Lister, the Secretary of State: 'My good friend, It is my intention to arrive in England about the end of June and I am eagerly looking forward to the opportunity of discussing matters affecting the interests of my people and country.' The Alake, it seems, wanted to do some sightseeing, but was wise enough to dress the visit up as an urgent matter of state.[60] Murray was soon complaining that the Alake 'seemed to be asking a lot'; the Yoruba chief now wanted to stay a week in the country for a 'rest' and required suitable accommodation. Murray was wondering whether it would be possible for the Alake to attend a court levee 'as a spectator' because 'bright dresses, uniforms and so on appealed to the negro mind, perhaps even more than an audience with His Majesty, the sobriety of which they found puzzling'.[61]

The Alake of Abeokuta postponed his planned visit to the summer of 1936; the Silver Jubilee celebrations of 1935 were used as an excuse for him not to be granted an audience with King George V. As one Colonial Office official wrote, the 'King has in the past . . . received Emirs and Sultans from the North, but the special fatigues of the Silver Jubilee make these precedents of no great importance'. He added the rider that the 'Alake of Abeokuta is, I believe, generally admitted to be a very important person in the Yoruba States'.[62] The visit of 1936 failed to take place too; the King died in January that year and the Alake decided not to visit at that time. The civil servant acidly remarked, 'I expect the Alake will want to come next year – unless the coronation is made an excuse for putting him off – though more probably *he* [emphasis in original] will regard it as the chief motive for his visiting this country.'[63]

This brief story shows how much the chiefs in the Yoruba west bought into the notion of empire. They were 'very important' people who enjoyed a power and authority directly granted to them by the British Empire. In the Igbo-dominated east of Nigeria, however, the system of indirect rule was less successful, since the Igbo, as Chinua Achebe has related, did not have chiefs, and the attempt to foist such leaders on them failed. The problem was that the system of Muslim emirates, which was adopted for the north of the country, became the 'model for the whole of united Nigeria'.[64] In 1937, Margery Perham, the Oxford academic and Nigeria expert who had befriended Lord Lugard in his old age, could speak of the 'democracy' of Igbo culture. She observed that the 'headship of any group' in the Igbo villages was 'never autocratic'. It was 'representative to an exceptionally full sense'. There was in the east of Nigeria a 'distribution of authority'. She was aware of reports which stated that 'younger men who have acquired high titles . . . or simply by virtue of their abilities, [were] able to raise their voice in council'. Perham could see in 1937 that 'the artificial system of the last thirty years or so' – the system of indirect rule and the promotion of the local chiefs and petty princes – had, in the south-east of Nigeria, 'been revealed as defective'.[65] It was this deficiency which would set Nigeria up for the crisis of civil war and which, in the form of tribalism and corruption, continues to exercise a malign influence on modern Nigeria.

15

Yellow Sun

The Second World War was a period of great upheaval for the British Empire. British officials could see that, by fighting Nazi Germany, they were actually undermining their own position among the colonial peoples they governed. Lord Moyne, the Colonial Secretary, warned the Governor of Nigeria about the high expectations raised by one of Clement Attlee's speeches: 'There is no doubt that in the minds of many coloured people we are fighting this war primarily to vindicate the doctrine of the equality of all races in contrast to the Nazi idea of the Herrenvolk.' He added, 'I feel that we must be very careful to live up to what is expected of us.'[1]

Nigeria itself was a backwater in the worldwide conflict, and the British officials there grew increasingly frustrated and found themselves side-lined. The Governor, Sir Bernard Bourdillon, was hankering after Khartoum and 'a closer contact with war'.[2] A career Colonial Office man who had spent time in Iraq in the 1920s, Bourdillon was now approaching sixty and was keen to get out of Nigeria. 'I am very fit, but there is no doubt that, after 34 years in the tropics, I am not as energetic, physically or mentally, as I was when I first came here.' It would be better, even if the end of the war is 'not clearly in sight', for there to be a change of governor. In June 1943, Sir Arthur Richards was appointed in his place. Richards was now fifty-eight. He had a mischievous sense of humour and a dry, cynical wit. A product of Clifton College and Christ Church, Oxford, he was just the kind of liberal administrator who so often presided over the last days of empire.

The native chiefs themselves continued to feel affection for the idea of empire. They were still trying to make money out of the British and, at home, they strutted with all their former confidence. At the height of the war, one Yoruba chief, who gloried in the title of the Akarigbo of Ijebu-Remo, was busy petitioning the Colonial Office for money which he claimed had been promised his father in the original treaty of 1894. The Chief believed that a subsidy of £100 a year had been stopped in 1914 and, consequently, he claimed accumulated arrears of £2,900 for the years 1914–42. The Colonial Office declined his request; the government argued that it had subsidized him and his lifestyle to a far greater extent than just £100 a year. Oliver Stanley, the aristrocratic Colonial Secretary, firmly put the upstart Chief in his place. 'Since 1916 the Akarigbo has been paid a salary from Native Authority funds, rising from £100 in 1916 to £600 at present,' Stanley wrote to his parliamentary under-secretary. This payment, as far as Stanley was concerned, fulfilled 'the obligation in the Treaty of 1894'. Another official laughingly believed that the Akarigbo was 'trying it on', a thing which the 'Ijebus are very prone to do'. While Britain faced the ultimate challenge to its survival from Nazi Germany, it seemed that everyone was 'trying it on', attempting to get money from the Treasury in Whitehall. The official remembered that 'shortly before the outbreak of war the City of Genoa raised a similar question on account of a debt incurred at compound interest by Edward III': 'I feel that the Ijebus have something in common with our Genoese creditors.'[3]

The Yoruba chiefs were not the only Nigerians who had something to lose from the demise of the empire. While the Nigerian independence movement was being led by southerners, such as Nnamdi Azikiwe, in the 1940s, the northern emirs were slow to recognize the new forces working on the Nigerian political scene. They had benefited significantly from British rule; their power and prestige had been buttressed by the policy of indirect rule, and, while they were suspicious of educating the mass of their people, they enjoyed the finer things which British rule had to offer. Some northern politicians had become ardent Anglophiles, one of whom was Ahmadu Bello, the Sardauna of Sokoto, an illegitimate son of the Sultan of Sokoto, the most revered of the Islamic chiefs who dominated the north of Nigeria.

Born in 1910, he had been educated at Katsina College, a teacher training academy, which was exactly the kind of boarding school that

Lugard had fondly imagined would educate the elite of Northern Nigeria. The college had been founded in 1922, with four British and two African masters. Its function was the 'teacher training of Muslims', and its emphasis was on the training of character. It became a leading educator of the northern elite, so much so that one British writer observed that 'one seldom makes a mistake when you comment, "You must have been to Katsina College," on hearing a now middle-aged Northern Nigerian speaking beautiful English'.[4] The Sardauna himself remembered his days at Katsina fondly; he looked back on a world of houses and all the paraphernalia of the British public school in its Edwardian heyday. He loved cricket, but his favourite game was fives, particularly 'the Eton variety of the game', which he noted had 'a little spur wall on one side which adds a great deal to the complexities of playing'. The Sardauna recommended Eton fives as a 'first-class game', which was the 'quickest way of getting exercise if you haven't much time'. Writing in the early 1960s, he observed that he and some of his colleagues 'still put in half an hour or so of an evening, whenever we get the chance'. He and his friends were also 'teaching young people to play it'. He was particularly honoured, on one of his visits to Great Britain, to be 'invited to play the game at Eton'.[5]

Katsina College was particularly effective in inculcating British values. Sir Hugh Clifford, the Governor of Nigeria, in the 1920s had envisaged special colleges for princes 'which they had in India'. This fitted the Muslim elite in Northern Nigeria very well. It also meant that many of the leading men in the north had started their 'working lives as teachers', because Katsina was nominally a teacher training college. The Sardauna felt he had more in common with the English than with his fellow Nigerians from the south of the country. He recalled his pleasure at staying with a family in Richmond, Yorkshire in 1948, where he had travelled to improve his English under the sponsorship of the British Council. In Yorkshire, he studied local government and also British methods of farming, and he stayed for a whole month. The Sardauna was 'delighted to live with an English family as part of their life'. He learned a 'great deal about the English and the way they lived and thought'. The whole experience 'had been of the greatest service to me ever since'.[6]

Men like Ahmadu Bello, Sardauna of Sokoto, were Anglophile conservatives. The Sardauna saw the emirs as being natural rulers and not merely 'effete, conservative and die-hard obstructionists'. As far as votes for women in Northern Nigeria were concerned, he was ambivalent. In his vivid autobiography, written in quaintly old-fashioned English, he noted, 'I daresay that we shall introduce it in the end here, but . . . it is so contrary to the customs and feelings of the greater part of the men of this Region that I would be very loath to introduce it myself.'[7] By 1948, however, while the Sardauna was staying with friends in Yorkshire, the tide had moved quickly in the direction of some kind of independence. Arthur Richards had already proposed the first post-war constitution of Nigeria; wary of the tribalism in the country, he had proposed a unitary (as opposed to federal) constitution to counter this feature of Nigerian politics.

After the war, there was a growing feeling that independence was just a matter of time. A hundred thousand Nigerians had served in the armed forces, and two divisions consisting of over 30,000 men had fought against the Axis powers in the Middle East, East Africa, Burma and India. The example of Indian independence in 1947 had 'a considerable impact in Africa'. By the early 1950s, the attainment of independence had become a 'foregone conclusion'.[8] Nigerian politics had, consequently, developed rapidly in the years immediately following the end of the Second World War, when three powerful political parties, each linked with the largest tribal group in the area, were formed in the three regions of Nigeria. In the east, the Igbo had their party, the NCNC; in the west, the Yoruba had the Action Group, while in the north the NPC represented the Hausa-Fulani Muslims. The northern leaders, conservative as they were in outlook, continued to be sceptical about independence. Northern nationalism differed from that of the south, since it was opposed not so much 'to British colonial rule as to the withdrawal of that rule making possible some form of southern domination'.[9]

The social differences between the three regions had actually become wider during the period of British rule, in the two or three decades before the independence of Nigeria in 1960. The roots of tribal nationalism lay to 'a great extent in the uneven educational development of the country'.

The western Yorubas had enjoyed earlier contact with European mission-aries. They were literate and had converted to Christianity, and now they had acquired a large degree of control over the businesses, the professions and the civil service. The eastern Igbos had started their own process of development in the 1930s and 1940s to eliminate what they perceived to be the economic and social gap between themselves and the Yorubas. In the north the emirs, the feudal lords and their retainers still maintained an iron grip on power and restricted Western educational opportunities, which they believed were corrupting influences, for their people.

The prevalence of Islam in the north was one of the reasons it had proved so attractive to Lugard and the early district commissioners. Islam was something they felt they understood, as many of the district commis-sioners had experience in the Sudan or had served in Asia. British officials appreciated the hierarchy and framework of Islamic society. The 'savages' of the south were, as we have seen, less well understood. There were, natu-rally enough, accusations that bias was shown by the British to the north. Frederick Forsyth, the novelist, would later write that 'the English loved the North; the climate is hot and dry as opposed to the steamy and malarial South; life is slow and graceful, if you happen to be an Englishman or an Emir'. The snobbery and class-consciousness that underpinned so much of British life in the early twentieth century found the idea of feudal rulers familiar and charming. The bias towards the north was a trait that the Foreign Office itself acknowledged in 1970: 'it was an article of faith in Eastern Nigeria, and had been for decades, that the British were hopelessly biased in favour of the feudal Emirs of the North; there was some basis for this, since the North retained the highest proportion of British officials, many of them coming from the Sudan with a romantic passion for Islam and for polo-playing aristocrats'.[10]

In the polo-playing north of the country, pageantry, royalty and invented traditions were combined in the institution of the durbars, imported from India. In 1959, the Duke and Duchess of Gloucester came to Nigeria, representing their niece Queen Elizabeth II. A durbar was held at Kaduna, the northern capital, during which 3,000 turbaned horsemen and 7,000 warriors dressed in medieval chain-mail, along with archers, lancers, musketeers, musicians, dancers, tumblers and snake-charmers, all presented themselves in a procession lasting three hours. The Duke and Duchess had come to celebrate the granting of self-government to Northern Nigeria, the last region to be given this degree of autonomy. This granting of self-government was regarded as the last step on the road to independence for the whole of Nigeria. 'The future may not be easy for you,' warned the Duke of Gloucester. 'You have a heavy task before you.' Each of the three regions now had its own prime minister. As Prime Minister of the Northern Region, the Sardauna of Sokoto took centre stage and played the perfect host to the royal couple. He was the dominant political player in the north, 'a land of ancient walled cities and feudal emirs', which was 'three times the size of the two other regions put together'.[11]

The 1950s had witnessed an intensification of the mutual suspicions and jealousies which characterized the relations between Nigeria's three regions. The original Richards constitution had given way to three more constitutions which all tried to address the same problem. Would Nigeria be a federation of independent regions, or would it be centrally administered under a strong unitary government?

Independence finally came on 1 October 1960. The new federal Prime Minister, responsible for the central government, was another northerner called Abubakar Tafawa Balewa, but everyone believed him to be a creature of the Sardauna, who had earlier told an American journalist that he would leave the job of being Nigeria's prime minister to 'one of my lieutenants'.[12] There had been elections in 1959 in which none of the three tribally based parties had secured an overall majority, but in which each had won handsome majorities in its home region. The Northern Region was the most populous of the three regions, with about 50 per cent of the country's population, so it was not surprising when the Northern People's Congress captured 134 out of 312 seats in the 1959 pre-independence parliament, all of which were in the north. In the east, the Igbos had won eighty-nine seats, while the Yoruba Action Group in the west won seventy-three.[13] The next five years were 'characterized by political crises' as each of the three main parties fought for 'supremacy over the federal government'. That there were three regions, each with its own ethnically based party, was wildly destabilizing and the perfect recipe for 'ethnic combat'.[14] The independence constitution had left the north strong. In this region, the Sardauna of Sokoto remained regional prime minister, and, so people said, the most powerful man in the country.

In the immediate period after independence, the Northern Party formed an alliance with the Igbos and allowed the Yorubas in effect to be an official opposition party. All parties were 'locked in a ferocious competition for a larger share from the national treasury': 'Tribalism became the ideology of politics.'[15] As population would influence the allocation of seats, censuses became keenly contested, the figures were disputed and sometimes the actual findings were repressed. The 1962 census took place in a climate of political tension and mounting confusion. In 1952, before the final constitution had been settled on, people had been under-counted in the census taken that year, because it was believed that the census was an instrument by which the colonial government would collect more taxes. In 1962, after independence, the census was now believed to affect political representation and so figures increased dramatically in many regions. The 1962 census was said to have cost £1.5 million, but the figures were never published. The Sardauna of Sokoto was reputedly upset by the findings when he saw that the unofficial figures showed that, while the north's population had gone up 30 per cent from 16.8 million in 1952 to 22.5 million, some of the eastern areas claimed increases of 200 per cent. The western returns also gave an increase of 70 per cent.[16] The implications of all this were clear: it was rumoured that the north no longer contained half the population and so could easily be dominated by a combination of the other two regions. When shown the results of the 1962 census, the Sardauna was said to have 'torn up the figures in disgust' and to have ordered Tafawa Balewa, the federal Prime Minister, 'to try again'.[17] Balewa did try again. Another census was conducted in November 1963, in which the Northern Region managed to 'find' another 7 million people more than the previous year and now, with a population of 29.8 million, there was no question of the north not having more than half of Nigeria's population of 55 million. Needless to say Dr Michael Okpara, Prime Minister of the Eastern Region, the Igbo-dominated area, rejected the census on the grounds that the 'Northern figures were fraudulent'.[18] Satisfied with the new figures, the Sardauna allowed the federal Prime

Minister to publish them, which he did without consulting the other regional premiers. Elections took place at the end of 1964 in an atmosphere of mutual suspicion and disillusionment. It was clear that the only issue at stake was whether the north would dominate Nigeria, or whether the two regions in the south could muster enough seats to counterbalance the northern bloc.

Outside purely electoral politics, there were other ethnic tensions. There was the problem of immigrants in the north, people who had come in search of work from the west and, in particular, from the east. The northern elites clearly resented these newcomers and managed to keep the immigrants in so-called strangers' communities, where, because of the difference of religion, schooling was segregated and two different societies existed side by side. As early as 1912, the British socialist E. D. Morel had observed that the 'Southern Nigerian system is turning out every year hundreds of Europeanized Africans', but the 'Northern Nigerian system aims at the establishment of an educational system based upon a totally different ideal'.[19] Fifty years of colonial rule had failed to bridge this gap. As ethnic tensions flared, the position of southerners in the north became more precarious. It was not possible to become a northerner by simply settling in the north, since an individual had to be born into a northern tribe to be considered a true northerner. Southerners were being systematically eliminated from the regional civil service in the north, 'and even Englishmen and other foreigners were preferred to them'.[20]

After the elections at the end of 1964, the easterners openly threatened secession and there was anarchy in the Western Region, while in the north the Sardauna was still trying to keep out southern influences in order to consolidate his power. It was obvious by 1964 that the Federation of Nigeria was falling apart. The mood of chaos deepened during 1965, as southerners became increasingly frustrated at being passed over in the civil service by northerners who, they believed, were less qualified than themselves. There were rumours of insurrection, even of a coup by disgruntled eastern officers in the army.

At the very beginning of 1966, the Sardauna of Sokoto planned to visit Saudi Arabia, where he hoped to spend a little more than a week, between

3 and 11 January, to pay his respects to the leaders of the Islamic faith. He had gone to Sokoto at the end of 1965 to say goodbye. Like a scene from a tragic play, there had been some grim forebodings and death threats, but the Sardauna's mood was composed and contemplative. He was in a fatalistic mood as he and his entourage of about twenty returned to Kano on the 11th after the successful visit to Mecca. The Sardauna went straight to Kaduna, the northern capital, where he was visited by Samuel Akintola, a distinguished Yoruba chief, who now served as the premier of the Western Region. Akintola had heard rumours of a coup, and was visiting his friend the Sardauna to discuss possible reactions to this new and alarming threat. On Friday 14 January the two regional premiers met at the Sardauna's house. Between 2.30 and 5.30 p.m., the two men discussed the plots and rumours they had heard. Akintola pointed out that he knew people in the army and that there were plans, now well advanced, to overthrow the federal government. Akintola, according to one source, argued with the Sardauna, saying, 'If the Prime Minister does not intervene with troops, we are all going to die.'

Chief Akintola left Kaduna to return to Ibadan, the capital of the Western Region, at 6 p.m. on the Friday evening. 'I will go back to Ibadan and face my death,' he declared. Once Akintola had gone, the Sardauna held a security meeting, then went out to play fives with some friends. Meanwhile the usual crowd of people came to the Sardauna's house between 8 and 10 p.m. – hangers-on, clients of the great feudal lord, who would petition for favours and money almost on a daily basis. Between 1.30 and 2 a.m. on the morning of Saturday the 15th, shots were heard outside the Sardauna's palace.[21] A twenty-nine-year-old Sandhurst-trained major, Patrick Nzeogwu, led his body of troops to the door of the palace and threw a hand grenade through the front gate as his men shot the gate itself from its hinges. The Sardauna was counting his prayer beads with his three wives. The Major, an Igbo by ethnic origin, educated in the north, had been holding night manoeuvres with his troops for six successive weeks. The city had become so used to the sound of gunfire during these manoeuvres that the police did not bother to investigate on the actual night of the rebellion. The men marched into the palace and dragged the Sardauna outside, propped him against a wall and shot him.

Similar scenes were enacted in Ibadan, the western capital, where Chief Akintola was shot and his house burned down. In the exclusive lagoon-front district of Lagos, a handful of men marched to the homes of the federal Prime Minister Sir Abubakar Tafawa Balewa, who was known to be a puppet of the Sardauna, and the Finance Minister Festus Okotie-Eboh, an Igbo man, known throughout Nigeria as the king of 'dash', a word which was used in West Africa at the time for bribery. Balewa was summoned from his prayers and submitted with dignity. He emerged, with his hands held aloft, ready for handcuffs. The corrupt Finance Minister behaved with less decorum. Producing a thick wad of bills, he tried to buy off the soldiers and then, still in his pyjamas, he ran outside, screaming, 'Don't kill me! Don't kill me!' Two soldiers knocked him down and jumped on him. His body was found three days later in a ditch thirty miles from Lagos. Near by lay the corpse of Sir Abubakar Tafawa Balewa. The army officers who had co-ordinated the successful coup were young men, largely educated at the Royal Military Academy at Sandhurst. The organization they showed prompted one resident Englishman to remark, 'Sandhurst training certainly leaves its mark.'[22]

The coup solved very little. Initially, it was welcomed, even in parts of the north, where the Sardauna had made too many enemies for his assassination to be widely mourned. The death of Tafawa Balewa, a well-respected figure, disturbed the north more deeply. In the south, by contrast, the coup was greeted with scenes of wild rejoicing.[23] There was an initial calm, although there remained the fear that the north would react in some violent way, waging, some feared, a 'Moslem holy war of reprisal'.[24] The young majors were open about who they regarded as the enemy; they were opposed, in the words of one contemporary Igbo writer, to the prevailing system, especially the 'hegemony which the Northern Region wielded at the behest of British neo-colonialism'. The northerners and the British were the particular culprits whose wickedness was frequently invoked to justify the coup.[25]

There was calm for the first few months after the coup, but this was largely deceptive as events moved swiftly after the new President, General Johnson Aguiyi-Ironsi, abolished the federation in May 1966 and proclaimed Nigeria to be a unitary state. He also announced that the regional civil services would be unified. From that point, Igbo immigrants in the north began to be victimized. The abolition of the federal constitution prompted calls for the north to secede. Crowds in Northern Nigeria began to shout 'Araba! Araba!' (Let us part). Almost inevitably, at the end of July, a group of northern army officers led a counter-coup. They killed General Ironsi, the man the majors had installed as president, and they also killed scores of eastern military officers. The motives of the northern officers in launching the counter-coup were simple: they wanted to reverse the unitary decree which had abolished the federation, and they wished to reassert northern dominance of the country. The time was ripe for yet more armed conflict. During the second half of 1966, hundreds of Igbo immigrants were slaughtered in a tide of violence which swept Northern Nigeria. The figures have been exaggerated over the years, and the 'massacres' formed part of the myth of the Igbo resistance, with some accounts claiming that between 80,000 and 100,000 Igbo immigrants were killed.[26] The truth was that not more than 7,000 had been killed between May and October. Sir David Hunt, the British High Commissioner at the time, writing in 1970, remembered that Chukwuemeka Ojukwu, the Igbo leader, had spoken to the Italian Ambassador in January 1967, only three months after the massacre, and had confided in him that the number killed was 'as high as 7,000'. Hunt added that 'whatever the figures, the massacre was a very great crime indeed'.[27]

By early 1967, it was clear that Nigeria, which had been independent for just over six years, was now in serious crisis. The new president whom the northern officers had installed was a thirty-one-year-old army officer, Yakubu Gowon, the son of a Methodist minister. A small, dapper man, Gowon hailed from the north, but from a minority tribe, so he had never really been part of the Muslim feudal aristocracy. The easterners remained unimpressed by his attempts to conciliate them. He immediately rescinded Decree no. 34 which had abolished the federation. In 1966 the government had installed a military governor in each of the regions of Nigeria and now there were four regions, as a new division named the Mid-Western Region had been created in July 1963. This new region did not change the overall weight of influence, since the Northern Region continued to have 'more land and a few more people than the

rest of the country combined'.[28] The military governors of each region
were in a powerful position and their personalities began to shape the
future of the country. As the British High Commissioner told the
Secretary of State for Commonwealth Affairs, in Africa 'personalities
generally speaking are more important than policies'.[29] This statement
may have been true, but its veracity extended far beyond Africa, right
through the entire British Empire.

It was at this time that the Igbo leader Chukwuemeka Ojukwu, Military
Governor of the Eastern Region, suddenly emerges as a central player in
the affairs of Nigeria. To the High Commissioner, he was a 'questionable
figure about whose sanity there could be some doubts'. Ojukwu was an
interesting man, the prime mover in the eventual secession of the Eastern
Region and the establishment of the nation of Biafra. He was the son of an
Igbo businessman who had been described as the richest man in Nigeria
and had been knighted for his achievements. Sir Louis Ojukwu had made
money in a road-haulage business in the 1940s; he then sold the business
and invested the proceeds in property, reputedly leaving a fortune of £8
million on his death in 1966.[30] The wealthy father had spared nothing in
educating his son and packed him off to England in the late 1940s to
continue his education at Epsom College, a public school in the stock-
broker belt of Surrey. The presence of Nigerians at British private boarding
schools, though commonplace by the 1970s, was unusual in the 1940s,
and Ojukwu remembered later that he had been 'swamped' by 'a sea of
white faces'. He claimed that he found it very difficult to recognize his
teachers. His powers of argument and his charisma won him a place on the
debating team at Epsom, where he also distinguished himself in sports,
playing rugby for the school and setting the school record for the discus
throw in 1952. School was followed by Oxford University, where he
started studying Law but then switched to Modern History, in which he
graduated with a third-class degree from Lincoln College in 1955. Ojukwu
remembered Oxford as the happiest days of his life; his father's wealth
allowed him to own a red MG sports car, in which he would 'burn up the
A40 between Oxford and London' at weekends.[31] The young man had
developed an extreme self-confidence and self-reliance in his schooldays,
as he had not got on with his housemaster in what must have been, for a

young Nigerian in an English boarding school in the late 1940s, a strange environment.

His background as a public schoolboy and Oxford undergraduate was, in itself, part of the fascination he held for members of the English establishment. Although Britain was steadily behind the federal government during the ensuing conflict, Ojukwu was a romantic character for whom the British had some instinctive sympathy. His education legitimized him in the eyes of many British officials. The High Commissioner, David Hunt, spoke of one of 'Colonel Ojukwu's invariable late night drinking and talking sessions'. Hunt reported that his own predecessor as high commissioner, 'who was himself educated at one of the best known universities in East Anglia, was apparently of the view that he [Ojukwu] had learnt these habits at Oxford'. 'One of the best-known universities in East Anglia' was a sly reference to Cambridge University, and the phrase reflects the jovial, rather smug and clubbish atmosphere of the British Foreign Office of that time.[32] Ojukwu himself, according to Hunt, was an 'outstandingly intelligent man', who was '34 and was educated at a public school in England and at Oxford'. One wonders if the official would have been so complimentary about his intelligence if, like Gowon, Ojukwu had been educated at a missionary school in Nigeria. In Hunt's view, Ojukwu was responsible for the propaganda campaign which had fomented an intense atmosphere of separatism in the Igbo-dominated Eastern Region. 'As soon as you cross the Niger bridge', the High Commissioner wrote, 'the atmosphere becomes more sulphurous and lurid.' There were 'warlike' posters which would 'certainly fall under the condemnation of the recent British Race Relations Act and [are] reminiscent of some of the ... manifestations of Der Stürmer', the Nazi newspaper of the 1930s and early 1940s. In the context of the tensions of early 1967, Hunt also observed that it was 'a melancholy fact that racialism (I almost wrote apartheid) is the primary political emotion in Africa south of the Sahara'.[33]

The atmosphere of suspicion was plain for all to see. In March 1967, Ojukwu had written to Harold Wilson, the British Prime Minister, that since July 1966, the Nigerian Federation has teetered on the brink of disintegration'. The murder of General Ironsi, the man who had been installed by the coup of January 1966, by 'Northern Nigerian Troops and the indiscriminate killing of Eastern Nigerian military officers' had 'destroyed the unity of the Army'. Ojukwu was clearly warning Wilson that war was likely: 'I have counselled Lt. Col. Gowon', Ojukwu added, 'against military action which can only lead to civil war and the disintegration of the country.'[34] By March 1967, in fact, Ojukwu's Eastern Region government had already employed an advertising company in New York to push its propaganda and an advertisement appeared in the *New York Times* with the heading 'Nigeria's Last Hope'. The agency was Ruder Finn, based on the Upper East Side of Manhattan. In April 1967, the High Commissioner reported a US assessment of Ojukwu: according to the Americans, he was now 'determined to obtain early de facto independence for the east'. Ojukwu was confident that Nigeria would break into four or more countries and was using his 'propaganda apparatus' in the east to 'stir up tribal animosities'.

As the tension grew, British and American diplomats in Nigeria believed that a vital determinant of the crisis would now be 'the attitude of foreign governments'. It was clear that the United Kingdom and the USSR supported the federal government, but according to British diplomats the position of the French was more uncertain: 'France seems willing to do business with the east through the back door,' even though it may have been unwilling to commit itself openly. The Americans would also support the federal government and they believed that, if other governments complied with its economic measures against the east, resistance would collapse 'within six months'. Ojukwu did not believe that the Americans were serious in their support for the unity of Nigeria. He was apparently convinced that 'the US government were only going through the motions of opposing Eastern secession', that 'true American sympathies were with the East' and that, if the secession came, the US 'would not be long in granting recognition' to the east. American officials were keen 'to dispel this impression'.[35] Hunt was now convinced that Ojukwu had 'decided to secede'. In his view, the Igbo leader was now 'paranoid'; he was also being increasingly dictatorial and had 'got the whole of the Eastern Region goose-stepping in violent demonstrations; his press and radio can only be compared to those of

Nazi Germany for their deliberate pursuit of the policy of the big lie'
and their 'poisonous incitement to racial hatred'.[36] Hunt was firmly
against secession and suspicious of the Igbo, who he believed were naturally inclined to paranoia. Other British officials were complaining of
'Ibo [sic] chauvinism'.[37]

As Nigeria slid into civil war during May and June 1967, Britain's position became more difficult, even though the final decision would be to
side with the federal government and support the unity of the Republic of
Nigeria, which Britain had created. The Commonwealth Office issued a
memorandum in May in which, obviously enough, it was declared that
the previous year's 'events in Nigeria, in which the government was twice
toppled by *coup d'état* and many thousands of Igbos from the Eastern
Region were massacred in the North have left an indelible scar on the
Eastern Region's relations with the Northern-orientated Federal
Government'. It was, according to the memorandum, clear where British
allegiance should lie: 'in these circumstances our policy has been to support
the Federal Government in all reasonable efforts to maintain a unified
Nigeria'.

The support of Britain for the federal government was unwavering: 'we
will do our utmost to avoid contributing to any measure which would lead
to the break-up of the country'. Typically, however, there was an escape
clause. The British government 'declined to give an assurance that we
would in no circumstances recognise a separate Eastern State'. This was a
classic case of diplomatic fence-sitting. While Britain 'sympathised' with
the federal government, it could not 'afford permanently to alienate the
East with whom we may one day have to do business as an independent
state'.[38] The problem with coming down unequivocally on the side of the
federal government was that, as so often, Britain's financial interests could
be compromised. The east of the country was where most of Nigeria's oil
was situated. 'Our investments [in Nigeria] are estimated at over £220
million,' of which £130 million was in oil, mostly in the east. British interests in the east were 'far larger than those of any other country' and 'an
open split between the Eastern Region and the rest of Nigeria' would 'face
us with an immediate dilemma'. Britain simply could not afford to 'alienate
either side'. The conclusion of this gutless state paper from the short-lived

Commonwealth Office (created by joining the old Colonial Office to the Commonwealth Relations Office) was that in the event of 'Eastern secession we should aim to keep in informal contact with the Eastern Government, having particular regard to our oil interests and the safety of British nationals', but 'we should be extremely cautious in recognising a separate Eastern State'. If possible, Britain should 'not move faster than other influential Governments'.[39]

At the end of May 1967, the final rupture between the Eastern Region and the federal state of Nigeria occurred. 'At 6 o'clock in the morning of 30 May, the Military Governor of Eastern Nigeria, Lieutenant-Colonel Ojukwu, made a broadcast declaring the Region, together with its continental shelf and territorial waters, to be an independent sovereign state under the name of the Republic of Biafra,' wrote Hunt, the High Commissioner. In Hunt's view, Ojukwu bore sole responsibility for what had happened. Ojukwu was an ambitious man who had 'a high opinion of his own talents'. Hunt did not believe that 'the impersonal forces . . . would necessarily have produced secession under a different Military Governor'. The attitude of Hunt was an important factor in Britain's position and he remained, while he resided in the federal capital, Lagos, as high commissioner, fully committed to the cause of Nigerian unity. His deputy, J. R. W. Parker, who was based in the Biafran capital of Enugu, was less convinced. The official papers reveal an open split between two of the highest-ranking British diplomats in Nigeria; as an official wrote in 1970, 'it is fairly unusual to detail for posterity differences between civil servants of this sort'. But it was useful for the 'historical record'.[40] Parker had a 'cordial personal relationship with Colonel Ojukwu'. He believed that eastern secession had not just been a matter of Ojukwu's personal ambition, as his superior Hunt believed, but reflected genuine fears felt by the Igbo people about northern aggression.[41] Ojukwu's view about Biafra's future prospects is neatly captured in a letter he wrote to Harold Wilson on the very day he declared independence for Biafra. 'In size, population, and potentialities the new state of Biafra compares with many countries of Africa in particular and the world in general.'[42] The new country, with a population of 14 million and large oil reserves, was indeed a viable country.

The difficulty of London's position was further reflected in the suspicion which both sides in the Biafran War, the easterners and the federal government, felt towards the British. Hunt would later confirm that it was 'widely believed in Lagos that Britain was behind secession in order to consolidate her control on Nigeria's oil resources'.[43] At the same time, the easterners were firmly convinced that the British favoured the Muslim emirs in the north.

On 7 July 1967 the federal government under Gowon finally moved against the east and started the Biafran War. The war itself has spawned dozens of books, memoirs and accounts. It has inspired many novels and remains one of the seminal events of modern African history. Much of the writing has been conceived from an Igbo standpoint. *Half of a Yellow Sun*, a novel published in 2007, portrays the lives of an Igbo professor and his girlfriend against the backdrop of the tragedy of Biafra. The story is set in a gentle, somewhat rarefied university campus whose tranquillity serves as a contrast to the terror of the war. The book reflects the well-rehearsed view that Biafra was a romantic experiment in civilized statecraft crushed by brute force. The atmosphere of the novel is sympathetic to the Biafrans, which is not surprising, given that the author, Chimamanda Adichie, is an Igbo who lost both her grandfathers in the war.[44] Biafra remains contentious, and, because many of the actors, in particular Gowon and Ojukwu, were still in their early thirties when the conflict started, some memories of the conflict have lasted a long time. It would be simplistic to blame the conflict entirely on the legacy of British rule, but it is not too bold to suggest that some of its causes originated in policies adopted in the colonial era.

Whatever policy Britain pursued was bound to be suspected by both sides. As David Hunt himself said, 'whatever Britain did there was little hope of it being regarded as neutral'.[45] Parker's position in Enugu was even more difficult. He was told by the Biafran authorities that 'the subordinate status of his relationship to the High Commissioner in Lagos was unacceptable' and, eventually, in October 1967, he and his staff were asked to leave the country. The war itself dragged on for thirty months, but it was apparent quite soon that the Biafrans were not going to get the recognition they wanted. The support the federal government enjoyed was overwhelming. Britain continued to supply it with weapons, as journalists like Frederick Forsyth accused the Labour government in London of supporting a 'military power clique in Lagos'.[46] Biafra, among right-wing circles in Britain, became a stick with which to beat Wilson's Labour government, though it is difficult to see how a Conservative administration would have acted differently. When Nigeria became independent in 1960, Iain Macleod, the Conservative Colonial Secretary in the government of Harold Macmillan, had declared that it was conducive to the 'mutual advantage' of Britain and Nigeria to co-operate in the 'field of defence'. He had pledged that each country would 'afford the other assistance in mutual defence' and that Britain would 'give Nigeria help in training, equipment and supplies'.[47] To have cut off these supplies during the Biafran War would have been interpreted as a hostile act. Once the war started, there were two questions confronting the British government: the first was whether 'Britain should supply arms and anti-aircraft weapons' to the federal government; the second was 'whether Shell and BP should pay the oil royalties owing to Nigeria to the Federal Government or to Biafra', where most of the oil was situated.

The solution to the first problem produced another typical piece of equivocation, but it was difficult to see what alternatives existed. Harold Wilson, in a letter of 16 July 1967, told Gowon that the British did not want to 'place any obstacle in the way of orders' for 'reasonable supplies of arms of types similar to those obtained in the past'. In other words, the supply of arms from Britain to Nigeria would continue as it had in the past, but no more sophisticated weapons would be supplied. The notion of 'reasonable supplies of arms' seems bizarre, and what it meant was that, according to Wilson, 'anti-aircraft guns' would be supplied, but 'requests for sophisticated weapons, a category which included aircraft bombs', would be refused. Britain's problems were compounded by the Cold War, during which the Russians constantly attempted to use international crises to increase their own influence and power in whichever region of the world was affected. The Soviet Union had already 'agreed to supply Nigeria with aircraft and other "sophisticated" offensive weapons'. There was, therefore, a realization in London that if 'British supplies to the Federal Military Government were cut off and the Federal Military Government were nevertheless victorious', the Russians would get the credit and would then be able to 'secure a further foothold in Nigeria'.[48]

The second problem, what to do with the oil revenues, touched on another perennial concern of British imperialism. The old colonial rivalry with the French over oil emerged once again, while the French government's attitude to Biafra was generally regarded as unhelpful by the British. In January 1968, David Hunt was concerned that, if Ojukwu won the war, he would 'cancel the Shell/BP oil concessions and turn over this immensely profitable area to the French company'. The French company in question was SAFRAP, a state oil concern which the Nigerians already believed had begun channelling French government funds covertly to Biafra. The British believed that the French were supporting Biafra, and that Charles de Gaulle, the French President, had an 'anti-Anglo-Saxon bias'. The Nigerians were also convinced that the French firmly supported Biafra.[49] Despite the general suspicion of French policy in Whitehall, there was scant proof of the activities of French mercenaries: 'There is little doubt that the French are up to no good in many parts of Africa, and it may well be that they are engaged in underhand activities in Biafra. But until concrete evidence of this can be supplied, I should have thought it irresponsible to claim that the French are involved either at official or Presidential level,' one British official wrote. There was no point in accusing French mercenaries of fighting on behalf of Biafra with the connivance of the French government because the French would only deny it.[50] Later that year, the French government went further and expressed support for Biafra, declaring on 31 July that the 'present conflict should be resolved on the basis of the right of peoples to self-determination'.[51]

Besides the French, by the end of 1967 Whitehall was also worried about 'Chinese experts and military supplies' coming into Biafra 'in great numbers' and 'prolonging the bloodshed'. The Biafrans were indulging in 'anti-Soviet propaganda' on their radio station, Radio Biafra, and British officials were worried that the anti-Soviet nature of the Biafran regime would draw them 'closer to the Chinese'. There was no evidence, however, to suggest that the Chinese were involved in Biafra to any great degree.[52] Everyone, it seemed, had an opinion on the conflict, and people were quick to take sides. At the end of October, the

Papal Office in the Vatican corresponded with the Foreign Office expressing 'great anxiety concerning the situation in Eastern Nigeria where there is a large Christian, principally Roman Catholic, community'. In Sweden there were demonstrations in favour of the Biafran cause, and in general the Swedes were perceived by British diplomats to be 'more sympathetic' to Biafra.[53]

The Biafran conflict, by causing famine and a humanitarian crisis, captured the imagination of many in the West, and the war was notable for the involvement of international aid agencies, like the Red Cross, which co-ordinated mass aid packages for the first time in an international crisis. Millions of dollars were poured into relief for Biafra; thousands of volunteers were mobilized. The normal annual budget for the International Committee of the Red Cross was £500,000, but by September 1968 the Committee's monthly budget for Nigeria alone was £1 million. The Red Cross's operations were assisted by various foreign governments' national Red Cross Societies and other agencies, as well as by an unprecedented number of individual donations. Biafra was one of the first media wars, if not the first, in which reporters such as Winston Churchill, grandson of the wartime leader, Jonathan Aitken, later a Conservative MP, and Frederick Forsyth, the author, learned their trade and gained useful exposure. There was a chic to the war. Forsyth befriended Ojukwu, whom he saw very much as an English minor public schoolboy, much like himself. Forsyth knew Ojukwu well enough to correct the mistaken belief that the Biafran leader had been educated at Sandhurst. He was at Eaton Hall, an infantry school in Cheshire, and not the more famous military academy, but this didn't matter. Everyone thought Ojukwu was a typical product of Sandhurst. 'Mad Mike' Hoare, the celebrated mercenary, got Ojukwu's academic provenance completely wrong when he described his manner and accent as those 'of an English squire' and claimed that his 'Sandhurst and Cambridge background predominated . . . his mind was clear and decisive'. Details did not detract from the central point that this Nigerian freedom fighter had apparently been educated at a decent public school and knew how to drink his whisky. As a result of Ojukwu's background, the natural snobbishness of some commentators made them sympathetic to the Biafran cause, just as

snobbishness had made the northern emirs attractive to an earlier generation of British imperial administrator.[54]

The foreign involvement, through the aid agencies and various pop
concerts held in support of Biafra, infuriated the Nigerian government. It
felt that Western reporters were ignorant of normal conditions in Africa
and had 'fanned public opinion in Europe and North America with exaggerated stories about the real suffering'. The Nigerians were appalled by
what they saw as the 'neo-imperialist and self-righteous attitude of the
international charitable organisations'. They remembered with bitterness
that neither the Pope nor the Red Cross had 'been equally brave in standing
up to Hitler'.[55] Nigerian resentment of the Pope was expressed immediately after the war in the *New Nigerian*, a newspaper based in the north of
the country, which predicted that 'accusations of atrocities' would be
levelled against the federal troops, and that the 'Pope [was] already leading
the way'. 'What', the newspaper asked, 'have we done to deserve this
pontifical injustice?' The following week, the same newspaper, in an article
entitled 'The Foreign Do-gooders', declared that the 'joint Church aid, the
French and Nordic Red Cross, Caritas' and other organizations could
'keep their blood money', since the relief work could be undertaken by
Nigerians themselves.[56]

The end of the war came at the very beginning of 1970. After thirty
months of fighting, the Biafrans surrendered, though the elusive Ojukwu
himself had been flown to Gabon by his Swedish pilot Carl-Gustav von
Rosen. Major General Philip Effiong, the forty-five-year-old emergency
leader, announced the surrender in a radio broadcast: 'any question of a
government in exile is repudiated by our people'. The aftermath of the
war inaugurated a remarkable period of reconciliation. There were no
trials or recriminations, and Gowon, the Nigerian federal leader, who had
devoured books about the American Civil War in the course of his own
country's conflict, adopted the attitude of Abraham Lincoln when he
declared that there would be 'no victors, no vanquished' in the war.
Behind the scenes, however, there was less magnanimity, and this less
generous attitude was reflected by the British government and by some
individual MPs in the Labour Party. In January 1970, Maurice Foley, a
Labour MP and self-appointed Africa expert, was in Lagos, where he

talked with the Permanent Secretary of the Ministry of Information: 'The conversation turned to the need to destroy the personal image of Ojukwu.' Foley suggested that 'a fully documented, comprehensive broadside followed by silence' might be the best way to achieve this.[57] Even in 1973, the Foreign Office was concerned to find out that Ojukwu's wife had been in Britain the previous Christmas. It was angry that the Home Office didn't seem to know when, or if, she had left the country. The Foreign Secretary, Sir Alec Douglas-Home, was 'very unhappy about the idea of her coming to this country at all and had agreed only with reluctance to her coming here for a visit of three weeks at the outside'. There was relief when it was learned that she had actually left Britain after only two weeks, on 20 December.[58] Meanwhile, after the Igbo defeat, other tensions were emerging. In January 1973, the Yorubas were now, according to M. H. G. Rogers, the Deputy High Commissioner in Lagos, 'regarded with much more suspicion in the North'. In a statement that indicated bias towards the Hausa-speaking north, Rogers wrote that the Yorubas were now 'inclined to show the same kind of arrogance towards the Hausas which the Ibos [sic] showed in earlier years and which in part led to the Ibo [sic] massacres of 1968'.[59]

Gowon himself was toppled in 1975, in one of the dozens of coups which have plagued Nigeria since independence. The institution of civilian rule made tribalism an even 'more important factor', according to a Foreign Office report in 1977. The report concluded that housing, loans, jobs, transport, nearly every area of Nigerian life were 'more blatantly dependent on family or tribal connections than before'. The armed forces were particularly affected by tribal antagonisms. The Yorubas, it was noted, did not like serving in the army, while northern officers tended to come from Hausa-Fulani aristocracy. In the mid-1970s, Nigeria's Brigade of Guards, which had been largely manned by members of minority tribes under General Gowon, was disbanded when General Murtala Mohammed, a northerner, deposed Gowon. The Guards were then replaced by units drawn largely from Hausas from the north. Unsurprisingly, it was an officer from one of these minority tribes, a Colonel Buka Suka Dimka, who in February 1976 led an abortive coup in which General Mohammed was assassinated. Between thirty and forty people, mainly relatively junior army officers, were tried and executed for this putsch, with 'almost all those executed' coming from 'a relatively small area' in the middle of the country.[60]

Modern Nigeria has been dogged by tribalism and corruption. The country's economic performance has been disastrous. More than five decades after independence, as one historian of modern Africa has written, Nigeria presents 'a sorry spectacle'. Wole Soyinka, the Nobel Prize-winner for literature, has described his own country as 'the open sore of a conti-nent'. Despite an oil boom which generated about $280 billion over thirty years, the economy was 'derelict'; public services were 'chronically ineffi-cient'; infrastructure was decaying. On average, Nigerians were poorer in 2000 than they had been at the start of the oil boom in the early 1970s; half of the population now lived on less than 30 cents a day. Successive governments had failed to provide even basic services for the people. Lagos, a city of around 10 million, had no more than 12,000 policemen on its payroll, whereas Greater London, with a population of 8 million, had 32,000 police officers in 2008. Corruption had played its part. Vast sums had been spent on prestige projects, but the money had merely lined the pockets of officials. Tales of Nigerian corruption were staggering, such was their scope. A total of $8 billion, for example, had been spent constructing a steel industry complex at Ajaokuta, which had conspicu-ously failed to produce steel in any significant quantities a decade after the project had started.[61]

Nigeria's rulers in the 1990s seemed to reach new levels of corruption. In 2003 Switzerland's highest court turned down an appeal by relatives of the Nigerian dictator Sani Abacha, who had ruled the country with an iron grip for four and a half years before his death, reportedly in the arms of two Indian prostitutes, in 1998. It was revealed that Abacha had diverted billions of dollars into personal bank accounts in Switzerland and London. The Swiss authorities froze accounts in their banks worth about $618 million, and pledged to help the Nigerian government track down other assets. In 2004, the British authorities were reported to have found traces of $1.3 billion handled by British banks on behalf of Abacha's family and friends, but the money had not remained in Britain.[62] The political process itself was dominated by money and violence. Governorship of one of

Nigeria's thirty-six states was an eagerly contested office, and in 2006 one gubernatorial candidate in the small province of Ekiti was stabbed and bludgeoned to death in his bed. This tiny state had a population of only 2 million, in a country whose population was then estimated to be 130 million, but the fact that the governor of each state received a monthly cheque, as part of that individual state's share of Nigeria's federal oil revenue, allowed the governors tempting opportunities to become very rich. Largely unaccountable, governors used the oil money to strengthen their own positions by bribing state legislators and other officials. One governor of Ekiti was alleged to have spent $7 million, mostly on contracts with political allies, 'supposedly set aside for a poultry farming project' which had not yet produced a single egg.[63]

Besides the endemic corruption that scarred Nigerian economic and political life, ethnic rivalries intensified, with religious animosity between Christians and Muslims aggravating tribal tensions. 'Everybody is sharpening his knife,' warned one state governor.[64] At the end of 2002, violence erupted in the northern capital, Kaduna, over the Miss World pageant that was supposed to be held in Nigeria, after an article appeared in a Lagos-based newspaper suggesting that the Prophet Mohammed would have approved of the pageant. The journalist, a woman staffer on the paper, asked, 'What would Mohammed think?' She answered her own question by asserting that 'in all honesty he would probably have chosen a wife from among them'. Four days of religious violence ensued, during which more than 200 people lost their lives. At least twenty-two churches and eight mosques were destroyed in Kaduna, causing the Miss World event to be relocated to London.[65]

The old hostility towards the Igbos still remained. Chinua Achebe described the situation in pessimistic terms: 'Nigerians of all other ethnic groups will probably achieve consensus on no other matter than their common resentment of the Ibo [*sic*]. They would all describe them as aggressive, arrogant and clannish.' A Western writer, travelling in Nigeria in the late 1990s, could claim that the '[Biafran] war was still in the mind of everyone in eastern Nigeria even among the majority of the Ibos [*sic*] who were born after the guns fell silent'. Ojukwu, in his 'impeccable upper class English accent', could tell the reporter that part of the Igbo problem was that 'we don't realize that we have survived'.[66] Ojukwu was now a successful businessman who claimed his old adversary, Gowon, as a personal friend, but the wounds still festered. He was in philosophical mood at the beginning of the twenty-first century when he observed that politicians were 'stirring up ethnic hatred because they have little else to offer'. His subsequent statement could be applied to many other situations, in lands far removed from the African scene: 'the more empty the leadership, the more reliance on primordial forces'.

It was clear, at the end of the first decade of the twenty-first century, that the structural problems that 'have bedevilled Nigeria since Lord Lugard's amalgamation in the name of the British Crown have not been resolved'.[67] That amalgamation had ushered in a period of indirect rule, in which a system that had been developed for one area of the country was indiscriminately foisted on to another part. Besides the problem of yoking together different areas with radically different traditions, there was a wider problem of decolonization and democracy itself. The whole tenor of British rule in Nigeria, as in other places, had been elitist and aristocratic. Northern emirs, Yoruba chiefs and business tycoons had been fêted and flattered by the colonial regime. Indirect rule itself deliberately elevated the so-called natural leaders of society and used them as instruments of imperial power. Nigeria was, as one high commissioner believed in 1968, 'one of the major British creations in Africa and hitherto the most successful'.[68] Nigerians felt an 'intense interest in Britain', in the view of one British deputy high commissioner in Lagos in the 1970s, because 'Britain created Nigeria out of the bush and . . . almost all the institutions which Nigerians value here were either imported from Britain or deliberately fostered by British administrators'. And yet, in a statement of great insight, the same official, Richard Parsons, observed that it was the elitist nature of many of the African leaders that made democracy so difficult to achieve: 'In retrospect the tragedy in modern Africa is perhaps that successive British Governments, when giving independence to their African territories, insisted on trying to transfer power to ostensibly democratic regimes based on the Westminster model. This has run counter to the views of many African leaders who are unashamedly elitist.'[69] This may have been true, but the whole premise of indirect rule in Nigeria had been 'unashamedly elitist'; indeed it was the very nature of British rule that had encouraged the elitism in the first place. Ojukwu, the Sardauna of Sokoto, the Yoruba chiefs and others had merely adopted the lofty, patrician style of their colonial masters; genuine democracy was as alien to them as it had been to Goldie and Lugard at the beginning of the twentieth century. Democracy, even without tribal conflict, never really stood a chance in Nigeria.

PART VI

Hong Kong: Money and Democracy

Hierarchies

By any measure, China and Great Britain were two of the great powers in the first half of the nineteenth century. Each nation felt itself to be superior to all other nations and races in the world, by virtue of its history, its traditions and the special character of its people, and it was this feeling of superiority that brought them, inevitably, into conflict with each other. The contact between these two superpowers of the age was brought about by trade. Ever since Lord Macartney's famous mission to Peking (as Beijing was then called in English) in 1793, the British had been trying to open China up to greater commerce.

By the early nineteenth century, British merchants were already making a great deal of money from China and, more importantly, they were well organized and politically astute. The main source of the commercial income of the British merchant in China was the trade in opium. It has been estimated that by 1830 the opium trade in Canton (modern Guangzhou) was 'the largest commerce of its time in any single commodity, anywhere in the world'.[1] Despite the riches to be made in the commerce with China, there was very little respect for the Chinese themselves. One of the men who would later symbolize the fabulous wealth of the British merchants was James Matheson, a tough Scot who was an avid campaigner on behalf of British traders. He urged the government in London to protect British trade and merchants from the Chinese. In a pamphlet, written in 1836, he boasted of having been 'engaged in active commercial pursuits at Canton for the last seventeen years'. Yet, despite his experience and increasing fortune, he found the Chinese to be 'a people characterised by a marvellous degree of imbecility, avarice, conceit and obstinacy'. It was unjust, he believed, that the Chinese should possess a 'vast portion of the most desirable parts of the earth' when they were not willing to share their wealth with foreigners by trading with them. The Chinese, in his view, were selfish; they merely wanted to 'monopolize all the advantages of their situation' and keep the foreigners, principally the British, out of their domestic market. Matheson greedily observed that, in China, there lived 'a population estimated as amounting to nearly a third of the whole human race'; then as now, businessmen were beguiled by the prospect of selling to the Chinese, who, in the early nineteenth century, were likely to have formed an even greater proportion of the world's inhabitants than they do today. (In 2010, China was estimated to constitute between a fifth and a quarter of the world's population.) Ten years before the repeal of the British Corn Laws in 1846, Matheson invoked free trade as a justification for opening up trade with China.[2]

Matheson was one of those Scots who typify the dynamism and commercial acumen of the British imperialist during this period. Born in Lairg in Sutherland in 1796, he had studied Science, Law and Economics at Edinburgh University, before going to Canton in 1819 to start his career in trade. A keen disciple of Adam Smith and his free-trade ideas, he was a writer of force and passion, convinced that it was the duty of the British government 'to make a firm and decisive demonstration in favour of our oppressed fellow-subjects in Canton'. The problem British merchants faced was simply that the Chinese government did not want them there, especially as the British were fuelling the trade in opium and thereby promoting drug addiction among the Chinese. In the context of the modern debate on drugs, Chinese officials were merely being prudent and responsible. To Matheson, however, they were showing 'contempt and injustice towards us', and were not playing fair, because they had already threatened to 'expel us from China', and such an act would 'not only be attended with the most destructive consequences to the trade', but would 'reflect intense dishonour upon the national character'. It would be dishonourable to surrender to the Chinese, because they were a weak nation; indeed, they were so weak that their emperor had 'neither the inclination nor the power to resort to hostile measures . . . if he saw us disposed to offer a serious resistance'. Gunboats and force would suffice to show which nation was the real master in the East. The Emperor was far too conscious of 'his weakness and our strength' to start disrupting what was already a lucrative trade.[3]

Initially, Matheson's plea of 1836 received little attention in Westminster or Whitehall. Merchants from Liverpool, Manchester and Glasgow were continually harping on the same theme, arguing that the Whig government, under the lackadaisical Lord Melbourne, needed to do something to place British trade on a 'more secure footing than it at present enjoys' in China. China was potentially an enormous market; everyone knew that. 'No country presents to us the basis of a more legitimate and mutually advantageous trade than China,' proclaimed the Manchester Chamber of Commerce and Manufactures in February 1836.[4] Britain's trade with China, noted another merchant in the same year, was already 'of equal if not greater importance than that with any other nation in the world' and, if properly encouraged, would be 'capable of almost unlimited increase'.[5]

The Foreign Secretary, Lord Palmerston, enjoying the second of three spells in that office, was very conscious of the importance of China. He ruled over the Foreign Office in an imperious manner, commenting sharply on notes submitted in bad handwriting, especially when contrasted with his own beautiful free-flowing script. He was aged fifty-two in 1836, and was, even at this relatively early date, viewed as the most dynamic and powerful minister in the government. Lord Melbourne, the elegant Whig aristocrat, was nominally prime minister, but it was to the Foreign Secretary that the entreaties of the Glasgow, Liverpool and Manchester merchants were so eagerly addressed. Even in the 1830s Palmerston was well on his way to becoming the legendary figure of his old age in the 1850s and 1860s. He was a famous seducer of women, who managed to marry his long-term mistress, the wife of Lord Cowper, only when he was fifty-five and she fifty-eight, even though smart society in London knew that they had been occasional lovers for twenty years. He was a sportsman who enjoyed boxing and field sports, but was also regarded as something of an intellectual and had, unusually, gone to Edinburgh University for a couple of years to learn some Philosophy and Economics, before resuming, at Cambridge University, the customary Classical studies he had pursued at Harrow.[6]

With a practised diplomat's eye, Palmerston could see that, in the early 1840s, competition among European manufacturers would make commercial markets on the continent of Europe difficult for British goods to penetrate. As a consequence of this competition, Britain should 'unremittingly endeavour to find in other parts of the world new vents for our industry'. In modern business parlance, British manufacturers needed new consumers for the goods they were now producing in such abundance. The most logical market was China, which 'at no distant period' would give Britain 'a most important extension to the range of our foreign commerce'.[7]

The Chinese Emperor and the scholarly officials who administered his empire were as contemptuous and dismissive of the British as the British were of them. The problem was a fine instance of the clash of civilizations, the inability of two cultures to understand one another. All Chinese officials had won their honoured positions by passing strenuous competitive examinations in the Confucian classics and they despised commerce. Britain, on the other hand, had, since at least the seventeenth century, identified itself as a trading nation. Commerce, to the Chinese mind, was a 'well-known barbarian idiosyncrasy', one of the things that 'made a barbarian what he was'.[8] The Emperor himself would observe in 1849 that 'it is plain that these barbarians always look on trade as their chief occupation' and it was true that the English, of all the Western powers, were the ones most addicted to this low pursuit, for it was their aristocracy who, among all European nations, had most intermarried with wealthy traders. In China, the merchant was a totally contemptible figure, taking his place in society far below the scholar, and below the farmer and even the craftsman.[9] This conflict of values lay behind the naval conflict now known as the first Opium War.

The merchants themselves were quite open about their desire for war. 'What, then, would be the force requisite to coerce the Chinese empire, with its countless millions of inhabitants?' asked one trader, an East India Company agent in China. Hugh Hamilton Lindsay answered his own question, confidently stating that a hostile power would need a seventy-four-gun ship, manned by 500 men, a large frigate and some troops, numbering about 3,000 in total.[10] Of course, the merchants' fond dreams of humbling the 'celestial empire' needed strong lobbying in London to prompt the otherwise lethargic ministers into action. Towards the end of

1839, an issue arose which was quickly exploited by another canny Scottish opium-dealer and stirred the young Queen Victoria's ministers into action.

William Jardine, Matheson's business partner, had been born in 1784, the same year as Lord Palmerston. He had been trained at the Royal College of Surgeons in Edinburgh and had spent the early part of his career as a ship's surgeon with the East India Company. At the age of thirty-four, he had given up this career and set up a trading business in Bombay, where he met James Matheson, who was already speculating in the opium trade, and from Bombay they both went to Canton, where they shrewdly believed much more money could be made. In their commercial activities, Jardine and Matheson were successful, Jardine in particular being a natural businessman, a man who never offered visitors a seat when they called upon him in his office. This lack of courtesy was prudent because it meant that visitors spent less time in his office; more business could be carried out if negotiators had the discomfort of having to stand up during the whole transaction.

By 1839, Jardine had grown rich and decided to leave China, while still maintaining his business interests. He took his leave in January that year and planned a leisurely trip back to London, passing through Bombay and crossing the isthmus of Suez. It was while he was on this return trip that he heard some startling news which, in its way, would change the history of the relationship between the two powers, Great Britain and China. When he stopped off at Naples, Jardine was informed that an energetic Chinese official, Lin Zexu, had seized and confiscated 20,000 cases of British-owned opium, worth £2 million. Jardine hurried on to London, where he arrived in early September; he lost no time in urging his friend John Abel Smith, an MP, to arrange a meeting with Lord Palmerston to explain the situation. The first interview, fixed for 16 September, was a fiasco, as the Foreign Secretary did not turn up. The next meeting, on the 27th, was more successful. Jardine spread out the maps and charts of the China coast on Palmerston's desk and described the scale of armaments needed to punish the Chinese. A naval force was prepared that included sixteen men-of-war, four armed steamers and twenty-seven transport ships which carried 4,000 Scottish, Irish and Indian troops to China. It was this force which seized the island of Hong Kong in January 1841. Jardine, whose commercial expertise was valued by Lord Palmerston, decided to have a real voice in Westminster and got himself elected as MP for Ashburton in Devon that same year.

After the Chinese fleet had been destroyed in a series of tragicomic battles, one of which lasted forty-five minutes, as twenty-nine Chinese junks were successively blown out of the water by British gunships, the Treaty of Nanking was signed in August 1842. This treaty confirmed British possession of the island.[11] The ostensible reason was the defence of free trade, but the war was really about freedom to trade in opium, which Jardine described in 1830 as the 'safest and most gentlemanlike speculation I am aware of'. The rich Jardine never married and died in 1843, but his values and drive had made their mark.

Hong Kong, from the start, fulfilled a basic commercial need. The idea of a free port in the East where goods could be warehoused and then resold was particularly appealing to a nation which was on the verge of adopting free trade. It was recognized that this free port would soon reap rich rewards. Even before the Treaty of Nanking, in April 1836, the *Canton Register*, an English newspaper founded by James Matheson and his brother in 1827, had recommended Hong Kong as the preferred site of a new British commercial base in the East: 'If the lion's paw is to be put down on any port of the south side of China, let it be Hong Kong.' The 'free' nature of Hong Kong was enshrined in the third article of the Treaty of Nanking.[12] The treaty also forced the Chinese to pay an indemnity to British merchants of 6 million silver dollars for the loss in opium-derived earnings, in addition to the war expenses incurred by the British, which would cost the Chinese government a further 12 million dollars; it was not surprising that the treaty was referred to as an 'unequal' one by the Chinese in the twentieth century.

Hong Kong may have started as a merchant's city, but it was soon encumbered by the formal structures of imperial rule. In April 1843, Sir Henry Pottinger was appointed governor but spent only a year in Hong Kong before returning to Britain. He was the first of a series of twenty-eight men who, ending with Lord Patten in 1997, set their mark in different ways on the island. More important than the figure of the governor was the idea of justice which the British worked hard, from the

beginning of their association with Hong Kong, to establish as a characteristic of their rule.

By 1857, the colony's population had grown to nearly 90,000, as against
the 5,000 inhabitants found on the island when the British took possession of it in 1841. The city was thriving and had already become a market
where East and West met, and where people of many nations could be
found selling their wares. There was the famous case in 1851 when a
brothel was advertised in a Hong Kong newspaper; an Australian 'actress'
had opened an establishment in Lyndhurst Terrace, her advertisement
announcing that 'at Mrs Randall's a small quantity of good HONEY [sic]'
was to be found 'in small jars'.[13] The most sensational scandal of the decade
occurred in January 1857, when bread produced in the main local bakery,
called Esing, was laced with arsenic and supplied to the expatriate community for breakfast. The proprietor of the bakery, a local Chinese of the
name Cheong Ahlum, had taken all the members of his extended family
to Macau earlier that morning. He was a confirmed Chinese patriot and
was alleged to have hatched a plot to wipe out the entire British population of Hong Kong. In the event, 400 people suffered from indigestion,
but, at the trial that followed, nothing could be proved. Even though the
presiding Chief Justice, J. W. Hulme, the attorney general and many of the
European members of the jury had been victims, Cheong was acquitted,
the burden of proof demanded being the customary common-law 'beyond
reasonable doubt'. The Chief Justice, though he had expressed his suspicions, famously declared that 'hanging the wrong man [would] not further
the ends of justice'. The baker Cheong was expelled from the island, but
the reputation of British justice had been established.[14]

Despite the Chinese trust in British justice, the merchants themselves
quickly established a reputation for arrogance and high living. Within
only a few years of the colony's settlement, dozens of merchant companies had come to Hong Kong and instituted a way of life which would
later come to represent the worst features of expatriate excess. Jardine's
famously imported a chef from London, whereas Dent's, at the time
Jardine's principal rivals, had brought a chef from Paris. The 'taipans'
themselves, the managers and partners of the business, along with their
assistants enjoyed in the mid-nineteenth century an extravagant lifestyle:

for example, claret for breakfast and champagne for dinner, accompanying dishes of pheasant, partridge, venison and all kinds of fish. A Shanghai doctor of the time, in advising a moderate dietary regime, suggested a light breakfast consisting of 'a mutton chop, fresh eggs, curry, bread and butter, with coffee or tea, or, preferably, claret and water'.[15] Even though the expression 'taipan' was a Cantonese word which meant 'general manager', the taipans themselves were exclusively European. This didn't mean that Chinese could not become very rich indeed. In fact, the richest inhabitants in Hong Kong were, from the earliest days of the colony, the Chinese businessmen who knew both the Chinese and Western mind, but European merchants quickly became known for their exclusivity and arrogance. As early as 1846, the Hong Kong Club had been established as the 'touchstone of social acceptability', from which 'shop keepers, Chinese, Indians, women and other undesirables were rigidly excluded'. The colony quickly, even by the 1860s, was known for its hierarchical and snobbish atmosphere, even though many of the most arrogant taipans were men who, in England, had not come from the 'best families' or been educated at the 'best schools'. A genuine aristocrat, in Hong Kong, with a proper title was rare, yet the social arrogance of the merchants in Hong Kong became a byword for pettiness. The first demand for democracy came in 1894 from the merchants, 362 of whom signed a petition sent to the House of Commons asking to be given the vote for candidates for the Legislative Council, whose members were appointed exclusively by the Governor.[16] Politicians in London dismissed this crude attempt to acquire power by an expatriate merchant class, who themselves disregarded the opinions of the Chinese, the overwhelming majority of the island's population. Joseph Chamberlain, the arch-imperialist Colonial Secretary, observed rather acidly of the petition that the 'Chinese community is the element which is least represented while it is also the most numerous'.[17]

There would be no elections in Hong Kong for 150 years. The colony was an example of benevolent paternalism, a place where hierarchy and status were enshrined to an almost absurd degree. The Governor and members of his staff formed an elite who, in their contempt for the taipan and merchant class, and in their own education in the Western Classics, very closely resembled the Chinese mandarin officials they had replaced. There were, in the early days at least, and right up to the outbreak of the Second World War, tensions between civil servants from the Governor down, who tended to be more pro-Chinese and could often speak Cantonese, and the less cerebral but more commercially astute merchants who staffed the offices of Jardine's and Dent's.

The cadets, the junior civil servants who helped the Governor run Hong Kong, were recruited and trained in a system which was instituted by Hercules Robinson, the then governor, in 1862. The introduction of this cadet system created in Hong Kong a bureaucratic elite to replace the old mandarins who ran the Chinese Empire. The Chinese mandarin, deeply imbued with the Confucian classics, believed in the idea of a *fumuguan*, or father and mother official, whose duty was to treat the people under his administration like his own children. In the Chinese political tradition, this paternal metaphor was central to the idea of how a good official should behave. In the 1880s, the system of cadets in Hong Kong attained a shape it would retain till the 1940s, and central to the system was the dispatch of the young cadet to Canton for two years, when he was expected to learn Cantonese.

The degree of progress individual cadets made in learning about Chinese society, as well as mastering the language, was determined by their own industry and talents. A future governor of Hong Kong in the 1950s, Sir Alexander Grantham, described how he had worked hard as a young cadet in the 1920s, but, after passing the examinations, he could 'do no more than make myself understood when shopping' or 'read the easiest parts of a Chinese newspaper'. Others gained considerably more knowledge; Cecil Clementi, a prize-winning Classical scholar from Balliol College, Oxford, was recruited to the Hong Kong service in the 1890s and rapidly gained a fluency in spoken and written Cantonese which astonished the Chinese inhabitants of the colony. As governor in the 1920s, he was comfortable making public speeches in Cantonese and his linguistic skills were sufficiently good for Lu Xan, a renowned Chinese writer before the Second World War, to have mistaken a speech of Clementi's for an awkwardly written piece by a former official of the imperial dynasty.[18] Some cadets used the two years to travel widely in China, while others, perhaps the majority, were quite happy to spend time socializing with their fellow cadets and among the expatriate community.

The term 'cadet officer' remained in official use for almost a century, until 1960. These cadets have been described as a *corps d'élite*, a 'minuscule band of officials' with the same values and from the same social background. Their sense of superiority did not, as in the case of the taipans, stem from wealth or race. In terms of their own society, back in Britain, they were not generally from a high social class. It is true that they were nearly all public-school educated, but, in the fine distinctions prevalent at that time, the schools they attended were 'minor public schools and obscure private schools, not listed in the Public Schools Yearbook': only one cadet from Eton and two from Harrow have been identified among the eighty-five cadets whose educational provenance is known, over the eighty years between 1862, when the scheme was started, and the Japanese invasion of 1941. The majority of the cadets were educated at Oxford and Cambridge, although a substantial contingent – about 30 per cent – came from universities in Ireland and Scotland. The fathers of the cadets were, for the most part, members of the older professions – the law, medicine and, especially, the Church; few of the fathers were businessmen or shopkeepers. It is important to notice that none was from an aristocratic background. Like so much of the snobbery in the British Empire, the superiority of the cadets lay in their education, not in their social status in Britain or their bank balances. The typical Hong Kong cadet was remarkably similar to his counterpart in the Sudan; he 'came from a solid, though not rich, upper middle class family, went to a public school, but not to the most prestigious, and then went up to one of the older universities where he read classics or history and was noted for his application to study and interest in healthy recreation'. The cadets were from what one might term the public school middle classes, their main distinguishing features being a skill in passing exams and attendance at a fee-paying school, no matter how lowly.[19]

The cadets displayed an arrogance, at times, that was breathtaking. Reginald Stubbs, who had been Cecil Clementi's predecessor as governor at the beginning of the 1920s, remembered them as being 'prepared to advance claims to act for the Almighty'. They saw themselves very much as prefects in the schools which had educated them. The model prefect was expected to be 'fair, just, upright, dignified'; ideas of equality were not really part of the public school prefect's mental universe. Authority, law and order were more likely to be concepts with which he would be familiar. In this hierarchical and intensely bureaucratic world, ideas of protocol and precedence were particularly important. The cadets also put a high premium on sociability, and their experiences involved endless picnics, swimming, polo, golf, tennis and bridge. When the New Territories (on the mainland and islands near by) were acquired on a ninety-nine-year lease in 1898, a further 350 square miles were added to the jurisdiction of Hong Kong. This newly acquired land offered the civil servants an opportunity to get out of the stifling atmosphere of Hong Kong itself, and walking expeditions in the New Territories became popular.[20]

Few of the officials in London knew anything about conditions in Hong Kong and the government in London relied very heavily on the judgement of successive governors of the colony.[21] One of the earliest, John Davis, had been famously shunned by the business community in the 1840s for being pro-Chinese. Davis had complained to Lord Stanley, the Colonial Secretary, that it was a 'much easier task to govern the 20,000 Chinese inhabitants of this colony, than a few hundred English', and, when he came to leave in 1848, the English merchants boycotted all the farewell ceremonies.[22] John Pope-Hennessy, something of an Irish political adventurer and a follower of Disraeli, who was governor in the 1880s, experienced similar treatment. He and his predecessor, Sir Arthur Kennedy, had offended the sensibilities of the English merchants, the taipans and their families, by inviting prominent members of the Chinese community to Government House, the elegant colonial-style mansion which had been build in 1855. The Europeans railed against Pope-Hennessy's 'Chinomania' and his 'native race craze'.[23] The Chinese businessmen were regarded as dishonest and malevolent by the English merchants, who felt that Pope-Hennessy, an impoverished Irish squire, was betraying their interests. Relations between the taipans and the Governor became so embittered that the English merchants and their wives refused invitations to Government House and when, in March 1882, Pope-Hennessy finally left Hong Kong he had much the same experience as Davis, with none of the business community presenting themselves at the wharf for the conventional leave-taking ceremony. Chinese business leaders did attend; Pope-Hennessy was known to be sympathetic to the Chinese, and he was called by them 'Number One Good Friend'.[24]

In its first hundred years as a Crown colony, Hong Kong was an incredibly divided society. There were the obvious racial divisions between the English and the Chinese, which were not merely a matter of class and money, since, as already noted, some of the richest people on the island were Chinese. As early as 1881, all but three of the twenty highest taxpayers in Hong Kong were Chinese. Despite their wealth, the rich Chinese businessmen did not socialize with their European counterparts of equal wealth and commercial attainments. On top of racial divisions, there were divisions among the British themselves, the most obvious of which was the split between the official class, with their elite culture, their Classical education and their competence in the Chinese language, and the class of wealthy expatriate merchants. All three of these elites, the British business classes, the Chinese business leaders and the colonial officials, more or less despised the vast mass of coolies, the working men without whom Hong Kong would never have been built. If anything, it was the colonial officers who showed the most liberal attitudes on race and class; the imperial civil servants were reflective enough to realize that, without the hard-working Chinese labourer, Hong Kong would die. In 1863, Hercules Robinson, another reforming governor, reported to the Colonial Office in London that 'it is the Chinese who have made Hong Kong what it is and not its connection with the foreign trade'. This contribution was widely recognized. As E. J. Eitel, a German missionary and scholar, observed in his classic account of Hong Kong, *Europe in China*, published in 1895, 'the rapid conversion of a barren rock into one of the wonders and commercial emporiums of the world has demonstrated what Chinese labour, industry and commerce can achieve under British rule'.[25]

The coolies, however, were the great invisible masses. In March 1901, a group of 'prominent Chinese residents asked Governor [Sir Henry] Blake to establish a special school exclusively for their own children'. These residents described themselves as 'an important and influential section of the Chinese community' and they were disappointed that education for the

Chinese had been 'directed almost exclusively' towards the 'lower and lower middle classes' at the expense of the higher classes. The renowned Central School, which had been renamed Queen's College, was excellent in its way, so the richer Chinese thought, but they objected to the 'indiscriminate and intimate mingling of children from families of the most various social and moral standing'. This 'mingling' made the school 'absolutely undesirable as well as unsuitable for the sons and daughters of respectable Chinese families'. Blake wrote to Chamberlain, the Colonial Secretary, that the 'better classes of Chinese are as anxious as any European to preserve their children from contact with children of a lower class'.[26]

The aspirations of the higher-class Chinese family were, of course, very low down on the list of priorities of the Hong Kong Club, which sought to imitate the smartest clubs in London's Piccadilly and St James's. In the Hong Kong Club, there reigned a social tyranny even more rigid and exclusive than that which prevailed in London. An illustration of this was the experience of the Sassoon family who, having lived in Baghdad for several centuries, had come to Hong Kong after a stint in Bombay. Although based mainly in Britain, the family, of which the war poet Siegfried Sassoon was a member, had diverse business and financial interests which spanned Asia and Europe. Frederick Sassoon sat on the Hong Kong Legislative Council in the 1880s but never joined the Hong Kong Club, 'the members of which were notorious for their propensity to blackball applicants on the least excuse'.[27] In London, the Sassoons could enter highest society, but in the stratified society of Hong Kong there were barriers which even a colossal fortune could not penetrate.

The Chinese had long ago realized that money by itself was not sufficient to admit anybody into the highest social circles. The case of Sir Robert Ho Tung illustrates this very clearly. He was born in 1862, the son of Walter Bosman, an English trader of dubious origins, and a Chinese woman, whom Bosman had arranged to come to Hong Kong from mainland China to be his wife. They had seven children, of whom Robert was the eldest son. Robert Ho Tung, with his fair skin and cobalt-blue eyes, looked like a European in his youth, but essentially made the choice to live and act like a Chinese gentleman. He wore silk robes and grew a long beard, using a Chinese last name. He had attended the famous Central

School, which had been founded in the same year as his birth. This school would produce an impressive roster of influential figures who would form the elite of Chinese Hong Kong. Ho Tung joined the Chinese Imperial Customs, but then in 1880, still only eighteen, he resigned to become a buyer, or *comprador*, for Jardine, Matheson and Company. By spanning two cultures, Ho Tung was an effective middleman and became very rich. By the age of thirty, he was already a millionaire and his business interests grew ever more extensive, as he used his trading profits to develop his own businesses in property, shipping and insurance.[28]

Conscious that they would never gain admittance to the Hong Kong Club, Ho Tung and some of his associates established the Chinese Club in 1899, of which Robert Ho Tung was the first chairman. In this way the Chinese elites responded to exclusion and discrimination by creating their own parallel world of exclusivity and privilege. The Chinese Recreation Club was set up as the parallel to the exclusively European Hong Kong Cricket Club.[29]

Perhaps the most sensitive racial issue for the wealthier Chinese residents was the difficult question of where to live. The most fashionable district of Hong Kong, the Peak, was effectively barred to Chinese until after the Second World War. Under the 1904 Peak District Reservation Ordinance, no Chinese, except for servants, were allowed to live there. The Peak, with its panoramic view of Hong Kong Island, was not only a beautiful place; it also symbolized privilege and exclusivity. In fact, the only Chinese resident in practice was Robert Ho Tung who, by 1917, owned three houses there, but he was never really accepted by his European neighbours.[30] Although a man of great wealth, Ho Tung was particularly sensitive to slights and, like many of his contemporaries, he was anxious to acquire titles from the imperial government. He had been made an ordinary Knight Bachelor in 1915 for his commercial activities and his help in the war effort, yet twelve years later he had come to feel that this honour was unsatisfactory.

At the beginning of 1927 Ho Tung entered into an extraordinary correspondence with the Colonial Office and the King's Private Office, in which he asked for a KBE, or Knight Commander of the Order of the British Empire, a notch above the ordinary knighthood he had received in 1915.

He told Sir Ronald Waterhouse, an official at the palace, that the New Year's Honours List, which had been published on 3 January, 'makes for my great disappointment', and this had been the third time 'in succession' that he had been disappointed. Ho Tung, now aged sixty-five, enclosed a detailed list of his 'services rendered to Hong Kong and the British Government after the conferment upon me of the honour of a Knight Bachelor'. The letter was direct and uncompromising in its self-confident claims: 'I make bold to assert that no Chinese resident has done more in the history of the Colony in aid of the Colonial services than I have.' Ho Tung also stated that, when he had been in England in 1925, he had every reason to believe that he 'might receive a K.B.E. from His Majesty's Government'. Such an honour, Ho Tung believed, 'would be acceptable even gratifying'.

The boldness of Sir Robert Ho Tung's letter is further revealed by the fact that in the same letter he even asked for a KCMG (the Order of St Michael and St George), a notch higher than the KBE: 'At the same time if the Prime Minister should be kind enough, after consideration of the special merits of the case, to recommend the conferment of a K.C.M.G. the honour, if conceded, would be even more greatly appreciated.' He then proceeded to list fifteen accomplishments which he felt had earned him the KBE; one of these was that 'after twelve years of experimental work by my wife and myself, at great cost and labour, we succeeded in producing mulberry leaves . . . and producing silk in the New Territory'. Another was that he had acted as an honorary associate commissioner of the Hong Kong section at the British Empire Exhibition at Wembley in 1924 and 1925; he had paid for 'all the expenses' of the journey and had guaranteed the exhibition against any losses the Hong Kong section might accrue.[31]

Waterhouse was stunned, and wrote to an official at the Colonial Office that the 'Eastern tranquillity of his effrontery' made it 'really very difficult to resist without rudeness'. The Prime Minister was being 'systematically bombarded on the subject'. Finally, at the end of 1927, another Honours List was submitted and still Sir Robert Ho Tung's name failed to appear. This time, the Colonial Office was ready simply to absorb the venting of Ho Tung's frustrated ambition. 'Sir Cecil Clementi has submitted his recommendations for the New Year 1928 but while recommending two other Chinese has made no reference to Sir Robert Ho Tung,' wrote E. H. Howell to Sir Gilbert Grindle, Deputy to the Permanent Under-Secretary. More damningly, Howell observed, 'no action [is] required until Sir Ho Tung again brings his claims forward'. Sir Gilbert believed that the Chinese themselves looked down on Ho Tung because he was 'a half-caste'.[32] In the end, Sir Robert Ho Tung got his KBE, but he had to wait another twenty-eight years to receive the honour, in January 1955, when he was ninety-two. The important point about the episode of Sir Robert and his KBE was how much a man who was known as the 'grand old man of Hong Kong', and who enjoyed tremendous business success, really cared about the titles and baubles of empire.

Ho Tung's correspondence about his knighthood would have been strictly confidential and, indeed, the documents were not released until 1978. Yet, in the status-conscious world of the Hong Kong colony, an exchange of this kind was unsurprising. Somerset Maugham, the great short-story writer, captured a great deal of the oppressive snobbery of Hong Kong between the wars in his novel *The Painted Veil*, in which a world of endless bridge parties, dinner parties and adultery is described with remorseless precision. In fact the whole plot of the book hinges around an adulterous affair, in which Kitty, the heroine, falls in love with the Assistant Colonial Secretary, Charles Townsend, deceiving her husband, Walter Fane. Fane is a doctor, a bacteriologist, and is therefore a man of little consequence in the colony: 'From a social point of view the man of science does not exist,' was one of Walter's more barbed remarks on the subject. The narrator observes that, as the wife of the 'Government bacteriologist', Kitty 'was of no particular consequence' and this 'made her angry'.

Kitty married Walter Fane in a panic, because she was then twenty-five and her younger sister, Doris, aged eighteen, was about to marry the son of a 'prosperous surgeon who had been given a baronetcy during the war'. Geoffrey (Doris's fiancé) would inherit the title: 'it is not very grand to be a medical baronet, but a title, thank God, is still a title – and a very consid-erable fortune'. Against this background of finely observed social distinctions, Kitty is appalled to discover that Hong Kong has its own rules. Status in London counted for very little in Hong Kong, while colonial grandeur did not necessarily translate into eminence in London. Dorothy Townsend, who, as Charles Townsend's hapless wife, was Kitty's rival, was an excellent example of a woman whose status was entirely defined by the empire. Her father 'had been a Colonial Governor and of course it was very grand while it lasted – everyone stood up when you entered a room and men took off their hats to you as you passed in your car – but what could be more insignificant than a Colonial Governor when he had retired?' Answering her own rhetorical question, Kitty observed that Dorothy Townsend's father lived in a 'small house at Earl's Court', whereas Kitty's father, Bernard Gastin, was 'a K.C. and there was no reason why he should not be made a judge one of these days. Anyhow they lived in South Kensington.' In Hong Kong, Kitty's status in London counted for nothing: 'It's too absurd,' she told her husband. 'Why, there's hardly anyone here that one would bother about for five minutes at home. Mother wouldn't dream of asking any of them to dine at our house.'

Hong Kong followed its own, highly developed rules. Despite the snobbery, life was jolly: 'there were clubs and tennis and racing and polo and golf'.[33] The 1920s and 1930s perhaps represented the high point of hierarchy and social snobbery. Labour was cheap. At the Peak, every family had a large staff of servants who each had a special uniform according to their role: houseboys wore black trousers and white jackets, while drivers wore white suits, socks and shoes. A fundamental part of Peak life was card-calling, which was perhaps unique to the British Empire at its short-lived apogee between the wars. The first duty of a new arrival in Hong Kong was to acquire cards printed with his name and his government department or business, and then drop the cards round the sumptuous residences of the Peak, in a circuit undertaken on foot. It was said that you would be lucky to get two dinner invitations for every hundred cards you dropped off, but at least that was a start.[34]

The 1920s also saw the only incident that, until the 1960s, seriously challenged the imperial regime. On 30 May 1925, Sikh police under British command opened fire on a crowd of Chinese demonstrators in Shanghai. This action precipitated a number of strikes in Hong Kong; on 18 June, most of the students at Queen's College were on strike. Then waiters and bellboys at the Peak Hotel and the Peak Club went on strike, and then labourers, shopkeepers and the workers on the trams joined them. By late June, most Chinese staff in restaurants, government agencies and newspapers were also on strike. Food prices soared, prompting a run on the banks, as people emptied their accounts and bought everything they could. Hong Kong's economy had faltered badly. On 22 June, the colonial government declared a state of emergency and, by early July, Hong Kong had become a ghost town. The strike lasted for more than a year, and the British government had to provide £3 million to keep the colony's economy afloat.[35]

There was the suspicion that the strikes of 1925–6 had much to do with the rigid social exclusiveness of the colony. There was an air of revolution. The coolies, people felt, had had enough, and their life in those inter-war years was not particularly enviable: they worked long hours for wages which 'barely kept them alive'; their homes were 'bedspaces in over-crowded, filthy tenement buildings'. Their clothing was minimal and 'they usually went without shoes' to the extent that, even in the late 1930s, Bob Yates, a British soldier stationed in Hong Kong, remembered, 'if you saw a Chinaman in a pair of shoes you wondered where he'd pinched them from'.[36] As we can gather from the reminiscences of soldiers and others, life in 1930s Hong Kong was not so different from what it had been in the 1920s, although some of the edge of arrogance had gone. The Peak Hotel, which was home for a number of elderly residents, shut its doors for the last time on 1 September 1936.[37]

The old world in Hong Kong survived the 1930s in attenuated form. One of the marks of social distinction in Hong Kong had been the 'posses-sion of a pew close to the altar in St. John's Cathedral'. In addition to a place on the Peak, an overdraft at the Hongkong and Shanghai Bank and being considered for membership of the Hong Kong Club, the pew was an important step on the 'inland hierarchy', but the renting of pews was brought to an end in 1928. Clementi, the Balliol Classicist, fluent in Mandarin and Cantonese, was a progressive on matters of race and class and, in May 1926, partly as a consequence of the strike, he appointed the first ethnic Chinese member to the Executive Council. The less exclusive Legislative Council, which, in very loose terms, played the part of a parliament to the Executive Council's cabinet, had admitted its first Chinese member in 1880. All these positions were, of course, appointed solely by the governor. Clementi further aroused the suspicions of the British community as being generally pro-Chinese because he was often sharply critical of the racial exclusiveness of many of Hong Kong's clubs, and even suggested replacing the Hong Kong Club with one which both British and Chinese members could join.[38]

The paternalism and bureaucracy which characterized the Hong Kong government were very much alive in the 1930s. Colonial Office records from the time cover such themes as the admission of 'Asiatics' to the Royal Hong Kong Golf Club, after an incident in Mombasa, Kenya, where a Japanese diplomat had been barred from playing golf at the club merely because of his race. At the beginning of January 1936, an official in Government House in Hong Kong was assuring the Colonial Office back in London that 'there is very little likelihood of any unpleasantness such as occurred at Mombasa happening in Hong Kong'. The rules at the Royal Hong Kong were simple: 'there is no rule against a person of any race being put up for full membership ... but it would be disingenuous to pretend that a Chinese or a Japanese resident would have much chance of election to full membership, for the Club already has as many members as it requires without bringing in Asiatics'. And besides, the Japanese had 'a Golf course of their own in the New Territories'. The ostensible reason for keeping 'Asiatic residents' out was simply that the members 'would be liable to be swamped in course of time if they did otherwise'. The position in relation to visitors, of course, was entirely different. The Captain of the club had 'full discretion to admit visitors of any race, and in point of fact I understand Mr Shudo [the Japanese diplomat] actually played at Fanling with the Captain, Mr S. H. Dodwell, on his recent visit to Hong Kong'.[39]

The 1930s saw grave tensions on the international scene, but in Hong Kong life went on in much the same way. Segregation between the Chinese and the Europeans was rigid. Even brothels were under different jurisdictions, depending on whether the prostitutes were Asian or European. In 1931, the position on this delicate subject needed to be clarified, as the Chief Justice Sir Joseph Kemp observed: 'the Secretary for Chinese affairs deals with the Chinese and Japanese brothels, and the Inspector General of Police deals with the few European brothels'. The white prostitutes on the China Coast (on mainland China opposite Hong Kong Island) were mainly Russian, and, although Shanghai was the great destination for them, white prostitutes were 'still permitted in Hong Kong'.⁴⁰ The incident shows how sensitive issues of race were in Hong Kong before the Second World War, but ideas about race need to be understood within the wider context of class and status.

That Hong Kong was intensely status-conscious is illustrated by the concern that was shown about the appointment of a trade commissioner in 1935. This was a new position in the imperial hierarchy in Hong Kong and it caused difficulty because people were asking 'where would he be placed in the table of precedence?' The Trade Commissioner would be placed, the new Governor decided, after the 'Manager of the Railway, No. 16, in the Table of Precedence' (see below).⁴¹ The Trade Commissioner, although placed at number 17, after the Manager of the Railway, would not be included in the official Table, as he was not an officer of the colonial government. Strictly speaking hierarchy applied only to the imperial servants, but the culture of hierarchy, of deference and status, was so deeply embedded in Hong Kong life that everyone knew his or, in Kitty Fane's case, her place.

HONG KONG Precedence Table,
approved by H[is] M[ajesty], September, 1931

1. The Governor or the Officer Administering the Government.
2. The Officer-in-Command of His Majesty's Naval Forces on the China Station, if of the rank of Flag Officer (Rear-Admiral or above); the Senior Officer-in-Command of the Troops, if of the rank of General Officer (Major General or above) and the Senior Officer of the Royal Air Force on the Station if of the rank of Air Officer, above the rank of Air Commodore, their own relative rank and precedence being determined by the King's Regulations on that Subject.
3. The Chief Justice.
4. a) The Commodore, His Majesty's Dockyard; b) The Officer-in-Command of His Majesty's Naval Forces on the China Station, if of

the rank of Commodore, Captain or Commander; c) The Officer-in-Command of the Troops, if of the rank of Brigadier, Colonel, or Lieutenant Colonel; d) The Senior Officer of the Royal Air Force if of the rank of Air Commodore, Group Captain or Wing Commander, their own relative rank and precedence being determined by the King's Regulations on that Subject.

5. Members of Executive Council in their order.

6. The Puisne Judge.

7. Members of Legislative Council in their order.

8. Cadet Officers of the First Class.

9. The Director of Public Works, if not included in the foregoing classes.

10. The Director of Medical and Sanitary Services, if not included in the foregoing classes.

11. The Inspector General of Police, if not included in the foregoing classes.

12. Commandant of the Volunteer Defence Corps (if of the rank of Colonel).

13. Cadet Officers of not less than 21 years' service.

14. The Director of Education, if not included in the foregoing classes.

15. The Harbour Master, if not included in the foregoing classes.

16. The Manager of the Railway.

17. The Crown Solicitor.

18. The Registrar, Supreme Court.

19. The Auditor.

20. Commandant of the Volunteer Defence (if below the rank of Colonel).

21. Cadet Officers of from 14 to 21 years' service.

22. The Land Officer.

23. The Superintendent of Prisons.

24. The Director of the Royal Observatory.

25. The Official Receiver.

26. The Superintendent of the Botanical and Forestry Department.[42]

Democracy Postponed

Towards the end of the Second World War, F. D. Roosevelt, the ailing American President, was conversing with Oliver Stanley, the younger son of the seventeenth Earl of Derby, who, in the Churchill-led coalition government, served as secretary of state for the colonies. Roosevelt, perhaps in a moment of light-hearted banter, indicated that he thought it would be a good idea for Britain to give up Hong Kong and make it an international free port. 'I do not wish to be unkind to the British,' he said, 'but in 1841 when you acquired Hong Kong, you did not acquire it by purchase.' Stanley seemed puzzled: 'Let me see, Mr President, that was about the time of the Mexican War, wasn't it?'[1] The Mexican War had been caused by the direct annexation of Texas by the United States.

Stanley, an assured member of the Conservative elite, was elegant and deft in his reply, gently reminding the President that international diplomacy in the nineteenth century had been a rough affair. The President, however, reflected common American opinion at the time. After the defeat of the Axis powers, colonialism had become unfashionable. The war, after all, had been a war against dictatorship in favour of democracy; President Roosevelt himself had pledged that the United States would be an 'arsenal for democracy'. Imperialism seemed to have had its day, and American sentiment was reflected in the press from New York to Chicago and Los Angeles. In August 1945, just after the war against Japan had concluded, the British Embassy in Washington was expressing concern to London about popular American feeling on the subject of Hong Kong: 'The future of Hong Kong has sprung dramatically into the headlines.' This was partly as a result of the current American infatuation with Chiang Kai-shek, the Generalissimo, whose American-educated wife was hugely influential and popular in the United States. The Embassy in Washington reported with dismay the opinion of the *Chicago Daily News*, and believed it spoke for 'a considerable segment of opinion' when it observed that 'the advantages of Hong Kong to the Empire seem to most Americans slight compared with the goodwill which the British could win from the Chinese and other Asiatics by relinquishing control of that great Chinese city to the Chinese people'. There was no desire in America for an 'unqualified and permanent return to the status quo'.[2] The problem, of course, was that there was an equally strong lobby in Britain which did not wish to give Hong Kong back. Like the Conservative leader, Winston Churchill, they had no desire to witness the 'liquidation of the British Empire'. The China Association, a group of businessmen with extensive dealings in China but based in London's Strand, were keen to stress to the Colonial Office 'the importance which is attached by the China Association to the retention of Hong Kong as part of the British Empire'.[3]

The China Association represented the hard-nosed businessmen who had always been an active lobby in British imperial politics, while the then Governor of Hong Kong, Sir Mark Young, was perhaps a quintessentially bureaucratic figure. He had become governor in the inauspicious year of 1941, when the Japanese overran the island and the territories and then proceeded to imprison Sir Mark with about 1,500 other British inmates. His experience at the hands of the Japanese in the Woosung Camp had, in his understated report of the experience, been 'most unsatisfactory', although, as governor, he had not experienced the worst of it. The prisoners were asked to sign an undertaking that they would not 'attempt to escape from the control of the Japanese Military Authorities'. Young and twelve other men, alone of the 1,500 prisoners, refused to sign. For the twelve men, conditions became harsh: they 'suffered very considerable hardship as a result of their refusal', in Young's assessment. He personally was 'not subjected to any ill treatment in consequence of my refusal to sign this certificate'. Yet he believed that his treatment at the hands of the Japanese had been 'almost invariably inconsiderate . . . very frequently objectionable, and . . . on occasions positively barbarous'.[4] In this formulation Sir Mark fulfilled William Johnson Cory's claim that a decent education should teach a man to express himself in 'graduated terms'.

Cory, of course, had been a master at Eton College, the school at which Sir Mark Young had been a King's Scholar, like his father and three brothers. More unusually, all four Young brothers had become imperial civil servants; the Youngs were the archetypal imperial family.

The Roman stoicism and stubbornness Sir Mark Young displayed in his blunt refusal to sign the Japanese certificate were a typical response from a man who, so to speak, had been born in the imperial purple. The Classical allusion would not have been lost on Young either, as he had graduated with a first in Classics from King's College, Cambridge in 1908. Yet after the war he could see that the world had changed. American pressure and new political forces led many observers to believe that the empire would have to change, and it was in this spirit that he ventured into the unknown, by trying to make Hong Kong more democratic. The Young proposals were tentative and, to later observers, hardly controversial. Yet in the context of Hong Kong's history they marked a radical departure from the benign authoritarianism which had been a characteristic feature of the colony's political life for more than a hundred years.

Hong Kong was ruled by a governor, chosen by Whitehall but enjoying considerable latitude once he arrived in Hong Kong. The governor was solely responsible for choosing members of both the Executive Council and the Legislative Council. By 1945 this arrangement had lasted more than a hundred years, and allowed for absolutely no democratic involvement at any stage of the process. Until the 1940s, the only appeals for democracy had come not from the Chinese masses, who constituted more than 98 per cent of the population, but from the British merchants, who for a time resented the power and authority of the bureaucrats, but who ultimately were content to confine themselves to commercial activities. The last significant movement to promote democracy in Hong Kong had occurred in 1894, more than fifty years before the end of the Second World War.

Young's proposals were simple. The main reform would be focused on the Urban Council (responsible for basic services and sanitation on Hong Kong Island and Kowloon), which would be turned into a Municipal Council of thirty members, twenty of whom would be elected and, unusually for Hong Kong, only ten appointed. The Municipal Council, Young envisaged, would be responsible for the day-to-day running of the colony. The most controversial aspect of his ideas, published in the second half of 1946, was the proposal that the seats on the council should be split 50–50 between the European and Chinese populations. Given that the Chinese community made up over 98 per cent of the population, it was clear that any proposal to split the representation evenly would deny them their fair share. By modern standards, there were many provisions that would fail to meet the requirements of pure democratic principles. Young not only proposed a franchise for those who had reached the age of twenty-five, he advocated a literacy qualification in English or Chinese and a property qualification. This was justified on the grounds that there was in Hong Kong 'a very large floating population (both literally and figuratively)' which made keeping an accurate electoral roll very difficult.[5] Young was a typical liberal mandarin of the period after the Second World War; now nearly sixty, he had never been a particularly fierce or trenchant imperialist. More relevantly, for Hong Kong's experience, he was not a Sinologist or, in the jargon of the day, a 'China hand'. He had served as a colonial civil servant in Ceylon, and as governor in Tanganyika and Barbados.[6] He knew very little of conditions in Hong Kong before he was appointed governor in 1941.

His lack of knowledge of Hong Kong perhaps filled him with an idealism which was not shared either by the British officials in Government House or by the Chinese population themselves. In his attempt to win local support for his reforms in the last months of 1946, he often expressed frustration, in his usual measured terms, about the lack of enthusiasm he found among the Chinese population. He complained to Arthur Creech Jones, the trade unionist who was now Labour's Colonial Secretary, of a 'decided lack of enthusiasm for any constitutional changes'. This 'lack of enthusiasm' had been apparent throughout the informal surveys of opinion he had undertaken. Young attributed the tepid response to his plans to apathy and in part to 'apprehension'. After the war, many Hong Kong Chinese believed that it would be only a matter of months before Hong Kong was handed over to the Chinese on the mainland. The majority of the Chinese in Hong Kong, in Young's view, had a 'vague feeling that it may be expedient to keep in with both sides', and they did not want to lose influence in China, after the handover of Hong Kong, by appearing to be enthusiastic supporters of a plan devised by British imperialists. Young had been particularly disheartened when a questionnaire canvassing local opinion, which had appeared in two newspapers with a combined readership of 20,000, elicited fewer than a hundred replies.[7] The attempt to bring a tiny bit of democracy to Hong Kong in 1946 was obstructed by local apathy and by the lack of any real conviction on the part of the British administrators themselves. Young himself retired from public service in May 1947. He had pursued a vision for democracy in Hong Kong but nothing had been achieved. He went to live in Winchester, where he devoted himself to his great love, music, especially in the form of choral singing, and occasionally dipped into the Classical texts which he had studied so diligently at Eton and Cambridge. He died, aged eighty-eight, in 1974. He was an excellent imperial servant, intelligent and humane, yet his hope for a more democratic Hong Kong was never realized in his lifetime.

The idea of democracy in Hong Kong persisted and found its most concrete expression in the formation of the Hong Kong Reform Club in January 1949. The club's objectives were bolder than Mark Young had ever been. It even petitioned his replacement as governor, Sir Alexander Grantham, for a directly elected Legislative Council. This was more radical than Young's own plans because he had envisaged only a Municipal Council which would act as a kind of super town council. The Reform Club also objected strongly to the idea of having two separate electorates, one European and the other Chinese.[8] The new governor, however, was not a man who found the idea of democracy particularly appealing, and, unlike Sir Mark, he had spent a large part of his career in Hong Kong and realized that local public opinion was probably largely indifferent to democratic reform.

Alexander Grantham was quite different from Young. Ten years younger than Sir Mark, he had been in the army at the end of the First World War. He was a product of Wellington College, one of the relatively new public schools, founded in 1853 as a national memorial to the Duke of Wellington. Unsurprisingly, given its origins, Wellington had a more overtly military ethos than older establishments like Eton or Winchester. There was about

Grantham an air of military efficiency, combined with a direct manner, which was practical and hard-edged. It is true that he had been educated at Cambridge, but his mind was not of the same cast as that of Cecil Clementi, who spoke nine different dialects of Chinese and wrote a Latin ode to commemorate the foundation of the University of Hong Kong in 1912. Neither was Grantham like Mark Young, who loved Bach and Classical literature. His practical mind had mastered enough Chinese to read the 'easiest parts' of the newspaper, and that was all he required.

Grantham's practical intelligence saw the problem of Hong Kong's future very clearly. He believed that Hong Kong 'could never become independent'. Either it would remain a British colony or it would be 'reabsorbed into China as part of the province of Kwangtung'. This being the case, he believed that the 'fundamental political problem of the British Colony of Hong Kong [was] its relationship with China and not the advancement to self-government and independence'.[9] The issue of democratic reform in Hong Kong was raised fitfully during the late 1940s and early 1950s, as the Grantham administration prevaricated and dodged the issue. Some articulate opinion in Hong Kong was scandalized by the way things were run in the colony, given that it remained the benign authoritarian state it had always been. Late in 1952, the *Far Eastern Economic Review* reported a speech by Percy Chen, a local barrister and political agitator, who declared, 'there is no other Colony where the system of Government is so archaic; where the system of nomination instead of election plays a bigger part in the selection of so-called representatives'. Chen concluded with the perfectly accurate observation that the 'Democratic system of Government has not been developed in Hong Kong'.[10]

Grantham's own views, though not initially favourable to the idea of democracy, were shaped by what he perceived to be apathy on the part of the local population. At the beginning of 1952, he believed that there was some appetite for limited reform. He had argued, in a meeting in London with Colonial Office officials, that 'those who do advocate' reform were in a strong position to stir up agitation based on the 'non-fulfilment of promises dating back to 1945'. It was only when there seemed to be less support for democracy in Hong Kong itself that Grantham became firmer in his opposition to this development. In the meantime, the Colonial Secretary,

Oliver Lyttelton, a large, jovial man whose political career had been very much subordinated to his financial interests in the City of London, followed the Governor almost blindly. In March 1952, Lyttelton accepted Grantham's view that 'we should now go ahead with the reforms'. Later in the year, in June, Grantham was singing a very different tune, reporting to Lyttelton, his nominal superior, that 'members of Executive Council now feel apprehensive regarding any major constitutional changes at the present time'. By September 1952, constitutional reform in Hong Kong was firmly put aside. Lyttelton observed to the Cabinet in September that 'my colleagues will remember that on the 20th May, the Cabinet approved of my proceeding with the measure of Constitutional Reform', but when 'the Governor of Hong Kong arrived in this country on leave I discussed the matter further with him. I do not propose to proceed with these reforms . . .'[11]

People in Hong Kong continued to agitate for democracy. In 1953, the Reform Club of Hong Kong intensified its campaign to bring some element of democracy into the colony. The London *Times* reported on 16 October that a petition had been signed by 12,000 Hong Kong residents urging the creation of just two elected seats on the Legislative Council. Yet, once again, the Hong Kong population was apathetic. The *China Mail*, in an editorial published on the same day as the *Times* report, remarked that 'deplorable though it may seem to enthusiasts, general public interest in constitutional reform of a major character is much less today than it was five years ago'.[12] People in Hong Kong, it seemed, were generally pleased with their government. Many, the *China Mail* editorial argued, thought the apathy was 'an expression of satisfaction with the post-war progressiveness of the Administration'. The paper concluded that there existed 'little more than academic interest' in constitutional reform. The *South China Morning Post*, on the same day, spoke scornfully of the Reform Club's petition: 12,000 – half of 1 per cent of the community – was hardly 'an enthusiastic endorsement of the zeal and enthusiasm of the reformers'. This newspaper believed that 'a relatively small group of polit- ically-minded persons is trying to foist upon the citizens rights and responsibilities to which the great majority are indifferent'. Democratic politics were unnecessary as the 'Government happens to enjoy very considerable prestige as it is'. What Hong Kong residents wanted was 'efficiency'. It was, the *South China Morning Post* believed, 'not a very adventurous outlook'.[13]

These views highlight a common perception about what made Hong Kong a special place. Trade and money-making were the principal activities that took place there, a theme that runs right through the history of Hong Kong. The British merchants themselves shared that attitude, although they were more likely to suggest that apathy to democracy was part of the Chinese character, and did not simply arise from particular circumstances. P. S. Cassidy was a pillar of the local community and had lived in Hong Kong since 1913. He had served as a member of the Legislative Council and as chairman of the Hong Kong Chamber of Commerce. To him, Hong Kong was like 'Amsterdam in the Middle Ages – the financial centre of Western Europe'. His history may have been suspect, as Amsterdam had enjoyed the summit of its prosperity in the seventeenth century, but the general point remained: Hong Kong was a commercial city, in which the Chinese were 'mainly concerned with their own affairs' and preferred 'to leave to trained administrators the management of public affairs'.[14]

The Reform Club's agitation in the last months of 1953 marked the conclusion of one particular episode in the evolution of democracy in Hong Kong. By the end of that year, Grantham dismissed the club as an institution that did 'not command wide support'. Lyttelton, as usual, was guided entirely by the Governor and, in response to a question from a Labour MP regarding the petition of the Hong Kong Reform Club, merely retorted that he had been 'advised by the Governor that the Reform Club of Hong Kong . . . is not representative of public opinion generally in the Colony and that there is no general demand for constitutional change in Hong Kong at the present time'. Lyttelton, in his characteristically blunt manner, further angered the Hong Kong Chinese by claiming that a large number of the 12,000 who had signed the petition were 'hawkers and others unlikely to understand the issues involved'.[15]

The abortive attempt to bring democracy to Hong Kong reveals once again a recurring feature of the British Empire: individuals mattered. It is likely that, if a more liberal-minded idealist like Mark Young had been governor in place of Grantham, more democratic reforms would have taken place. A leading historian of Hong Kong has even suggested that the 'most important factor which altered the direction of Hong Kong was the difference in attitude and approach of the two Governors involved – Young and Grantham'. It was this radical difference in outlook which determined Hong Kong's course in the subsequent decades and ensured that, between 1952 and 1981, both the British and Hong Kong governments 'ruled out any possibility of developing the Hong Kong constitution' along democratic lines. This difference of outlook between Mark Young and Alexander Grantham shows the anarchic individualism which dominated the empire: individuals who had been granted large responsibility and power were largely unchecked. Each colonial administrator was given a wide latitude to pursue his own policies, and was only rarely overruled by unusually confident ministers like Randolph Churchill in the case of Burma. Generally, the man on the spot had sole responsibility and yet, because another man would soon take over, there was no consistent line of policy that was developed over time. Thus anarchic individualism led to instability because there was no policy coherence or strategic direction. A liberal governor like Sir Mark Young promoted greater democracy in Hong Kong, only for a more pragmatic and less idealistic governor, like Sir Alexander Grantham, to push those reforms to one side.

From the evidence of his memoirs, Grantham obviously enjoyed being a governor in what was perhaps the most authoritarian colony of the British Empire. His account of the powers and authority granted to the governor were straight from the pages of Somerset Maugham, who had written about Hong Kong in the 1920s. 'In a crown colony the Governor is next to the Almighty. Everyone stands up when he enters a room,' Grantham remembered, with some nostalgia. He was 'deferred to on all occasions'. Grantham's view of Hong Kong was wholly in accord with received opinion in Hong Kong ever since its beginning as a British colony in 1841: Hong Kong was exclusively concerned with trade and commerce; the Chinese were not interested in politics or democracy, and the British could provide them with the stable background, the law and order, necessary for them to make money. 'Provided that the government maintains law and order, does not tax them too much and that they can get justice in the courts, they [the Chinese inhabitants of Hong Kong] are content to leave the business of government to the professionals,' Grantham asserted. He was unsentimental about Hong Kong, the colony in which he had spent the first twelve years of his career, and where he would serve as governor for nine years. He believed that the Chinese had no loyalty to the place, any more than Europeans had ties there: the Chinese came 'to Hong Kong to work until they retired home to China, just as the Europeans returned home to Europe'. In a striking metaphor, he compared Hong Kong to 'a railway station, and its inhabitants to the passengers who pass in and out of the gates'. He believed with equal conviction that politicians in Britain were 'quite ready to abandon constitutional reform for Hong Kong' on the grounds that the 'matter did not interest the British electorate'.[16]

Of course, Grantham was right. A colonial governor exercised enormous power, in many cases literally a power of life and death. This was shown, to graphic effect, in the case of Dalton and Douthwaite, two British soldiers who were arrested in 1953 for the murder of a Chinese woman the previous December. The soldiers belonged to the 35th Infantry Brigade stationed in Hong Kong. Lance-Corporal George Robert Douthwaite, the older man, aged twenty-four, had fought in the Korean War, while Dalton was only nineteen. They were alleged to have pulled a woman, Ho Sze-mui, off her bike, to have beaten her with a pair of handcuffs in a seemingly unprovoked attack, and then to have left her body in a ditch on the side of a military road known as Route 7. In April 1953, just as Britain was preparing for the coronation of Queen Elizabeth II, the two men were convicted and sentenced to death by Mr Justice Gould, a New Zealand-born judge. The case went to the Court of Appeal, which dismissed the case of the two soldiers that June. There followed a further appeal to the Privy Council in early October, which was similarly unsuccessful. In the meantime, Dalton's mother wrote a personal letter to the Queen asking for her to intervene. Private Dalton had been a loving son and his parents lived as poor tenants on an estate where the soldier's father had worked as a dairyman. At this point the Colonial Office adopted a firmly neutral position; in a businesslike letter, British officials told the mother of the younger soldier in unequivocal language that the 'prerogative of mercy in cases of this nature is delegated by Her Majesty to the Governor of Hong Kong and your petition has accordingly been sent to him for consideration'. It is doubtful that Her Majesty would even have seen the letter addressed to her. Peter Smithers, the Daltons' local MP, lobbied the government, but was firmly told by Oliver Lyttelton that it was not the Secretary of State's 'duty to advise Her Majesty on the exercise of the prerogative of mercy in this case: it is for the Governor of Hong Kong to decide whether it should be exercised'. Lyttelton considered that it would be 'improper for me to seek to influence him in coming to his decision'. The two soldiers spent the summer of 1953 in a humid cell in Hong Kong awaiting their deaths. Then, on 20 October, the Acting Governor, Robert Black, announced that he had commuted the sentence and had ordered that Douthwaite be imprisoned for twenty years and Dalton for twelve. The men had spent six months on death row and at every stage of their appeals the death sentence had been confirmed. It was only after this lengthy process that the Governor saved the soldiers in an act of clemency which no one had foreseen. The story had a final sad consequence. The elder soldier's mother, Priscilla Douthwaite, a widow, was found dead in a stream in May near her home. She was sixty-nine and had been traumatized by the news of her son's impending fate.[17]

The 1950s are generally remembered in the West as years of steady conservatism, but there was perhaps no other society in which an atmosphere of paternalism and authority was so prevalent as that of Hong Kong, where the role of the state had not evolved since the nineteenth century. Social provision was minimal and welfare support was organized by voluntary bodies or kaifong associations, which reflected the Chinese reputation for 'assisting those in need through either the family or through Clan associations'.[18]

Drug abuse continued to be an endemic problem in Hong Kong in the 1950s, and the colony's government sought to counter the problem by getting the Acting Secretary for Chinese Affairs, the Honourable P. C. M. Sedgwick, to give an evening broadcast on the subject in November 1959, in which he urged the public to 'co-operate in the official campaign against the terrible social evil of drug addiction'. He cited the alarming statistic that 'over 50,000 persons committed to prison during the past five and a half years have been found to be drug addicts'. He went on to suggest that the number of addicts could be as high as 'three to five times that figure'; a figure of 'between 150,000 and 200,000' in an estimated total population of 2.8 million was intolerably high. This method of public admonishment was crude, and officials deliberately contrasted Hong Kong unfavourably with the law-abiding conditions in Britain, where in 1959 it was claimed there existed 'only a few hundred drug addicts in a total population of 50 million'. In the United Kingdom, as Sedgwick explained, the drug addict was 'looked down upon'; even 'in the criminal classes this is so', he boasted.[19]

Paternalism had governed Hong Kong for more than a hundred years and little had changed in the years immediately after the war, which witnessed remarkable economic expansion in the colony, accompanied by considerable immigration. When Hong Kong surrendered to the Japanese on Christmas Day 1941, its population was estimated at 1.6 million. In less than three years under Japanese rule that population had sunk below 600,000; the future of the colony seemed bleak, and yet, by a process of growth in which the government had little direct involvement, it would develop in the 1950s and 1960s to become one of the great commercial centres of the world. The communist takeover of mainland China in 1949, by ensuring that Hong Kong's great rival, Shanghai, was no longer open to foreign capital, gave the colony an unexpected boost. Yet, even during the struggle which raged within China from 1945 until 1949, financiers, merchants and industrialists had started the flight to Hong Kong from the chaos and uncertainty of Shanghai.[20] Immigration was such that by 1960 the population of the colony had reached nearly 3 million people. The industrial sector grew at impressive rates; Hong Kong now became famous for its textiles, for its banking and for the uncanny ability of its manufacturers to mimic luxury goods from outwardly more sophisticated cities like Milan, Paris or London. It was during the 1950s and 1960s that the image of Hong Kong in Europe and Japan became indelibly associated with the manufacture of 'cheap shirts and plastic flowers'.[21]

The dynamic days of Hong Kong's economic expansion have been attributed by many to the activity, or rather the non-activity, of one civil

servant, the Financial Secretary of the colony from 1961 to 1971, John
Cowperthwaite, who died in 2006 at the age of ninety. He became
unwittingly a minor cult figure among the new conservative right in
America for the uncompromising nature of his laissez-faire views. He
was a rather rigid disciple of his fellow Scot Adam Smith, and developed
a doctrine of 'positive non-intervention' in which the state's role would
be minimal, consisting only of keeping taxes low, maintaining open
markets and abolishing restrictions on the movement of capital.
Cowperthwaite had never taken a degree in Economics, but was yet
another Oxbridge Classics graduate, so common in the administration
of Hong Kong. He had graduated from Christ's College, Cambridge
with a double first in 1939, before going to Edinburgh University to
learn some Economics. A statement of his doctrines came in his maiden
budget speech in 1961, which, in itself, was one of the clearest exposi-
tions of the gospel of the free market in practical affairs: 'In the long run,
the aggregate of decisions of individual businessmen, exercising individual judgement in a free economy, even if often mistaken, is less likely
to do harm than the centralized decisions of a government, and certainly
the harm is likely to be counteracted faster.'[22]

Cowperthwaite was passionate about Hong Kong, and declared himself
to be a 'Hong Kong chauvinist'. He has been described by the American
right-wing commentator P. J. O'Rourke as a 'master of simplicities' and
was clear and direct in his manner, although there always lurked a hint of
mischief in his style, which has been characterized as 'polished and
amusing'.[23] Personal taxes he kept at a maximum of 15 per cent. His rigid
determination always to balance the budget and never to borrow money
would have impressed Gladstone. Red tape and bureaucracy were reduced,
it was said, to such an extent that a new company could be registered with
a one-page form. Cowperthwaite, by background and inclination, was the
ultimate conservative bureaucrat, giving – with a slight air of superiority
– a controlled display of measured efficiency. He was naturally sceptical
about all human ability to improve society as a whole and, during his
administration, Adam Smith's invisible hand was a far better guide to
policy than the more direct approaches favoured by most states in the
twentieth century.

Milton Friedman, the Nobel Prize-winning champion of free-market capitalism, remembered with affection a visit which he and his wife made to Hong Kong in 1963. While enjoying his stay in Hong Kong's finest hotel, the Peninsula, and while his wife Rose indulged her tastes in what she described as 'a shopper's paradise', Friedman got a chance to meet Cowperthwaite. During this memorable encounter between the most famous theoretical advocate of laissez-faire in the twentieth century and the doctrine's most successful practical exponent, Cowperthwaite explained that he had resisted requests from civil servants to provide economic statistics because 'he was convinced that once the data was published there would be pressure to use them for government intervention in the economy'.[24] Famously, in what seems to be an apocryphal story, Cowperthwaite greeted and then immediately sent back on the next plane a delegation of civil servants who had arrived in Hong Kong from London to find out why employment statistics had not been collected in the colony.[25]

The partisans of free-market economics were not slow to point out the contrast between the entrepreneurial, business-friendly Hong Kong and the socialist state that many of them believed Britain had become in the decades after 1945. Milton Friedman observed that 'by following a policy opposite to that of its mother country' Hong Kong had thrived, 'while the mother country did not'.[26] Cowperthwaite's obituarist in the Hong Kong *Standard* pointed out that while 'Britain was moving to a socialist and welfare state', the colony 'had the fortune to have Cowperthwaite'.[27] It is true that Hong Kong's growth during Cowperthwaite's tenure was spectacular, and that he often decried the influence of governments on society and the economy, yet the irony was that, for all his distrust of bureaucracy, he was the archetypal bureaucrat of the British Empire: he was Scottish by birth – the high number of Scots in the imperial administration was well known – he was educated at a public school, in his case Merchiston Castle in Edinburgh, and he had studied Classics – the imperial subject par excellence – with considerable success at Cambridge.

Hong Kong, as Cowperthwaite's supporters never fail to observe, grew at an average of 13.8 per cent in every year of his tenure as the colony's financial secretary, and its foreign currency reserves quadrupled. When he died in 2006, his successor (and the last to hold the post of financial secretary), Donald Tsang, later the Special Administrative Region's second chief executive after Hong Kong's return to Chinese rule, paid a fulsome tribute to Cowperthwaite: 'We shall always remember Sir John for the pioneering and dominant role he played in the birth of the legend of Hong Kong as the freest market economy.'[28] The picture, however, was not one of unalloyed sunlight and harmony. Milton Friedman described Cowperthwaite as a 'benevolent dictator', yet, owing to the lack of infrastructure, new immigrants to Hong Kong were housed in shacks and squatter huts, built on hillsides and in cemeteries.[29] Even more alarmingly, Cowperthwaite's period of office saw a banking crisis in 1965 and the most destabilizing political riots in the colony's history in 1967, both of which undermined international confidence in Hong Kong.[30]

The British possession of Hong Kong had always been an embarrass-ment to the Chinese. Indeed, many people had believed that the Chinese, first under Chiang Kai-shek, in the years immediately after the Second World War, and then under Mao Zedong, after 1949, were poised simply to overrun the colony and take it over by force. That this never happened was surprising and, all through the first two decades after 1945, British officials in Hong Kong and in London remained aware of this potential threat. It is likely that the pressure of internal politics prevented China from expanding its borders, as it underwent a period of intensive industri-alization in 1953–7, accompanied by a shift to more widely practised socialism, as well as the introduction of its first Five-Year Plan.[31] In addi-tion to the Chinese military threat, there was also the growing realization that the lease of the New Territories, which comprised the vast majority of the land area of the colony, was due to expire; Hong Kong Island and Kowloon would remain legally British, but in practical terms their continued retention would be impossible. Contrary to a commonly held view in the UK in the 1980s, even ordinary Hong Kong residents grew increasingly aware during the 1960s of the significance of 1997 and the need to prepare for it. Robert Black, Grantham's successor as governor, observed in 1964 in a letter to the Colonial Office that 'people, of course, are by no means unaware of the significance of the date 1997', and referred to an article in the *Sunday Times* colour supplement about 'the future of Hong Kong in relation to the end of the New Territories' lease'.[32]

The growing consciousness of the significance of 1997 in the 1960s was coupled with an air of resignation, even of defeatism, which clung around the old Colonial Office, as it lingered on till its ultimate abolition in 1966, and also around the Foreign Office. There was no point making a declaration about 1997 because any announcement would simply cause a panic, in which people might flee the colony, but some sort of plan was needed. In 1962 Black wrote gloomily, in his best official, circumlocutory style, that we 'would deceive ourselves grossly if we failed to acknowledge that we hold our position in Hong Kong at China's sufferance'. This, in his view, had been the case since 1950. He added that there 'can be no doubt whatever that many people here are even now discussing and speculating upon the situation that lies little more than a generation ahead'. Black was a devotee of the principle of 'masterly inactivity' which had been a guiding notion in Britain's handling of foreign and colonial affairs from the time of Lord Salisbury. His 'single conclusion' was that there 'should be no official or authorised pronouncement on Hong Kong's future until and unless this becomes clearly unavoidable'. He could see very clearly in 1962 something which some British officials never fully grasped, that 'eventual incorporation with China is the only feasible long-term future for Hong Kong'.[33]

What Churchill had once called the 'drawling tides of drift and surrender' had, by the mid-1960s, nearly submerged the once confident imperial bureaucrats in London and the formerly proud British diplomats overseas. The Queen's proposed visit to South-east Asia in 1965 was carefully scheduled to avoid Hong Kong on the grounds that if she stopped over here this could 'provoke' the Chinese. Lord Palmerston would have been horrified by the British diplomat in Beijing who stated before the Queen's tour that although 'we have for the past 18 months had comparatively easy going with the Chinese over Hong Kong, I believe that this period may be drawing to a close'. The diplomat advised against her visiting Hong Kong, concluding that 'all in all, pusillanimous though [this] may appear, I believe discretion is, in this case, the better part of valour'.[34]

British diplomats were also afraid that rivalry between the Soviet Union and China might goad the Chinese into rash action. T. W. Garvey, the man in Beijing who had counselled against the Queen's visit to Hong

Kong in 1965, noticed that the Soviet propaganda machine was now using Hong Kong as a stick with which to beat the Chinese. At the end of May 1964, *Pravda*, the official Russian newspaper, carried a feature entitled 'The Ill Fame of Hong Kong' which criticized the British imperialists while taunting the Chinese:

> In this society the rifts between rich and poor are especially deep. On the sweat of the dockers, the coolies, rickshaw men, fishermen and factory workers live the bourgeois Chinese, the bosses of British firms and foreign businessmen. And all this goes on [at] the doorstep of the PRC [People's Republic of China] and on soil which has been Chinese from time immemorial.[35]

Pravda mocked Beijing's inertia in relation to Hong Kong, claiming that the Chinese press 'displays extreme indifference to the fate of the unfortunates living in the floating quarters of Hong Kong or in the shanties of Kowloon'. The Chinese, the Russians sneered, were not good communists, since 'talk of principles dies away when the call of the dollar is heard'.[36] Britain was worried, during the 1960s, that the Chinese, merely to prove their anti-imperialistic good faith, would act in an aggressive way over Hong Kong.

The year 1967 is one which people in Hong Kong would rather forget. The background to the disturbances of that time did not lie in anything John Cowperthwaite did or omitted to do, but rather in the precarious nature of the relationship between Britain and the People's Republic of China. The actual cause of the unrest that shook Hong Kong was a labour dispute at a plastic-flower factory in May of that year. The industrial dispute quickly widened into a series of demonstrations and riots, and to the laying of bombs, both real and dummy. In Beijing, the *People's Daily* fulminated against the British, urging the Chinese to 'tell the British imperialists that not only have Chinese peasants the right to fill the land in the New Territories, but the whole of Hong Kong must return to the motherland'. Sir David Trench, the Governor of Hong Kong since 1964, managed to keep up a front of characteristic British insouciance by playing his weekly game of golf, but the official messages that flew between London and Hong Kong betrayed grave concern on the part of British officialdom. The brokers on the floors of the Hong Kong Stock Exchange experienced real fear as the Hang Seng index, a crude but powerful measure of local sentiment, plunged to a low of 59 points in 1967.[37] In between his weekly rounds of golf, Sir David Trench, in a telegram of May 1967 marked 'Top Secret', showed his true feelings, admitting 'that in the face of an *all-out* confrontation we probably could not last very long', as the Chinese could always cut off the water supply. The Governor was sufficiently calm, however, to observe that the communists in China would probably want merely to humiliate the British and not 'force us out of Hong Kong'.[38] The extent to which Beijing was involved in the disturbances was unclear, although the Governor was cautious about blaming the Chinese directly.[39] The incidents that May led to a long summer in which relations between China and Britain sank to their lowest ebb in decades. In August, the *People's Daily* denounced the British in inflammatory language, promising that the 'debt of blood which British imperialism has accumulated will certainly be paid off'. Much of the denunciation of the British was openly racist: in October, the same newspaper denounced British hypocrisy in lurid terms, claiming that the 'barbarous bald-pates of British imperialism on the one hand carry out fascist barbarities . . . and on the other hand assume the airs of gentlemen with talk of British democracy and freedom'. The 'bald-pates' of Europeans were the equivalent of the Western view of the Chinese as 'slit-eyed'.[40]

The crisis of 1967 was taken sufficiently seriously in London for the Treasury to draw up secret plans for evacuation. In a paper written in August on the 'Possible Economic Effect on the UK of the Disturbances in Hong Kong', Treasury officials pointed out that the Chinese, if they occupied Hong Kong, would probably seize the assets of the residents of Hong Kong and the assets of the banks. They recommended that, in that event, the British government should immediately block all the Hong Kong sterling balances, which included the money held by Hong Kong institutions on deposit in London; this would be a 'grave step', but it would essentially freeze all the deposits of Hong Kong banks in London and keep their money out of Chinese hands. In the context of a 'forced evacuation', it was decided that the sterling balances would be frozen by the government, although there would be 'no possibility of protecting British property' in the form of 'fixed physical assets', such as buildings, in the colony itself.[41]

These plans were top secret and it was vital that 'absolutely no hint should be given to Mr Cowperthwaite that we have been considering contingency plans' for evacuation. In the event, Cowperthwaite displayed his usual calm confidence and seemed, in the words of the official who met him in London in September 1967, 'entirely unworried'.[42] To Treasury officials in London, the most likely scenario in the face of continued disturbances would be a 'loss of confidence and flight of capital'. The contingency plan had been carefully considered, but the pragmatic view was that there would probably be 'no alternative but to sweat it out in the hope that in time a Chinese regime will emerge with which at a suitable moment we could negotiate an orderly and mutually satisfactory withdrawal from Hong Kong'.[43] At this time Whitehall still believed that the withdrawal should occur 'in advance of the expiry of the lease on the New Territories in 1997', since the common opinion at the time was that capital flight and panic, once people knew the British were leaving, would be such that Hong Kong would be of little value when the year 1997 itself finally arrived.[44]

Throughout 1967, Hong Kong remained Britain's 'main problem in relation to China'.[45] The situation was tense and difficult, as rioters were confronted by an equally determined police force. By December, there was a 'steady decrease in the use of genuine bombs', but the police remained the 'main target for bomb attacks and other acts of violence', and the communist press still continued to produce large quantities of 'anti-British propaganda'.[46] At this time, China was experiencing the worst days of the Cultural Revolution, and to the colony's government the likelihood of Maoist revolutionaries taking over Hong Kong seemed high. A Special Branch report of the Hong Kong Police, dating from January 1968, surveyed the scene with alarm. The 'local Communists here have no intention of abandoning their long term aim of obtaining a victory over the Hong Kong Government', the police believed. Of nine communist newspapers three had been suppressed, but the communists still had 'a forceful propaganda machine'. Radio broadcasts from Macau, from the radio station Villa Verde, attacked the Hong Kong government every day, though it was noted that the nature of these attacks had softened since December 1967. The police were also worried about widespread interest in the thought of Mao; the police report painted a lurid picture of study groups, large-scale meetings and exhibitions at 'Communist premises', which aimed to make the whole Hong Kong community 'red'. 'It should not be forgotten', the report observed, 'that the continual study of the "little red book" – a handbook of Mao's political philosophy – breeds fanatics with no respect for law and order.'[47] Even though, by the beginning of 1968, the situation had quietened down, the police were concerned that the communists had now adopted a policy of the 'friendly hand and the smiling face' in order to ingratiate themselves with a sceptical local community.

This wide-ranging report was perhaps a typical product of police forces everywhere, which often exaggerate dangers in order to justify their own powers. Yet the report offered constructive suggestions for how to improve Hong Kong's internal security and oppose the communist threat: 'To counter this new phase of communist confrontation the government must, in addition to maintaining law and order', bring about 'genuine and lasting improvements in standards of living, especially among the poorer classes'. 'Trade disputes' needed to be avoided, and a sophisticated public relations machine had to be established which could 'meet the challenge of communist propaganda'.[48]

In February 1968, the ban on the three suppressed newspapers was lifted. The nine communist daily newspapers now had a combined daily circulation of only 250,000, compared to a figure nearer 350,000 the year before. Trade had been seriously affected by the confrontation, as there had been a 45 per cent decrease in imports from China in the period from May to September 1967, compared to the same period in 1966, but the police felt that the battle for 'hearts and minds' was turning in the Hong Kong government's favour. During the confrontation, the Hong Kong community had gained 'considerable confidence' in the 'Government's ability to contain communism'. The tension had been defused by initiatives of the Chinese government. As always, the police report of March 1968 continued, 'everything depends on the attitude of China'. So long as the Chinese government supported local Hong Kong communists only with propaganda and 'limited financial aid', the communist problem was containable. This seemed to be the path the Chinese were likely to follow, 'so long as the economic value of the colony remains an over-riding factor in the eyes of Peking'.[49]

And what of democracy? Democracy played an even smaller part in the thinking of the Hong Kong government in the 1960s than it had done in the late 1940s. There was the issue of local apathy, since, as one official had crudely noted as early as 1952, the man in the street in Hong Kong wanted only a 'full belly'.[50] But more relevantly to the colony's actual situation in the late 1960s, any move to democracy could result in Hong Kong falling into the wrong, communist hands. This had always been a worrying consideration, from the days when Chiang Kai-shek and his Kuomintang held power in China before 1949. In a memorandum on the history of the Young proposals, the argument was explicitly stated: 'These proposals, though approved, were never implemented chiefly because they would have resulted in effective control of many essential services passing to a body whose British character and loyalty could not necessarily be guaranteed during a period of strained relations with China'.[51] This argument carried even more weight after the communists had taken over China in 1949. Hilton Poynton, a Colonial Office veteran, had been unequivocal about this in a letter to the Governor in 1964: 'Hong Kong's constitutional development cannot be along normal lines leading to self government and independence,' since this would leave it 'open to communist penetration and control'.[52] The events of 1967 made this line of argument even more compelling; as a consequence, democracy in Hong Kong was never seriously contemplated.

18

Red Dawn

As Hong Kong entered the 1970s, Britain was leaving its imperial past behind. The upheaval of decolonization had left large tracts of Africa and Asia to fend for themselves as newly independent states, but Hong Kong remained in much the same condition. As a consequence of the failure of any movement towards self-government, the governor continued to be an all-powerful figure. In 1971 a new governor, Murray MacLehose, had been appointed not from the ranks of the Colonial Office, but from those of the Foreign Office, yet in all other respects his background was very similar to that of his immediate predecessors. Like many others who served in the Hong Kong government, MacLehose was Scottish, but he had been educated in the very English institutions of Rugby and Balliol College, Oxford, perhaps the most imperially minded Oxford college, where he had taken a third-class degree in Modern History in 1939.[1] 'Big Mac', as he was fondly called, has been described as the 'last of the great British proconsuls', but the start to his tenure as governor of Hong Kong was modest.

There was nothing to indicate that Big Mac would differ in any way from his predecessors. He was just another Scottish diplomat who had been made governor of Hong Kong, but as the 1970s went on it was clear that he would have to face fresh challenges, negotiating relations between Hong Kong and London, while attempting not to irritate the communist regime in Beijing. Commercially, the early 1970s were years of expansion and confidence, after the low point of the 1967 disturbances. The Hang Seng index leaped from its low of 59 in 1967 to 1,775 in March 1973, making this six-year period one of the greatest bull runs in international stock-market history.[2]

Politically, MacLehose's nominal bosses in Whitehall were less optimistic. As late as 1972, officials in London remained gloomy about the
future of Hong Kong, and were considering plans to evacuate the colony,
or at least for a managed withdrawal, before the official end of British rule
in 1997. The Foreign and Commonwealth Office, a new department
created in 1968 from an amalgamation of the old Commonwealth and
Foreign Offices, was realistic about the prospect of holding on to Hong
Kong. Officials in the newly created department argued, no doubt
correctly, that 'if the Chinese allowed the lease of the New Territories to
run its full term, we could not expect to renegotiate it in 1997'. 'Sovereignty
in Hong Kong', a Foreign Office official wrote in 1972, 'will have to be
handed over to China and this is likely to become an issue in the 1980s.'
The prospects for Hong Kong in the 1980s seemed bleak, as 'confidence
and the economy' would 'inevitably start to run down'. In the event of a
general economic decline, which officials in London anticipated, Hong
Kong could 'become a major liability'.[3]

The early 1970s were a bleak time for Britain, as constant threats of
industrial disputes and strikes dominated the headlines, and the country
was still trying to find a role in the world after the rapid decolonization of
the 1960s. Much of this pessimistic outlook is reflected in the pronounce-
ments of officials. Since Hong Kong's economy would wind down in the
1980s, so it was presumed, one official drew the obvious conclusion that
'the disadvantages of our remaining in Hong Kong up to 1997 seem greatly
to outweigh the advantages'. The only problem was that any hint that the
British intended to leave 'could well precipitate the collapse of confidence
that we want to avoid'.[4] Others in the new FCO joined in the chorus of
doom: 'we should withdraw as soon as we can reasonably do so' because
there was a 'lack of defence for Hong Kong' and because of the 'drain
which our presence there imposes on our financial balance of payments
and manpower'. Another could only observe that 'to stay in Hong Kong
would be contrary to our general colonial policy'.[5] Organized retreat seems
to have been the favoured policy with regard to Britain's imperial commit-
ments at the Foreign Office in the early 1970s. The Chinese, by contrast,
after the excesses of the Cultural Revolution in the late 1960s, had become
more reconciled to current circumstances than their harassed counterparts

in London's Foreign Office. Showing admirable pragmatism, the Chinese were now content to allow the current situation to continue, as they waited patiently for 1997. In 1971, the veteran Chinese politician Zhou Enlai informed the former Colonial Secretary Malcolm MacDonald that China would not seek to recover Hong Kong until the expiry of the New Territories' lease in 1997.[6]

Strong economic growth in Hong Kong had led to an epidemic in corruption that threatened to destabilize the colony, and it was for his fight against corruption that much of MacLehose's subsequent reputation was gained. 'Fast money' in Hong Kong encouraged a culture in which the police took bribes from Triad gangs and other known criminals, allowing the gangsters to run gambling syndicates, drug rings and brothels without any interference.[7] The most notorious case involved Peter Godber, a police chief superintendent, who had fled the colony in June 1973, whereupon the slogan 'Fight Corruption, Catch Godber' became widely heard. Godber had escaped the colony just at the moment he was about to be charged for corrupt practices. Four days before his flight to London, police investigators had raided Godber's car and house, where they found boxes full of silver bars and what they described as 'a trail of fortune', leading them to bank accounts in Singapore, Australia, Canada and other countries. Godber's escape was the sensation of the year, but he was brought back from London and sentenced to four years in jail in Hong Kong. He served thirty-one months of his term and then, on his release in October 1977, he disappeared. Ernest, otherwise known as 'Taffy', Hunt was an associate of Godber who later turned against his old mentor: 'Make no mistake about it,' he assured the *Daily Express* in 1975, 'I was a villain.' He candidly told the BBC later in the same year that being corrupt in Hong Kong was 'as natural as going to bed at night and brushing your teeth in the morning'.[8]

The scale of corruption prompted MacLehose to establish the Independent Commission Against Corruption, or ICAC, in 1974. This body was 'flabbergasted' by the scale of corruption in the police force, where policemen were found to be 'salting away sizeable fortunes to acquire villas in Spain', and it was discovered that highly organized police syndicates took 'breath-taking' sums of money, 'amounting to hundreds of millions of US dollars'. The key figure in each police syndicate was known as the 'caterer', and he alone possessed all the information on the deals, acting as a sort of banker in the distribution of kickbacks and bribes to the other members of the syndicate. This was the other, seamier side of the laissez-faire culture which Cowperthwaite and his superiors in Government House had promoted.[9] The air of corruption in Hong Kong was part of a wider malaise in the colony which stemmed partly from the free-wheeling nature of its capitalism and partly from the ossified nature of its society, which remained snobbish and static. In such an environment, where free enterprise was promoted but society stagnated, a criminal underworld, with its own rules, rapidly emerged. This was the time when it was said that 'the Jockey Club, the Hong Kong and Shanghai Bank, and the Governor' ruled Hong Kong '*in that order*'.[10] The Jockey Club had, by the 1960s, replaced the Hong Kong Club as the colony's most elite social institution, though the Hong Kong Club kept its gentlemen's club atmosphere until 1997.

But it wasn't from the Chinese, the gentlemen's clubs or even the corrupt police force that MacLehose experienced the most acute political pressure. It was the advent of the Labour government in Britain in 1974 which put Hong Kong's rather anomalous position as a benign dictatorship, or at best a benevolent oligarchy, in the spotlight. Democracy in Hong Kong was back on the discussion table, in the corridors of Whitehall at least. The 1970s in Britain was probably the decade when inverse snobbery, a hostile suspicion of many of the elite presuppositions which had underpinned the British Empire, was at its strongest. It was the time when the top rate of tax on earned income reached 83 per cent, and when grammar schools, which selected their pupils by rigorous examinations at the age of eleven, were mostly abolished in Britain. British Labour MPs had started noticing the archaic flavour of Hong Kong when they visited the colony as opposition MPs in the early 1970s. At the end of 1973, the Labour MP Robert Hughes wrote to his even more left-wing colleague Ian Mikardo that he had been 'recently in Hong Kong and no one who has visited the colony can fail to have been greatly concerned at the manner in which the Hong Kong Government runs affairs'. Hughes's letter enumerated the usual left-wing objections to Hong Kong in a litany which recalled the *Pravda* article of 1964 entitled 'The Ill Fame of Hong Kong'. Hughes complained to Mikardo of the 'tremendous disparities of wealth, of working conditions, of housing conditions' – disparities which would not be tolerated in Britain. He compared the state of affairs in Hong Kong to that in South Africa and attributed this to the 'lack of Trade Union rights and organization'. More importantly, in a classically Marxist critique of the Hong Kong government, he said that 'all the nominees to the Legislative Council represent the commercial and business interests of the Colony' and that there was no 'democratic right of people to influence their way of life'. This had been the case for the 130 years before Robert Hughes had come to this realization. At the conclusion of his letter, he added astutely that '[we] forget that [Hong Kong] is a colony because of its autonomy'.[11]

In a series of meetings which took place when the Governor visited Britain in April 1975, MacLehose was told very clearly what the Labour Party thought of Hong Kong. The Governor, of course, was treated in a civilized manner; he often met officials for lunch in London at gentlemen's clubs like Brooks's or the Travellers, but real business was conducted in the Foreign Office where, on Friday 11 April at 11.30 in the morning, MacLehose met James Callaghan, the Foreign Secretary. Callaghan was a stalwart of the Labour movement who had been elected to Parliament in 1945 and was very much in touch with the grass roots of the party, in contrast to his more privileged colleagues, such as Anthony Crosland and Roy Jenkins, who had enjoyed more financial security in their upbringing and had earned first-class degrees at Oxford University. 'Sunny Jim', as Callaghan was popularly known, had left school at fifteen and had served in the navy before becoming active in Labour politics. His interview with MacLehose on that April morning was characteristically frank. Callaghan opened the meeting by baldly stating that 'the reputation of Hong Kong did not stand particularly high in the Labour movement in the United Kingdom'.

Interestingly, the objections of the 'Labour movement' to Hong Kong did not really stem from the lack of democracy in itself, but rather from the poor labour rights which existed in the colony, the low wage rates of Hong Kong seamen and the narrow social composition of the Legislative Council, which continued to be handpicked by the Governor. The embattled

MacLehose argued that the Legislative Council 'more closely approximated to a Cabinet than to a Parliament' and, as a consequence of this, a 'high calibre of member' was essential. He did however accept that members 'from lower income brackets' would need to be included 'in due course'. Callaghan conceded the need for 'high calibre in the members', but made the obvious retort that such arguments would not 'carry much weight politically' in the Labour Party in Britain. At an earlier meeting with the Foreign Office minister Goronwy Roberts, Callaghan's junior in the department, MacLehose had played the stalling game beloved of natural conservatives when faced with a radical onslaught, insisting that he did not think that any 'precipitate action should be taken . . . to broaden the membership of the Legislative Council'. Given time, he told Roberts, 'one or two of the natural leaders' of the workers could emerge. Roberts was unimpressed, continuing to harangue the Governor; and in his summary of the conversation he claimed that MacLehose shared his view 'that Hong Kong must continue to move towards more progressive taxation and social security policies'. These were the very measures which Cowperthwaite had so vigorously opposed in the 1960s, and which Milton Friedman believed had made Britain less prosperous in the period after 1945.[12]

Unsurprisingly, the Governor earned the same polite rebuke when he came back to Britain in July the following year. Yet he clearly knew how to handle his political superiors in London. Labour ministers had by then become fixated with the idea of placing a trade union representative on the Legislative Council, and had abandoned any interest, if they ever had any, in establishing real democracy in Hong Kong. They 'recognized the difficulties in Hong Kong terms of appointing a trade unionist to the Legislative Council' but contended that it 'would be virtually impossible to defend a decision not to do so here'. The 'Labour movement' was still very concerned that the 'interests of wage earners [should] . . . be represented in the Hong Kong government'. The government ministers were polite enough to show understanding of the difficulty the Governor was in, but 'ministers were under severe pressure' in Britain, especially from the TUC (the Trades Union Congress) and from the NEC (the National Executive Committee of the Labour Party). Towards the end of his visit to Britain, MacLehose met Ted Rowlands, who had replaced Goronwy Roberts at the Foreign

Office in March 1976, when Callaghan moved from the Foreign Office to become prime minister.

Rowlands showed considerable aggression at the meeting, asking about corruption in Hong Kong. MacLehose acknowledged that there had indeed been corrupt practices in the Hong Kong police force, to which Rowlands, in an extraordinary attack, responded that 'Victorian attitudes sometimes seemed to prevail in the Colony.' MacLehose objected to this, by pointing out that Victorians did not provide 'housing or health on the scale that was being provided in Hong Kong'. The next day, MacLehose saw Tony Crosland, the Foreign Secretary, who told him in schoolmasterly fashion that the 'matter of a trade unionist on Council had now assumed symbolic importance here and it was, in his view, essential that such an appointment should be made now'. Crosland was prone to seeing Hong Kong politics in terms of tension between social classes. The notion of class conflict had, of course, been the legacy of Karl Marx to progressive political thought. In this context, Crosland asserted that there had to be a 'representative of working class interests' on the Legislative Council.[13]

It was unlikely that many people in Hong Kong saw their society in such narrowly defined social categories. There was grotesque inequality in Hong Kong, but the Chinese hawkers and traders had never subscribed to a Marxist philosophy which saw everything in terms of class. In this respect, the Hong Kong Chinese were more like Victorian liberals who believed, as Deng Xiaoping later said, that 'to grow rich is glorious' and that wealth was a reward for industry and individual initiative.

The issue of the death penalty revealed how out of touch the Labour government in London was with sentiment in Hong Kong. In the 1970s, despite its abolition in Britain, the death penalty still existed in Hong Kong and, although the Governor and his predecessor had commuted every death sentence since the late 1960s, 'public opinion there [was] still strongly in favour of its being applied'.[14] In 1975, the Foreign Office had noticed that there was 'no sign that public pressure in Hong Kong for the implementation of death sentences is yet diminishing' and capital punishment was so popular that the Executive Council accepted that 'they would be unwise to press their proposal that the death penalty in Hong Kong should be suspended'.[15]

The feelings of the left wing of the Labour Party were well articulated by the Reverend John Gingell, the self-styled Industrial Adviser to the Bishop of Derby, who wrote the Foreign Office a series of letters on the issue of Hong Kong in the mid-1970s. Gingell had been a member of the Labour Party for many years and was concerned that 'Hong Kong continues to be ruled as a colony with no democratic involvement on the part of its citizens,' and that a Labour government had 'no business maintaining colonial anachronisms'. The observation of the pragmatic Foreign Office was more sensitive to the realities of the situation in Hong Kong itself: 'Gingell seems to assume that the people in Hong Kong would welcome a more democratic Government and that the Chinese government would also prefer a democracy to a colonial regime in Hong Kong.' The idealism of the Labour Party faithful contrasted with the pragmatic realism of the British Foreign Office, and directly contradicted the views of the Governor, as he sat in his study back in Government House.[16]

There still remained some political activists in Hong Kong who were more committed to the ideal of democratic participation than the British officials. These activists were people like Brook Bernacchi, the chairman of the Hong Kong Reform Club, who had been beating the drum for constitutional reform since the 1950s. At the beginning of 1978 he wrote eagerly to Dr David Owen, Britain's young Foreign Secretary, that the results of a survey showed that 50 per cent of the adult population of Hong Kong 'positively want a measure of elected representation' to the Legislative Council, and that this proportion would rise to 62 per cent if the survey were confined to those aged eighteen to thirty-four. The Reform Club warned the British government that 'if the voice of the people is not taken heed of now' there could be 'disturbances'. Such threats, however, did little to convince London of the need for reform. Bernacchi and his associates had been saying the same thing for thirty years, and their arguments could be rebutted in a matter of minutes by the well-trained mandarins of the Foreign and Commonwealth Office. As one official observed, 'there is clearly a difference between being in favour of something and positively wanting it'. This was demonstrated by the fact that 'only half of those in favour of elections say that they would be likely to vote if elections were to be held'. The old argument of Hong Kong apathy was wheeled out once again to prevent genuine democratic reform. The clincher was, of course, the attitude of China. As 1997 approached, the British Foreign Office was only too well aware of the need to keep Beijing happy. 'The present system is understood and accepted by the Chinese Government and any change would be bound to arouse their suspicions.'[17]

The efforts of the Reform Club were politely rebuffed; they were simply told that 'although there are no plans to introduce elections to the Legislative Council, we are grateful to you for keeping us informed of your findings which have been studied with great interest'. This formula of words was a polite diplomatic expression of exasperated contempt. Denys Roberts, the Chief Secretary of Hong Kong, who in 1978 was appointed chief justice by MacLehose, concluded this episode with a firm rejection of democracy in the colony. The people of Hong Kong, he argued, were 'indifferent' and there 'was no substantial tradition of the democratic process as we know it'. The argument that there was 'no substantial tradition' could be applied in every country in the world where democracy did not exist: it simply justified prevailing circumstances. To compound this bureaucratic conservatism, Roberts also said that there was 'a fairly widespread view that the boat should not be rocked' at this time. The people of Hong Kong, in his rather complacent judgement, were 'content not to have elections on any substantial scale, and would not welcome the uncertainties that would accompany them'.[18]

The background of international politics had, by 1978, shifted against the democratic movement in Hong Kong. With the death of Mao and the accession of Deng Xiaoping, a new era of economic liberalization had begun in China, which was accompanied by friendlier relations with the West, coupled with a more pragmatic attitude to Hong Kong. In the 1960s, Beijing had accused the British of hypocrisy because they had not let the people of Hong Kong rule themselves, but by the late 1970s the Chinese were anxious for the old order to remain. Beijing's greater tolerance of colonial rule was reflected in the British press, which observed with delight the 'unprecedented toasting of the Queen's health by China's unofficial "ambassador" to Hong Kong' at the Chinese National Day Celebration in October 1978; Bank of China executives, it was also noticed, no longer entertained their Western counterparts in the workers' canteen in the basement, but took them to one of the 'modern American-run hotels' in Hong Kong.[19]

The Chinese on the mainland were only too well aware of the advantages derived from Hong Kong business, and, as 1997 loomed ever larger on the horizon, they were particularly anxious to preserve the colony's prosperity. A group of Hong Kong businessmen, on a visit to mainland China at the end of 1977, were told to 'work for the prosperity of Hong Kong' and that they should be 'at ease'. They were also entreated, 'don't sell your property and go elsewhere'. At this time, Taiwan had become a bigger concern for China than Hong Kong, and Gordon Wu, a major property developer and a member of the business delegation, was told that 'China would settle the Taiwan problem first before it decides what to do with Hong Kong'.[20] China was also eager to purchase equipment and technology from the West to strengthen 'her economy and military capacity'. The new détente between the West and China made any progress on the issue of democracy for Hong Kong unlikely. The point of which everyone was conscious, in the late 1970s, was that any abrupt change to the way in which Hong Kong had been governed for nearly 150 years would upset Beijing, and would inevitably increase uncertainty immediately before the colony was handed over. Even the Labour government concerned itself only with trade union representation and not with actual democracy. Genuine democracy in Hong Kong was simply not a consideration that absorbed many people's interest: Beijing did not want it, the government in London was indifferent, while British civil servants in London and Hong Kong were decidedly against the idea, as were the Governor and most of the business interests in Hong Kong. In the late 1970s, the pro-democracy in Hong Kong movement, if it could be described in such terms, consisted only of a few radical democrats in the Hong Kong Reform Club and the ideological democrats among the left of the Labour Party in Britain.

The unspoken alliance between London and Beijing was further strengthened by a perception in London that Hong Kong itself was of very little value to Britain any more. 'Hong Kong', wrote W. E. Quantrill, a Foreign Office official, in 1978, 'is no longer of crucial importance to us: if it did not exist, we should not now need to invent it.' Obviously, Britain could not 'simply abandon the territory and its population', but an understanding with the Chinese would be possible 'before 1985, and possibly as early as 1980 or 1981'. The assumption was that 'the People's Republic of China will continue to be ruled by the sort of rational, pragmatic men who have emerged as the country's leaders since the death of Mao Tse Tung'. Agreement with the Chinese was therefore extremely likely since China had 'turned away' from the 'extremism' of Chairman Mao. The main difficulty in diplomatic relations with China concerning Hong Kong's fate was the need for strict secrecy. In 1978 it was clear that the '1997 problem has become a fairly common subject of discussion in Hong Kong', but 'any leaks about our studies or intentions could do great damage'. There was an organized attempt not to say anything publicly which might incite a mood of panic among the people of Hong Kong. There was never any doubt that the colony's future would largely be a matter for the Chinese: 'The Chinese have let it be known in Hong Kong that Chinese interests will require the maintenance of the status quo for the foreseeable future.' China was also backing its word 'with concrete actions in the form of substantial investment in Hong Kong', which had helped to create 'a new climate of confidence in the future of the colony'.[21]

The paternalism of MacLehose was actually popular in Hong Kong and in London. In the colony itself, the government boasted of its achievements in the twenty-five years since 1955; it had accomplished much in 'providing housing, social services, education and employment for the rapidly increasing population'. The government had made primary and junior secondary education both compulsory and free; there were only minimal charges for medical treatment, while 'more than 2 million people lived in 400,000 government provided or government subsidised flats'.[22] Hong Kong was probably the most successful exercise in benevolent dictatorship in history. Its success could be measured by the vast influx of immigrants which, every year, descended upon the colony from China. During 1979, some 70,000 legal immigrants entered Hong Kong, while 90,000 illegal immigrants were arrested and repatriated to China. Perhaps the most startling fact of all was that 110,000 illegal immigrants had actually escaped arrest that year and had been merely absorbed into the population. An 'annual influx of nearly 200,000' people into Hong Kong

could not be 'sustained without serious social and economic consequences'.[23] These figures represented about 5 per cent of the total
population of Hong Kong. It would be the equivalent of 15 million people
entering the United States today, or 3 million entering Great Britain. This
influx would probably have been unacceptable in most democracies, but,
under the benevolent paternalism of Hong Kong, people just got on with
their lives and let the government tackle the problem. Indeed, it was one
of the ironies of Hong Kong's autocratic system of government that
MacLehose's humanitarian response to the plight of the Vietnamese boat
people was praised by Western liberals. By October 1979, Hong Kong was
housing over 62,000 Vietnamese, and, as one historian of the colony has
pointed out, there can be 'little doubt that had Hong Kong possessed a
more democratic government with its leaders answerable to elections . . .
it would have been obliged to adopt sterner measures'.[24]

Everything seemed to augur well for the handover in 1997. By the late
1970s, the Chinese and the British seemed to have reached a cordial
understanding. Much about Hong Kong's position was not publicly stated
as no one wanted to upset the existing arrangements, but there was a tacit
understanding that things would not change much in Hong Kong, which
had historically enjoyed one of the most stable regimes in Asia. The
contrast between the upheavals in China and the tranquil fate of Hong
Kong could not have been more striking, since China had, in the period
after 1841, experienced two violent revolutions, many years of civil war,
the abolition of a monarchy which had lasted thousands of years, the
violence of Mao's Cultural Revolution and then, finally, an economic revolution inaugurated in 1978 in which capitalism was openly embraced.
Hong Kong had meanwhile lived under the administration of twenty-five
governors of similar background, who had preserved the same way of
government over the entire period from 1841.

It was the arrival of Margaret Thatcher as prime minister in 1979 that
began to challenge the happy understanding between China and Britain.
This is not the place to chart Mrs Thatcher's rise to power, but her gender
and education at a northern grammar school made her an outsider. She
had disdain for the traditions of the Foreign Office, as she believed that
they had consistently failed to fight for British interests. Indeed, one of the

China veterans in the Foreign Office, Percy Cradock, described her attitude towards the policy of the Foreign Office on Hong Kong as being encapsulated in the line 'Here is another colonial outpost they want to sell off.'[25] Thatcher famously saw the world in simple, even stark terms. There was good and there was evil; there was freedom and democracy, on the one side, and tyranny and oppression, on the other. The more nuanced views of the British Foreign Office were often just swept aside or ignored.

Margaret Thatcher had first visited China as leader of the opposition in 1977. Most politicians, when they actually visited China, were entranced and fascinated by its ancient civilization and culture. Mrs Thatcher was different; she was an exception to the general rule among political and business leaders that, once in Beijing having 'their tummies tickled, they [were] captivated by the place, seeing themselves as latter-day Marco Polo figures'. On her first visit in 1977, she found China to be a 'rather unpleasant place governed by rather unpleasant people'.[26] It was in the late 1970s that she was famously defined by her uncompromising stance against communism and was dubbed the 'Iron Lady of the Western World' by the state-controlled media in the Soviet Union.

To Mrs Thatcher, the Chinese were as bad as the Russians; they were communists who practised political repression and lived under a dictatorship. They represented to her the antithesis of what she believed Britain stood for. In her mind, Britain upheld freedom and democracy, while the Chinese believed in brutal repression. At a later date, such aggressive liberalism would be dubbed neo-conservatism, and it was radically different from the more conciliatory traditions of the Foreign Office and the British Empire, as these had evolved in the twentieth century. In Hong Kong, the most consistently powerful obstacle to democracy had been the Governor's office itself. Over 150 years, of the twenty-five or so governors who had ruled Hong Kong, only Sir Mark Young had actually initiated a plan for greater democracy, and his plans had been shelved by his successor. Thatcher's view of the British Empire, however, bore very little relation to the reality of empire, which, as I have argued in this book, was a pragmatic affair, governed more by notions of intellectual and social elitism, deference and privilege than by any abstract ideal of democracy or political liberalism.

Thatcher's second visit to Beijing, as prime minister, occurred in September 1982. The date was significant because she had recently defeated Argentina in the Falklands War, which had ended in June of that year. She herself acknowledged the confidence that her recent victory in the South Atlantic had given her on the international stage. She recalled in her memoirs that 'Britain's standing in the world and my own had been transformed as a result of victory in the Falklands.'[27] In the course of the discussions, it appeared that the British Prime Minister rejected the presumption since 1945 that all of Hong Kong really belonged to China and would be given back when the lease on the New Territories expired in 1997. As the *South China Morning Post* reported, citing 'Chinese sources', Margaret Thatcher was 'probably the first British statesman in the past decade to dispute China's sovereignty over Hong Kong'.[28]

In the course of his interview with Mrs Thatcher, Deng Xiaoping reiterated that the 'Chinese were not prepared to discuss sovereignty'.[29] In this statement Deng implied that the sovereignty of Hong Kong was an issue which Mrs Thatcher believed to be a subject of negotiation in the early 1980s. Yet by the late 1970s, there was a considerable degree of agreement between Britain and China on the issue of Hong Kong and China's sovereignty had been fully accepted in the 1950s and 1960s, when Robert Black and Alexander Grantham had ruled out independence for Hong Kong, recognizing that the colony's future lay in China. Margaret Thatcher had read Chemistry at Oxford, and boasted of being the first British prime minister with a science degree; intellectually, too, she had a different background from the British official class, steeped as it was in history and the classics. Regardless of her educational background, she brought very little historical understanding to bear on the issue of Hong Kong; she framed the question of sovereignty simply in terms of a battle between democracy and tyranny, between right and wrong. At her meeting in September, she was surprised that 'the Chinese refused to budge an inch', and they were surprised that she seemed to be turning her back on an understanding between China and Great Britain which had lasted several decades. All sides were conscious that China could take the colony by force; even in 1949, the British expected the communists to seize Hong Kong, and, before that, in 1945, the Americans had thought that the Chinese

Nationalists, under Chiang Kai-shek, would accomplish the same end. These experiences formed the background to Deng's rather brutal observation that the Chinese could 'walk in and take Hong Kong later today if they wanted to'.[30] It was a raw statement of realpolitik, but it was merely the unspoken assumption which had existed between the two countries, whose bureaucrats liked to conduct their diplomacy in subtle, covert ways. As Robert Black, the governor at the time, had observed as long ago as 1962, Britain was deluded 'if we failed to acknowledge that we hold our position in Hong Kong at China's sufferance'.[31] This was exactly the point Deng made to Mrs Thatcher, though with considerably less subtlety, twenty years later.

Mrs Thatcher challenged Deng on this point, arguing that if China did invade then the world would see 'what followed from British to Chinese rule', implying that the true nature of China's totalitarian system would be exposed for the world to see. Deng was taken aback, she later wrote, and 'his mood became more accommodating'. Yet he was shocked less by her firmness than by her refusal to acknowledge a reality which had been recognized since the end of the Second World War. In her memoirs, Margaret Thatcher concludes the section on her trip to China in September 1982 in an uncharacteristically elegiac tone: 'I had been able to visit the extraordinarily beautiful Summer Palace on the north-western outskirts of Peking, known in Chinese as the Garden of Peaceful Easy Life. I felt that this was a less than accurate description of my own visit to the Far East.'[32] The stock market was less sentimental than Mrs Thatcher. The Hang Seng index fell 21 per cent in the week after her visit. It was felt that her intransigence could jeopardize the economic stability of Hong Kong.[33]

Margaret Thatcher's visit was followed by two years of negotiations between the British Foreign Office and its Chinese counterparts. The conclusion of this diplomacy was the Joint Declaration of 1984, which formed the basis of many disputes between London and Beijing in the years immediately before 1997. The principle underlying the Joint Declaration was that 'current' institutions of Hong Kong were to remain unchanged for fifty years, but it gave no definition of what the term 'current' actually signified. The Chinese, perhaps understandably, argued that Hong Kong should return to China as it stood in 1984, when the

Joint Declaration was signed. The British, in both London and Hong Kong, insisted that Hong Kong could not be frozen in time for thirteen years, and that the term 'current' had to reflect developments which might occur after the Declaration had been signed.[34] In the context of Hong Kong's 150-year history as a British colony, the British position seemed disingenuous. The colony had been ruled as a benign autocracy for 150 years. Murray MacLehose, who was still governor as late as 1982, had gently but firmly set himself against widening the democratic process. The fact that Hong Kong had never substantially changed its political or legal institutions was perhaps its most defining characteristic. Even the British constitution itself had changed more since 1841 than had Hong Kong's method of government. In Britain, there had passed the Second Reform Bill in 1867, the Third Reform Bill in 1884, the extension of the franchise to all adult males in 1918, the granting of votes for women at the same age as men in 1928, even a lowering of the voting age to eighteen in 1967. In contrast, apart from the addition or subtraction of a few seats on the Legislative and Executive Councils, absolutely nothing had changed in Hong Kong, which continued to be an outpost of benign authoritarianism while the world around it had been reshaped. And then, just as the final act unfolded, the British tried to rush through reforms, in order to give the impression that the empire had been about democracy all along. It seemed to the Chinese like a desperate sleight of hand.

The first elections in Hong Kong's history took place in 1985, after the Joint Declaration. By any international standards, they were a muted affair, as there was no universal suffrage, but rather a system in which members of district, urban and regional councils and representatives of various professional bodies could participate. There was a member of the Legislative Council who represented the legal profession, another who represented industry, one for medicine and another for architecture.[35] This was a corporate view of democracy, more in line with thinking in the Middle Ages; it was a belated start, and more agitation was to come.

In 1989 the Tiananmen Square massacre occurred in Beijing, when hundreds of student demonstrators were killed by the repressive Chinese regime. Tiananmen Square helped distort the debate on Hong Kong because it seemed to justify the concept of a Manichaean struggle between good and evil, between Western democracy and Chinese autocracy, which had formed so large a part of Margaret Thatcher's thinking. Yet, in the context of Hong Kong, the division was a false one. The traditions of British imperial rule were much more akin to Chinese, Confucian concepts of law and order, social hierarchy and deference than to any idea of liberal democracy. Some astute observers had always been aware of the central irony of British rule in Hong Kong, that the British civil servants were even more 'Chinese' in their philosophy of government than the Chinese themselves. Hong Kong was described in 1977 as the 'last remaining place where Chinese people are governed on principles traditional to their civilization'.[36] Tiananmen Square harmed China and obscured the fact that British rule in Hong Kong shared many of the values espoused by Confucius and other authoritarian thinkers in the Chinese tradition, particularly prizing the traditional Confucian ideals of order, hierarchy, stability and continuity.

Chris Patten, the last principal character in the history of British rule in Hong Kong, was, like Mrs Thatcher, an ideological warrior. Although, in British terms, he had been a centrist figure, he remains passionately committed to liberal political philosophy. In his book, *East and West*, his personal account of the last days of colonial rule in Hong Kong, he freely quotes De Tocqueville, among other heroes of the liberal tradition. This is admirable, but it is historically inaccurate to project those values on to the British Empire. Patten was made governor of Hong Kong in 1992 as a consolation prize. As the general election strategist for the Conservative Party, he had helped ensure that John Major, his friend and contemporary, was re-elected prime minister, but he himself had lost his seat as MP for Bath. On arrival in Hong Kong, Patten immediately made an impact. He was firm in his conviction that 'the people of Hong Kong should be consulted, and progress would reflect their wishes'.[37]

It was fitting that the last imperial governor of any significance should have been a graduate of Balliol, Oxford, which had produced so many imperial civil servants in the century since Benjamin Jowett, a late nineteenth-century master of the college, had promised to 'inoculate England with Balliol'. Yet Patten's philosophy and manner were very different from the calm and considered manner of the Imperial Civil Service. He had a glib turn of phrase, but knew very little about China or diplomacy. He rather perversely thought that his lack of knowledge of Chinese was a good thing, and boasted of having visited Hong Kong 'three times' before he became governor.[38] He described himself as a 'democratic politician, through and through', and this was true. If he had not been voted out by his constituents in Bath, he would never have become governor of Hong Kong, so he owed his career, even more than most politicians, to the decisions of democratic electorates.

It would be inaccurate to say that Patten was not conscious of Hong Kong's history. He was one of the first to call the colony's form of government 'benign authoritarianism'.[39] Immediately after leaving Oxford he had joined Conservative Central Office, where he showed his abilities as an organizer and originator of policy. He ended up as head of the research department there, before being elected to Parliament, at the age of thirty-five, in 1979. He went on to acquire extensive experience in domestic British politics, but spoke no foreign languages, had never lived outside Britain and had no professional training in law; nor had he undergone the usual Balliol grounding in the Classics which, although Greek and Roman civilization had long perished, did at least, its devotees argued, expose the student to a rigorous discipline in the languages and mentality of alien cultures. The cadet in Hong Kong was expected to spend two years in Canton and learn Cantonese. In other colonial jurisdictions, district commissioners were expected to learn some local languages and the rudiments of law. Thus, in many ways, Patten was among the least qualified graduates of Balliol College, Oxford ever to hold high office in the British Empire.

With his passionate belief in democracy and his dogmatic manner, Patten infuriated the Foreign Office mandarins and members of the Hong Kong business community. As Percy Cradock observed, China was a fact of life: 'if we wished to serve Hong Kong we had to remain able to talk to Peking'. His realism made fun of the 'chimerical alternative policy, which would somehow be tougher with Peking and at the same time more beneficial to Hong Kong'.[40] Cradock, a former Cambridge law don, who became a diplomat in his early thirties, was of the old school. He believed that the general approach of Foreign Office officials from 1979 to 1992 of trying to accommodate China on the question of Hong Kong could not be 'seriously faulted'. He recognized that it would have been better if 'democracy could have been long rooted in Hong Kong', but democracy had been actively opposed by Grantham, Black and MacLehose, who had collectively ruled Hong Kong for twenty-seven of the thirty-five years between 1945 and 1980.[41] Henry Keswick, the hereditary chairman of Jardine Matheson, Hong Kong's greatest merchant company, had made the same claim before a House of Commons Select Committee in May 1989, a couple of weeks before the Tiananmen Square massacre: 'the fact is, we have not introduced democracy in Hong Kong, so that Hong Kong [could] choose its own leaders and its own future'.[42]

Patten sought to consolidate democracy in Hong Kong, which he believed to be a legacy of British imperialism, but which was certainly unhistorical with regard to Hong Kong and much of the imperial past. In this attempt, he managed to antagonize the Chinese on the mainland, as well as the colony's business community who simply wanted to carry on making money in their 'merchant city'.[43] Having being appointed governor in July 1992, Patten promptly upset the Chinese, in October, by announcing proposals to make the legislative system in Hong Kong more democratic. This not only, in the Chinese view, went against 150 years of British tradition, it also violated the tacit assumption that China would have the ultimate say in Hong Kong's future, because Patten had failed to inform Beijing in advance of the democratic reforms he announced. Even as late as 1991, the first time elections were properly free and openly contested, forty-two of the sixty members of the Legislative Council were either appointed by the Governor or selected 'by "election committees" and from the "functional constituencies" which represented powerful professional bodies in the colony'.[44] Patten's attempts to impose greater democracy in Hong Kong, at this eleventh hour of British rule, baffled and surprised the Chinese. Patten saw himself as a champion of democratic rights, but the Foreign Office establishment, typified by Percy Cradock, viewed him as, at best, a nuisance and, at worst, a grave threat to Sino-British relations. Cradock was conscious that a Hong Kong without China was inconceivable; whatever happened, Hong Kong would have to be part of China. He believed therefore that 'it was one thing to be defiant when we in Britain would bear the consequences ourselves', but to be 'defiant at the expense of a third party, particularly one to whom we stood in a position of trust, as with Hong Kong, was something very different, an inexcusable self-indulgence'.[45]

Patten continued to be defiant. Like any democratic politician, he courted the popularity of the masses and used his skill as a publicist to good effect. He was portrayed in the media as the champion of the little man's rights against the big bully, China. Yet, as Cradock pointed out, Patten would be leaving Hong Kong in a royal yacht within five years, while the people of Hong Kong would have to live with the consequences of his schoolboy politics. In 1995, by redefining the 'functional constituencies', Patten more or less extended the vote in Hong Kong to a full democratic franchise. His friends argued that he had brought democracy to Hong Kong; his detractors thought it was a pointless and futile gesture. In terms of what actually happened, the detractors were proved right. The Legislative Council which was elected under Patten's governorship was dissolved upon the handover of Hong Kong to China and replaced by a Provisional Legislative Council until elections were held under the old pre-Patten rules in 1998. Patten left Hong Kong as a popular figure; he was energetic and charismatic and had, in his wife and three young attractive daughters, a photogenic family which would be the envy of any Western democratic politician, but, in terms of a legacy, it is difficult to see what he achieved.

On 15 June 2005, Donald Tsang handed in his nomination form for the post of chief executive of Hong Kong; the form bore the signatures of 674 members of the 800-strong Election Committee. Hong Kong after June 1997 was designated a Special Administrative Region, under the 'one country, two systems' concept enshrined in the Joint Declaration of 1984. Tsang's almost unanimous election revealed the emptiness of the 'one country, two systems' slogan. As Hong Kong resumed its status as a benevolent dictatorship, and as China moved towards capitalism with increasing alacrity, it was difficult to see how different the systems actually were. More relevantly to the history of the British Empire, it was difficult to see how different Donald Tsang himself was from the British governors who had preceded him as autocrats of Hong Kong. Tsang was Chinese, whereas the British were all white European men, but, in his manners and style, he was virtually indistinguishable from them. A devout and disciplined Roman Catholic, he had joined the Hong Kong Civil Service in 1967 and had served under British rule for thirty years, during which time he became the first ethnic Chinese to serve as financial secretary of the colony. His outlook was similar to that of John Cowperthwaite, whom he praised as the architect of the 'colony's prosperity as an international business centre'. Tsang always wore bow ties, and sent his two sons to English boarding schools.[46] He was pleased to receive a knighthood in recognition of his services to the British Crown, and he was not embarrassed to use Government House as his residence despite its Southern plantation style. Hong Kong in the first decade of the twenty-first century had simply continued its life as a colony, with Beijing as its master in the place of London. The 'new cadres', one observer noted, 'coming down from [China's capital] are reminiscent of the early British administrators in the 1800s, with their own language, their own clubs, and their own condescending attitudes towards their new subjects'.[47]

Hong Kong's history goes to the heart of the nature of the British Empire. Its reversion to China under a regime of 'benign authoritarianism', the term Chris Patten used to describe British rule, shows a remarkable continuity. Hierarchy, deference, government by elite administrators, united by education in the same institutions, in largely the same subjects, were all features of British imperial rule which were also characteristic of officials in imperial China. The story of Hong Kong also confirms the enormous power wielded by colonial governors. If Sir Mark Young had been succeeded by administrators who shared his vision, the history of Hong Kong might well have been very different. Lastly, Hong Kong showed, in many ways, how changes in Britain were not reflected by changes in the wider empire. Patten was a child of the liberal 1960s and blindly believed a version of his country's history that presented the British Empire as an enlightened liberal force, spreading democracy and freedom to the furthest shores of the earth. Margaret Thatcher had grown up through the Second World War, listening to, and believing, Churchill's late Victorian rhetoric that invoked Shakespeare's 'sceptred isle' imagery; she genuinely shared the Whiggish notion that British history, with its

Magna Carta and Glorious Revolution, was the story of the development of 'freedom' and liberal democratic ideas of government. So far as this idea was true for Britain, it did not apply to any real extent to the administration of the British Empire, which was always a wholly different political organization from Britain itself. The British Empire had nothing to do with liberal democracy, and, particularly in Hong Kong, was administered along lines much closer to the ideals of Confucius than to the vivid, impassioned rhetoric of Sir Winston Churchill, or even Shakespeare.

Conclusion

When Benjamin Disraeli, by then Earl of Beaconsfield, wound up the debate on the Congress of Berlin in the House of Lords on 18 July 1878, he made his final appeal to 'the consciousness that in the Eastern nations there is confidence in this country, and that, while they know we can enforce our policy, at the same time they know that our Empire is an Empire of liberty, of truth, and of justice'.[1]

It is revealing that Disraeli said nothing about democracy or liberal economics. Subsequent generations of politicians, historians and campaigners have made the British Empire in their own image, promoting it as a vehicle for whatever cause they happened to espouse. One example of different people appropriating the empire for their own purposes occurs in the field of economic theory. For old-fashioned economic liberals like Winston Churchill, the British Empire was an empire of free trade; for Joseph Chamberlain, on the other hand, the empire was perfect for protectionism, known as 'imperial preference', in that goods from the British colonies were 'preferred', more lightly taxed, in comparison with goods from Britain's industrial competitors, such as Germany and the United States. The empire has been invoked to support a multitude of causes.

Perhaps the key to understanding the British Empire is the idea of natural hierarchy. Class and status were absolutely integral to the empire, and notions of class were important in forming alliances with local elites, the chiefs, the petty kings and maharajas who crowded the colonial empire. The dominance of ideas of class and status made it easy for the British to establish local chiefs as hereditary rulers. In Kashmir, a Hindu family were established as rulers over an overwhelmingly Muslim kingdom. The Dogras ruled Kashmir for a hundred years, and the effects of their rule are still felt today. In Iraq, a new monarchy was established in 1921 under the Hashemite family, who had no historic links to the country. Once again, notions of royalty and status prompted policy without regard to local opinion. The French in Syria were more pragmatic; they established not a monarchy but a series of states which would form the Republic of Syria in 1930. Monarchy was a particularly British instrument of policy. The British established a monarchy in Jordan and supported the monarchy in Egypt. The French by contrast, under the Third Republic, were less enthusiastic about that form of government, and they had actually deposed Faisal, Iraq's future king, as King of Syria in 1920. It was the British who compensated Faisal by making him King of Iraq, and yet the events of the summer of 1958, only thirty-seven years after Faisal I's coronation, revealed the imprudence of the British policy. The unpopular monarchy was overthrown in Iraq and led to the establishment of governments in that country which were successively nationalist regimes that often ranged themselves against Western interests.

The so-called natural leaders, the maharajas, the sultans and nawabs, even the local chiefs, were flattered and cultivated. Individual rulers were set up in the Middle East, in India and in Africa. The irony of this generally pro-monarchical policy was that it was not consistent. A centuries-old monarchy in Burma was torn down by an abrupt change of policy, while monarchies were set up in Kashmir and Iraq which had no real tradition of independent monarchy. Behind monarchy lay ideas of class, which made aristocracies and natural leaders a favourite theme of Colonial Office civil servants, governors and chief secretaries. Natural leaders were explicitly an integral part of Lord Lugard's policy of indirect rule, a policy which prevailed in large parts of the Indian subcontinent, where a third of the Indian Empire was formed by the princely states.

Of course, in this context, any notion of democracy was far from anyone's mind. The British Empire was hierarchical and highly structured in its social organization. Mere snobbery formed an important part of this organization, as many of the tribal leaders and local potentates, like Yoruba chiefs in 1930s Nigeria, vied for audiences with the King in London, or lobbied extensively, like Sir Robert Ho Tung in Hong Kong, for differing ranks of knighthood. To the likes of Sir Robert Ho Tung there was a world of difference between being a mere knight bachelor and being a KBE or the even more exalted KCMG.

Despite hierarchy and class being central to the British Empire, we cannot be blind to the fact that the British Empire did bring justice and order to often anarchic parts of the world. To say that the empire was undemocratic is not to say that its effects were wholly negative. It is common for people involved in history and politics to see institutions, with the best intentions, as wholly good or wholly bad. Such institutions as slavery, or ideas such as fascism, can be put into these simple categories with some justification. Other institutions have a more mixed legacy; they are neither wholly good nor wholly bad, and these must be understood within their own terms and in their own context. I place the British Empire in this category. By putting institutions in their own context, I am arguing against a rather Whiggish view of history in which the past is merely a prologue to the present, where one thing leads inevitably to another, in a steady ascent of progress. History is more interesting and complicated than that. The British Empire is not some prelude to a modern twenty-first-century Western world of democracy, multiculturalism and liberal economics. The British Empire was something different. Some of its aspects, its hierarchy, its open disavowal of the idea of human equality and its snobbery, would strike the metropolitan reader of twenty-first-century London or New York as unpleasant and alien.

Others, while recognizing the hierarchical nature of the British Empire, have said that conditions in the empire merely matched conditions in Britain itself. This is not strictly true. While Britain was a country famously obsessed by class, after 1918 there existed mass democracy, and certainly, by the 1930s, democracy existed in Britain on the same basis as it does today, except for the lowering of the voting age in 1967. If one were to look at the British prime ministers of the 1920s and 1930s, the discrepancy between heads of government in Britain and colonial governors in places like Sudan and Hong Kong becomes obvious. David Lloyd George, the son of a Baptist minister from Wales, could become prime minister in 1916. It is inconceivable that a man of his background, without a university education or a military career, could have become governor of Nigeria, for example. The same could be said of Ramsay MacDonald, the illegitimate son of a Scottish housemaid, who became the Labour Party's first prime minister in 1924. Without a public school education, and without a university degree, it is very unlikely that anyone like Ramsay MacDonald could have got anywhere in the colonial empire. The British Empire was undoubtedly more snobbish, more hierarchical and more deferential than the mother country. It is wrong to argue, as some have done, that British administrators were merely projecting the class distinctions of Britain's society on to the colonial empire. Britain was changing at a much faster rate than the empire, and recruits to the Imperial Civil Service towards the end of the empire, in the 1950s, were only too conscious of this.

In the colonies themselves, distinct rules of precedence applied which bore no relation to status in the mother country. If these distinctions were derived from Britain, they took on a totally independent life in the colonies which, by the early twentieth century, had a completely different scale of values and preoccupations. This realization forms part of Kitty Fane's frustration in Somerset Maugham's *The Painted Veil*, and it informs her observation that 'it is rather funny when you think of all the people who used to come to our house at home [in South Kensington] that here [in Hong Kong] we should be treated like dirt'.[2] Hong Kong, as Fane saw, had its own rules of hierarchy and precedence. It is important to remember that, at a time of increasing democracy and Labour governments in Britain, the colonial empire, especially in places like Hong Kong, remained much the same. Hong Kong would be governed in the same autocratic way for 150 years. In the Sudan, public schoolboys still dominated the administration in a way that often surprised civil servants in London.

The power exercised by district commissioners in places like the Sudan, where young men in their mid-twenties would rule a land the size of Wales, as judges, lawgivers and policemen rolled into one, was immense. The arrogance of provincial governors in Sudan was legendary. This aspect of empire shows the extent to which there was a predisposition to strong individuals, leaders who, by sheer force of character, could impose their will on circumstances. The late Victorian hero-worship of Lord Kitchener is a conspicuous example of this tendency.

This individualism was, I have noted, anarchic, in that there was very often no policy coherence or strategic direction behind the imperial government as experienced in individual colonies. Often strong-minded officials and governors would, by a metaphoric sweep of the hand, reverse the policy of decades, thereby creating more confusion and instability. Such reversals occurred in Burma, in Sudan and in Hong Kong. In Burma, the policy which the British government had pursued in India, since the Mutiny of 1857, was reversed by Lord Randolph Churchill, who was committed to the outright annexation of the country. This step was not only contrary to the policy followed since 1857, but had been opposed by the Earl of Mayo when he was viceroy of India in the early 1870s, and had been viewed suspiciously by the Marquess of Ripon, viceroy in the 1880s. Even as late as the 1940s, officials were not convinced that Lord Randolph had done the right thing when he abolished the Burmese monarchy. In Sudan, the 'Southern Policy' of Harold MacMichael was reversed in the late 1940s. That policy has been seen by the Sudanese in the north as the cause of many of the problems which their country has confronted in the half-century since independence, years which have been dominated by civil war. In Hong Kong, Sir Mark Young's sincere plans for greater democracy were reversed by his successor, Sir Alexander Grantham, and this suspended any progress towards democracy in Hong Kong for thirty years. As it happened, democracy, even by the late 1980s, had never been seriously practised in Hong Kong. This lack of any democratic progress in the colony, over the three decades immediately after the Second World War, made Chris Patten's aggressive stance in the 1990s bewildering not only to the Chinese government in Beijing, but to British diplomats in China and in Whitehall.

Individualism was a guiding principle of the British Empire. This is shown by the career of Herbert Horatio Kitchener. Withdrawn and aloof, repressed and driven, Kitchener was an idiosyncratic loner who became a hero of empire. His administrative talents were uneven, and he was clearly bored by the routine of day-to-day government, but his image, the drooping moustache and clear blue, wide-set eyes, was compelling, while his autocratic manner gave people assurance in uncertain times. The cry for Lord Kitchener to be given high office at the outbreak of the war in

1914 was deafening and prompted Asquith, the Prime Minister, to appoint him secretary for war, a decision which Asquith often regretted.

The British Empire allowed individuals, the civil servants and imperial administrators who worked within it, a wide degree of freedom; the man on the spot was often, quite literally, the master of all he surveyed. A Kitchener in the Sudan, or a Lugard in Nigeria, for example, could rule like a benign dictator with very little supervision from Whitehall. Even as late as the 1950s, when he was in office in Hong Kong, Sir Alexander Grantham described the power and authority of the governor in terms usually reserved for the Almighty.

In the Classical Greek sense, the British Empire was an aristocratic empire, and it openly celebrated 'rule by the best people'. There was a meritocratic element to imperial government; selection for the imperial service followed rigorous exams or interviews, designed to select those believed to be the best. Yet that selection was confined to a very narrow range of schools and universities; the products from a magic circle of public schools – the fifteen schools George Orwell remembered from his prep-school days – enjoyed the lion's share of the best imperial postings. This process produced a class of colonial administrators drawn overwhelmingly from the upper-middle, professional classes, and yet there was a broad range within this class, as Orwell himself knew. In the Sudan, the sons of peers might serve as district commissioners; in Hong Kong the sons of impoverished clergymen or schoolmasters could be cadets; the imperial class did have some wide variations within it, even though, compared to the rest of the country, the pool from which it was drawn outwardly seems shallow.

This was only natural, in the thinking of the time. Such people were born leaders. They were the 'best of our race' and represented the 'highest athletic and mental culture' of the British people, as Lord Cromer said of the Sudan Political Service. These administrators would rule over native populations like Plato's guardians – whom, given the Classical education many of the civil servants had received, they consciously imitated. In this sense of natural rulers, or rule of the best, whether those 'best' men came from the British Isles or from the colonies, an aristocratic principle ran right through the empire. Coupled with the idea of rule by the best there

is also the implication, in many of the letters written by colonial governors, that the empire was seen as something of a school of virtue, where
character, discipline and willpower would be trained to prevail. The colonies were regarded as providing a suitable arena for the display of talent for
the best of the imperial breed. Like any aristocratic oligarchy, imperial
administrators believed theirs to be a high calling, requiring self-discipline
and ability.

In its individualism, its elitism and its snobbery, in the audacity of its
self-belief, the British Empire was not the precursor of the world of the
early twenty-first century. Its values and the mental universe of its administrators, educated as many of them were in the languages and culture of
ancient Greece and Rome, could not be further removed from the largely
Americanized world we now inhabit. The British Empire, in its scale and
ethos, was completely unlike any system of government that the world has
known. It is highly unlikely that such an enterprise will be undertaken by
any nation, no matter how powerful, ever again. The phenomenon of
British imperial rule must be understood in its own terms.

Notes

Introduction

1 Cannadine, David, *Ornamentalism*, London, 2001, p. xx.
2 Ibid., p. 4.
3 Quoted in Judd, Gerrit Parmele, *Members of Parliament 1734–1832*, Chicago, 1972, p. 36.
4 Stone, Norman, introduction to Wells, H. G., *A Short History of the World*, London, 2006, p. xiii.
5 *Dictionary of National Biography* (*DNB*).
6 Orwell, George, *Essays*, London, first published 1984, new edn 2000, p. 425.
7 Cannadine, *Ornamentalism*, p. xix.
8 Ferguson, Niall, *Empire: How Britain Made the Modern World*, London, 2003, p. xxii.
9 Ferguson, Niall, *Colossus*, London, 2005, p. 24.

Chapter 1: The Spoils of War

1 Yergin, Daniel, *The Prize: The Epic Quest for Oil, Money, and Power*, New York, 1991, 2nd edn 1992, p. 183; Delaisi, Francis, *Oil: Its Influence on Politics*, trans. C. Leonard Leese, London, 1922, p. 86.
2 For Curzon, see Gilmour, David, *Curzon*, London, 1994; Nicolson, Harold, *Curzon: The Last Phase 1919–1925. A Study in Post-War Diplomacy*, London, 1934, p. 49.
3 TNA, CAB 21/119.
4 Ibid.
5 Stivers, William, *Supremacy and Oil: Iraq, Turkey and the Anglo-American World Order 1918–1930*, London, 1982, p. 47.
6 Lawrence, T. E., letter to *The Times*, 22 July 1920.
7 Leslie, Shane, *Mark Sykes: His Life and Letters*, London, 1923, pp. 13, 17.
8 Ibid., pp. 163, 94.
9 Ibid., p. 62.
10 Ibid., pp. 147, 151.
11 Fromkin, David, *A Peace to End All Peace: The Fall of the Ottoman Empire and the Creation of the Modern Middle East*, New York, 1989, p. 375; Hewins, Ralph, *Mr Five Per Cent: The Biography of Calouste Gulbenkian*, London, 1957, p. 128.

12 Monroe, Elizabeth, *Britain's Moment in the Middle East 1914–1956*, London, 1963, p. 60; Kent, Marian, *Oil and Empire: British Policy and Mesopotamian Oil 1900–1920*, London, 1976, p. 146.

13 Marlowe, J., *Late Victorian: The Life of Sir Arnold Talbot Wilson*, London, 1967, pp. 35, 36.

14 TNA, CAB 21/119.

15 TNA, CAB 21/61.

16 Ireland, Philip Willard, *Iraq: A Study in Political Development*, New York, 1937, p. 451.

17 Quoted in Mejcher, Helmut, *Imperial Quest for Oil: Iraq 1910–1928*, London, 1976, p. 49.

18 TNA, CAB 24/4.

19 House of Lords debate 20 February 1919, quoted in Wilson, A. T., *Mesopotamia 1917–1920: A Clash of Loyalties. A Personal and Historical Record*, London, 1931, p. 163.

20 Bell, Gertrude, *Letters of Gertrude Bell*, selected and edited by Gladys Bell, London, 1987, pp. 468, 400.

21 Philby, H. St J., *Arabian Days*, London, 1948, p. 131.

22 MECA, Bowman papers.

23 Storrs, Sir Ronald, *Great Britain in the Near and Middle East*, Cust Foundation Lecture, University College, Nottingham, 1932.

24 MECA, Bell papers, box 1, letter to Lord Allenby, 13 August 1920.

25 Philby, *Arabian Days*, pp. 173–4.

26 Bell, *Letters*, p. 460, letter to Sir Hugh Bell, 1 November 1920.

27 MECA, Bowman papers, diary entry, Basra, 24 August 1918.

28 Abdullah, Thabit A. J., *Dictatorship, Imperialism and Chaos*, London, 2006, p. 13.

29 Bell, *Letters*, p. 393.

30 Luizard, Pierre-Jean, *La Formation de l'Irak contemporain*, Paris, 1991, pp. 373, 380 (translations are my own).

31 Quoted in Stivers, *Supremacy and Oil*, p. 35.

32 Haldane, Sir Aylmer, *The Insurrection in Mesopotamia 1920*, Edinburgh, 1922, pp. 30, 314.

33 MECA, Bowman papers.

34 Simon, Reeva Spector, and Tejirian, Eleanor H. (eds), *The Creation of Iraq 1914–1921*, New York, 2004, p. 29.

35 Wilson, *Mesopotamia*, p. 253.

36 Luizard, *La Formation de l'Irak*, pp. 374, 422.

37 Bell, *Letters*, p. 404.

38 Quoted in Ireland, *Iraq*, p. 243.

39 Luizard, *La Formation de l'Irak*, p. 402.

40 Marr, Phebe, *The Modern History of Iraq*, 2nd edn, Boulder, Colorado, 2004, p. 23.

41 Simon, Reeva Spector, *Iraq between the Two World Wars: The Militarist Origins of Tyranny*, New York, 1986, rev. edn 2004, p. 46.

42 *The Times*, 7 August 1920, quoted in Bennett, G. H., *British Foreign Policy during the Curzon Period 1919–1924*, London, 1995, pp. 106, 107–9.

43 MECA, Bell papers, letter dated 23 March 1921.

44 For Churchill remark, see Simon, *Iraq between the Two World Wars*, p. 1; Kedourie, Elie, *England and the Middle East: The Destruction of the Ottoman Empire*, London, 1987, p. 88.

45 Lawrence, T. E., *The Letters of T. E. Lawrence*, selected and edited by Malcolm Brown, London, 1988, p. 384, letter to Sir Gilbert Clayton, 9 October 1928.

46 Ibid., pp. 349–50, letter to Mrs Charlotte Shaw, 18 October 1927.

47 Bell, *Letters*, p. 468.

48 Ibid., p. 500.

49 Main, Ernest, *Iraq from Mandate to Independence*, London, 1935, p. 44.

50 Howell, Georgina, *Daughter of the Desert: The Remarkable Life of Gertrude Bell*, London, 2006, pp. 447–8.

51 Bell, *Letters*, p. 536, letter to Sir Hugh Bell, 30 January 1923.

52 Lawrence, *Letters*, p. 353, letter to Sir Hugh Bell, 4 November 1927.

Chapter 2: Rivals

1 Mejcher, Helmut, *Imperial Quest for Oil: Iraq 1910–1928*, London, 1976, Preface.

2 Ibid., p. 136.

3 Kent, Marian, *Moghuls and Mandarins: Oil, Imperialism and the Middle East in British Foreign Policy 1900–1940*, London, 1993, p. 1.

4 Earle, Edward Meade, 'The Turkish Petroleum Company: A Study in Oleaginous Diplomacy', *Political Science Quarterly*, vol. 39, no. 2, June 1924, pp. 265–79, at pp. 272–3.

5 McMurray, Jonathan S., *Distant Ties: Germany, the Ottoman Empire and the Construction of the Baghdad Railway*, London, 2001, p. 134, n. 5.

6 McBeth, B. S., *British Oil Policy 1919–1939*, London, 1985, p. 7.

7 Nicolson, Harold, *Curzon: The Last Phase 1919–1925. A Study in Post-War Diplomacy*, London, 1934, p. 330.

8 Hewins, Ralph, *Mr Five Per Cent: The Biography of Calouste Gulbenkian*, London, 1957, pp. 129, 77.

9 Gulbenkian, Nubar, *Pantaraxia*, London, 1965, p. 38.

10 Ibid., p. 38.

11 Ibid., p. 229.

12 Bennett, G. H., *British Foreign Policy during the Curzon Period 1919–1924*, London, 1995, p. 115.

13 Delaisi, Francis, *Oil: Its influence on Politics*, trans. C. Leonard Leese, London, 1922, pp. 15–17.

14 McBeth, *British Oil Policy*, p. 34.

15 Stivers, William, *Supremacy and Oil: Iraq, Turkey and the Anglo-American World Order 1918–1930*, London, 1982, p. 59.

16 Monroe, Elizabeth, *Britain's Moment in the Middle East 1914–1956*, London, 1963, p. 66.

17 Meade, 'The Turkish Petroleum Company', p. 274.

18 Delaisi, *Oil*, pp. 42–3.

19 Quoted in Mejcher, *Imperial Quest*, p. 106.

20 *New York Times*, 18 November 1920, quoted in Fischer, Louis, *Oil Imperialism: The International Struggle for Petroleum*, London, 1926, p. 219.

21 Ibid., p. 220.

22 Ibid., pp. 220–1.

23 McBeth, *British Oil Policy*, p. 59.

24 Quoted in Shwadran, B., *The Middle East, Oil and the Great Powers*, New York, 1955, 3rd edn, 1973, p. 219.

25 TNA, CAB 24/125.

26 TNA, CAB 24/134, quoted in Bennett, *British Foreign Policy*, p. 116.

27 Ibid., p. 136; TNA, CO 730/29/60539.

28 TNA, CAB 21/119, letter of Edwin Montagu to Viscount Harcourt, 23 December 1918.

29 Stivers, *Supremacy and Oil*, pp. 30, 110; TNA, CAB 23/43.

30 TNA, ADM 116/2692, letters to Shuckburgh, 19 November, 4 December and 8 December 1928.

31 *DNB.*

32 MacMillan, Margaret, *Paris 1919*, New York, 2001, p. 373; BL, MSS Eur F 112/274.

33 Quoted in Earle, 'The Turkish Petroleum Company', p. 273.

34 TNA, ADM 116/2652, pp. 16–66.

35 Ibid., pp. 77, 84–5.

36 Fischer, *Oil Imperialism*, p. 244.

37 TNA, ADM 116/2692, p. 60.

38 Ibid., pp. 290–1, letter from M. Berthelot, 31 May 1929.

39 TNA, CAB 27/436.

40 Ibid., p. 45, Iraq Oil Committee, 4 February 1931.

41 TNA, ADM 116/2692, p. 407.

42 TNA, CAB 27/436, p. 137.

Chapter 3: Monarchy and Revolution

1 *Iraq Times*, 16 November 1933, quoted in MECA, Sinderson papers.

2 Khadduri, Majid, *Independent Iraq 1932–1958: A Study in Iraqi Politics*, London, 1960, pp. 40–3.

3 MacMillan, Margaret, *Paris 1919*, New York, 2001, pp. 387, 389.

4 Lawrence, T. E., *The Letters of T. E. Lawrence*, selected and edited by Malcolm Brown, London, 1988, p. 350, letter dated 18 October 1927.

5 Morris, James, *The Hashemite Kings*, London, 1959, p. 83.

6 Bell, Gertrude, *Letters of Gertrude Bell*, selected and edited by Gladys Bell, London, 1987, p. 537, letter to Sir Hugh Bell, 1 March 1923; ibid., p. 538, letter dated 10 April 1923.

7 Ibid., p. 576, letter to Florence Bell, her stepmother, 14 December 1924.

8 Sluglett, Peter, *Britain in Iraq 1914–1932*, London, 1976, pp. 221–2.

9 Samara, Ihsan Hani, 'The Economic Growth of Iraq: The Role of Oil Revenues, Government Policies and Strategies since 1950', unpublished PhD thesis, University College of Swansea, University of Wales, 1980, pp. 83–7, 90.

10 Longrigg, Stephen Hemsley, *Iraq 1900 to 1950: A Political, Social and Economic History*, London, 1953, p. 278.

11 Main, Ernest, *Iraq from Mandate to Independence*, London, 1935, pp. 20–1.

12 Ibid., p. 33.

13 Batatu, Hanna, *The Old Social Classes and the Revolutionary Movements of Iraq*, Princeton, 1978, p. 1115.

14 *Time*, 17 April 1939; Morris, *The Hashemite Kings*, p. 145; Simon, Reeva Spector, *Iraq between the Two World Wars: The Militarist Origins of Tyranny*, New York, 1986, rev. edn 2004, p. 38; *Iraq Times*, 4 February 1937, in MECA, Sinderson papers.

15 Mansfield, Peter, *Kuwait: Vanguard of the Gulf*, London, 1990, p. 22.

16 *Iraq Times*, 7 April 1939, in MECA, Sinderson papers.

17 Gulbenkian, Nubar, *Pantaraxia*, London, 1965, p. 167.

18 Caractacus, *Revolution in Iraq: An Essay in Comparative Public Opinion*, London, 1959, p. 78.

19 *Iraq Times*, 20 February 1936, in MECA, Sinderson papers; *Encyclopaedia Britannia*, 1911 edn.

20 Marr, Phebe, *The Modern History of Iraq*, 2nd edn, Boulder, Colorado, 2004, p. 51.

21 Ibid.; Morris, *The Hashemite Kings*, p. 158.

22 Khadduri, *Independent Iraq*, pp. 184–5.

23 Marr, *The Modern History of Iraq*, pp. 53–5; Khadduri, *Independent Iraq*, p. 175.

24 Khadduri, *Independent Iraq*, p. 224.

25 TNA, CAB 80/28.

26 *Time*, 17 June 1957.

27 Birdwood, Lord, *Nuri As-Said: A Study in Arab Leadership*, London, 1959, p. 2.

28 Gallman, Waldemar J., *Iraq under General Nuri: My Recollections of Nuri al-Said, 1954–1958*, Baltimore, 1964, pp. 90, 172.

29 MECA, Perowne papers.

30 Morris, *The Hashemite Kings*, pp. 169, 189–90.

31 Samara, 'The Economic Growth of Iraq', p. 69.

32 For the annual reports of the IPC, see BP Archive, University of Warwick.

33 Samara, 'The Economic Growth of Iraq', p. 104.

34 Ibid., p. 85.

35 Batatu, *The Old Social Classes*, p. 34.

36 Salter, Lord, *The Development of Iraq: A Plan of Action*, London, 1955, pp. 115, 146.

37 Gallman, *Iraq under General Nuri*, pp. 17, 53.

38 *Iraq Times*, 2 May 1953; *Liwa al-Jihad*, 5 May 1955, in MECA, Sinderson papers.

39 Gallman, *Iraq under General Nuri*, p. 203.

40 Fernea, Robert A., and Louis, William Roger (eds), *The Iraq Revolution of 1958: The Old Social Classes Revisited*, London, 1991, p. viii.

41 Marr, *The Modern History of Iraq*, p. 78; Gallman, *Iraq under General Nuri*, p. 203; Morris, *The Hashemite Kings*, p. 198.

42 Caractacus, *Revolution in Iraq*, pp. 126–7; Birdwood, *Nuri As-Said*, p. 266; Batatu, *The Old Social Classes*, p. 801.

43 Forbes, Colin D., *Innocent in a Revolution*, Lewes, 1999, p. 76.

44 Astarjian, Henry, *The Struggle for Kirkuk: The Rise of Hussein, Oil and the Death of Tolerance in Iraq*, London, 2007, p. 53.

45 Morris, *The Hashemite Kings*, p. 199.

46 Gallman, *Iraq under General Nuri*, p. 203.

Chapter 4: Saddam Hussein and Beyond

1 MECA, Cornwallis papers.

2 James, Morris, *The Hashemite Kings*, London, 1959, pp. 186, 17.

3 Ferneu, Robert A., and Louis, William Roger (eds), *The Iraqi Revolution of 1958: The Old Social Classes Revisited*, New York, p. vi (Foreword by Albert Hourani).

4 Shwadran, B., *The Middle East, Oil and the Great Powers*, New York, 1955, 3rd edn, 1973, pp. 242–4.

5 Ibid., p. 267.

6 Astarjian, Henry, *The Struggle for Kirkuk: The Rise of Hussein, Oil and the Death of Tolerance in Iraq*, London, 2007, p. 157.

7 Marr, Phebe, *The Modern History of Iraq*, 2nd edn, Boulder, Colorado, 2004, p. 111.

8 Ibid., p. 102.

9 Astarjian, *The Struggle for Kirkuk*, p. 158.

10 TNA, PREM 13/2171, letter from Tom Bridges to J. O. Wright, Foreign Office, 2 February 1965.

11 TNA, FCO 54/35.

12 Ibid., letter from H. St J. B. Armitage at British Embassy in Beirut to Foreign and Commonwealth Office, 21 December 1967.

13 *The Times*, 28 December 1967, 'Russia moves into middle east oil', quoted in TNA, FCO 54/35.

14 TNA, FCO 67/179, telegram from Baghdad to Foreign and Commonwealth Office, 30 October 1968.

15 Ibid., telegram from Baghdad to Foreign and Commonwealth Office, 17 October 1968.

16 Marr, *The Modern History of Iraq*, p. 139.

17 TNA, FCO 67/179, quoted in telegram from Baghdad to Foreign and Commonwealth Office, 21 November 1968.

18 Ibid., telegram from Baghdad to Foreign and Commonwealth Office, 22 October 1968.

19 TNA, FCO 67/180, letter from J. T. Fearnley to N. C. Hibbs, Foreign and Commonwealth Office, 17 January 1969.

20 Interview with Dr Rifa'i, in *Middle East Economic Survey*, vol. XII, no. 14, 31 January 1969, p. 2.

21 Brown, Michael, E., 'The Nationalization of the Iraq Petroleum Company', *International Journal of Middle East Studies*, 1979, vol. 10, pp. 107–24, at pp. 114, 123.

22 Coughlin, Con, *Saddam: The Secret Life*, London, 2002, p. 106.

23 Chabrun, Laurent, and Heriot, Franck, *Les Corrompus de Saddam Hussein*, Paris, 2006, p. 20.

24 Quoted in Saint-Prot, Charles, *Saddam Hussein: un gaullisme arabe?*, Paris, 1987, p. 109.
25 Matar, Fuad, *Saddam Hussein: The Man, the Cause and the Future*, London, 1981, p. 31.
26 Ibid., pp. 168–9.
27 Saddam Hussein, *On Oil Nationalisation in Iraq*, Baghdad, 1973, pp. 8, 10.
28 TNA, FCO 55/1116, letter from Tom Boardman to Sir Alec Douglas-Home, [n.d.] August 1973.
29 Ibid., letter from Robin Butler, 10 August 1973.
30 Ibid., memo by Anthony Parsons, 26 July 1973.
31 Ibid., 2nd draft memorandum, 17 July 1973.
32 Ibid., letter from Robin Butler, Cabinet Office, to Charles Cruickshank, 20 August 1973; letter from C. J. A. Chivers, Treasury, to Richard Dales, Energy Department, 23 August 1973.
33 Ibid., 'Proposal for an Oil and Agricultural Development Project for Iraq', 1st draft, 26 September 1973.
34 Ibid., letter from P. R. H. Wright, 30 October 1973.
35 Ibid., letter from S. L. Egerton to Anthony Parsons, 3 December 1973.
36 Ibid., letter from P. R. H. Wright to S. L. Egerton and A. Parsons, 21 November 1973.
37 Saint-Prot, *Saddam Hussein*, pp. 215, 222.
38 Matar, *Saddam Hussein*, p. 181.
39 Ibid., p. 165.
40 Alnasrawi, Abbas, *The Economy of Iraq: Oil, Wars, Destruction of Development and Prospects 1950–2010*, London, 1994, p. 70.
41 Marr, *The Modern History of Iraq*, p. 162.
42 Chabrun and Heriot, *Les Corrumpus de Saddam Hussein*, p. 20.
43 Tripp, Charles, *A History of Iraq*, Cambridge, 2000, 3rd edn, 2007, p. 206.
44 Fuerlig, Henner, *Saddam Hussein – der neue Saladdin? Irak und der Golf Krieg*, Berlin, 1991, p. 101.
45 Wakin, Edward, *Contemporary Political Leaders of the Middle East*, New York, 1996, p. 20.
46 Matar, *Saddam Hussein*, p. 7.
47 Alnasrawi, *The Economy of Iraq*, p. 105; Galbraith, Peter, *The End of Iraq: How American Incompetence Created a War without End*, New York, 2006, p. 37.
48 Marr, *The Modern History of Iraq*, p. 221; Tripp, *A History of Iraq*, p. 242.
49 Verma, Sonia, 'Iraq could have largest oil reserves in the world', *The Times*, 20 May 2008.
50 *Gulf Oil and Gas*, 'Iraq issues tenders to drill 40 oil wells', 16 February 2009.
51 *International Herald Tribune*, 'Iraq reopens its oil reserves to foreign companies, but few rush in', 3 February 2009.

Chapter 5: Land for Sale

1 BL, MSS Eur F 85/29A, H. M. Lawrence papers, Punjab Intelligence, Lahore, 1 March 1846.
2 Caroe, Sir Olaf, *The Pathans 550 B.C.–A.D. 1957*, Oxford, 1959, p. 257.

3 Allen, Charles, *The Soldier Sahibs*, London, 2000, p. 60.

4 Hardinge, Viscount, *Life of Hardinge*, Rulers of India Series, Oxford, 1891, p. 71.

5 BL, MSS Eur F 85/48, Hardinge papers, letter from Hardinge to Lawrence, 27 April 1846.

6 Younghusband, Francis, *Kashmir*, London, 1924, p. 147.

7 Napier, Sir William, *The Life and Opinions of General Sir Charles James Napier*, 4 vols, London, 1857, vol. IV, p. 128, letter dated 28 October 1846.

8 Ibid., vol. III, p. 419, letter from Charles Napier to his brother William Napier, 8 November 1846; ibid., p. 475, letter from Charles Napier to his brother, 15 November 1846.

9 Ibid., pp. 410, 455.

10 BL, MSS Eur F 213/23, Dalhousie papers, letter from Queen Victoria, 30 July 1849.

11 Singh, Khushwant, *The Sikhs*, London, 1953, p. 79.

12 BL, MSS Eur F 213/23, letter from Dalhousie to Sir Charles Napier, [n.d.] November 1849; letter from Dalhousie to Queen Victoria, 20 January 1851.

13 Napier, *Life of Charles Napier*, vol. IV, p. 27.

14 Hardinge, *Hardinge*, p. 138.

15 Allen, *Soldier Sahibs*, pp. 10–12, 47.

16 Napier, *Life of Charles Napier*, vol. III, p. 459, in a letter dated 6 November 1846.

17 BL, MSS Eur F 213/25, letter from Colonel Henry Steinbach to Lord Dalhousie, 4 August 1851.

18 Morgan, Gerald, *Anglo-Russian Rivalry in Central Asia 1810–1895*, London, 1981, p. 107.

19 *DNB*.

20 Hopkirk, Peter, *The Great Game: On Secret Service in High Asia*, London, 1990, p. 1.

21 BL, MSS Eur B 380/2, Mayo papers, letters to the Duke of Argyll, letter from Mayo to Argyll, 1 July 1869.

22 Warikoo, K., *Central Asia and Kashmir: A Study in the Context of Anglo-Russian Rivalry*, New Delhi, 1989, pp. 206–7.

23 BL, MSS Eur B 380/4, Mayo papers, letter to Duke of Argyll, 10 May 1870.

24 *DNB*.

25 BL, MSS Eur B 380/4, letters dated 31 January 1870, 8 February 1870, 10 May 1870.

26 Khan, Mohammad Ishaq, *History of Srinagar 1846–1947: A Study in Socio-Cultural Change*, Srinagar, 1978, p. 79.

27 Ibid., p. 80.

28 Ibid., p. 24.

29 Warikoo, *Central Asia and Kashmir*, p. 147.

30 Lamb, Alastair, *Kashmir: A Disputed Legacy 1846–1990*, Hertingfordbury, 1991, p. 29.

31 Cannadine, David, *Ornamentalism*, London, 2001, pp. 43–5.

32 Lethbridge, Sir Roper, *The Golden Book of India: A Genealogical and Biographical Dictionary of the Ruling Princes, Chiefs, Nobles, and Other Personages, Titled or Decorated of the Indian Empire*, London, 1893, pp. xi, xix–xxiii.

33 Copland, Ian, *The Princes of India in the Endgame of Empire 1917–1947*, Cambridge, 1997, pp. 8, 21.

34 Ibid., p. 45; Ramusack, Barbara N., *The Indian Princes and their States*, Cambridge, 2004, p. 90.

35 Wavell, Lord, *The Viceroy's Journal*, ed. Penderel Moon, London, 1973, p. 463.

36 Fisher, Michael H., 'Indirect Rule in the British Empire: The Foundations of the Residency System in India (1764–1858)', *Modern Asian Studies*, vol. 18, no. 3, 1984, pp. 393–428, at p. 403.

37 Teng, M. K., Bhatt, R. K. K., and Bhatt, S. K., *Kashmir Constitutional History and Documents*, New Delhi, 1977, p. 248, Report on the affairs of the State of Jammu and Kashmir by the Resident in Kashmir, 5 March 1888.

38 French, Patrick, *Younghusband: The Last Great Imperial Adventurer*, London, 1994, p. 264.

39 Schofield, Victoria, *Kashmir in the Crossfire*, London, 1996, p. 81; Ramusack, Barbara N., *The Princes of India in the Twilight of Empire: Dissolution of a Patron–Client System 1914–1919*, Columbus, Ohio, 1978, p. 138; Copland, Ian, *State, Community and Neighbourhood in Princely North India c. 1900–1950*, Basingstoke, 2005, p. 53.

40 BL, MSS Eur F 111/256, Curzon papers.

41 See French, *Younghusband*, title-page.

42 Ibid., p. 402.

43 BL, MSS Eur F 197/111, Younghusband papers.

44 Ibid., speech at state banquet, 26 June 1908.

45 Ibid., speech at state banquet, 8 December 1909; letters of Younghusband to his wife, [n.d.] 1906 and 4 November 1907.

46 BL, IOR R/1/1/633, 'Enhancement of the administrative powers of his highness the Maharaja of Jammu and Kashmir subject to certain conditions', memo written by R. E. Holland, 19 September 1918.

47 BL, MSS Eur Photo Eur 33, letter in German with Indian and English translation from Count Theobald von Bethmann-Hollweg (1856–1921), German Chancellor 1909–17, to the Maharaja of Jammu and Kashmir.

48 BL, IOR R/1/1/633, Memorandum from Resident Lieutenant Colonel A. D'A. G. Bannerman, 9 October 1918; letter from Bannerman to Holland.

49 Schofield, *Kashmir in the Crossfire*, p. 57.

Chapter 6: The World of Sir Hari Singh

1 French, Patrick, *Younghusband: The Last Great Imperial Adventurer*, London, 1994, pp. 270, 269.

2 Quoted from the Mayo College website, www.mayocollege.com.

3 BL, IOR R/1/1/917, letter from J. B. Wood to Lieutenant Colonel Bannerman, 17 November 1917; letter from Bannerman to Wood, 19 November 1917.

4 Ibid., letter from Bannerman to Wood, 26 December 1917.

5 Ibid., collection of papers entitled 'Kashmir affairs, 1917'.

6 BL, MSS Eur F 118/83, Lord Reading papers, letter from Hari Singh to Sir Pratap Singh, 1 October 1921.

7 *Time*, 5 May 1961, 'The Shivering Maharaja'.

8   BL, IOR R/1/1/1788, letter from the Earl of Birkenhead, Secretary of State for India, to the Viceroy, 19 January 1928.

9   Ibid., E. B. Howell, 'Note on Colonel Ward's Case'.

10 Ibid., letter from Viscount Peel, Secretary of State for India, to the Viceroy, 8 May 1928.

11 *New York Times*, 9 April 1922, 'Montagu's successor'.

12 BL, IOR R/1/1/1788, letter of Viscount Peel, Secretary of State for India, to the Viceroy, 29 November 1928.

13 Ibid., letter from Maharaja Hari Singh to Viscount Peel, 4 March 1929.

14 Ibid., letter from the Resident to Charles Watson, 9 February 1928.

15 BL, IOR R/1/1/2123, letters from the Resident to Charles Watson, 18 May, 11 June and 28 November 1931.

16 BL, IOR R/1/4/166, memorandum by B. J. Glancy, 23 January 1940; memorandum dated 5 February 1940.

17 BL, IOR R/1/1/293, memorandum by B. J. Glancy, 28 January 1939.

18 Singh, Karan, *Autobiography*, Bombay, 1989, pp. 15–16.

19 Wakhlu, Somnath, *Hari Singh: The Maharaja, the Man, the Times*, New Delhi, 2004, p. 54.

20 Singh, *Autobiography*, p. 31.

21 Khan, Mohammad Ishaq, *History of Srinagar 1846–1947: A Study in Socio-Cultural Change*, Srinagar, 1978, pp. 204, 159.

22 Ibid., p. 174.

23 Birdwood, Lord, *Two Nations and Kashmir*, London, 1956, p. 21.

24 Neve, Ernest F., *Beyond the Pir Panjal: Life and Missionary Enterprise in Kashmir*, London, 1914, p. 28.

25 Younghusband, Francis, *Kashmir*, London, 1924, pp. 113, 107.

26 BL, MSS Eur C 419, Burton papers, Doris Hargreaves Burton, 'Two months leave in Kashmir written in 1910–1914'.

27 BL, MSS Eur D 1003/1, Morton papers.

28 Lamb, Alastair, *Kashmir: A Disputed Legacy 1846–1990*, Hertingfordbury, 1991, p. 84.

29 Neve, *Beyond the Pir Panjal*, p. 47.

30 Lamb, *Kashmir*, p. 87.

31 Singh, Bawa Satinder, *The Jammu Fox: A Biography of Maharaja Gulab Singh of Kashmir 1792–1857*, Carbondale and Edwardsville, 1974, p. 176.

32 BL, MSS Eur F 164/25A, Mudie papers, 'Kashmir before Accession'.

33 Singh, *Autobiography*, p. 3.

34 Lamb, *Kashmir*, p. 89.

35 Copland, Ian, 'Islam and Political Mobilization in Kashmir 1931–1934', *Pacific Affairs*, vol. 54, no. 2, summer 1981, pp. 228–59, at p. 243. This article is perhaps the most thorough account of the 1931 disturbances.

36 BL, IOR R/1/1/2261 (2) Govt. of India Foreign and Political Department paper, file no. 204, 1932; letter from Kashyap Bandhu, 25 January 1932.

37 Ibid., 'Draft Address to be presented to his excellency the Viceroy by the members of the all-India Kashmir Committee', 25 February 1932.

38 Ibid., 'Reply to Muslim delegation', [n.d.] April 1932.

39 Birdwood, *Two Nations and Kashmir*, pp. 34–5.

40 Copland, 'Islam and Political Mobilization', p. 246.

41 BL, MSS Eur D 862, Powell papers, 'Jammu & Kashmir State, 1947'.

42 Teng, M. K., Bhatt, R. K. K., and Bhatt, S. K., *Kashmir Constitutional History and Documents*, New Delhi, 1977, 'Presidential Address of Dr Sir Muhammad Iqbal delivered at the Allahabad Session of the All India Muslim League', [n.d.] December 1930, p. 336.

43 BL, MSS Eur D 704, Ahmed Shah papers, 'Political Note on the Kashmir Problem', given to Morgan Price MP, 20 October 1948.

44 Singh, *Autobiography*, p. 39.

45 Quoted in Kapur, M. L. (ed.), *Maharaja Hari Singh*, New Delhi, 1995, p. 52.

46 Teng, Bhatt and Bhatt, *Kashmir Documents*, 'Proclamation of Maharaja Hari Singh', 9 July 1931, p. 342.

47 Copland, Ian, 'The Abdullah Factor: Kashmiri Muslims and the Crisis of 1947', in Low, D. A. (ed.), *The Political Inheritance of Pakistan*, London, 1991, pp. 218–54, at pp. 220–1.

48 BL, MSS Eur D 862, Powell's papers. This rather bizarre episode is recounted fully in Powell's manuscripts.

49 Wavell, Lord, *The Viceroy's Journal*, ed. Penderel Moon, London, 1973, p. 177, entry dated 17 October 1945.

50 Lamb, *Kashmir*, p. 117.

51 Ziegler, Philip, *Mountbatten*, London, 1985, p. 473.

52 Roberts, Andrew, *Eminent Churchillians*, London, 1994, p. 104.

53 BL, MSS Eur D 862, Powell's papers.

54 Wakhlu, *Hari Singh*, pp. 163–4.

55 BL, MSS Eur Photo Eur 393, Wavell papers, letter to H. M. Close, 13 December 1949. Wavell died on 24 May 1950.

Chapter 7: Deadlock

1 Lamb, Alastair, *Kashmir: A Disputed Legacy*, Hertingfordbury, 1991, p. 101.

2 Collins, Larry, and Lapierre, Dominique, *Freedom at Midnight: The Epic Drama of India's Struggle for Independence*, London, 1975, p. 444.

3 Ziegler, Philip, *Mountbatten*, London, 1985, p. 445.

4 Patel, Sardar, *Sardar Patel's Correspondence 1945–1950*, ed. Darga Das, vols I–VIII, Ahmedabad, 1971–3, vol. I, p. 45, letter from Nehru to Sardar Patel, 27 September 1947.

5 Ibid., p. 57, letter to Baldev Singh, 7 October 1947.

6 BL, MSS Eur D 670/6, George Cunningham diary, 1947.

7 Hodson, H. V., *The Great Divide: Britain–India–Pakistan*, Karachi, 1969, p. 445.

8 Birdwood, Lord, *Two Nations and Kashmir*, London, 1956, p. 57; BL, MSS Eur F 164/25A, Mudie papers, 'Kashmir before Accession', letter by Maharaja of Kashmir to Lord Mountbatten, 26 October 1947.

9 Collins and Lapierre, *Freedom at Midnight*, p. 447.

10 BL, MSS Eur D 670/6, Cunningham diary, 1947, entry dated 25 October 1947.

11 Collins and Lapierre, *Freedom at Midnight*, p. 449.

12 BL, MSS Eur F 164/24, Mudie papers, 'Intelligence reports concerning the tribal repercussions to the events in the Punjab, Kashmir and India', report

week ending 11 October 1947; Guha, Ramachandra, *India after Gandhi: The History of the World's Largest Democracy*, London, 2007, p. 66.

13 Patel, *Correspondence*, vol. I, p. 63, letter from Nehru to the Maharaja of Kashmir, 1 December 1947.

14 BL, MSS Eur D 670/6, Cunningham diary, 1947, entries dated 18 and 29 October 1947.

15 *DNB*.

16 BL, MSS Eur D 670/6, Cunningham diary, 1947, entry dated 28 October 1947.

17 Dasgupta, C., *War and Diplomacy in Kashmir 1947–48*, New Delhi, 2002, p. 9.

18 BL, MSS Eur D 670/6, entry dated 7 November 1947.

19 BL, MSS Eur D 714/84, 'Correspondence and Minutes on Kashmir 1947–48'.

20 Ibid., 'Note on the situation in India & Pakistan', 1 December 1947.

21 BL, MSS Eur D 862, Powell's papers.

22 BL, MSS Eur F 164/24, Mudie papers, 'Intelligence reports concerning the tribal repercussions to the events in the Punjab, Kashmir and India', reports week ending 8 and 22 November 1947.

23 Guha, *India after Gandhi*, pp. 72–3.

24 BL, MSS Eur D 714/86, 'Governor-General's Personal Report No. 8', 3 February 1948.

25 Patel, *Correspondence*, vol. VI, p. 387, letter from Sardar Patel to Arthur Henderson, 3 July 1948.

26 Ibid., vol. I, p. 163, letter from Nehru to Sardar Patel, 8 February 1948.

27 Ibid., pp. 159–62, letter from the Maharaja of Kashmir to Sardar Patel, 31 January 1948.

28 Ibid., p. 181, letter from the Maharaja of Kashmir to Sardar Patel, 13 April 1948; ibid., p. 191, letter from Nehru to Sardar Patel, 30 May 1948.

29 Ibid., p. 225, letter from the Maharaja of Kashmir to Sardar Patel, 9 September 1948.

30 Schofield, Victoria, *Kashmir in the Crossfire*, London, 1996, p. 161.

31 Patel, *Correspondence*, vol. I, p. 201, letter from Nehru to Sardar Patel, 6 June 1948.

32 Abbas, Ahmad, *Kashmir Fights for Freedom*, Bombay, 1948, p. 12.

33 Patel, *Correspondence*, vol. I, p. 293, letter from V. Shankar to V. P. Menon, 16 August 1949.

34 Ibid., p. 268, letter from Sardar Patel to Nehru, 11 May 1949; ibid., p. 269, letter from the Maharaja of Kashmir to Sardar Patel, 6 May 1949; ibid., p. 272, letter from Nehru to Sardar Patel, 18 May 1949; ibid., p. 298, letter from the Maharani of Kashmir to Sardar Patel, 6 September 1949.

35 Wakhlu, Somnath, *Hari Singh: The Maharaja, the Man, the Times*, New Delhi, 2004, pp. 250, 253.

36 Brown, Judith M., *Nehru: A Political Life*, London, 2003, p. 214.

37 Collins and Lapierre, *Freedom at Midnight*, p. 448.

38 Smith, Donald, 'Bloody Kashmir: Peril in Paradise', *National Geographic News*, 22 March 2000.

39 Schofield, *Kashmir in the Crossfire*, p. 238.

40 Bose, Sumantra, *Kashmir: Roots of Conflict, Paths to Peace*, London, 2003, p. 6.

41 Abbas, *Kashmir Fights for Freedom*, p. 6.

42 Bose, *Kashmir*, pp. 102–3.

43 Ibid., pp. 104–5.

44 Joshi, Manoj, *The Lost Rebellion: Kashmir in the Nineties*, New Delhi, 1999, p. 2.

45 Ibid., pp. 442–3.

46 *Time*, 'What did Kashmir have to do with the Mumbai Attacks?', 7 December 2008.

47 J. Korbel, quoted in Guha, *India after Gandhi*, p. 79.

48 Patel, *Correspondence*, vol. I, p. 249, letter from Nehru to Sardar Patel, 27 October 1948.

49 Orwell, George, 'Wells, Hitler and the World State', in Orwell, George, *Essays*, London, new edn. 2000, p. 190.

50 Ibid., vol. I, p. 157, letter of Maharaja of Kashmir to Sardar Patel, 25 January 1948.

Chapter 8: White Elephant

1 Browne, Horace A., *Reminiscences of the Court of Mandalay: Extracts from the Diary of General Horace A. Browne, 1859–1879*, Woking, 1907, p. 179, entry dated 25 July 1879.

2 Ibid., p. 19, entry dated 1 September 1859.

3 Ibid., p. 14, entry dated 1 September 1859.

4 BL, MSS Eur E 290/20, Sladen papers, 'The Present Political Situation in Burma', report dated 17 September 1885.

5 Browne, *Reminiscences*, p. 37, entry dated 24 April 1872.

6 Ibid., p. 35, entry dated 24 April 1872.

7 Maung Htin Aung, *The Stricken Peacock: Anglo-Burmese Relations 1752–1948*, The Hague, 1965, p. 66.

8 Quoted in Woodman, Dorothy, *The Making of Burma*, London, 1962, p. 184.

9 Browne, *Reminiscences*, pp. 45–6, entry dated 31 July 1874.

10 Ibid., p. 46, entry dated 31 July 1874.

11 Maung Htin Aung, *Lord Randolph Churchill and the Dancing Peacock: British Conquest of Burma, 1885*, New Delhi, 1990, p. 34.

12 Anonymous, *Burma, the Foremost Country: A Timely Discourse*, London, 1884, p. 16; Ali, Mohammed Shamsher, 'The Beginnings of British Rule in Upper Burma: A Study of British Policy and Burmese Reaction 1885–1890', unpublished PhD thesis, University of London, 1976, pp. 32–3.

13 Maung Htin Aung, *Lord Randolph Churchill*, p. 19.

14 BL, MSS Eur E 290/20, Sladen papers, 'The Present Political Situation in Burma', report dated 17 September 1885, p. 1.

15 Browne, *Reminiscences*, p. 145, entry dated 26 September 1878.

16 Thant Myint-U, *The Making of Modern Burma*, Cambridge, 2001, p. 156.

17 Quoted in Stewart, A. J. Q., *The Pagoda War*, London, 1972, p. 64.

18 Marks, John Ebenezer, *Forty Years in Burma*, London, 1917, pp. 223–4.

19 Colbeck, James, *Mandalay in 1878–1879: The Letters of James Alfred Colbeck, Originally Selected and Edited by George H. Colbeck in 1892*, ed. Michael W.

Charney, Knaresborough, 1892, p. 62, letter dated 18 September 1878; ibid., pp. 62, 65, letter dated 28 September. The recipients of Colbeck's letters are unknown.

20 Thant Myint-U, *The Making of Modern Burma*, p. 157.

21 Ibid., p. 55.

22 Colbeck, *Letters*, p. 66, letter dated 12 October 1878.

23 Ibid., p. 65, letter dated 28 September 1878.

24 Browne, *Reminiscences*, p. 171, entry dated 8 July 1878.

25 Colbeck, *Letters*, p. 72, letter dated 16 November 1878.

26 Geary, Grattan, *Burma, after the Conquest, Viewed in its Political, Social and Commercial Aspects from Mandalay*, London, 1886, p. 99.

27 Ibid., p. 128; Stewart, *The Pagoda War*, p. 61; Thant Myint-U, *The Making of Burma*, p. 162.

28 Colbeck, *Letters*, p. 73, letter dated 24 February 1879.

29 Stewart, *The Pagoda War*, p. 61.

30 Browne, *Reminiscences*, p. 159, entry dated 27 June 1879.

31 BL, MSS Eur E 290/25, Sladen papers, 'Memorandum of the Burmese Minister of the Interior', written up by Sladen, dated 22 January 1886.

32 Thant Myint-U, *The Making of Modern Burma*, p. 59.

33 Geary, *Burma*, pp. 175–6.

34 Colbeck, *Letters*, p. 75, letter dated 11 May 1879.

35 *DNB*.

36 BL, MSS Eur D 912, Letter book of Sir Charles Edward Bernard, letter to Lord Ripon, 1 July 1880; letters to A. C. Lyall, 8 and 27 July 1880.

37 *DNB*; BL, MSS Eur D 912, letter to Lord Ripon, 17 September 1880.

38 BL, MSS Eur D 912, letter to Lord Ripon, 6 April 1881.

39 BL, MSS Eur E 290/20, Sladen papers, 'The Present Political Situation in Burma', p. 29.

40 BL, MSS Eur D 912, letter to Lord Ripon, 22 February 1882.

41 *DNB*.

42 Colquhoun, A. R., *Burma and the Burmans or the Best Unopened Market in the World*, London, 1885, p. vi.

43 Ibid., pp. 21, 31, 40.

44 Browne, *Reminiscences*, p. 161.

45 Anonymous, *Burma, the Foremost Country*, p. viii.

46 Browne, Edmond, *The Coming of the Great Queen: A Narrative of the Acquisition of Burma*, London, 1988, pp. 103–4.

47 *DNB*.

48 *DNB*.

49 BL, MSS Eur E 254/10, Thirkell White papers, 'letter from Secretary to the Chief Commissioner of British Burma to Secretary of the Government of India Foreign Department', 28 July 1885.

50 Ibid., letter from E. S. Symes to Indian Foreign Secretary, 16 October 1885.

51 Quoted in Woodman, *The Making of Burma*, p. 3.

52 BL, MSS Eur E 290/20, pp. 36, 33, 40–1.

53 Thant Myint-U, *The River of Lost Footsteps*, London, 2007, p. 12.

54 Ali, 'The Beginnings of British Rule in Upper Burma', p. 30.

55 BL, MSS Eur E 290/65, Sladen papers, diary January to December 1885, entries dated 29 October and 7 November 1885.

56 BL, MSS Eur E 290/26, Sladen papers, letter from E. B. Sladen to H. M. Durand, Secretary to the Government of India, Foreign Department, 21 December 1885.

57 BL, MSS Eur E 290/65, Sladen diary, entry dated 9 December 1885.

58 Ibid., entry dated 16 December 1885.

Chapter 9: The Road from Mandalay

1 BL, MSS Eur B 380/2, Mayo papers, letter to Colonel Fytche, 11 June 1869.

2 Churchill, Winston S., *Lord Randolph Churchill*, 2 vols, London, 1906, vol. I, p. 48.

3 Ibid., pp. 524–5.

4 McCord, Norman, *British History 1815–1906*, Oxford, 1991, p. 378.

5 *Parliamentary Debates*, vol. 302, p. 339, House of Commons debate, 25 January 1886.

6 Ibid., p. 322, House of Commons debate, 25 January 1886.

7 Ibid., pp. 850–3, House of Lords debate, 22 February 1886.

8 *DNB*.

9 *Parliamentary Debates*, vol. 302, pp. 948–52, House of Commons debate, 22 February 1886.

10 Ibid., p. 963, House of Commons debate, 22 February 1886.

11 Ibid., p. 974, House of Commons debate, 22 February 1886.

12 Thant Myint-U, *The River of Lost Footsteps: A Personal History of Burma*, London, 2007, pp. 22–3.

13 Blackburn, Terence R., *Executions by the Half-Dozen: The Pacification of Burma*, New Delhi, 2008, p. 13.

14 BL, MSS Eur E 290/26, Sladen papers, 'Memorandum by his Excellency the Viceroy and Governor-General', 25 February 1886.

15 Ibid.

16 *Parliamentary Debates*, vol. 302, p. 182, House of Lords debate, 22 January 1886; ibid., p. 189, House of Commons debate, 22 January 1886.

17 BL, MSS Eur E 290/26, Sladen papers, 'Memorandum by his Excellency the Viceroy and Governor-General', 25 February 1886.

18 Geary, Grattan, *Burma, after the Conquest, Viewed in its Political, Social and Commercial Aspects from Mandalay*, London, 1886, p. 219.

19 Kipling, Rudyard, 'The Taking of Lungtungpen', in Kipling, Rudyard, *Plain Tales from the Hills*, London, 1888, pp. 99–104.

20 Geary, *Burma*, p. 234.

21 Ibid., p. 236. The correct quotation is 'when lenity and cruelty play for a kingdom, the gentler gamester is the soonest winner'.

22 BL, MSS Eur E 290/26, Sladen papers, 'Minuted Conversation with Mr Bernard', 20 December 1885; letter from Colonel Sladen to the Chief Commissioner, 27 December 1885.

23 Ibid., letter from the Chief Commissioner to Colonel Sladen, 27 December 1885; letter from Sladen to the Chief Commissioner, 28 December 1885.

24 Ibid., telegram from the Chief Commissioner to the Indian government, 10 January 1886.

25 Ibid., 'Memorandum by his Excellency the Viceroy and Governor-General', 25 February 1886.

26 BL, MSS Eur E 290/28, Sladen papers, papers relating to the visit of Lord and Lady Dufferin to Mandalay, February 1886, statement of Lord Dufferin to the Council, signed Mandalay, 18 February 1886.

27 BL, MSS Eur E 290/27, Sladen papers.

28 Stewart, A. J. Q., *The Pagoda War*, London, 1972, p. 157.

29 Crosthwaite, Sir Charles, *The Pacification of Burma*, London, 1912, pp. 13–14.

30 BL, MSS Eur E 254/1, Thirkell White papers, letter from Charles Crosthwaite to Herbert Thirkell White, 6 August 1909.

31 Crosthwaite, *The Pacification of Burma*, p. v.

32 Ibid., p. 2.

33 Browne, Edmond Charles, *The Coming of the Great Queen*, London, 1888, p. 235.

34 Minayeff, I. P., *Travels in and Diaries of India and Burma*, trans. Hirendwanath Sanyal, Calcutta, 1958, p. 145, entry dated 25 January 1886.

35 *The Times*, 13 July 1886; Thant Myint-U, *The River of Lost Footsteps*, p. 28.

36 Browne, *The Coming of the Great Queen*, pp. 245–6, 248–9.

37 BL, MSS Eur E 254/10, Thirkell White papers, Major General Sir George White in the *Burma Gazette*, 2 July 1887.

38 Ibid., A. H. Hildebrand, Political Officer, Shan States, diary entry dated 25 January 1887; J. G. Scott, Assistant Superintendent, diary entry dated 6 March 1887.

39 Stewart, *The Pagoda War*, p. 180.

40 BL, MSS Eur E 254/10, Thirkell White papers, 'Translation of papers found on the body of Bo Swe, the notorious dacoit leader in the Minbu district who was killed in October, 1887'.

41 Ibid., 'Appendix 1 to note by Chief Commissioner from H. T. White', dated 29 September 1889.

42 Crosthwaite, *The Pacification of Burma*, pp. v–vi.

43 Charles Crosthwaite, letter to Captain Raikes, 4 April 1888, quoted in Ali, Mohammed Shamsher, 'The Beginnings of British Rule in Upper Burma: A Study of British Policy and Burmese Reaction, 1885–1890', unpublished PhD thesis, University of London, 1976, pp. 284, 288.

44 BL, MSS Eur E 254/1, Thirkell White papers, letter from Charles Crosthwaite to Herbert Thirkell White, 2 January 1902.

45 BL, MSS Eur E 254/10, 'Note by H. T. White, Secretary for Upper Burma, on the settlement of Pegu Province in 1852–55', [n.d.] July 1886.

46 Geary, *Burma*, p. 245.

47 Ali, 'The Beginnings of British Rule', p. 314.

48 Ibid., p. 319.

49 Ni Ni Myint, *Burma's Struggle against British Imperialism 1885–1895*, Rangoon, 1983, p. 158.

50 Ali, 'The Beginnings of British Rule', p. 330.

51 Stewart, *The Pagoda War*, p. 180.

52 Ibid., p. 164.

Chapter 10: 'Twilight over Burma'

1 BL, MSS Eur E 362/3, Sir Arthur Bruce, Memoirs, p. 4.
2 Crick, Bernard, *George Orwell: A Life*, London, 1980, p. 156.
3 Thant Myint-U, *The River of Lost Footsteps: A Personal History of Burma*, London, 2007, p. 187.
4 Thirkell White, Herbert, *A Civil Servant in Burma*, London, 1913, pp. 24–5.
5 Copland, Ian, *India 1885–1947*, London, 2001, p. 19.
6 Thirkell White, *A Civil Servant*, pp. 55, 58, 66.
7 Kipling, Rudyard, *Complete Verse*, ed. M. M. Kaye, London, 1990, p. 260.
8 Browne, Edmond, *The Coming of the Great Queen*, London, 1888, p. 247.
9 BL, MSS Eur E 362/3, Sir Arthur Bruce, Memoirs, p. 4.
10 Geary, Grattan, *Burma, after the Conquest, Viewed in its Political, Social and Commercial Aspects from Mandalay*, London, 1886, p. 11; Thirkell White, *A Civil Servant*, pp. 69–70.
11 BL, MSS Eur D 912, Bernard papers, memorandum from Government House, Rangoon, [n.d.] January 1881.
12 BL, MSS Eur E 254/1, Thirkell White papers, letter from Crosthwaite to Thirkell White, 5 October 1888.
13 Crick, *Orwell*, p. 164; BL, MSS Eur E 362/8, Lord Ogmore, Memoirs, ch. 6, p. 8. The latter source gives details of U Tin Tut's favoured position on the rugby field.
14 Collis, Maurice, *Trials in Burma*, London, 1945, new edn 1978, pp. 205–8; Solomon, Robert A., 'Saya San and the Burmese Rebellion', *Modern Asian Studies*, vol. 3, no. 3, 1969, pp. 209–23, at p. 210.
15 Collis, *Trials in Burma*, pp. 208–9.
16 Ibid., p. 212.
17 Solomon, 'Saya San and the Burmese Rebellion', pp. 212, 210.
18 Sarkisyanz, Manuel, 'Messianic Folk-Buddhism as Ideology of Peasant Revolts in Nineteenth and Early Twentieth Century Burma', *Review of Religious Research*, vol. 10, no. 1, Autumn 1968, pp. 32–8, at p. 35.
19 Taylor, Robert H., *The State in Burma*, London, 1987, p. 203.
20 Hyam, Ronald, *Britain's Declining Empire: Decolonization 1918–1968*, Cambridge, 2006, p. 82.
21 BL, MSS Eur E 362/5, T. L. Hughes, Memoirs, pp. 2–10.
22 BL, MSS Eur E 362/2, A. G. Bottomley, Recollections of last days in Burma, p. 3.
23 BL, MSS Eur E 362/3, Sir Arthur Bruce, Memoirs, pp. 30, 32, 46.
24 BL, MSS Eur E 362/10, B. R. Pearn, Memoirs, p. 15.
25 BL, MSS Eur F 169/20, Sir Hubert Rance, 'The Memoirs and Personal Papers of Major General Sir Hubert Rance'.
26 Charney, Michael W., *A History of Modern Burma*, Cambridge, 2009, p. 57.
27 BL, MSS Eur E 362/10, B. R. Pearn, Memoirs, pp. 1–10.
28 BL, MSS Eur F 169/20, Sir Hubert Rance, Papers.
29 *DNB*.
30 BL, MSS Eur E 215/1–2, Dorman Smith papers, letter from Leo Amery to Reginald Dorman-Smith, 1 December 1942; letter from Leo Amery to Reginald Dorman-Smith, 29 December 1942.

31 BL, MSS Eur E 362/5, T. L. Hughes, Memoirs, p. 57.

32 Gilbert, Martin, *Churchill: A Life*, London, 1991, p. 734.

33 BL, MSS Eur E 362/3, Sir Arthur Bruce, Memoirs, p. 71.

34 Ibid., pp. 5, 4.

35 Maung Htin Aung, *A History of Burma*, New York, 1967, p. 269.

36 Silverstein, J. (ed.), *The Political Legacy of Aung San*, rev. edn, Ithaca, New York, 1993, pp. 78–9.

37 BL, MSS Eur E 362/5, T. L. Hughes, p. 41; MSS Eur E 362/3, Sir Arthur Bruce, p. 79.

38 BL, MSS Eur E 362/5, T. L. Hughes, p. 41; MSS Eur E 362/3, Sir Arthur Bruce, p. 84.

39 BL, MSS Eur E 362/18, Sir John Wise, Memoirs, pp. 4, 52.

40 Ibid., p. 49.

41 BL, MSS Eur F 169/20, Sir Hubert Rance, Papers.

42 BL, MSS Eur E 362/7/1, Philip Nash, Memoirs, p. 39.

43 Ibid., appendix, letter from Hubert Rance to Pethick-Lawrence, 13 November 1946.

44 BL, MSS Eur E 362/8, Lord Ogmore, Memoirs, ch. 4, pp. 2–3.

45 *DNB*.

46 BL, MSS Eur E 362/2, A. G. Bottomley, 'Recollections of Last Days in Burma', p. 9; MSS Eur E 362/18, Sir John Wise, Memoirs, p. 47.

47 BL, MSS Eur E 362/8, Lord Ogmore, Memoirs, ch. 4, p. 4.

48 Ibid., ch. 6, pp. 3–5.

49 Ibid., p. 12.

50 BL, MSS Eur F 169/20, Sir Hubert Rance, Papers; MSS Eur E 362/7/1, Philip Nash, Memoirs, p. 110.

51 BL, MSS Eur E 362/3, Sir Arthur Bruce, Memoirs, p. 100.

52 *Time*, 'Strength through Weakness', 5 March 1965.

53 Sargent, Inge, *Twilight over Burma*, Honolulu, 1994, p. xi.

54 *Time*, 'Strength through Weakness'.

55 *Daily Telegraph* obituary, 6 December 2002.

56 Turrell, Robert V., 'Conquest and Concession: The Case of the Burma Ruby Mines', *Modern Asian Studies*, vol. 22, no. 1, 1988, pp. 141–63, at p. 144.

57 *The Times*, 'Blood rubies bankroll Burmese Junta', 30 September 2007.

58 *Time*, 'Burma's Faceless Leaders', 1 October 2007.

59 See http://www.bbc.co.uk/news/world-asia-pacific-12362745.

60 BL, MSS Eur E 362/8, Lord Ogmore, Memoirs, ch. 6, pp. 2–3.

Chapter 11: Kitchener: An Imperial Hero

1 Magnus, Philip, *Kitchener: Portrait of an Imperialist*, London, 1958, new edn 1968, p. 15.

2 Pollock, John, *Kitchener*, London, 2001, p. xxi.

3 Ibid., p. 12.

4 Warner, Philip, *Kitchener: The Man behind the Legend*, London, 1985, p. 7.

5 Pollock, *Kitchener*, p. 16; *DNB*.

6 Pollock, *Kitchener*, p. 12.

7   Shepperd, Alan, *Sandhurst: The Royal Military Academy*, London, 1980, p. 64.

8   Pollock, *Kitchener*, p. 19.

9   Ibid., p. 19.

10 Magnus, *Kitchener*, p. 23.

11 Sandes, E. W. C., *The Royal Engineers in Egypt and the Sudan*, London, 1937, p. 510.

12 TNA, PRO 30/57/1, Kitchener papers.

13 Ibid., letter from Herbert Kitchener to Sir R. Biddulph, 2 August 1882.

14 Churchill, Winston S., *The River War*, London, 1899, new edn 1997, pp. 64–5.

15 Pollock, *Kitchener*, pp. 71–2.

16 TNA, PRO 30/57/6, Kitchener papers, Major H. H. Kitchener, 'The Fall of Khartoum', 14 February 1885.

17 Slatin, Rudolf, *Fire and Sword in the Sudan: A Personal Narrative of Fighting and Serving the Dervishes 1879–1895*, London, 1896, new edn 1897, p. 55.

18 Churchill, *The River War*, p. 12.

19 TNA, PRO 30/40, Sir John Ardagh's papers, 'The insurrection of the False Prophet, 1881–1883', c. 1883.

20 Churchill, *The River War*, p. 16.

21 Ibid., p. 17.

22 Raugh, Harold E., *The Victorians at War: An Encyclopedia of British Military History*, Santa Barbara, 2004, p. 166.

23 *DNB*.

24 TNA, PRO 30/57/12, 'General Report on the Sudan, 1890', Intelligence Report for the War Office, Cairo, 30 December 1890.

25 Beatty, Charles, *His Country was the World: A Study of Gordon of Khartoum*, London, 1954, p. 215.

26 Churchill, *The River War*, p. 29.

27 TNA, PRO 30/57/6, Kitchener papers, Major H. H. Kitchener, 'The Fall of Khartoum', 14 February 1885.

28 Churchill, *The River War*, p. 39.

29 TNA, PRO 30/57/6, 'The Fall of Khartoum'.

30 Ibid.

31 Ibid.

32 Slatin, *Fire and Sword*, p. 228.

33 Ibid., p. 233.

34 Churchill, *The River War*, p. 48.

35 TNA, PRO 30/57/12, 'General Report on the Sudan, 1890'.

36 TNA, FO 633/86, Cromer papers, 'The Reconquest of Sudan: October 1895– September 1898', pp. 1, 3.

37 TNA, PRO 30/57/9, letter from Sir Evelyn Baring in Cairo to the Marquess of Salisbury, 9 February 1892, p. 24.

38 Ibid., pp. 24–5.

39 Pollock, *Kitchener*, pp. 59, 63–4.

40 Ibid., p. 76.

41 TNA, PRO 30/57/13, Kitchener papers, 'Intelligence Reports, 1890–1899', Intelligence Report, August 1894.

42 TNA, FO 633/86, Cromer, 'The Reconquest of Sudan', p. 9.

43 Ibid., pp. 9–10.

44 Steevens, G. W., *With Kitchener to Khartoum*, London, 1898, new edn 1990, p. 45.

45 Ibid., p. 51.

46 TNA, PRO 30/57/9, Kitchener papers, letter from Sir Evelyn Baring to the Marquess of Salisbury, 9 February 1892, p. 24.

47 Churchill, *The River War*, p. 193.

48 Steevens, *With Kitchener*, p. 282.

49 Churchill, *The River War*, p. 206.

50 TNA, FO 633/86, Cromer, 'The Reconquest of Sudan', p. 30.

51 Steevens, *With Kitchener*, p. 301.

52 TNA, PRO 30/57/16, Kitchener papers, letter from Queen Victoria to Lord Kitchener, 24 March 1899.

53 TNA, PRO 30/57/15, Kitchener papers, *New Penny Magazine*, Saturday 26 November 1898.

54 TNA, PRO 30/57/16, Kitchener papers, letters from Queen Victoria to Lord Kitchener, 24 June and 17 November 1899; telegram from Queen Victoria to Lord Kitchener, 26 July 1899.

55 Steevens, *With Kitchener*, pp. 325–6.

56 Cromer, Earl of, *Political and Literary Essays 1908–1913*, 1st Series, London, 1913, 'The Government of Subject Races', p. 15.

57 Ibid., p. 17.

58 Ibid., pp. 27–30.

59 Magnus, *Kitchener*, p. 450.

Chapter 12: 'The Finest Body of Men'

1 Warburg, Gabriel, *The Sudan under Wingate*, London, 1971, p. 2.

2 Keun, Odette, *A Foreigner Looks at the British Sudan*, London, 1930, p. 53.

3 Jackson, H. C., *Sudan Days and Ways*, London, 1954, pp. 24–5.

4 *DNB*.

5 Wingate, Sir Ronald, *Wingate of the Sudan*, London, 1955, p. 45.

6 Steevens, G. W., *With Kitchener to Khartoum*, London, 1898, new edn 1990, p. 64.

7 Daly, M. W., *The Sirdar: Sir Reginald Wingate and the British Empire in the Middle East*, Philadelphia, 1997, pp. 3–4.

8 Warner, Philip, *Kitchener: The Man behind the Legend*, London, 1985, p. 100.

9 MacMichael, Sir Harold, *The Sudan*, London, 1954, pp. 102–3.

10 TNA, FO 373/5/20, 'Handbook of Anglo-Egyptian Sudan', handbooks prepared under the direction of the Historical Section of the Foreign Office, No. 107, London, 1919, p. 59.

11 MECA, Bowman papers, diary entry dated 10 November 1911.

12 Vansittart, Lord, *The Mist Procession: The Autobiography of Lord Vansittart*, London, 1958, p. 91.

13 Warburg, *Sudan*, p. 81.

14 Symes, Sir Stewart, *Tour of Duty*, London, 1946, p. 213.

15 Cromer, Earl of, *Political and Literary Essays*, 2nd Series, London, 1914, 'Egypt and the Sudan', p. 224.

16 Kirk-Greene, A. H. M., 'The Sudan Political Service: A Profile in the Sociology of Imperialism', *International Journal of African Historical Studies*, vol. 15, no. 1, 1982, pp. 21–48, at p. 27.

17 Collins, Robert, 'The Sudan Political Service', *African Affairs*, vol. 71, no. 284, July 1972, pp. 293–303, at p. 296.

18 Collins, Robert O., and Deng, Francis M., *The British in the Sudan 1898–1956: The Sweetness and the Sorrow*, London, 1984, p. 61; Warburg, *Sudan*, p. 84.

19 Symes, *Tour of Duty*, p. 213.

20 Kirk-Greene, 'The Sudan Political Service', p. 37; Collins, 'The Sudan Political Service', p. 296.

21 Jackson, *Sudan Days*, p. 15.

22 Kirk-Greene, 'The Sudan Political Service', p. 40.

23 Mangan, J. A., 'The Education of an Elite Imperial Administration: The Sudan Political Service and the British Public School System', *International Journal of African Historical Studies*, vol. 15, no. 4, 1982, pp. 671–99, at p. 689.

24 Collins, 'The Sudan Political Service', p. 301.

25 Ibid., p. 297.

26 TNA, CO 877/11/2, 'Sudan Political Service', Information for Candidates, reprinted, January 1933, pp. 5, 1.

27 Ibid., pp. 4–5.

28 Jackson, *Sudan Days*, p. 17.

29 Thesiger, Wilfred, *The Life of my Choice*, London, 1987, p. 171.

30 Keun, *A Foreigner Looks*, p. 50.

31 Ibid., p. 52.

32 Collins, 'The Sudan Political Service', p. 300.

33 MECA, MacMichael Papers, letter from Sir John Maffey, Governor General of Sudan, to Harold MacMichael, 27 April 1927.

34 TNA, CO 877/11/2, Information for Candidates, p. 3.

35 Jackson, *Sudan Days*, pp. 26–7.

36 Kenrick, Rosemary, *Sudan Tales: Recollections of Some Sudan Political Service Wives 1926–1956*, Cambridge, 1987, p. 9.

37 Ibid., pp. 25–6.

38 Ibid., p. 26.

39 TNA, FO 141/647/16, 'General Situation in the Sudan', 9 June 1935.

40 Symes, *Tour of Duty*, p. 220.

41 Steevens, *With Kitchener*, p. 2.

42 TNA, FO 373/5/20, 'Handbook of Anglo-Egyptian Sudan', p. 57.

43 Ibid., p. 43.

44 Buchan, John, *Greenmantle*, London, 1916, new edn 1964, p. 18.

45 TNA, FO 633/110, Cromer papers, 'Sudan Book of Loyalty', pp. 1–2.

46 TNA, FO 141/426/9, 'Darfur Situation and Ali Dinar', Cursory Review of our Political Relations with the Sultan of Darfur, 10 August 1915, p. 1.

47 Ibid., pp. 3–4.

48 Ibid., 'Confidential Dispatch' from Wingate to Sir Henry MacMahon, Resident in Cairo, 12 February 1916, pp. 1–3.

49 Ibid., telegram from Wingate to Gilbert Clayton in Cairo, 26 February 1916, pp. 1–4.

50 Ibid., translation of a letter addressed to Sultan Ali Dinar by Enver Pasha, 3 February 1915.

51 Ibid., letter from Ali Dinar to the Governor of Kordofan, 7 February 1916.

52 Ibid., 'Proclamation to all the natives of Darfur translated from Arabic', [n.d.] April 1916.

53 Ibid., letter from Wingate to Gilbert Clayton, 25 May 1916.

54 Ibid., letter from Ali Dinar to the Sirdar (Wingate), c. 17 May 1916.

55 Ibid., letter from Ali Dinar to the Sirdar (Wingate), c. end of May 1916.

56 Ibid., 'Final Despatch Western Frontier Force Sudan', [n.d.] November 1916.

57 TNA, FO 141/805/2, translation of a letter to H. M. Saad Pasha Zaghloul, Prime Minister of Egypt, 9 July 1924.

58 *DNB*.

59 Collins, Robert, *Shadows in the Grass: Britain in the Southern Sudan 1918–1956*, New Haven, 1983, pp. 44–5.

60 Quoted in MECA, MacMichael papers, 'Review of the Anglo-Egyptian Sudan', *Oxford Times*, 26 October 1934.

61 Ibid.

62 Johnson, Douglas H., *The Root Causes of Sudan's Civil Wars*, Oxford, 2003, p. 11.

63 TNA, FO 141/624/4, 'Spread of Arabic Language in the Southern Sudan', memorandum by Lord Lloyd, Resident in Cairo, to Arthur Henderson, Secretary of State for Foreign Affairs, 19 June 1929.

64 TNA, FO 141/647/16, 'General Situation in the Sudan', 'Political Memorandum on the Anglo-Egyptian Sudan', written by Stewart Symes, 9 June 1935, Khartoum.

65 TNA, FO 141/544/1, 'Education in Sudan', memorandum by A. F. G. Huddleston, Acting Governor General of the Sudan, 4 June 1932.

Chapter 13: North and South

1 Daly, M. W., *Imperial Sudan: The Anglo-Egyptian Condominium*, Cambridge, 1991, p. 235.

2 Henderson, K. D. D., *The Making of the Sudan: The Life and Letters of Sir Douglas Newbold*, London, 1953, p. 55, letter to Frank Cottrell, 29 October 1933.

3 Thomas, Graham F., *Sudan 1950–1985: Death of a Dream*, London, 1990, pp. 15, 31.

4 Ibid., p. 21; Thomas, Graham F., *Sudan: Struggle for Survival*, London, 1993, p. 6.

5 TNA, FO 371/73472, 'Political Situation in Sudan, 1949', letter from F. Roberts to M. Wright, Foreign Office, 18 April 1949.

6 Thomas, *Sudan: Death of a Dream*, p. 29.

7 Meredith, Martin, *The State of Africa: A History of Fifty Years of Independence*, London, 2005, p. 5.

8 Collins, Robert O., *Shadows in the Grass: Britain in the Southern Sudan 1918–1956*, New Haven, 1983, p. x.

9 Ibid., pp. 175, 261.

10 Robertson, Sir James, *Transition in Africa: From Direct Rule to Independence*, London, 1974, p. 110.

11 Ibid.

12 Daly, *Imperial Sudan*, p. 236.

13 Ibid., pp. 242–3.

14 TNA, FO 371/80358, 'The Political Situation in the Sudan, 1950', Report on the Southern Provinces of the Sudan covering 1948 and 1949, to African Department of the Foreign Office, by Sir James Robertson, 9 March 1950.

15 Ibid., letter from Sir R. Howe to Sir W. Strang, personal, 8 March 1950.

16 TNA, FO 371/73472, 'Political Situation in the Sudan, 1949', Background to Sudan News, The First Session of the Legislative Assembly (opened December 1948), prepared by E. N. Corbyn, May 1949.

17 Thomas, Graham F., *From the Last of the Proconsuls: Letters from Sir James Robertson*, London, 1994, p. 83, letter from Sir James Robertson to Graham Thomas, 30 January 1974.

18 Ibid., p. 64, letter from Sir James Robertson to Graham Thomas, 15 January 1956.

19 Johnson, Douglas H., *The Root Causes of Sudan's Civil Wars*, Oxford, 2003, p. 26.

20 Johnson, Douglas H. (ed.), *British Documents on the End of Empire*, Series B, vol. 5: *Sudan*, London, 1998, p. 506, dispatch no. 128 from Sir E. Chapman Andrews to Selwyn Lloyd, 30 October 1956.

21 MECA, Davies papers, G. Warburg interview with R. Davies, held on 28 September 1970.

22 Meredith, *The State of Africa*, p. 345.

23 TNA, CO 822/1185, 'Mutinies in Southern Sudan', Omdurman Radio Political Diary by Muhammad Yusuf Hashim, September 1955, enclosed in a note from Evelyn Shuckburgh to Henry Hopkinson MP, 9 September 1955.

24 Ibid., *Ayam*, 3 September 1955.

25 O'Ballance, Edgar, *Sudan, Civil War and Terrorism 1956–99*, London, 2000, p. 8.

26 TNA, CO 822/1185, draft letter from T. I. K. Lloyd, Colonial Office, to Sir Ivone Kirkpatrick, c. September 1955.

27 Ibid.

28 Johnson (ed.), *British Documents*, p. 506, dispatch no. 128 from Sir E. Chapman Andrews to Selwyn Lloyd, 30 October 1956.

29 *Sudan Tribune*, 31 August 2007.

30 O'Ballance, Edgar, *The Secret War in the Sudan 1955–1972*, London, 1977, p. 149.

31 TNA, FO 1090/1, *Daily Telegraph*, 'Extermination Army from Khartoum', 21 March 1967; *The Times*, 'Where Racialism is Ignored', 7 April 1967, letter from Sir David Renton QC, MP.

32 TNA, Fo 1090/1, letter from D. J. Speares, Foreign Office, to Sir Hugh Greene, Broadcasting House, 8 April 1967.

33 TNA, FCO 29/295, 'Malawi Political Affairs', President Welcomes Autonomy for Southern Sudan, by Alfred Mkandawine, 11 June 1969.

34 Eprile, Cecil, *War and Peace in the Sudan 1955–1972*, London, 1974, p. 49.

35 Lawrence Joffe, obituary of Jaafar Nimeiri, *Guardian*, 5 June 2009.

36 TNA, FCO 39/510, 'Sudan Economic Affairs, Bilateral Relations with USSR', letter from G. O. Roberts to Mrs Eirene White MP, 26 August 1969.

37 TNA, FCO 93/1186, 'Valedictory Dispatch – Sudan', J. F. S. Phillips to David Owen, 30 September 1977.

38 Meredith, *The State of Africa*, p. 312.

39 TNA, FCO 93/1659, 'Oil in the Sudan, 1978', letter from Brian Pridham to P. J. Torry, 3 October 1978; letter from Brian Pridham to P. J. Torry, 6 July 1978.

40 TNA, FCO 93/1652, 'Military Relations between UK and Sudan', memorandum dated 22 June 1978.

41 TNA, FCO 93/1636, D. C. Carden on North–South Relations, 18 December 1978, details of a meeting with Hassan Turabi, held on 28 November 1978.

42 Meredith, *The State of Africa*, p. 357.

43 Joffe, obituary of Nimeiri, *Guardian*, 5 June 2009.

44 Thomas, *Sudan: Struggle for Survival*, pp. xiii–xiv.

45 Steevens, G. W., *With Kitchener to Khartoum*, London, 1898, new edn 1990, p. 2.

46 Daly, M. W., *Darfur's Sorrow: A History of Destruction and Genocide*, Cambridge, 2007, p. 254.

47 Meredith, *The State of Africa*, p. 588; Wright, Lawrence, *The Looming Tower: Al Qaeda's Road to 9/11*, London, 2006, p. 164.

48 Ibid., pp. 166–8.

49 Ibid., pp. 214, 220.

50 Flint, Julie, and de Waal, Alex, *Darfur: A Short History of a Long War*, London, 2005, p. 13.

51 Daly, *Darfur's Sorrow*, pp. 273, 314.

52 Ibid., p. 3.

53 *Time*, 'The Tragedy of Sudan', 4 October 2004.

54 *Time*, 'Sudanese President Omar Hassan al-Bahir', 5 March 2009.

55 Quoted in Jackson, H. C., *Sudan Days and Ways*, London, 1954, p. 249.

56 O'Ballance, *The Secret War*, p. 151.

57 Eprile, *War and Peace in the Sudan*, p. 17.

58 TNA, FO 633/86, 'The Reconquest of Sudan, October, 1895–September, 1898', pp. 5–6.

Chapter 14: Indirect Rule

1 Schwarz, Frederick A. O., Jr, *Nigeria: The Tribes, the Nation, or the Race*, Cambridge, Massachusetts, 1965, p. 20n.

2 *DNB*.

3 Myer, Valerie Grosvenor, *A Victorian Lady in Africa: The Story of Mary Kingsley*, Southampton, 1989, p. vii.

4 Ibid., p. 1.

5 Kingsley, Mary, 'Imperialism: A Lecture Delivered in Liverpool', in *West African Studies*, 2nd edn, London, 1901, pp. 416–18.

6 Kingsley, Mary, *The Story of West Africa*, London, 1899, pp. 153–4.

7 Shaw, Flora, *A Tropical Dependency: An Outline of the Ancient History of Western Soudan with an Account of the Modern Settlement of Northern Nigeria*, London, 1905, pp. 364–5.

8 Wellesley, Dorothy, *Sir George Goldie, Founder of Nigeria: A Memoir*, London, 1934, pp. vii–viii.

9 Ibid., p. 93.

10 Flint, John E., *Sir George Goldie and the Making of Nigeria*, London, 1960, p. 4.

11 Wellesley, *Goldie*, p. 94; Flint, *Goldie*, p. 5.

12 *DNB*; Flint, *Goldie*, p. 5.

13 *DNB*.

14 Robinson, Gallagher, with Alice Denny, *Africa and the Victorians: The Official Mind of Imperialism*, 2nd edn, London, 1981, p. 395.

15 Vandeleur, Seymour, *Campaigning on the Upper Nile and Niger*, London, 1898, p. 263.

16 Ibid., p. xxvii.

17 TNA, FO 403/75, correspondence respecting the Royal Niger Company, Part I, 1885–1886, p. 36b, letter dated 8 November 1886 from George Goldie to the Earl of Iddesleigh.

18 TNA, FCO 403/75, Royal Niger Company correspondence, pp. 64–8, letter from company to Sir J. Pauncefote, 20 December 1886.

19 Ibid.

20 TNA, FCO 403/76, correspondence respecting the Royal Niger Company, Part II, 1888, pp. 12–13, letter from German Embassy, 27 January 1888; ibid., p. 56, letter from George Goldie to the Foreign Office, 21 February 1888.

21 Ibid., p. 115, letter from Goldie to the Foreign Office, 1 May 1888.

22 Ibid., p. 167, extract from *North German Gazette*, 18 July 1888.

23 TNA, FO 403/75, correspondence respecting the Royal Niger Company, Part I, 1885–1886, pp. 90–3, letter from Messrs Stuart and Douglas to W. F. Lawrence MP, 15 December 1886.

24 Ibid., p. 112, letter from W. F. Lawrence to the Foreign Office, 15 December 1886; letter from the Foreign Office to W. F. Lawrence, 27 January 1887.

25 TNA, FO 403/149, correspondence respecting the Royal Niger Company, Part IV, 1890, p. 8, letter from the Duke of Westminster to the Marquess of Salisbury, 9 January 1890.

26 Wellesley, *Goldie*, pp. 23, 31–4, 25.

27 Ibid., p. 113; Flint, *Goldie*, pp. 311, 319.

28 Cecil, Lady Gwendolen, *Life of Robert, Marquis of Salisbury*, vol. IV, London, 1933, p. 323.

29 Achebe, Chinua, *Things Fall Apart*, Penguin edn, London, 2006, p. 8.

30 Ibid., pp. 130–1.

31 Ibid., p. 197.

32 Robinson, C. N., *Nigeria: Our Latest Protectorate*, London, 1900, p. 105.

33 Ibid., p. 106.

34 Schwarz, *Nigeria*, p. 35.

35 Kingsley, *The Story of West Africa*, p. 182.

36 TNA, FO 403/217, p. 4, Sir John Kirke to the Marquess of Salisbury, 25 August 1895.

37 Perham, Margery, *Lugard: The Years of Adventure*, vol. I: *1858–1898*, London, 1956, pp. 5–6; *DNB*.

38 Perham, Margery, *Lugard: The Years of Authority*, vol. II: *1898–1945*, London, 1956, p. 139.

39 Ibid., p. 136.

40 Lugard, Lord, *The Dual Mandate in British Tropical Africa*, London, 1965 (with an introduction by Margery Perham), 1st edn, London, 1922, p. 617.

41 Lord Salisbury in House of Lords debate, 14 February 1895, quoted in ibid., p. 612.

42 Ibid.

43 Lugard, Lord, *The Dependencies of the British Empire and the Responsibilities They Involve, Address on the Occasion of the 105th Anniversary of the Foundation of Birkbeck College*, London, 1928, pp. 4–5.

44 Ibid., pp. 8–10.

45 Ibid., pp. 10, 16.

46 Lugard, *The Dual Mandate*, p. 199.

47 Gervis, Pearce, *Of Emirs and Pagans: A View of Northern Nigeria*, London, 1963, p. xiii.

48 Dudley, B. J., *Parties and Politics in Northern Nigeria*, London, 1968, p. 16.

49 TNA, CO 822/27/16, Lugard, 'Education in Tropical Africa', originally published in the *Edinburgh Review* in July 1925, pp. 2–9.

50 Ibid., p. 10.

51 Ibid., pp. 10, 13.

52 Ibid., p. 11.

53 TNA, FCO 51/125, Miss V. Ryan, 'A Study of Events in Nigeria 1954–1969', 28 November 1969, p. 9.

54 Lugard, *The Dual Mandate*, p. 223.

55 Gervis, *Of Emirs and Pagans*, p. 36.

56 TNA, CO 879/119/8, Lugard, Report on the Amalgamation of Northern and Southern Nigeria, and Administration, 1912–1919.

57 Ibid., p. 12.

58 Perham, Margery, *Native Administration in Nigeria*, London, 1937, p. 89.

59 TNA, CO 583/201/10, letter of J. A. Maykin to Sir Philip Cunliffe-Lister, Secretary of State for the Colonies, 28 December 1934.

60 Ibid., letter from A. E. F. Murray to the Under-Secretary of State at the Colonial Office, 11 February 1935; ibid., letter from Alake of Abeokuta to Sir Philip Cunliffe-Lister, 4 February 1935.

61 Ibid., memorandum by I. M. R. Maclennan, 7 March 1935.

62 Ibid., memorandum by A. Fiddian, 2 February 1935.

63 Ibid., memorandum by I. M. R. Maclennan, 17 March 1936.

64 Perham, *Native Administration*, p. 81.

65 Ibid., pp. 231, 241.

Chapter 15: Yellow Sun

1 TNA, CO 967/117, Semi-official and Personal Correspondence between Secretary of State and Governors, letter from Lord Moyne to Sir Bernard Bourdillon, 2 October 1941.

2 Ibid., letter to Lord Lloyd, 5 October 1940.

3 TNA, CO 583/255/8, letter from Oliver Stanley to the Permanent Under-Secretary of State, 31 January 1944; letter to A. Cohen, 8 January 1944.

4 Gervis, Pearce, *Of Emirs and Pagans: A View of Northern Nigeria*, London, 1963, pp. 64–5.

5 Bello, Sir Ahmadu, *My Life*, Cambridge, 1962, pp. 29–31.

6 Ibid., pp. 31, 35, 64.

7 Ibid., pp. 229, 232.

8 TNA, FCO 51/125, 'Nigeria, 1954–1969', p. 13.

9 Ibid., pp. 16–17.

10 TNA, FCO 51/125, p. 6.

11 *Time*, 'The Sardauna', 25 May 1959.

12 Ibid.

13 Meredith, Martin, *The State of Africa: A History of Fifty Years of Independence*, London, 2005, p. 194.

14 TNA, FCO 51/125, p. 31; Meredith, *The State of Africa*, p. 194.

15 Meredith, *The State of Africa*, p. 194.

16 Ibid., p. 197.

17 Forsyth, Frederick, *The Biafra Story*, London, 1969, p. 27.

18 TNA, FCO 51/125, p. 38.

19 Morel, E. D., *Nigeria and its Peoples and its Problems*, London, 1912, p. 186.

20 Schwarz, Frederick A. O., Jr, *Nigeria: The Tribes, the Nation, or the Race*, Cambridge Massachusetts, 1965, p. 115.

21 Paden, John N., *Ahmadu Bello, Sardauna of Sokoto: Values and Leadership in Nigeria*, London, 1986, pp. 656–7.

22 *Time*, 'The Men of Sandhurst', 28 January 1966.

23 TNA, FCO 51/125, p. 52; Meredith, *The State of Africa*, p. 199.

24 *Time*, 'Men of Sandhurst'.

25 Ekwe-Ekwe, Herbert, *The Biafra War: Nigeria and the Aftermath*, Lampeter, 1990, p. 48.

26 Ibid., p. 28.

27 TNA, FCO 51/125, letter from David Hunt to E. E. Orchard, 6 November 1970.

28 Schwarz, *Nigeria*, p. 1.

29 TNA, FCO 25/232, 'The Secession of Eastern Region', letter from the British High Commissioner to the Secretary of State for Commonwealth Affairs, 23 March 1967.

30 Forsyth, *The Biafra Story*, p. 68.

31 *Time*, 'Agony in Biafra', 2 August 1968.

32 TNA, FCO 25/232, letter from the High Commissioner in Lagos to the Secretary of State for Commonwealth Affairs, 9 June 1967.

33 Ibid., letter from the High Commissioner to the Secretary of State for Commonwealth Affairs, 23 March 1967.

34 Ibid., letter from Colonel Ojukwu to Harold Wilson, 16 March 1967.

35 Ibid., telegram from Lagos to the Commonwealth Office, 14 April 1967.

36 Ibid., letter from the High Commissioner to E. G. Norris at the Commonwealth Office, 15 April 1967.

37 Ibid., 'Paper on Eastern Nationalism' by D. F. Hawley at the British High Commission in Lagos, 15 April 1967.

38 Ibid., memorandum by the Secretary of State for Commonwealth Affairs, 8 May 1967.

39 Ibid.

40 TNA, FCO 51/125, P. W. Heap, comment on draft of 'Nigeria 1954–1970', 14 August 1970.

41 Ibid., 'Nigeria, 1954–1970', p. 87.

42 TNA, FCO 25/232, letter from Colonel Ojukwu to Harold Wilson, 30 May 1967.

43 TNA, FCO 51/125, letter from David Hunt to E. E. Orchard, 6 November 1970.

44 Adichie, Chimamanda Ngozi, *Half of a Yellow Sun*, London, 2007.

45 TNA, FCO 51/125, 'Nigeria 1954–1970', p. 88.

46 Forsyth, *The Biafra Story*, p. xi.

47 TNA, PREM 11/3048, 'Mr Macleod statement in the House of Commons relating to the talks in London held from 10 May to 19 May, 1960, to discuss Nigerian independence and membership of the Commonwealth'.

48 TNA, FCO 51/125, 'Nigeria 1954–1970', p. 86.

49 TNA, FCO 25/232, letter from David Hunt to George Thomson, Secretary of State for Commonwealth Affairs, 19 January 1968.

50 Ibid., note by J. R. Young, 31 January 1968.

51 TNA, FCO 38/211, 'French Arms Supplies to Nigeria'.

52 TNA, FCO 25/232, letter from Donald Tebbit to Martin Le Quesne, 24 November 1967; letter from Le Quesne to Tebbit, 4 January 1968.

53 Ibid., letter from the Holy See to the Foreign Office, 10 October 1967; letter from R. B. Bone to the Foreign Office, 7 June 1968.

54 Forsyth, *The Biafra Story*, p. 65; *The Times*, 'Mad Mike Hoare', 1 December 1967.

55 TNA, FCO 65/1194, Richard Parsons, 'General Comments on Political Situation in Nigeria', 4 July 1972.

56 TNA, FCO 65/735, 'Position of Ibo after end of Civil War in Nigeria', newspaper cuttings in telegram from Sir Leslie Glass, High Commissioner in Lagos, to the Foreign Office, 14 January 1970; newspaper cuttings in telegram from Sir Leslie Glass, 17 January 1970.

57 TNA, FCO 65/735, 'Position of Ibo after end of civil war in Nigeria', telegram from Lagos to the Foreign Office, 15 January 1970.

58 TNA, FCO 65/1362, 'Position of Former Rebel Leader of Biafra, Colonel C. O. Ojukwu', letter from A. A. Acland, Foreign Office, to G. L. Angel, Home Office, 12 January 1973.

59 TNA, FCO 65/1363, letter from M. H. G. Rogers, Deputy High Commissioner, to J. de Courcy Ling, 12 January 1973.

60 TNA, FCO 65/1920, 'Tribalism in Nigeria', 21 October 1977.

61 Meredith, *The State of Africa*, pp. 580–1.

62 Langley, Alison, 'Court allows access to ex-leader's files', *New York Times*, 2 May 2003; *New York Times*, 'Late Nigerian dictator looted nearly $500 million, Swiss say', 19 August 2004.

63 Polgreen, Lydia, 'Money and violence hobble democracy in Nigeria', *New York Times*, 24 November 2006.

64 Meredith, *The State of Africa*, p. 582.

65 *New York Times*, 'Hundreds flee Nigerian city swept by riots', 25 November 2002.

66 Maier, Karl, *This House Has Fallen*, London, 2001, pp. 271–3.

67 Ibid., p. 287.

68 TNA, FCO 25/232, letter from David Hunt to George Thomson, Secretary of State for Commonwealth Affairs, 19 January 1968.

69 TNA, FCO 65/1194, Richard Parsons, 'General Comments on Political Situation in Nigeria', 4 July 1972; ibid., Richard Parsons, 'Valedictory Remarks', 30 June 1972.

Chapter 16: Hierarchies

1 Beeching, Jack, *The Chinese Opium Wars*, London, 1975, p. 39.

2 Matheson, James, *Present Position and Prospects of the British Trade with China*, London, 1836, p. 1.

3 Ibid., pp. 56, 39, 61.

4 *Memorials to his Majesties Government soliciting Protection to the British Trade in China, from the Merchants of Manchester, Liverpool, Glasgow and Canton*, London, 1836, p. 121.

5 Lindsay, H. Hamilton, *Letter to the Rt. Hon. Viscount Palmerston*, London, 1836, pp. 18–19.

6 *DNB*.

7 Palmerston letter to Lord Auckland, dated January 1841, quoted in Beeching, *The Chinese Opium Wars*, p. 95.

8 Fairbank, J. K., 'Chinese Diplomacy and the Treaty of Nanking, 1842', *Journal of Modern History*, March 1940, vol. XII, no. 1, pp. 1–30, at p. 6.

9 Costin, W. C., *Great Britain and China, 1833–1860*, Oxford, 1937, p. 11.

10 Lindsay, *Letter to Viscount Palmerston*, p. 12.

11 Beeching, *The Chinese Opium Wars*, pp. 96–8; *DNB*.

12 Eitel, E. J., *Europe in China*, London, 1895, pp. 60, 156.

13 Morris, Jan, *Hong Kong*, London, 1997, p. 56.

14 Ibid., p. 52; Tsang, Steve, *A Modern History of Hong Kong*, London, 2004, p. 53.

15 Morris, *Hong Kong*, p. 85; Crisswell, Colin N., *The Taipans: Merchant Princes*, Hong Kong, 1981, p. 5.

16 Tsang, *A Modern History of Hong Kong*, p. 27.

17 Ibid.

18 Tsang, Steve, *Governing Hong Kong: Administrative Officers from the Nineteenth Century to the Handover to China, 1862–1997*, London, 2007, pp. 27, 30–1.

19 Lethbridge, H. J., 'Hong Cadets 1862–1941', in Lethbridge, H. J., *Hong Kong*, London, 1978, pp. 37, 43.

20 Ibid., p. 50.

21 Tsang, *Governing Hong Kong*, p. 170.

22 Morris, *Hong Kong*, p. 88.

23 *DNB*.

24 Pope-Hennessy, James, *Half-Crown Colony: A Hong Kong Notebook*, London, 1969, pp. 78–9.

25 Eitel, *Europe in China*, p. v.

26 Carroll, J. M., *Edge of Empires: Chinese Elites and British Colonials in Hong Kong*, Cambridge, Massachusetts, 2005, pp. 87–8.

27 Crisswell, *Taipans*, p. 137.
28 *Los Angeles Times*, 'A Family's Priceless Legacy', 15 June 1997; Carroll, *Edge of Empires*, p. 79.
29 Carroll, *Edge of Empires*, pp. 100–1.
30 Ibid., p. 95.
31 TNA, CO 448/34, letter from Sir Robert Ho Tung to Sir Ronald Waterhouse KCB, 12 January 1927.
32 Ibid., letter from Sir Ronald Waterhouse to J. A. P. Edgcumbe, 8 February 1927; letter from E. H. Howell to Sir Gilbert Grindle, 21 October 1927; note by G. Grindle, 10 February 1927.
33 Maugham, W. Somerset, *The Painted Veil*, London, 1925, new edn 2001.
34 Gillingham, Paul, *At the Peak: Hong Kong between the Wars*, Hong Kong, 1983, pp. 23–8.
35 Carroll, *Edge of Empires*, pp. 132–4.
36 Gillingham, *At the Peak*, p. 79.
37 Ibid., p. 28.
38 Ibid., pp. 45–6.
39 TNA, CO 129/555/10, letter from W. J. Southorn to H. R. Cowell, 3 January 1936.
40 TNA, CO 129/533/10, note on the legal and practical position of brothels in Hong Kong by Chief Justice Sir Joseph Kemp, 16 May 1931; letter from Clementi to Wilson, 19 September 1931. This letter was written when Clementi had moved to Singapore.
41 TNA, CO 850/63/20, letter from the Governor to Philip Cunliffe-Lister, Secretary of State for the Colonies, 3 May 1935.
42 Ibid.

Chapter 17: Democracy Postponed

1 Quoted in Blake, Robert, *Jardine Matheson: Traders of the Far East*, London, 1999, p. 240.
2 TNA, CO 129/592/8, 'Future Policy in Hong Kong', telegram from Washington to London, 26 August 1945.
3 Ibid., letter from the China Association to the Secretary of State for the Colonies, 4 April 1945.
4 TNA, CO 968/98/6, 'Treatment of Sir Mark Young as a Prisoner of War in Japanese Hands', letter from Sir Mark Young to the Colonial Office, 12 December 1945.
5 TNA, CO 527/1651, '1946 Reforms', letter from Hazlerigg to the Colonial Office, 18 November 1946.
6 *DNB*.
7 TNA, CO 527/1651, '1946 Reforms', letter from Sir Mark Young to Arthur Creech Jones, Secretary of State for the Colonies, 22 October 1946.
8 TNA, CO 1023/41, 'Constitutional Reforms', *Far Eastern Economic Review*, 'Constitutional Reform in Hong Kong', 4 September 1952.
9 Grantham, A., *Via Ports: From Hong Kong to Hong Kong*, Hong Kong, 1965, pp. 111, 105.

10 TNA, CO 1023/41, extract from *Far Eastern Economic Review*, 'Speech by Mr Percy Chen', 6 November 1952.

11 Ibid., letter from J. B. Sidebottom to C. H. Johnston, 19 March 1952; telegram from Hong Kong (A. Grantham) to the Colonial Office, 26 June 1952; Cabinet memorandum by the Secretary of State for the Colonies, 'Constitutional Reform in Hong Kong', [n.d.] September 1952.

12 Ibid., *The Times*, 16 October 1953; *China Mail*, 16 October 1953.

13 Ibid., *South China Morning Post*, 16 October 1953.

14 Ibid., Cassidy, P. S., 'Asian Affairs', 31 July 1953.

15 Ibid., explanatory note by J. B. Johnston, 14 November 1953; telegram from Oliver Lyttelton, Secretary of State for the Colonies, to Alexander Grantham, 11 December 1953.

16 Grantham, *Via Ports*, pp. 107, 112.

17 Details of the entire Douthwaite–Dalton case are found in TNA, CO 1023/227, 'Trial of British Soldiers: Douthwaite and Dalton in Hong Kong'.

18 TNA, CO 1023/41, P. S. Cassidy, 'Asian Affairs', 31 July 1952.

19 TNA, CO 1030/899, 'The Drug Problem in Hong Kong 1957–59'; broadcast appeal by P. C. M. Sedgwick, 12 November 1959.

20 Schenk, Catherine, *Hong Kong as International Financial Centre: Emergence and Development 1945–65*, London, 2001, p. 25.

21 Buckley, Roger, *Hong Kong: The Road to 1997*, Cambridge, 1997, pp. 17, 48.

22 *Standard* (Hong Kong), 'Farewell Hong Kong Chauvinist', 31 January 2006.

23 Ibid.; *Daily Telegraph*, obituary of John Cowperthwaite, 25 January 2006.

24 Friedman, Milton and Rose, *Two Lucky People: Memoirs*, Chicago, 1998, pp. 316, 318.

25 Alex Singleton, obituary of John Cowperthwaite, *Guardian*, 8 February 2006.

26 Friedman and Friedman, *Two Lucky People*, p. 318.

27 *Standard* (Hong Kong), 31 January 2006.

28 Ibid.

29 *The Times*, obituary of John Cowperthwaite, 3 February 2006.

30 Schenk, *Hong Kong*, p. 3.

31 Fenby, Jonathan, *The Penguin History of Modern China: The Fall and Rise of a Great Power 1850–2009*, London, 2009, p. 376.

32 TNA, FO 371/175888, 'Future of Hong Kong', letter from Robert Black to Hilton Poynton, Colonial Office, 29 January 1964.

33 TNA, CO 1030/1300, 'Future of Hong Kong', letter from Robert Black to Hilton Poynton, Colonial Office, 30 October 1962.

34 TNA, FO 371/175912, 'Possibility of HM Queen visiting Hong Kong; Chinese Reaction', letter from T. W. Garvey, British Embassy in Beijing, to C. M. MacLehose, Foreign Office, dated 2 June 1964; telegram from Garvey to the Foreign Office, 16 December 1964.

35 TNA, FO 371/175888, *Pravda*, 27 May 1964, 'The Ill Fame of Hong Kong', quoted in letter from Garvey to Murray MacLehose, 2 June 1964.

36 Ibid.

37 Cottrell, Robert, *The End of Hong Kong*, London, 1993, pp. 29–30, 32.

38 TNA, FCO 21/196, 'Hong Kong Political Affairs: General Situation and Policy', telegram from Sir David Trench to the Secretary of State for the Commonwealth Office, 19 May 1967.

39 Ibid.

40 TNA, FCO 21/205, 'Hong Kong, Political Affairs, Chinese Attitude Towards', *People's Daily*, 7 August 1967, quoted in telegram from Beijing to the Foreign Office, 7 August 1967; *People's Daily*, 10 October 1967, quoted in telegram from Beijing to the Foreign Office, 11 October 1967.

41 TNA, T 317/902, 'Possible Economic Effect on the UK of the Disturbances in Hong Kong, 1967', memorandum by the Treasury for the Cabinet Defence and Overseas Policy Committee, 29 August 1967; T 317/903.

42 TNA, T 317/903, 'Possible Economic Effect on the UK of the Disturbances in Hong Kong, 1967', letter from A. Mackay to D. F. Hubback, 14 September 1967.

43 Ibid., memorandum by A. Mackay, 4 September 1967.

44 Ibid.

45 Ibid.

46 TNA, FCO 21/196, 'Hong Kong Political Affairs: General Situation and Policy', draft notes for use of the Secretary of State in Cabinet on Thursday 14 December 1967.

47 Ibid., 'Hong Kong Political Affairs: General Situation and Policy', Special Branch Hong Kong Police Report, 15 January 1968, pp. 7–8.

48 Ibid., p. 12.

49 Ibid., Special Branch Hong Kong Police Report, 5 March 1968, pp. 15, 26–7.

50 TNA, CO 1023/41, 'Note of a meeting in Mr Raskin's rooms at 11am February 1952 to discuss "Constitutional Reform in Hong Kong"'.

51 Ibid., 'Brief for the Secretary of State on the Hong Kong Constitution', 15 May 1952.

52 TNA, FO 371/175888, 'Future of Hong Kong', letter from A. H. Poynton to Robert Black, 13 January 1964.

Chapter 18: Red Dawn

1 *DNB*.

2 Cottrell, Robert, *The End of Hong Kong*, London, 1993, p. 32.

3 TNA, T 317/1775, 'Future of Hong Kong', memorandum by J. P. L. Gwynn, 12 April 1972.

4 Ibid., memorandum by H. S. Lee for the Defence and Overseas Policy Committee, [n.d.] January 1973.

5 Ibid., letter from J. E. Hansford to M. C. Scholar, 14 April 1972.

6 Yahuda, Michael, *Hong Kong: China's Challenge*, London, 1996, p. 48.

7 Buckley, Roger, *Hong Kong: The Road to 1997*, Cambridge, 1997, p. 87.

8 *Standard* (Hong Kong), 1 June 2006.

9 Buckley, *Hong Kong*, pp. 87–9.

10 Keay, John, *Last Post: The End of Empire in the Far East*, London, 1997, p. 85.

11 TNA, FCO 40/617, letter from Robert Hughes MP to Ian Mikardo MP, 7 December 1973.

12 Ibid., 'Discussions with Governor of Hong Kong during visit to UK', 8–11 April 1975, record of conversation between the Foreign Secretary and the

Governor of Hong Kong, 11 April 1975; record of meeting with Goronwy Roberts, 9 April 1975.

13 TNA, FCO 40/711, 'Discussions with MacLehose', visit by the Governor 19–24 July 1976.

14 TNA, FCO 40/764, 'Policy of UK on status of Hong Kong', general brief on Hong Kong, September 1977.

15 TNA, FCO 40/617.

16 TNA, FCO 40/957, 'The Future of Hong Kong', letter from John Gingell to David Owen, 13 September 1978; 'Note on letter from the Bishop of Derby's Industrial Adviser', 9 October 1978.

17 TNA, FCO 40/937, 'Representations of the Reform Club of Hong Kong', from Brook Bernacchi letter to David Owen, 5 January 1978; letter from J. A. B. Stewart to Denys Roberts, Chief Secretary of Hong Kong, 7 February 1978.

18 Ibid., letter from Denys Roberts to J. A. B. Stewart, 17 April 1978.

19 TNA, FCO 40/957, Dick Wilson, 'Hong Kong losing its "Berlin complex"', *Financial Times*, 8 November 1978.

20 TNA, FCO 40/764, 'Policy of UK on Status of Hong Kong', letter from D. C. Wilson to R. C. Samuel, 2 December 1977, quoting an article by Frank Ching in *Asian Wall Street Journal*, 25 November 1977.

21 TNA, FCO 21/1634, 'Relations between Hong Kong and China', draft paper 'Policy Towards Hong Kong in the 1980s' by W. E. Quantrill, dated November 1978, pp. 1, 5; note by R. J. Maclaren, 20 November 1978.

22 TNA, FO 973/119, 'Pressure on Hong Kong Resources', [n.d.] September 1980.

23 Ibid.

24 Buckley, *Hong Kong*, p. 96.

25 Dimbleby, Jonathan, *The Last Governor*, London, 1997, p. 43.

26 Cottrell, *The End of Hong Kong*, p. 83.

27 Thatcher, Margaret, *The Downing Street Years*, London, 1993, p. 259.

28 Cottrell, *The End of Hong Kong*, p. 90.

29 Thatcher, *The Downing Street Years*, p. 261.

30 Ibid., p. 262.

31 TNA, CO 1030/1300, 'Future of Hong Kong', letter from Robert Black to Sir Hilton Poynton, Colonial Office, 30 October 1962.

32 Thatcher, *The Downing Street Years*, p. 262.

33 *Time*, 11 October 1982, 'Countdown to a Crisis'.

34 Carroll, John M., *A Concise History of Hong Kong*, Lanham, Maryland, 2007, p. 185.

35 Morris, Jan, *Hong Kong*, London, 1997, p. 201.

36 TNA, FCO 40/764, quoted from Dennis Duncannon, *Asian Affairs*, vol. VIII, part II, June 1977, p. 198.

37 Patten, Chris, *East and West*, London, 1998, p. 36.

38 Ibid., pp. 15–16.

39 Ibid., p. 25.

40 Cradock, Percy, *Experiences of China*, London, 1994, p. 224.

41 Ibid., p. 258.

42 Cottrell, *The End of Hong Kong*, p. 177.

43 Dimbleby, *The Last Governor*, p. 85.

44 Ibid., p. 90.
45 Cradock, *Experiences*, p. 251.
46 *Time*, 14 March 2005, 'Bow-Tied Bureaucrat'.
47 Carroll, *Edge of Empires*, p. 192.

Conclusion

1 *Parliamentary Debates*, vol. 241, p. 1774, House of Lords debate, 18 July 1878.
2 Maugham, W. Somerset, *The Painted Veil*, London, 1925, new edn 2001, p. 8.

Bibliography

Manuscripts

The National Archives (TNA)
ADM 116
CAB 21
CAB 23
CAB 24
CAB 27
CAB 80
CO 129
CO 448
CO 527
CO 583
CO 730
CO 822
CO 850
CO 877
CO 879
CO 967
CO 968
CO 1023
CO 1030
FCO 21
FCO 25
FCO 29
FCO 38
FCO 39
FCO 40
FCO 51
FCO 54
FCO 55
FCO 65
FCO 67
FCO 93

FCO 403
FO 141
FO 371
FO 373
FO 403
FO 633
FO 973
FO 1090
PREM 11
PREM 13
PRO 30
T 317

Middle East Centre Archive, St Antony's College, Oxford (MECA)
Bell papers
Bowman papers
Cornwallis papers
Davies papers
MacMichael papers
Perowne papers
Sinderson papers

University of Warwick
BP Archive, University of Warwick

India Office Records and Private Papers, British Library (BL)
IOR R
MSS Eur B 380
MSS Eur C 419
MSS Eur D 670
MSS Eur D 704
MSS Eur D 714
MSS Eur D 862
MSS Eur D 912
MSS Eur D 1003
MSS Eur E 215
MSS Eur E 254
MSS Eur E 290
MSS Eur E 362
MSS Eur F 85
MSS Eur F 111
MSS Eur F 112
MSS Eur F 118
MSS Eur F 164
MSS Eur F 169
MSS Eur F 197

MSS Eur F 213
MSS Eur Photo Eur 33
MSS Eur Photo Eur 393

Unpublished PhD Theses

Ali, Mohammed Shamsher, 'The Beginnings of British Rule in Upper Burma: A Study of British Policy and Burmese Reaction 1885–1890', unpublished PhD thesis, University of London, 1976.

Samara, Ihsan Hani, 'The Economic Growth of Iraq: The Role of Oil Revenues, Government Policies and Strategies since 1950', unpublished PhD thesis, University College of Swansea, University of Wales, 1980.

Published Sources

Articles

Brown, Michael, E., 'The Nationalization of the Iraq Petroleum Company', *International Journal of Middle East Studies*, 1979, vol. 10, pp. 107–24.

Chen, Percy, 'Speech by Mr Percy Chen', *Far Eastern Economic Review*, 6 November 1952.

Collins, Robert, 'The Sudan Political Service', *African Affairs*, vol. 71, no. 284, July 1972, pp. 293–303.

Copland, Ian, 'Islam and Political Mobilization in Kashmir 1931–1934', *Pacific Affairs*, vol. 54, no. 2, summer 1981, pp. 228–59.

Daily Telegraph, obituary of Ne Win, 6 December 2002.

Earle, Edward Meade, 'The Turkish Petroleum Company: A Study in Oleaginous Diplomacy', *Political Science Quarterly*, vol. 39, no. 2, June 1924, pp. 265–79.

Fairbank, J. K., 'Chinese Diplomacy and the Treaty of Nanking, 1842', *Journal of Modern History*, March 1940, vol. XII, no. 1, pp. 1–30.

Fisher, Michael H., 'Indirect Rule in the British Empire: The Foundations of the Residency System in India (1764–1858)', *Modern Asian Studies*, vol. 18, no. 3, 1984, pp. 393–428.

Gulf Oil and Gas, 'Iraq issues tenders to drill 40 oil wells', 16 February 2009.

International Herald Tribune, 'Iraq reopens its oil reserves to foreign companies, but few rush in', 3 February 2009.

Joffe, Lawrence, obituary of Jaafar Nimeiri, *Guardian*, 5 June 2009.

Kingsley, Mary, 'Imperialism: A Lecture Delivered in Liverpool', *West African Studies*, 2nd edn, London, 1901, pp. 416–18.

Kirk-Greene, A. H. M., 'The Sudan Political Service: A Profile in the Sociology of Imperialism', *International Journal of African Historical Studies*, vol. 15, no. 1, 1982, pp. 21–48.

Langley, Alison, 'Court allows access to ex-leader's files', *New York Times*, 2 May 2003.

Los Angeles Times, 'A Family's Priceless Legacy', 15 June 1997.

Mangan, J. A., 'The Education of an Elite Imperial Administration: The Sudan Political Service and the British Public School System', *International Journal of African Historical Studies*, vol. 15, no. 4, 1982, pp. 671–99.

Middle East Economic Survey, vol. XII, no. 14, Interview with Dr Rifa'i, 31 January 1969.

New York Times, 'Hundreds flee Nigerian city swept by riots', 25 November 2002.

New York Times, 'Late Nigerian dictator looted nearly $500 million, Swiss say', 19 August 2004.

New York Times, 'Montagu's successor', 9 April 1922.

New York Times, 18 November 1920, quoted in Fischer, Louis, *Oil Imperialism: The International Struggle for Petroleum*, London, 1926, p. 219.

Polgreen, Lydia, 'Money and violence hobble democracy in Nigeria', *New York Times*, 24 November 2006.

Sarkisyanz, Manuel, 'Messianic Folk-Buddhism as Ideology of Peasant Revolts in Nineteenth and Early Twentieth Century Burma', *Review of Religious Research*, vol. 10, no. 1, Autumn 1968, pp. 32–8.

Singleton, Alex, obituary of John Cowperthwaite, *Guardian*, 8 February 2006.

Smith, Donald, 'Bloody Kashmir: Peril in Paradise', *National Geographic News*, 22 March 2000.

Solomon, Robert A., 'Saya San and the Burmese Rebellion', *Modern Asian Studies*, vol. 3, no. 3, 1969, pp. 209–23.

Standard (Hong Kong), 'Farewell Hong Kong Chauvinist', obituary of John Cowperthwaite, 31 January 2006.

Standard (Hong Kong), 1 June 2006.

Sudan Tribune, 31 August 2007.

The Times, 'Blood rubies bankroll Burmese Junta', 30 September 2007.

The Times, obituary of John Cowperthwaite, 3 February 2006.

The Times, 7 August 1920, quoted in Bennett, G. H., *British Foreign Policy during the Curzon Period 1919–1924*, London, 1995, pp. 106, 107–9.

Time, 'Agony in Biafra', 2 August 1968.

Time, 'Bow-Tied Bureaucrat', 14 March 2005.

Time, 'Burma's Faceless Leaders', 1 October 2007.

Time, 'Countdown to a Crisis', 11 October 1982.

Time, 'The Men of Sandhurst', 28 January 1966.

Time, 'The Sardauna', 25 May 1959.

Time, 'The Shivering Maharaja', 5 May 1961.

Time, 'Strength through Weakness', 5 March 1965.

Time, 'Sudanese President Omar Hassan al-Bahir', 5 March 2009.

Time, 'The Tragedy of Sudan', 4 October 2004.

Time, 'What did Kashmir have to do with the Mumbai Attacks?', 7 December 2008.

Time, 17 April 1939.

Time, 17 June 1957.

Turrell, Robert, V., 'Conquest and Concession: The Case of the Burma Ruby Mines', *Modern Asian Studies*, vol. 22, no. 1, 1988, pp. 141–63.

Verma, Sonia, 'Iraq could have largest oil reserves in the world', *The Times*, 20 May 2008.

Books

Abbas, Ahmad, *Kashmir Fights for Freedom*, Bombay, 1948.

Abdullah, Thabit A. J., *Dictatorship, Imperialism and Chaos*, London, 2006.

Achebe, Chinua, *Things Fall Apart*, Penguin edn, London, 2006.

Adichie, Chimamanda Ngozi, *Half of a Yellow Sun*, London, 2007.

Allen, Charles, *The Soldier Sahibs*, London, 2000.

Alnasrawi, Abbas, *The Economy of Iraq: Oil, Wars, Destruction of Development and Prospects 1950–2010*, London, 1994.

Anonymous, *Burma, The Foremost Country: A Timely Discourse*, London, 1884.

Astarjian, Henry, *The Struggle for Kirkuk: The Rise of Hussein, Oil and the Death of Tolerance in Iraq*, London, 2007.

Batatu, Hanna, *The Old Social Classes and the Revolutionary Movements of Iraq*, Princeton, 1978.

Beatty, Charles, *His Country was the World: A Study of Gordon of Khartoum*, London, 1954.

Beeching, Jack, *The Chinese Opium Wars*, London, 1975.

Bell, Gertrude, *Letters of Gertrude Bell*, selected and edited by Gladys Bell, London, 1987.

Bello, Sir Ahmadu, *My Life*, Cambridge, 1962.

Bennett, G. H., *British Foreign Policy during the Curzon Period 1919–1924*, London, 1995.

Birdwood, Lord, *Nuri As-Said: A Study in Arab Leadership*, London, 1959.

——, *Two Nations and Kashmir*, London, 1956.

Blackburn, Terence R., *Executions by the Half-Dozen: The Pacification of Burma*, New Delhi, 2008.

Blake, Robert, *Jardine Matheson: Traders of the Far East*, London, 1999.

Bose, Sumantra, *Kashmir: Roots of Conflict, Paths to Peace*, London, 2003.

Brown, Judith M., *Nehru: A Political Life*, London, 2003.

Browne, Edmond, *The Coming of the Great Queen: A Narrative of the Acquisition of Burma*, London, 1888.

Browne, Horace A., *Reminiscences of the Court of Mandalay: Extracts from the Diary of General Horace A. Browne 1859–1879*, Woking, 1907.

Buchan, John, *Greenmantle*, London, 1916, new edn 1964.

Buckley, Roger, *Hong Kong: The Road to 1997*, Cambridge, 1997.

Cannadine, David, *Ornamentalism*, London, 2001.

Caractacus, *Revolution in Iraq*, London, 1959.

Caroe, Sir Olaf, *The Pathans 550 B.C.–A.D. 1957*, Oxford, 1959.

Carroll, J. M., *Edge of Empires: Chinese Elites and British Colonials in Hong Kong*, Cambridge, Massachusetts, 2005.

Carroll, John M., *A Concise History of Hong Kong*, Lanham, Maryland, 2007.

Cecil, Lady Gwendolen, *Life of Robert, Marquis of Salisbury*, vol. IV, London, 1933.

Chabrun, Laurent, and Heriot, Franck, *Les Corrompus de Saddam Hussein*, Paris, 2006.

Charney, Michael W., *A History of Modern Burma*, Cambridge, 2009.

Churchill, Winston S., *Lord Randolph Churchill*, 2 vols, London, 1906.

Churchill, Winston S., *The River War*, London, 1899, new edn 1997.

Colbeck, James, *Mandalay in 1878–1879: The Letters of James Alfred Colbeck, Originally Selected and Edited by George H. Colbeck in 1892*, ed. Michael W. Charney, Knaresborough, 1892.

Collins, Larry, and Lapierre, Dominique, *Freedom at Midnight: The Epic Drama of India's Struggle for Independence*, London, 1975.

Collins, Robert O., *Shadows in the Grass: Britain in the Southern Sudan 1918–1956*, New Haven, 1983.

Collins, Robert O., and Deng, Francis M., *The British in the Sudan 1898–1956: The Sweetness and the Sorrow*, London, 1984.

Collis, Maurice, *Trials in Burma*, London, 1945, new edn 1978.

Colquhoun, A. R., *Burma and the Burmans or the Best Unopened Market in the World*, London, 1885.

Copland, Ian, 'The Abdullah Factor: Kashmiri Muslims and the Crisis of 1947', in Low, D. A. (ed.), *The Political Inheritance of Pakistan*, London, 1991, pp. 218–54.

——, *India 1885–1947*, London, 2001.

——, *The Princes of India in the Endgame of Empire 1917–1947*, Cambridge, 1997.

——, *State, Community and Neighbourhood in Princely North India c. 1900–1950*, Basingstoke, 2005.

Costin, W. C., *Great Britain and China 1833–1860*, Oxford, 1937.

Cottrell, Robert, *The End of Hong Kong*, London, 1993.

Coughlin, Con, *Saddam: The Secret Life*, London, 2002.

Cradock, Percy, *Experiences of China*, London, 1994.

Crick, Bernard, *George Orwell: A Life*, London, 1980.

Crisswell, Colin N., *The Taipans: Merchant Princes*, Hong Kong, 1981.

Cromer, Earl of, *Political and Literary Essays 1908–1913*, 1st Series, London, 1913

——, *Political and Literary Essays*, 2nd Series, London, 1914.

Crosthwaite, Sir Charles, *The Pacification of Burma*, London, 1912.

Daly, M. W., *Darfur's Sorrow: A History of Destruction and Genocide*, Cambridge, 2007.

——, *Imperial Sudan: The Anglo-Egyptian Condominium*, Cambridge, 1991.

——, *The Sirdar: Sir Reginald Wingate and the British Empire in the Middle East*, Philadelphia, 1997.

Dasgupta, C., *War and Diplomacy in Kashmir 1947–48*, New Delhi, 2002.

Delaisi, Francis, *Oil: Its Influence on Politics*, trans. C. Leonard Leese, London, 1922.

Dictionary of National Biography (*DNB*).

Dimbleby, Jonathan, *The Last Governor*, London, 1997.

Dudley, B. J., *Parties and Politics in Northern Nigeria*, London, 1968.

Eitel, E. J., *Europe in China*, London, 1895.

Ekwe-Ekwe, Herbert, *The Biafra War: Nigeria and the Aftermath*, Lampeter, 1990.

Eprile, Cecil, *War and Peace in the Sudan 1955–1972*, London, 1974.

Fenby, Jonathan, *The Penguin History of Modern China: The Fall and Rise of a Great Power 1850–2009*, London, 2009.

Ferguson, Niall, *Colossus*, London, 2005.

——, *Empire: How Britain Made the Modern World*, London, 2003.

Fernea, Robert A., and Louis, William Roger (eds), *The Iraq Revolution of 1958: The Old Social Classes Revisited*, London, 1991.

Fischer, Louis, *Oil Imperialism: The International Struggle for Petroleum*, London, 1926.

Flint, John E., *Sir George Goldie and the Making of Nigeria*, London, 1960.

Flint, Julie, and de Waal, Alex, *Darfur: A Short History of a Long War*, London, 2005.

Forbes, Colin D., *Innocent in a Revolution*, Lewes, 1999.

Forsyth, Frederick, *The Biafra Story*, London, 1969.

French, Patrick, *Younghusband: The Last Great Imperial Adventurer*, London, 1994.

Friedman, Milton and Rose, *Two Lucky People: Memoirs*, Chicago, 1998.

Fromkin, David, *A Peace to End All Peace: The Fall of the Ottoman Empire and the Creation of the Modern Middle East*, New York, 1989.

Fuerlig, Henner, *Saddam Hussein – der neue Saladdin? Irak und der Golf Krieg*, Berlin, 1991.

Galbraith, Peter, *The End of Iraq: How American Incompetence Created a War without End*, New York, 2006.

Gallman, Waldemar J., *Iraq under General Nur: My Recollections of Nuri al-Said 1954–1958*, Baltimore, 1964.

Geary, Grattan, *Burma, after the Conquest, Viewed in its Political, Social and Commercial Aspects from Mandalay*, London, 1886.

Gervis, Pearce, *Of Emirs and Pagans: A View of Northern Nigeria*, London, 1963.

Gilbert, Martin, *Churchill: A Life*, London, 1991.

Gillingham, Paul, *At the Peak: Hong Kong between the Wars*, Hong Kong, 1983.

Gilmour, David, *Curzon*, London, 1994.

Grantham, A., *Via Ports: From Hong Kong to Hong Kong*, Hong Kong, 1965.

Guha, Ramachandra, *India after Gandhi: The History of the World's Largest Democracy*, London, 2007.

Gulbenkian, Nubar, *Pantaraxia*, London, 1965.

Haldane, Sir Aylmer, *The Insurrection in Mesopotamia 1920*, Edinburgh, 1922.

Hardinge, Viscount, *Life of Hardinge*, Rulers of India Series, Oxford, 1891.

Henderson, K. D. D., *The Making of the Sudan: The Life and Letters of Sir Douglas Newbold*, London, 1953.

Hewins, Ralph, *Mr Five Per Cent: The Biography of Calouste Gulbenkian*, London, 1957.

Hodson, H. V., *The Great Divide: Britain–India–Pakistan*, Karachi, 1969.

Hopkirk, Peter, *The Great Game: On Secret Service in High Asia*, London, 1990.

Howell, Georgina, *Daughter of the Desert: The Remarkable Life of Gertrude Bell*, London, 2006.

Hussein, Saddam, *On Oil Nationalisation in Iraq*, Baghdad, 1973.

Hyam, Ronald, *Britain's Declining Empire: Decolonization 1918–1968*, Cambridge, 2006.

Ireland, Philip Willard, *Iraq: A Study in Political Development*, New York, 1937.

Jackson, H. C., *Sudan Days and Ways*, London, 1954.

Johnson, Douglas H. (ed.), *British Documents on the End of Empire*, Series B, vol. 5: *Sudan*, London, 1998.

Johnson, Douglas H., *The Root Causes of Sudan's Civil Wars*, Oxford, 2003.

Joshi, Manoj, *The Lost Rebellion: Kashmir in the Nineties*, New Delhi, 1999.

Judd, Gerrit Parmele, *Members of Parliament 1734–1832*, Chicago, 1972.

Kapur, M. L. (ed.), *Maharaja Hari Singh*, New Delhi, 1995.

Keay, John, *Last Post: The End of Empire in the Far East*, London, 1997.

Kedourie, Elie, *England and the Middle East: The Destruction of the Ottoman Empire*, London, 1987.

Kenrick, Rosemary, *Sudan Tales: Recollections of Some Sudan Political Service Wives 1926–1956*, Cambridge, 1987.

Kent, Marian, *Moghuls and Mandarins: Oil, Imperialism and the Middle East in British Foreign Policy 1900–1940*, London, 1993.

——, *Oil and Empire: British Policy and Mesopotamian Oil 1900–1920*, London, 1976.

Keun, Odette, *A Foreigner Looks at the British Sudan*, London, 1930.

Khadduri, Majid, *Independent Iraq 1932–1958: A Study in Iraqi Politics*, London, 1960.

Khan, Mohammad Ishaq, *History of Srinagar 1846–1947: A Study in Socio-Cultural Change*, Srinagar, 1978.

Kingsley, Mary, *The Story of West Africa*, London, 1899.

Kipling, Rudyard, *Complete Verse*, ed. M. M. Kaye, London, 1990.

——, 'The Taking of Lungtungpen', in Kipling, Rudyard, *Plain Tales from the Hills*, London, 1888.

Lamb, Alastair, *Kashmir: A Disputed Legacy 1846–1990*, Hertingfordbury, 1991.

Lawrence, T. E., *The Letters of T. E. Lawrence*, selected and edited by Malcolm Brown, London, 1988.

Leslie, Shane, *Mark Sykes: His Life and Letters*, London, 1923.

Lethbridge, H. J., 'Hong Cadets 1862–1941', in Lethbridge, H. J., *Hong Kong*, London, 1978.

Lethbridge, Sir Roper, *The Golden Book of India: A Genealogical and Biographical Dictionary of the Ruling Princes, Chiefs, Nobles, and Other Personages, Titled or Decorated of the Indian Empire*, London, 1893.

Lindsay, H. Hamilton, *Letter to the Rt. Hon. Viscount Palmerston*, London, 1836.

Longrigg, Stephen Hemsley, *Iraq 1900 to 1950: A Political, Social and Economic History*, London, 1953.

Low, D. A. (ed.), *The Political Inheritance of Pakistan*, London, 1991.

Lugard, Lord, *The Dependencies of the British Empire and the Responsibilities They Involve*, Address on the Occasion of the 105th Anniversary of the Foundation of Birkbeck College, London, 1928.

——, *The Dual Mandate in British Tropical Africa*, London, 1965 (with an introduction by Margery Perham), 1st edn, London, 1922.

Luizard, Pierre-Jean, *La Formation de l'Irak contemporain*, Paris, 1991.

McBeth, B. S., *British Oil Policy 1919–1939*, London, 1985.

McCord, Norman, *British History 1815–1906*, Oxford, 1991.

MacMichael, Sir Harold, *The Sudan*, London, 1954.

MacMillan, Margaret, *Paris 1919*, New York, 2001.

McMurray, Jonathan S., *Distant Ties: Germany, the Ottoman Empire and the Construction of the Baghdad Railway*, London, 2001.

Magnus, Philip, *Kitchener: Portrait of an Imperialist*, London, 1958, new edn 1968.

Maier, Karl, *This House Has Fallen*, London, 2001.

Main, Ernest, *Iraq from Mandate to Independence*, London, 1935.

Mansfield, Peter, *Kuwait: Vanguard of the Gulf*, London, 1990.

Marks, John Ebenezer, *Forty Years in Burma*, London, 1917.

Marlowe, J., *Late Victorian: The Life of Sir Arnold Talbot Wilson*, London, 1967.

Marr, Phebe, *The Modern History of Iraq*, 2nd edn, Boulder, Colorado, 2004.

Matar, Fuad, *Saddam Hussein: The Man, the Cause and the Future*, London, 1981.

Matheson, James, *Present Position and Prospects of the British Trade with China*, London, 1836.

Maugham, W. Somerset, *The Painted Veil*, London, 1925, new edn 2001.

Maung Htin Aung, *A History of Burma*, New York, 1967.

——, *Lord Randolph Churchill and the Dancing Peacock: British Conquest of Burma 1885*, New Delhi, 1990.

——, *The Stricken Peacock: Anglo-Burmese Relations 1752–1948*, The Hague, 1965.

Mejcher, Helmut, *Imperial Quest for Oil: Iraq 1910–1928*, London, 1976.

Memorials to his Majesties Government soliciting Protection to the British Trade in China, from the Merchants of Manchester, Liverpool, Glasgow and Canton, London, 1836.

Meredith, Martin, *The State of Africa: A History of Fifty Years of Independence*, London, 2005.

Minayeff, I. P., *Travels in and Diaries of India and Burma*, trans. Hirendwanath Sanyal, Calcutta, 1958.

Monroe, Elizabeth, *Britain's Moment in the Middle East 1914–1956*, London, 1963.

Morel, E. D., *Nigeria and its Peoples and its Problems*, London, 1912.

Morgan, Gerald, *Anglo-Russian Rivalry in Central Asia 1810–1895*, London, 1981.

Morris, James, *The Hashemite Kings*, London, 1959.

Morris, Jan, *Hong Kong*, London, 1997.

Myer, Valerie Grosvenor, *A Victorian Lady in Africa: The Story of Mary Kingsley*, Southampton, 1989.

Napier, Sir William, *The Life and Opinions of General Sir Charles James Napier*, 4 vols, London, 1857.

Neve, Ernest F., *Beyond the Pir Panjal: Life and Missionary Enterprise in Kashmir*, London, 1914.

Nicolson, Harold, *Curzon: The Last Phase 1919–1925. A Study in Post-War Diplomacy*, London, 1934.

Ni Ni Myint, *Burma's Struggle against British Imperialism 1885–1895*, Rangoon, 1983.

O'Ballance, Edgar, *The Secret War in the Sudan 1955–1972*, London, 1977.

——, *Sudan, Civil War and Terrorism, 1956–99*, London, 2000.

Orwell, George, *Essays*, London, new edn 2000.

Paden, John N., *Ahmadu Bello, Sardauna of Sokoto: Values and Leadership in Nigeria*, London, 1986.

Parliamentary Debates (Hansard).

Patel, Sardar, *Sardar Patel's Correspondence 1945–1950*, ed. Darga Das, vols I–VIII, Ahmedabad, 1971–3.

Patten, Chris, *East and West*, London, 1998.

Perham, Margery, *Lugard: The Years of Adventure*, vol. I: *1858–1898*, London, 1956.

—, *Lugard: The Years of Authority*, vol. II: *1898–1945*, London, 1956.

—, *Native Administration in Nigeria*, London, 1937.

Philby, H. St J., *Arabian Days*, London, 1948.

Pollock, John, *Kitchener*, London, 2001.

Pope-Hennessy, James, *Half-Crown Colony: A Hong Kong Notebook*, London, 1969.

Ramusack, Barbara N., *The Indian Princes and their States*, Cambridge, 2004.

Ramusack, Barbara N., *The Princes of India in the Twilight of Empire: Dissolution of a Patron–Client System 1914–1919*, Columbus, Ohio, 1978.

Raugh, Harold E., *The Victorians at War: An Encyclopedia of British Military History*, Santa Barbara, 2004.

Roberts, Andrew, *Eminent Churchillians*, London, 1994.

Robertson, Sir James, *Transition in Africa: From Direct Rule to Independence*, London, 1974.

Robinson, C. N., *Nigeria: Our Latest Protectorate*, London, 1900.

Robinson, Gallagher, with Alice Denny, *Africa and the Victorians: The Official Mind of Imperialism*, 2nd edn, London, 1981.

Saint-Prot, Charles, *Saddam Hussein: un gaullisme arabe?*, Paris, 1987.

Salter, Lord, *The Development of Iraq: A Plan of Action*, London, 1955.

Sandes, E. W. C., *The Royal Engineers in Egypt and the Sudan*, London, 1937.

Sargent, Inge, *Twilight over Burma*, Honolulu, 1994.

Schenk, Catherine, *Hong Kong as International Financial Centre: Emergence and Development 1945–65*, London, 2001.

Schofield, Victoria, *Kashmir in the Crossfire*, London, 1996.

Schwarz, Frederick A. O., Jr, *Nigeria: The Tribes, the Nation, or the Race*, Cambridge, Massachusetts, 1965.

Shaw, Flora, *A Tropical Dependency: An Outline of the Ancient History of Western Soudan with an Account of the Modern Settlement of Northern Nigeria*, London, 1905.

Shepperd, Alan, *Sandhurst: The Royal Military Academy*, London, 1980.

Shwadran, B., *The Middle East, Oil and the Great Powers*, New York, 1955, 3rd edn 1973.

Silverstein, J. (ed.), *The Political Legacy of Aung San*, rev. edn, Ithaca, New York, 1993.

Simon, Reeva Spector, *Iraq between the Two World Wars: The Militarist Origins of Tyranny*, New York, 1986, rev. edn 2004.

Simon, Reeva Spector, and Tejirian, Eleanor H. (ed.), *The Creation of Iraq 1914–1921*, New York, 2004.

Singh, Bawa Satinder, *The Jammu Fox: A Biography of Maharaja Gulab Singh of Kashmir 1792–1857*, Carbondale and Edwardsville, 1974.

Singh, Karan, *Autobiography*, Bombay, 1989.

Singh, Khushwant, *The Sikhs*, London, 1953.

Slatin, Rudolf, *Fire and Sword in the Sudan: A Personal Narrative of Fighting and Serving the Dervishes 1879–1895*, London, 1896, new edn 1897.

Sluglett, Peter, *Britain in Iraq 1914–1932*, London, 1976.

Steevens, G. W., *With Kitchener to Khartoum*, London, 1898, new edn 1990.

Stewart, A. J. Q., *The Pagoda War*, London, 1972.

Stivers, William, *Supremacy and Oil: Iraq, Turkey and the Anglo-American World Order 1918–1930*, London, 1982.

Stone, Norman, introduction to Wells, H. G., *A Short History of the World*, London, 2006.

Storrs, Sir Ronald, *Great Britain in the Near and Middle East*, Cust Foundation Lecture, University College, Nottingham, 1932.

Symes, Sir Stewart, *Tour of Duty*, London, 1946.

Taylor, Robert H., *The State in Burma*, London, 1987.

Teng, M. K., Bhatt, R. K. K., and Bhatt, S. K., *Kashmir Constitutional History and Documents*, New Delhi, 1977.

Thant Myint-U, *The Making of Modern Burma*, Cambridge, 2001.

——, *The River of Lost Footsteps: A Personal History of Burma*, London, 2007.

Thatcher, Margaret, *The Downing Street Years*, London, 1993.

Thesiger, Wilfred, *The Life of my Choice*, London, 1987.

Thirkell White, Herbert, *A Civil Servant in Burma*, London, 1913.

Thomas, Graham F., *From the Last of the Proconsuls: Letters from Sir James Robertson*, London, 1994.

——, *Sudan 1950–1985: Death of a Dream*, London, 1990.

——, *Sudan: Struggle for Survival*, London, 1993.

Tripp, Charles, *A History of Iraq*, Cambridge, 2000, 3rd edn 2007.

Tsang, Steve, *Governing Hong Kong: Administrative Officers from the Nineteenth Century to the Handover to China, 1862–1997*, London, 2007.

——, *A Modern History of Hong Kong*, London, 2004.

Vandeleur, Seymour, *Campaigning on the Upper Nile and Niger*, London, 1898.

Vansittart, Lord, *The Mist Procession: The Autobiography of Lord Vansittart*, London, 1958.

Wakhlu, Somnath, *Hari Singh: The Maharaja, the Man, the Times*, New Delhi, 2004.

Wakin, Edward, *Contemporary Political Leaders of the Middle East*, New York, 1996.

Warburg, Gabriel, *The Sudan under Wingate*, London, 1971.

Warikoo, K., *Central Asia and Kashmir: A Study in the Context of Anglo-Russian Rivalry*, New Delhi, 1989.

Warner, Philip, *Kitchener: The Man behind the Legend*, London, 1985.

Wavell, Lord, *The Viceroy's Journal*, ed. Penderel Moon, London, 1973.

Wellesley, Dorothy, *Sir George Goldie, Founder of Nigeria: A Memoir*, London, 1934.

Wilson, A. T., *Mesopotamia 1917–1920: A Clash of Loyalties. A Personal and Historical Record*, London, 1931.

Wingate, Sir Ronald, *Wingate of the Sudan*, London, 1955.

Wright, Lawrence, *The Looming Tower: Al Qaeda's Road to 9/11*, London, 2006.

Woodman, Dorothy, *The Making of Burma*, London, 1962.

Yahuda, Michael, *Hong Kong: China's Challenge*, London, 1996.

Yergin, Daniel, *The Prize: The Epic Quest for Oil, Money, and Power*, New York, 1991, 2nd edn 1992.

Younghusband, Francis, *Kashmir*, London, 1924.

Ziegler, Philip, *Mountbatten*, London, 1985.

Acknowledgements

While writing this book I have incurred many debts of obligation to scholars, friends and librarians. I would like to thank, in particular, the staff of the British Library and the National Archives, whose efficiency and good nature made the task of writing the book more pleasant. I am also grateful for the assistance provided by the highly professional staff at the BP Archive, based at the University of Warwick. Debbie Usher, the archivist at the Middle East Centre Archive at St Antony's College, Oxford, was also extremely helpful with the research I conducted at that excellent institution.

In addition, I am indebted to the generosity of my readers who were selflessly enthusiastic about reading specific chapters, adding many useful and instructive notes. Eugene Rogan was a meticulous reader for Iraq; David Washbrook helped with Kashmir; Michael Charney managed to send me some very detailed comments about Burma while on holiday in South East Asia; Cherry Leonardi, at the Sudan Archive in Durham, improved the chapters relating to that country; John Peel's remarks on Nigeria were scholarly and to the point; Rana Mitter, despite differences of opinion, was incredibly efficient and generous with his time in correcting some of my more basic mistakes on Hong Kong.

I would like to thank many friends who provided encouragement while I wrote the book. It would be invidious to mention everybody by name, but a special debt of gratitude is owed to Sarah Fitch, Henry Hitchings, Amber Rudd, Charles Steel, Rachel Wrangham and Alice Yates.

The production of a book like this necessarily involves a great deal of commitment from a number of professionals. Anna Simpson, amongst others at Bloomsbury, worked tirelessly on the editorial side. Peter James lived up to his reputation as an exemplary copy editor. My editor, Michael Fishwick, always provided encouragement and support for a project which he believed in from the very beginning.

Lastly I would like to extend special thanks to my parents, to whom the book is dedicated, and to my agent, Georgina Capel, whose boundless energy and dauntless optimism sustained the project right through to its completion.

Index

A NOTE ON THE TYPE

The text of this book is set in Adobe Garamond. It is one of several versions of Garamond based on the designs of Claude Garamond. It is thought that Garamond based his font on Bembo, cut in 1495 by Francesco Griffo in collaboration with the Italian printer Aldus Manutius. Garamond types were first used in books printed in Paris around 1532. Many of the present-day versions of this type are based on the *Typi Academiae* of Jean Jannon cut in Sedan in 1615.

Claude Garamond was born in Paris in 1480. He learned how to cut type from his father and by the age of fifteen he was able to fashion steel punches the size of a pica with great precision. At the age of sixty he was commissioned by King Francis I to design a Greek alphabet; for this he was given the honourable title of royal type founder. He died in 1561.